THE
MAJOR
PROPHETS

THE SERIES

INTERPRETER'S CONCISE COMMENTARY

THE MAJOR PROPHETS

A COMMENTARY ON
ISAIAH, JEREMIAH, LAMENTATIONS,
EZEKIEL, DANIEL

By
Peter R. Ackroyd
Stanley Brice Frost
Harvey H. Guthrie, Jr.
William Hugh Brownlee
George A. F. Knight

Edited by Charles M. Laymon

Abingdon Press
Nashville

Interpreter's Concise Commentary
Volume IV: THE MAJOR PROPHETS

Copyright © 1971 and 1983 by Abingdon Press

Library of Congress Cataloging in Publication Data

Main entry under title:
The Major Prophets.
  (Interpreter's concise commentary; v. 4)
  Originally published as part of. The Interpreter's one-volume
commentary on the Bible. 1971.
  Bibliography: p.
  1. Bible. O.T. Prophets—Commentaries. I. Ackroyd,
Peter R. II. Laymon, Charles M. III. Series.
BS1505.3.M34   1983   224'.07   83-7090

The Major Prophets ISBN 0-687-19235-8

(Previously published by Abingdon Press in cloth as part of
The Interpreter's One-Volume Commentary on the Bible, regular ed.
ISBN 0-687-19299-4, thumb-indexed ed. ISBN 0-687-19300-1.)

MANUFACTURED BY THE PARTHENON PRESS AT
NASHVILLE, TENNESSEE, UNITED STATES OF AMERICA

EDITOR'S PREFACE

to the original edition

A significant commentary on the Bible is both timely and timeless. It is timely in that it takes into consideration newly discovered data from many sources that are pertinent in interpreting the Scriptures, new approaches and perspectives in discerning the meaning of biblical passages, and new insights into the relevancy of the Bible for the times in which we live. It is timeless since it deals with the eternal truths of God's revelation, truths of yesterday, today, and of all the tomorrows that shall be.

This commentary has been written within this perspective. Its authors were selected because of their scholarship, their religious insight, and their ability to communicate with others. Technical discussions do not protrude, yet the most valid and sensitive use of contemporary knowledge underlies the interpretations of the several writings. It has been written for ministers, lay and nonprofessional persons engaged in studying or teaching in the church school, college students and those who are unequipped to follow the more specialized discussions of biblical matters, but who desire a thoroughly valid and perceptive guide in interpreting the Bible.

The authorship of this volume is varied in that scholars were chosen from many groups to contribute to the task. In this sense it is an ecumenical writing. Protestants from numerous denominations, Jews, and also Roman Catholics are represented in the book. Truth cannot be categorized according to its ecclesiastical sources. It is above and beyond such distinctions.

It will be noted that the books of the Apocrypha have been included and interpreted in the same manner as the canonical writings. The value of a knowledge of this body of literature for understanding the historical background and character of the Judaic-Christian tradition has been widely recognized in our time, but commentary treatments of it have not been readily accessible. In addition, the existence of the Revised Standard Version and the New English Bible translations of these documents makes such a commentary upon them as is included here both necessary and significant.

The commentary as a whole avoids taking dogmatic positions or representing any one particular point of view. Its authors were chosen throughout the English-speaking field of informed and recognized biblical scholars. Each author was urged to present freely his own interpretation and, on questions where there was sometimes a diversity of conclusions, each was also asked to define objectively the viewpoints of others while he was offering and defending his own.

Many persons have contributed to the writing and production of this volume. One of the most rewarding of my personal experiences as editor was corresponding with the authors. On every hand there was enthusiasm for the project and warmth of spirit. The authors' commitment to the task and their scholarly sensitivity were evident in all of my relationships with them. The considerate judgments of the manuscript consultants, Morton S. Enslin, Dwight M. Beck, W. F. Stinespring, Virgil M. Rogers, and William L. Reed, were invaluable in the making of the character of the commentary. The copy editors who have worked under the careful and responsible guidance of Mr. Gordon Duncan of Abingdon Press have contributed greatly to the accuracy and readability of the commentary.

—Charles M. Laymon, Editor

PUBLISHER'S PREFACE

The intent of *The Interpreter's Concise Commentary* is to make available to a wider audience the commentary section of *The Interpreter's One-Volume Commentary on the Bible*. In order to do this, the Publisher is presenting the commentary section of the original hardback in this eight-volume paperback set. At the same time, and in conjunction with our wish to make *The Interpreter's One-Volume Commentary* more useful, we have edited the hardback text for the general reader: we have defined most of the technical terms used in the original hardback text; we have tried to divide some of the longer sentences and paragraphs into shorter ones; we have tried to make the sexually stereotyped language used in the original commentary inclusive where it referred to God or to both sexes; and we have explained abbreviations, all in an attempt to make the text more easily read.

The intention behind this paperback arrangement is to provide a handy and compact commentary on those individual sections of the Bible that are of interest to readers. In this paperback format we have not altered the substance of any of the text of the original hardback, which is still available. Rather, our intention is to smooth out some of the scholarly language in order to make the text easier to read. We hope this arrangement will make this widely accepted commentary on the Bible even more profitable for all students of God's Word.

WRITERS

Peter R. Ackroyd
Samuel Davidson Professor of Old Testament Studies, University of London, King's College, England

Stanley Brice Frost
Professor of Old Testament Studies and Dean of the Faculty of Graduate Studies and Research, McGill University, Montreal, Canada

Harvey H. Guthrie, Jr.
Dean, Episcopal Theological School, Cambridge, Massachusetts

William Hugh Brownlee
Professor of Religion, Claremont Graduate School and University Center, Claremont, California

George A. F. Knight
Principal (President) of the Pacific Theological College, Suva, Fiji

CONTENTS

THE BOOK OF ISAIAH

Peter R. Ackroyd

INTRODUCTION

The Unity of the Book

It has long been recognized that only part of the book of Isaiah actually belongs to the period of the prophet Isaiah ben Amoz, who lived in the latter half of the eighth century B.C. and presumably died early in the seventh. It is only in the first half of the book, chapters 1-39, that material from that period may be found. Even here there is much that can hardly belong to so early a date. From chapter 40 onward the historical background is that of the sixth century. Some parts of chapters 56-66 possibly belong to an even later date. Thus the material of the book extends over a period of at least two hundred years, and probably three hundred or even more. The individual sections reveal sharp divisions of content and background, and a full understanding of the book can be reached only if account is taken of these.

In spite of the differences of historical background and content there is an important sense in which the book is a unity. Its present form cannot be regarded as mere accident. At some stage in its formation it may have consisted of only part of the present work. Chapters 36-39 are a historical insertion taken from II Kings, with some important differences in the text.

Possibly these chapters were appended to a collection already existing before chapters 40-66 were added.

But the idea that chapters 40-66 formed a separate collection of prophecy entirely unrelated to the Isaiah material does less than justice to the facts. It fails to account for points of contact among the various parts of the book. While these points do not prove unity of authorship, they nevertheless suggest a continuity of tradition.

The belief that Isaiah wrote the whole book is not the only ancient tradition concerning its composition. There is a late Jewish tradition that the book was written by the "Men of Hezekiah." In Proverbs 25:1 this group is said to have been responsible for copying a collection of Solomon's proverbs. Hezekiah has a reputation in some of the records as a reforming king (cf. II Kings 18:3-6 and Jeremiah 26:19, where his pious activities are associated with the influence of the prophet Micah, a contemporary of Isaiah). It would not be impossible to suppose that the words of Isaiah were handed down by his associates or followers and that this process continued in a group which considered itself in some way linked with the reforming activities of Hezekiah.

There is evidence to show that the words of Isaiah were reapplied to later situations, especially to the problems of the Babylonian exile. Possibly the unknown author of chapters 40-55—commonly called Second Isaiah—gave what could be regarded as a further reapplication of the message of Isaiah, though it is clear that at the same time it represents a great new prophetic message. Subsequently other prophetic material came to be associated with this tradition. The eventual formation of the book is the result of a long and complex process. We can never hope to know fully all that was involved.

But it is not sufficient to take each small section of the book and look at it by itself. We must also try to visualize the whole picture. Nor can we get away from the fact that the individual sections derive their meaning not simply from the original utterances which they contain but also from the way in which the whole passage is set in a larger context. When we try to understand the meaning of a passage today, we are continuing a process which goes back virtually to the time of the original Isaiah himself. He was, as we can sometimes see, his own first interpreter.

The Historical Setting

It should be clear that there is no one historical moment to which the material of the book can be attached. For its full interpretation we need a knowledge of the period from around 740 B.C. to about 500 B.C. when the later sections were probably written. Even beyond this, the final shaping of the book is not seen until around 200 B.C. Possibly no substantial additions were made in the later years. But the process by which the book came to be regarded as canonical—that is, belonging to a recognized collection of sacred books—assumes that it was seen to be continually relevant. The reapplication of the older material to new situations, seen in the New Testament, shows that the preservation of the text is more than a matter of copying. It involves active interpretation.

The clearly datable material in Isaiah belongs to two main periods. The first is that of the prophet Isaiah. This included two great crises in the history of Judah—the Syro-Ephraimitic War of *ca.* 734-732, during the reign of Ahaz, and the invasion of Judah by Sennacherib in 701, during the reign of Hezekiah. The political and religious aspects of these crises are important factors in the understanding of the prophet.

The second period is that of the Second Isaiah, the great unknown prophet of the Exile, author of chapters 40-55. His activity is probably to be placed within the reign of Nabonidus, the last Babylonian ruler (around 555-539). At this time the rise of Cyrus the Persian and his rapid series of victories caused the Babylonian Empire to collapse and led to high hopes of restoration among the Jewish exiles.

The period overlaps naturally into the years that followed, which are reflected perhaps in the prophecies in chapters 56–66. In these years attempts were made at reestablishing the life of the Jewish community in and around Jerusalem. During this time the temple was rebuilt. Adjustments had to be made to a new situation. Instead of being a more or less independent nation ruled by a king, the community found itself a subject district of a great empire. Its main center was in Jerusalem, but many of those who owed allegiance to it were scattered members of the community and the significance of this "dispersion" is reflected in some prophecies of the book.

The Prophet and His Successors

Isaiah himself is portrayed for us in narratives and prophecies in the opening chapters of the book. We see him in his conflict with the politically minded Ahaz, in his encouragement of the timorous Hezekiah, in the shattering experience of finding himself in the very presence of God. God is revealed in the stark and brutal words of judgment against the people and their leaders. The portrait is an incomplete one, and it is not entirely unified. As with other Old Testament characters, differing traditions have come down to us. To smooth over the inconsistencies is to do less than justice to the material.

In some passages Isaiah's message is of uncompromising judgment. In others, especially chapters 36–39, he appears as one utterly confident that God will protect the city and people. This confidence bears the marks of the more popular tradition, but it contains within it a true expression of the tremendous faith of the prophet. Here was a man who could face the worst disasters and the prospect of utter devastation and still maintain faith. He could see that for his people the way to life lay, not through easy maneuvering for security, but in the discipline of obedience and trust.

It is this faith, so characteristic of the prophet, which provides the link to the unknown figures of the later parts of the book. Here and there—for example, in chapters 40, 49, and 61—we seem to get glimpses of one or another of these figures, impressions of the impact on them of the power of God's presence, the relentless control of God's spirit. But there is no description of their lives or persons. The Second Isaiah was almost certainly among the exiles in Babylonia. Some of his later successors may well have been active in Palestine. Greater precision is impossible to attain.

But these are not all the successors of Isaiah. Among his immediate associates there must have been those who appropriated his word and, in handing it on, added their own insights into the nature and purpose of God. The later editors of the material were not mechanical manipulators of what had come down to them. They were creative handlers, and through them the material retained its vivid message. The book witnesses not only to great people of crisis moments in Israel's history. It reveals also how rich was the continuity of faith of those who were bearers of the tradition and maintainers of its truth.

Structure

For the purposes of this commentary the book has been divided into seven sections:

chapters 1-12;
chapters 13-23;
chapters 24-27;
chapters 28-35;
chapters 36-39;
chapters 40-55 (subdivided into chapters 40-48 and 49-55);
chapters 56-66.

There is a major division after chapter 39. This is justified on the ground that no material in chapters 40-66 belongs to Isaiah. In chapters 1-39 there is a considerable amount which must be associated directly with him, and there is other material which may be his or based on his original utterances. The first part of the book also contains the narrative material concerned with Isaiah.

Differences in content mark the further subdivisions. Chapters 36-39 are immediately marked off by the fact that they are found also in II Kings 18–20. Chapters 13-23 contain almost exclusively oracles on foreign nations. The component parts are marked by the distinctive use of the title "oracle" (literally "burden"). This section is closely followed by chapters 24–27.

Here the judgment on the nations is elaborated into a picture of the final age of both judgment and promise.

In chapters 1–12 and 28–35 are found the main oracles of Isaiah. These are concerned almost exclusively with Judah and to a limited extent with the northern kingdom of Israel. Chapters 13–27 divide these two collections. But there are no hard and fast lines to be drawn here. The handing down of Isaiah's oracles involved considerable reinterpretation. For example, the element of promise within judgment, so bound up with Isaiah's message, has been elaborated with oracles of hope, some of which clearly reflect a later period. This can be seen especially in the concluding sections of both the collections of Isaiah's oracles (chapters 1–12 and 28–35). This feature is to be found also in other prophetic collections—for example, Amos and Micah.

Analysis of the second part of the book (chapters 40-66) is not so readily made. It is common practice now to divide the book after chapter 55. Chapters 40–55 are seen as the oracles of Second Isaiah and chapters 56–66 as those of Third Isaiah. This is convenient and has been followed here. Chapters 40–55 are divided into two sections—chapters 40–48 and 49–55. But the divisions are less clear than in the first part of the book. No titles appear to assist the reader.

The differences between the sections of Second Isaiah are partly of content. Chapters 40–48 are more concerned with the political situation and have direct reference to Cyrus the Persian. Chapters 49–55 are more concentrated on the place of Israel in the purposes of God. Attempts have been made to trace direct historical connections for the various passages in chapters 40–48 and to show that they are in chronological order. But their overlaps in content and the extreme difficulty of deciding at what precise points they should be divided make such interpretations very uncertain.

Chapters 56-66 are even more problematic since the material is very difficult to date at all. A reasonable case can be made for allocating most if not all of it to the period around 540-500. But there may well be some earlier material, and quite possibly some that is later. Arguments for a single prophet Third Isaiah are not very convincing. In all probability the collection is made up of material from various dates and from various personalities or groups. Nor is the division between chapters 40–55 and chapters 56–66 quite so clear as has sometimes been suggested. There are overlaps of thought and style—for example chapters 60–62—which strongly suggest a close connection between the two.

If we see the formation of the book as an organic growth within circles closely linked with the tradition of the original Isaiah, it becomes unnecessary to try to make hard and fast divisions among the so-called three Isaiahs.

This interconnection in fact cuts right across all the dividing lines. Chapter 35, with its strongly expressed hopes of restoration and a way through the desert, is obviously connected with chapter 40. It is difficult to avoid the impression that here we are dealing with poems from the same school if not actually from the same prophet. The poems on the downfall of Babylon in chapters 13–14 are not entirely out of contact with the pronouncements of chapters 46–47, though language and style suggest that these cannot be from the same author. The interpretation of the vineyard theme of 5:1-7 in 27:2-6 and the relationship between 11:1-9 and 65:17-25 indicate connections between different parts of the book which must be taken into account in any description of its formation and structure.

Interpretation is one of the characteristics of the evolution of the prophetic material which may be illustrated within Isaiah. The structure is in part due to such interpretative activity. Isaiah himself, as we may see in chapter 28, reapplied his own oracles to new situations. Probably there are many such examples less obvious to us. Those who followed him gave new shape to his teaching by their explanation of it. Chapters 24–27 offer an explanation of chapters 13–23 by providing those foreign-nation oracles with a wider setting. Chapters 56–66 may be regarded as providing in some measure an interpretation of the teaching of Second Isaiah for the generation immediately after the Exile.

The history of the formation of the book and the study of its present structure involve considerations of interpretative activity. This means that no purely literary description is adequate to the understanding of the work. However exalted its poetry and however important the study of literary forms for the analysis of its separate units, the book is not a work of literature. It is the record of a long process of theological interpretation of the experience of a community.

Interpretation and Significance

The very familiarity of certain well-known phrases from Isaiah makes the discussion of interpretation difficult. The New Testament use of 7:14 or of the so-called "servant" passages in Second Isaiah; the associations gathered around such passages as 40:1-11, especially because of their use in Handel's *Messiah;* the precise interpretation of royal oracles such as 9:2-7 and 11:1-9—all these give an initial bias to the understanding of the book which can easily result in missing its full significance. This sense of its relevance to later events has not been restricted to Christian interpretation. To the Jewish community too its promises have been a rich source of encouragement and faith. But any narrow understanding of the relationship between the contents of Isaiah and later Jewish and Christian experience must inevitably lead to a too limited appreciation of its full significance.

To isolate particular passages and concentrate on them without full appreciation of their context leads to a failure to see what the book has to reveal about the nature and purpose of God in the broadest sense. To limit our assessment of it by some artificial scheme of prophecy and fulfillment means that many things in the book either must be twisted from their proper sense to fit the scheme or must be left on one side as belonging only to the past and irrelevant to our present situation.

Isaiah belongs to the period in which it was formed. The defining of this period and the dating of the sections of the book are not easy matters. Sometimes a clear historical situation is indicated—as in the vitally important experience of Isaiah described in chapter 6. At other points only the most general indications of date can be given. Ideally, discovery of the original situation is essential for full understanding. In practice such a discovery is rarely possible. Ideally we should endeavor to say of each passage not only where and when it originated but also how and when and in what ways it has been modified and reinterpreted. In practice such a description can be given only tentatively.

If we are concerned to discover the fullest meaning of a given passage, we need a knowledge of the entire Old Testament and the life and world to which it belongs. For example, judgment of what chapter 6 tells us about Isaiah and about God must be made in the light of the fuller picture of the prophet. This in turn must be derived not only from the book but also from an understanding of Old Testament prophecy as a whole. Our judgment must also be made in the light of other affirmations about God. We must not pick out what we regard as highlights and misinterpret these by looking at them out of context, as if they were statements immediately comparable with New Testament affirmations about God. This not only provides us less than the true meaning of these passages. It also inevitably leads to the assumption that the rest of the book is less important because it is apparently at a lower standard theologically.

This problem of interpretation is particularly acute in regard to the so-called "servant songs" of Second Isaiah. There is a general agreement among scholars that four passages in chapters 40–55 should be so described. These are usually given as 42:1-4 (or 1-8 or 9); 49:1-6 (or 7); 50:4-9; and 52:13–53:12. These are not the only passages in chapters 40–55 in which "servant" is used; also, in 50:4-9 the term itself does not occur.

The isolating of these passages is based on the assumption—which may or may not be justified—that chapters 40–55 consist of small separate units. There is also the subjective impression that what is said in these passages differs sufficiently from the remainder of the prophecies for them to be separate. It may be that they are by a different author, as some have maintained. Or they represent particular stages in the prophet's thought, perhaps even standing in chronological order. The varieties of interpretation arising from this approach have been so great as to raise questions concerning its validity. Opinion in recent years holds that there is no good ground for regarding these passages as of different authorship. To study them in isolation from the remainder of the prophecies is to miss their full significance.

Jewish interpreters have not been influenced by the discovery of points of apparently direct contact between these passages and the New Testament. Therefore they have always been more able to see the interrelationship of these servant songs, the other "servant" passages, and the prophecies in which the term is not used even though the same or similar thoughts are present. In spite of the illumination that has resulted from the detailed studies of these passages, the isolation of the servant songs has been one of the blind alleys of modern Old Testament criticism.

Only a full assessment of the teaching of Second Isaiah can do justice to the real meaning of the servant songs. Only then does the depth of the prophet's insight into the nature and purpose of God, gained in the experience of exile in Babylonia, come out clearly. The significance of what is said about the "servant of God" becomes clearer as it is seen to be bound up in the prophet's appreciation of the meaning of the divine judgment on the people. This judgment is acknowledged to be the rightful outcome of the people's failure. It is shown to be the moment both of divine promise and of divine action. God's promise is revealed to the world through a people who have apparently failed. Thus the prophet of the Exile stands out as one who most fully appreciated what the Old Testament repeatedly emphasizes that "man's extremity is God's opportunity."

Such an understanding of God is one of the human factors which made possible the kind of entry into the human condition which the New Testament describes. It made possible the presentation and appropriation of the understanding of God which is to be seen in the cross of Christ. The relationship between the prophecies of Second Isaiah and the New Testament is at a much fuller and deeper level than mere correspondence. It is at the level of insight into the nature of God, the revelation of God through the personality of a man who stands in so many ways head and shoulders above his associates in the Old Testament.

This example only pinpoints the general principle. In every passage what the book says about God must be seen through as sound an understanding of the text as we can reach, with as adequate an assessment of the situation as we can make. If we let its words point us to God, we shall certainly be aware that in the light of the revelation of God in Christ it is never an unshadowed picture of God that we obtain. But we shall also be aware of some of the richness of that revelation of God which was granted to the people of faith who gave us this book. In the process our own limited understanding of the God revealed in Christ may be enlarged.

I. THE FIRST COLLECTION (1:1–12:6)

A. THE TITLE (1:1)

The opening verse sets the prophet in historical context by listing the **kings of Judah** of his lifetime. **Vision** is a general term which emphasizes the prophet's insight into the divine purpose—an insight which is made clear in the description of his experience of divine commission in chapter 6. Perhaps the title originally referred only to chapters 1–12. But it appropriately heads the first part of the book (chapters 1–39), which is closely linked with the eighth century prophet. It may also serve to remind the reader that the whole book is associated with the prophetic tradition initiated by Isaiah (see Introduction).

B. FAITHLESS AND FAITHFUL JERUSALEM (1:2–2:5)

1:2-6. *Indictment of the City.* The failure of the people and the expression of hope and confidence for the future are

11

concentrated in the picture of the city of Jerusalem. In her present state she is faithless, having lost the rightness of life which should be hers. The prospect is of judgment. But this judgment is linked with the divine purpose to restore, and her future glory is far to outshine anything she has known. Jerusalem's condition epitomizes that of the whole people. Thus it is appropriate that the passage opens with an invocation to **heavens** and **earth** to act as witnesses, as often in prophetic judgment sayings. They are to attest the divine care lavished on Israel and the unnaturalness of its disobedience. The fatherly care which has watched over the people from its beginnings is met with a failure to acknowledge the activity of God (verses 2-3).

1:4-6. The life of the people is wholly corrupt. It is depicted as a body wounded from **head** to **foot** with no alleviation offered. Characteristically the corruptness is linked with the spurning of **the Holy One of Israel.** This title, which is frequent in this book but little used elsewhere in the Old Testament, expresses the deep sense of both the separation of God from humanity by reason of the divine nature and also the mystery of the divine action in regard to Israel.

1:7-9. *The Devastation of Judah.* The general failure infects the whole land as is shown by a detailed picture of Judah. This probably refers to the devastation wrought by the armies of Sennacherib in 701, when he claims to have captured forty-six cities of Judah and to have shut up Hezekiah like a bird in a cage. Jerusalem is left isolated in the center of the devastated land, and the prophet makes the people acknowledge divine grace: **If the LORD of hosts had not left us a few survivors, we should have been like Sodom.** The people's failure could have brought about a total collapse. Such dire judgment is frequent in the prophet's message. The remnant here is all that is left, and it exists only as an act of mercy, totally unexpected and totally unmerited (cf. 37:33-37).

The prophet recalls the ancient tradition of the destruction of the cities of the plain (Genesis 19) to indicate vividly again what Judah and her capital have deserved. Possibly verse 7 also contains an allusion to this, since the word for **overthrown** is used most often of this disaster. It has been proposed that the phrase should read "as the overthrow of Sodom."

1:10-17. *Perverse Worship.* Jerusalem's failure is so terrible that her rulers can be described as **rulers of Sodom,** her people as **people of Gomorrah.** They are exhorted to **hear** the divine **word,** the term so often used for the prophetic message, and the **teaching,** the law which is often associated with the priests. It is in this context that the nature of the failure is more closely defined. As in verse 4, the relationship with God is linked with the need for right dealings.

When a people comes to worship with its hands **full of blood,** the performance of ritual becomes an utter weariness to God. This point is emphasized by several of the prophets (cf. Jeremiah 7:21-26; Hosea 6:6; Amos 5:21-26), though various interpretations have been placed on their words. It has sometimes been thought that in such pronouncements the prophets rejected all the forms of sacrificial worship.

But there can be no doubt of the meaning here. God indicates an unwillingness to listen even to their **many prayers.** The whole of their present worship is unacceptable. The text lists a great variety of observances (perhaps **iniquity** in verse 13 should be "fasting"). Cf. Psalm 15, where the conditions on which the worshiper may be in the shrine are laid down.

Those who are disobedient to the basic requirements of God's law are unfit to engage in worship. Far from receiving blessing and favor when they appear before God, they inevitably call down judgment on themselves. The people's condition is unforgivable because their understanding of worship is so totally wrong. They conceive it as a way of winning, indeed earning the right to, divine favor. They find themselves faced by the demand that they show obedience by abandoning their forms of false worship. Above all they are to protect the **fatherless** and the **widow** and insure the maintenance of right.

1:18-20. *Promise of Forgiveness.* The gloomy picture of alienation is followed by an exhortation and promise, combined with a further warning. Verse 18 has indeed been variously interpreted. Is it an ironic question: Can your sins be forgiven? Is it a concession for the sake of argument: Let us for the moment ignore their reality? The context strongly suggests that it is a word of promise. Thus it provides an answer to what otherwise might seem an insoluble problem. Men and women have no right to stand in the presence of God with guilt on them. But how can they be released from the sin which besets their lives?

Up to a point the Old Testament prophets seem to present an optimistic view. They suggest that we have only to be **willing and obedient** for all to be well. They do not always see the depths of human failure. But, without precisely explaining the relationship, they set the problem of our willingness or unwillingness to respond in the context of divine promise, and here the promise is of forgiveness.

1:21-31. *Restoration to Former Faithfulness.* The theme of the failure of Jerusalem returns in verses 21-23, contrasting her present condition with a time when **righteousness lodged in her.** For this failure judgment must come, but it will be like the refining of **silver** (verses 22, 25). It will lead to a restoration of justice as in an ideal past. Here there is perhaps an allusion to the growing tradition of the idyllic reigns of David and Solomon. The city will be renamed **city of righteousness, the faithful city.**

1:27-31. A further series of sayings speaks of the purity of the new population of the city—those who **repent** (literally "return," perhaps meaning from captivity). Those who rebel against the divine will are to be destroyed. The theme of those who **forsake the LORD** is elaborated in words of judgment which seem to refer to alien cult practices (verse 29). The powerlessness of the idolaters is described in verse 30. Verse 31 is not altogether clear. Perhaps it refers to the destruction of idolaters and their images. The text found in the Dead Sea Isaiah scroll has plural forms, "your strength, your work," and thereby gives a more general application to the saying.

2:1-5. *Jerusalem, a Blessing for the World.* Since chapter 2 begins with a new heading, (cf. 1:1), it is usually thought that the following verses form the introduction to a new section. These verses are found also in a slightly different form in Micah 4:1-5.

There they give a contrasting climax to the judgment of Jerusalem depicted in the final verses of Micah 3. It seems likely that in Isaiah too the oracle is meant to provide a concluding comment to the opening chapter with its theme of faithless and faithful Jerusalem. The full promise is only now reached.

Since this oracle appears in two prophetic books, the words in 2:1 were perhaps originally a marginal note suggesting that the saying really is Isaiah's. This may have been a first scholarly attempt to deal with the problem of authorship of this passage, which probably should be regarded as an independent saying.

The place of Jerusalem in the Old Testament tradition is here richly illustrated. As the capital of the Davidic kingdom it had political significance. As the city in which the royal shrine for Yahweh was built by Solomon, and where the ancient religious symbol, the ark, was to be found, it called for devotion, as many of the psalms reveal. But above all it was the place which God chose. Therefore it must become the very center of the world's life—supernaturally the **highest of the mountains,** to which the **nations** will come. It would be the source of the divine **law** and of the divine blessing of peace for the whole world. Here is expressed in vivid symbol the reality of God's presence and God's judgment of the world—and the hope of new life which is God's promise. The section closes, echoing its beginning (1:2-3), with an appeal to Israel to respond and find its true way of life.

The whole passage links together oracles of the prophet and other sayings, some of which may be of later origin. It presents a unified picture. It carries a powerful message of warning and promise.

C. THE DAY OF THE LORD (2:6–4:6)

2:6-22. *A Time to Hide.* This section is marked off by the recurrence of a sort of refrain (verses 10, 19, 21). Each part of the poem is punctuated by a return to the theme of human humiliation—of hiding like **moles** and **bats** in the **caves** and rock clefts before the terror of God in the **glory of his majesty.** The means of judgment is not described here—only the sense of awe at the presence of God. It is doubtful whether these three parts originally belonged together. But the common theme of the refrain and the close interlinkage of thought makes understandable why they are combined, whether by Isaiah himself or by his followers. This passage is appropriately placed after the opening section of the book. It reechoes the theme of absolute allegiance and obedience to God's laws and shows the consequences of failure.

2:6-11. The first part portrays a people involved in alien practices (verse 6), priding itself in the wealth of its possessions (verse 7), and engaged in idolatry (verse 8). But humiliation must come (verses 9-11). Verse 6 presents considerable difficulty. Since it appears to begin in the middle of a condemnation, perhaps the opening of the poem is missing. Possibly verse 6a should be linked with verse 5 and read: "For you have rejected your strength [or "your kinsman," that is, God], O house of Jacob." Despite the uncertain text it seems clear that verse 6b refers to magical practices. In verse 6c a small change would give "traders like the Philistines," a good parallel to the bargaining suggested by **strike hands with foreigners.**

2:12-19. The second part speaks in highly poetic language of the coming of Yahweh's own **day** of judgment. It depicts this disaster in terms of the overthrow of glorious trees, mountains, towers, and ships. Again the picture of humiliation and hiding follows. The day of Yahweh is a concept found earlier, clearly in Amos (cf. Amos 5:18-20). Popular thought seems to have seen it as a day of victory for Israel. But to Isaiah, as to Amos, it is a day of divine intervention. It is the day of judgment for those who are unfit to be God's people—who fail to trust in God, indulge in pride and self-sufficiency, and are involved in social evil. The Holy One of Israel will be found to be holy in judgment.

2:20-22. The third part returns briefly to the theme of the futility of idolatry. After again speaking of humiliation, it ends with a warning note—perhaps a scribal comment—against any kind of trust in **man.**

3:1-15. *Collapse of Civil Order.* The coming of the divine judgment is here described more precisely. All support is to be removed from **Jerusalem** and **Judah,** and civil order will come to an end. The leadership will be lost. Military, civil, and religious authority will be undermined. The inexperienced will rule, and social disorder will follow (verses 1-5). **Magician** and **expert in charms** may indicate that all those on whom the people rely for counsel will be removed. But it is possible that these refer to the skilled "craftsmen" taken into exile in 597 (cf. II Kings 24:14).

The theme is continued with emphasis on the hopeless situation, in which no one is willing to take responsibility. The disaster no longer appears to be in the future. Jerusalem and Judah have already come to disaster for their defying of the holy majesty of God (verses 6-8). The combination of phrases suggests a coming day of judgment. This is seen in terms of removal of leaders and chaos in government, for this was what occurred in the northern kingdom.

The prophet may be looking back on the fall of Samaria in 722 and seeing disaster coming on Jerusalem in the same form. But interwoven into this is an interpretation of judgment in terms of siege and famine (verse 1). The indication that **Jerusalem has stumbled and Judah has fallen** and that the city has become a **heap of ruins** (perhaps better "fallen one") suggests that Isaiah's words against Jerusalem have been seen as meaningful again in the time of the disaster of exile in 586. The significance of the prophetic word is not exhausted in its original situation.

3:9-12. The theme of civil chaos continues in verses 9 and 12. A new point is added, bringing home the nature of Judah's failure in justice and her insolent sin (verse 9). On **Sodom** see above on 1:7-9. Verse 12 should perhaps begin: "As for my people, his rulers are wrongdoers, and exactors [or "creditors"] rule over him." Between these two verses stands a wisdom saying (verses 10-11), moralistic in tone, which should probably be emended to read: "Happy are the righteous, for it shall be well . . ." The blessing of the righteous at the coming of God is contrasted with the inevitable judgment which falls on the wicked.

3:13-15. The judge, God, is ready to pass sentence (cf. Psalm 82). God is in the law court to condemn the leaders who have oppressed. The oracle is linked to the opening proclamation of judgment on the ruling groups.

3:16–4:1. *Judgment on Women.* A further saying is concerned with women—evidently the wealthy women, perhaps the wives of the rulers who are condemned (cf. Amos 4:1-3). Their pride, their love of finery, will be destroyed. Their fashionable hair styles and their rich clothing will become **baldness** and **sackcloth,** the signs of mourning and perhaps also of exile. A long list of **finery** is included in verses 18-23. Not every item is clear, but it reveals the kind of rich attire and jewelry which a wealthy Judean woman might possess. Verse 17*c* might better be rendered: "the LORD will lay bare their foreheads." In verse 24*e* **shame** appears in the famous Dead Sea scroll of Isaiah. Without this word the text may be translated "branding for beauty."

3:25–4:1. This judgment on the women of Jerusalem suggests the picture of Jerusalem as the mother of her sons (cf. Lamentations 1:1, 18). It probably comes from a later interpreter in the exilic period. The **men** have fallen **in battle** and the city is taken. The situation of the surviving women is so desperate that they seek the protection of the few men remaining, asking only the protection of a **name,** not the full care of the marriage relationship.

4:2-6. *Hope in Judgment.* But this terrible series of pictures is not God's last word. God enters the human sphere in holiness to judge and to save. The day of the Lord, which is gloom and terror to those who merit it, will also bring blessing and hope. There will be a new sprouting up of life in the final age for the remnant of Israel. The term **branch** is sometimes used to denote the leader of the new age (cf. Jeremiah 23:5; 33:15 and Zechariah 3:8; 6:12). Here it seems to have a more general sense. The survivors will be sanctified, for Jerusalem will be a **holy** city, a place of **life** (cf. Zechariah 14:20-21). The wind of divine judgment, as a **burning** fire, will purify the people and remove their defilement. The presence of God will protect the holy mountain, and it will be a **refuge** and **shelter.**

The opening chapter, picturing the faithlessness of the city, issues in the vision of Jerusalem as the center of the world's life (2:2-5). Also here the proclamation of judgment—as the coming day of the Lord, the day of siege and exile, the time of total downfall—issues in a further vision of hope. Such visions seem to point to a background of disaster and perhaps of exile such as finally overtook Judah in the sixth century. Set in the context of judgment, they provide a fitting interpretation of the nature of divine promise, placed against the background of human failure and sin.

D. THE LORD'S VINEYARD (5:1-30)

The vineyard song covers only the opening seven verses. However, it has been appropriately linked with two further elements—a long series of woes exemplifying the failure of Judah indicated in the song (verses 8-23) and a final word of disaster (verses 24-30).

5:1-7. *The Vineyard Song.* This song is reminiscent of the marriage poetry of the Song of Solomon, where "vineyard" may actually be used to signify the bride (Song of Solomon 8:11-12). The poem may thus be based on a love song, highly poetic in its imagery and with a twist imparted at the end of verse 2. The carefully tended vineyard, provided with everything needful, produces **wild grapes** (literally "stinking things," perhaps meaning putrid fruit). The speaker establishes the relationship of obligation. One part has been fulfilled. The community is summoned to give judgment. As in the parables of Nathan (II Samuel 12) and of Jesus, the hearers are invited to pass judgment, to concur in the sentence passed on the vineyard. It is to be condemned to destruction, deprived of fertility.

But, as in the parables, the judges are in reality judging themselves. They cannot help concurring in the sentence. But the sentence is on Judah, on themselves. God's care for the people has brought the response not of **justice** but **bloodshed,** not **righteousness** but a **cry.**

Was the word of judgment intended to come as a surprise to Judah? We cannot be sure, but it seems likely that the symbol of the vineyard for the land and people was of older origin than the time of Isaiah. It is found in Psalm 80:14-15, and Hosea possibly knew the analogy (cf. Hosea 2:3-6). Later it is used by Ezekiel (Ezekiel 19:10-14) and by Jesus (Matthew 21:33-46; Mark 12:1-9; Luke 20:9-19).

5:8-23. *Woes of Judah.* This series of woes depicts in detail the people's failure. The first two concern matters of social failure and thus link closely to the judgment in the preceding verse. There are those who make wrong use of the **land,** which is given by God to the people, an inheritance of God, not theirs. The result is loss of true status for those deprived of their family inheritance (cf. I Kings 21). The luxury **houses** become **desolate** and their fields unproductive. An **ephah** was only a tenth of a **homer,** which was five bushels. Similarly concern with feasting and drinking leads away from a true regard for what God does. The judgment takes the form of deprivation of true leadership and true knowledge of God.

5:14-17. The pattern here is **Woe to those . . .** followed by **therefore** (which introduces the word of judgment). Sometimes the stronger word **surely** is used instead of "therefore" (verse 9). Verse 14 begins again with **therefore** and includes another judgment closely similar to that of verse 13. Probably either a "woe" has been accidentally omitted or, in view of the similarity, two alternative forms of the judgment pronouncement have been preserved.

The essential part of the refrain from the day of Yahweh poem in chapter 2 is introduced in verses 15-16. This perhaps indicates the close of one small collection of woes and emphasizes the absolute supremacy and holiness of God. Verse 17 is obscure. We expect a continuance of the judgment idea. It has been suggested that this may be seen more clearly by rendering the second part: "and the ruins of those who have been wiped out young beasts shall eat up."

5:18-23. This new series of woes overlaps the first series with its mention of drunkenness. Verses 18-21 are concerned with the wrongheadedness of those who fail to see the true nature of God's action. They set right standards at nought, and trust in their own cleverness. Verses 22-23 return to the theme of social evils.

5:24-30. *Culminating Disaster.* The series of woes in verses 18-23 has no judgment pronouncement corresponding to each woe. But the omission is remedied and the whole section is drawn together in this concluding passage. The gloomy refrain at the end of verse 25 shows that this conclusion is actually the final stanza of the long poem in 9:8–10:4. Its placement here may be due to accidental dislocation, since 6:1–9:7 could have been inserted into the poem after its stanzas had got out of order. But it seems more probable that the stanza has been used deliberately here to provide the necessary final judgment on the people.

The poem as found in 9:8–10:4 consists of a series of judgments. Each culminates in the warning that this is not the last—that the divine anger still blazes. But here, in what appears to be the last stanza, there is no indication of further future judgment. The picture is of a foreign power summoned by God. The strength of its army appears almost supernatural. There is no escape from its relentless onslaught. The final note is of utter **darkness.**

5:26. The singular **nation** may well be the original form of the text, referring to the coming of Assyria. But the Hebrew has the plural "nations," which is probably due to a reinterpretation of the phrase. The judgment of God, as the Old Testament prophets frequently describe it, is expressed not just in terms of this or that historical moment. It has a finality which is seen in the picture of the nations of the world engaging in a final catastrophic battle against Jerusalem.

E. The Vision in the Temple (6:1-13)

The events described in this chapter are often said to represent Isaiah's call to be a prophet. But there is no precise indication that it is his first experience, and it is possible that some of Isaiah's prophecies should be dated before it. What is significant is the strength of the prophet's sense of being commissioned by God. An uncongenial message is laid on him by divine compulsion. Here is no casual encounter with God—nor is there a voluntary respone to a divine call. The hand of God rests heavily on Isaiah. Finding himself in the presence of Yahweh, he can do no other than accept what is laid on him.

6:1-3. *The Setting.* Uzziah (Azariah) **died** in 740 or 739 B.C. Isaiah's experience is set in the Jerusalem **temple,** perhaps on some notable occasion, some great annual feast. The stress on the divine kingship suggests the great autumnal festival which ushered in the new year with a ceremony of covenant renewal and a recommittal of king and people to their God. In the earthly temple—the chosen place of the divine dwelling—Isaiah sees the heavenly court, for heavenly and earthly dwelling are intimately bound up together. He becomes aware of the dread holiness of God, conscious of the acclamation of that holiness by the attendant beings. This sense of God's holiness is clearly a marked characteristic of Isaiah's understanding of God.

6:2-3. The **seraphim** (Hebrew plural of "seraph"; no indication is given of their number) are members of the heavenly court. They utter praise and carry out the divine command. Like the cherubim, they may have been thought of as human-animal creatures—perhaps winged snakes with human hands and faces, betraying an ancient and alien origin. Here they are subordinated to Yahweh, who is the Lord of the heavenly beings and also ruler of the whole earth.

6:4-7. *The Divine Presence.* The presence of God is expressed by the earthquake which shakes the earthly building. A great earthquake was remembered from the reign of Uzziah (cf. Amos 1:1 and Zechariah 14:5), but smaller tremors were not uncommon and became a natural symbol for the divine approach. The effect on the prophet of discovering himself in God's presence is shattering. He is conscious of the condition both of himself and of his people, of an uncleanness—including but not to be equated with sinfulness—which cannot stand in the face of that holiness. To see God is to die (cf. Exodus 33:20) unless God offers protection. Here the heavenly being mediates cleansing. The way is opened for Isaiah to hear the heavenly deliberations which reveal the reason for the vision.

6:8-13. *The Prophet's Commission.* The experience as described closely parallels Micaiah's vision in I Kings 22. But Isaiah is more involved in his experience. He not only speaks of what he sees taking place but finds himself caught up into it. As the deliberation of the heavenly court proceeds he knows that he is being commissioned. It is for this that he is being shown the secret purposes of God (cf. Amos 3:7). There is laid on him the commission to proclaim disaster, to speak a message which will fall on deaf ears, a message which will reveal more clearly the disobedience of Judah. The details of the message are not given, but its grimness calls out from the heart of the prophet the lamentation, so often the cry of the psalmists, **How long, O Lord?** Isaiah is shown a picture of a desolate land, of exile and destruction, of further ruthless judgment even on those who survive.

6:13. The text as it stands pictures total judgment. Perhaps the **tenth** is intended to refer to the sparing of Judah in the first cataclysm, the destruction of the nothern kingdom in 722, and to point to a further catastrophe which will overtake the southern kingdom. But the last words are problematic. The manuscript of Isaiah found in the Dead Sea Scrolls has a different reading, perhaps meaning: "as the oak and the terebinth when the sacred pillar of a high place is overthrown."

The total judgment is, however, modified by the last phrase: **The holy seed is its stump** (literally "pillar," perhaps meaning "sacred pillar"). There has been much discussion whether this is original to the chapter. That Isaiah thought in terms of a remnant which would survive disaster is clear—though it is also clear that he saw this as an act of divine grace (cf. 1:9). Possibly he himself offered this reinterpretation of his own message, but it seems more probable that it is a later gloss. The Greek translators reveal another stage in the interpretation of the material. They present a modified text of verse 12 which introduces the idea of divine mercy even there.

Both these later interpretations are still part of the tradition. The text is interpreted in the light of later needs. A word of God was discovered which was perhaps especially relevant to the generation which saw the ultimate disaster to Judah and Jerusalem at the hands of Babylon—and was also able to see in that disaster the working out of a divine purpose for God's people which could lead to their reestablishment in a new and better relationship.

F. Faith and Power Politics (7:1-25)

The threat of Assyria produced many shifts in policy and changes in alliance during the second half of the eighth century. The problem for the politicians—in this case Ahaz and his advisers—is to maneuver into security by whatever means offered. The prophet sees each situation as an occasion for divine judgment and promise. So faith and politics are set alongside one another.

7:1-9. *The Meeting at the Conduit.* As II Kings 16:5 shows, the attempt is being made by the two kingdoms of **Syria** and **Israel** to coerce Judah into an alliance against Assyria. Ahaz, being alarmed, appeals to Assyria, and not without good reason. His enemies both outside and within the state may depose him and replace him by a willing rebel. To the panic of king and court, gathered at the water conduit, the prophet speaks the assurance that the divine judgment is on Syria and Israel. They are frail rather than powerful. Security in the deepest sense lies in faith in God.

7:3-4. Isaiah is accompanied by his son **Shearjashub**—a name which would appear to be deliberately symbolic, though its interpretation can be variously given. Is it "a remnant shall return," as in the Revised Standard Version footnote? Or "only a remnant will return"? In any case the name is one of judgment—and of promise only insofar as judgment comes first.

Possibly the naming of the child belongs to a lost incident in Isaiah's contact with Ahaz. The king is being reminded of what has earlier been said. No clue is available, for the child is not mentioned again, though the name is reinterpreted in 10:21.

7:5-6. The opponents of Ahaz threaten to put the **son of Tabeel** on the throne. In the vocalized Hebrew text the name is spelled with a wrong vowel point, probably deliberate, that changes its meaning from "God is good" to "no good." The reference to the man by his father's name suggests a dignitary who has succeeded to his father's office and is therefore an influential person. The danger is obviously great that anti-Assyrian groups within the kingdom will see here their opportunity and assist in the overthrow of Ahaz.

7:8-9. These verses are not altogether clear. Perhaps **the head of** was a proverbial phrase suggesting that destruction would begin with the leaders. Verse 8*c* is put in parentheses in the Revised Standard Version because it clearly interrupts the context. This threat is probably an addition, but it is very obscure, since a threat of disaster **sixty-five years** later would seem to have no precise relevance. An ingenious suggestion is to read "yet six, yea five years more." This would indicate the imminence of the disaster vividly. But it must remain very uncertain, since numerical phrases of this kind are normally in the reverse order (cf. Amos 1:3). The pun in verse 9*cd* might be rendered "If you are not firm in faith you will not be firm."

7:10-17. *The Sign of Immanuel.* This is a new situation, perhaps in the court since the address is to the whole **house of David.** To confirm his faith Ahaz is offered any **sign** from **heaven** above to **Sheol,** the abode of the dead beneath the earth. His show of false piety conceals his lack of faith, but the prophet answers with his own sign—that of the child to be named **Immanuel** ("God is with us"). Without knowing who the child was we cannot be certain of the meaning of the sign. It seems probable that it represents an act of faith by some unknown woman—perhaps the prophet's wife, who appears in the next chapter.

But, as in chaper 6, the assurance of divine presence does not bring simple blessing. To those who have faith it is assurance. To those like Ahaz who do not have faith it is the token of a judgment at the hands of the Assyrians which will overtake the whole land. This theme of faith is echoed again in 8:8, 10.

7:18-25. *Judgment at the Hands of the Assyrians.* The day of judgment is described in terms suggestive of the day of the Lord in chapter 2. It is relentless. There is no escape, and the devastation of the land will be complete (cf. 6:11-13). The day, described in 2:12-22 in general terms, is here precisely identified as the Assyrian invasions which were to devastate the land in the time of Ahaz' successor Hezekiah (cf. 1:7-8 and chapters 36–37).

G. Judgment and Promise (8:1–9:7)

Many different elements make up this passage. Yet there can be seen certain linkages of thought which suggest that they may appropriately be treated together. The theme of judgment is interwoven with the expression of confidence in the saving power of God. The failure of his people finds the prophet confessing his faith, with the assurance that his message and indeed his life bear witness to the purposes of God. The darkness of ignorance and superstition will be answered by the light and rejoicing of a new age when a true Davidic king will reign in justice and righteousness.

8:1-4. *The Birth of a Son.* A renewed message of the overthrow of Syria and Israel is centered on the birth of a son to the prophet and the **prophetess.** This is a sign of the imminent disaster, for his name **Maher-shalal-hash-baz** (literally "speed spoil haste booty") confidently announces the judgment of God at the hands of Assyria. The name is written on a placard and attested—possibly instead of **in common characters** we should read "indelibly." The birth of the child, like the birth of Immanuel in 7:14, proclaims the truth of the message.

8:5-10. *A Warning to Judah.* Judah's lack of faith provides the counterpart to this, so that what might appear to be a message of pure hope becomes a warning of disaster. The **waters of Shiloah** are perhaps to be linked not simply with the ordinary water supply of Jerusalem but rather with the hidden river of God (cf. Psalm 46:4). The rejection of these waters brings on Judah the flood waters of the **River**, the Euphrates, which is identified as the power of **Assyria**. In verses 9-10 the **Immanuel** theme is picked up again. The planned onslaught of the nations is brought to nothing.

8:11-18. *A Warning to the Prophet.* The **strong hand** of God rests on his prophet to warn him against accepting the **way of this people.** Their values are wrong, and their awe is misplaced. So God's holiness becomes to the people, not a source of strength and refuge, but a stumbling block and a snare. The word which should be a word of life becomes to the disobedient a word of death, falling on deaf ears. But for the prophet the assurance of the divine purpose is there. It is preserved in the teaching which acts as an enduring witness to the divine will. Using the metaphor of a tied and sealed document (verse 16) he confidently proclaims that what has been said by God through him will be preserved safely. So too his **children** and **disciples** will be a sign to his people.

It has sometimes been thought that these verses indicate Isaiah's withdrawal from public activity, but there is no real suggestion of this. What is significant is the enduring testimony of his message, preserved **among** his **disciples**—or perhaps, if the Greek translators were right, preserved "so that it should not be understood," making the minds of the hearers dull (cf. 6:9-10) because their lack of faith prevents their acceptance of the divine word.

8:19-22. *Apostasy of the People.* In sharp contrast to the prophet's faith and his willingness to wait on God (verse 17) is the people's panicky search for security. They resort to magic and necromancy, turning to **consult the dead** for what they cannot find elsewhere (cf. I Samuel 28:7-19). The obscurity of these verses prevents precise indication of what is involved. But it is clear that here is a people so distressed they they turn against both king and God in their uncertainty.

9:1-7. *Restoration of the Davidic Kingdom.* The darkness finds its answer in a word of hope. The outlying parts of the ancient kingdom of David which have been lost will be restored ("the circuit of the nations" is perhaps more correct than **Galilee of the nations**). **Joy** will prevail at the overthrow of the oppressors. Over this reestablished Davidic kingdom there will rule an ideal king. He is acclaimed as a "wonder of a counselor," one whose counsel will be effective for his people's well-being; a "divine [hero] warrior"; a "father [of his people] from of old" (or perhaps "father of plunder," who by his conquests brings benefit to them); and a "prince who brings prosperity." His rule is to be established **for evermore,** and its character will be **justice** for all.

The picture of such a reign of justice is an important element in the conceptions of kingship in the Old Testament (cf. 11:2-5; II Sam. 23:3-7). It is expressed in the stories of the founding of the monarchy and particularly in the figure of **David.** This element becomes embodied in the hopes for the future, for an ideal king. But it would be wrong to think of this only in terms of the future. Insofar as each king enshrines the Davidic promises in himself he can be described in such exalted terms.

The form in which the promises are expressed, and their setting as an answer to the judgment oracles of the prophet, suggest that they may be later than Isaiah. Nevertheless they form an important part of the tradition which has come to be associated with him. They bring assurance of divine mercy mediated through the Davidic monarchy.

H. RELENTLESS DOOM (9:8–10:4)

This section is closely unified by the occurrence in 9:12, 17, 21 and 10:4 of the refrain:

> For all this his anger is not turned away
> and his hand is stretched out still.

This refrain also appears in 5:25. It appears likely that the three stanzas thus marked off in chapter 9 form the earlier part of a long poem of which 5:24 (or 25)-30 is the conclusion. It proclaims the relentness judgment of God in successive stages. In each stage an opportunity of repentance is possible. But Israel proves recalcitrant, and the warnings are unavailing. The structure, and indeed the wording, of the refrain resemble closely the poem in Amos 4:6-12. In the present form of the book the concluding stanza has been utilized to provide a final word of judgment to the woes of chapter 5. The remaining stanzas here have been linked with another woe (10:1-4) which provides a final note. Many suggestions have been made to explain this arrangement, but nothing can be established with any certainty (see above on 5:24-30).

9:8-21. *Judgment on the Northern Kingdom.* The three stanzas of the poem speak of different aspects of the people's life. In the first stanza (verses 8-12) the beginning of the moment of judgment is shown in relation to the confidence of those who regard their present setbacks as only temporary. What has **fallen** they **will build** again and better. The exact historical situation is not evident, but the sense of overconfidence of the people of **Samaria** is a theme fully elaborated in chaper 28. In verse 9 **will know** should be rendered "will be brought low."

9:13-17. Verse 13 could be the opening of the second stanza. But it is possible to read it as a comment, perhaps a marginal note of warning, designed to round off the first stanza. The fate of the leaders and the total failure of the people are indicated in the second stanza. In verse 14 the metaphors **head** and **tail** mean rulers and subjects, and express total overthrow. They are explained in verse 15 by precise reference to political leaders and false prophets. The **honored man** is perhaps to be taken as the courtier.

9:18-21. The third stanza describes the disaster of civil war that has brought utter chaos to the land. In verse 19 an alternative textual form suggests "is in confusion" for **is burned,** and this is certainly appropriate to the context.

These three pictures reflect aspects of the life of the truncated northern kingdom in the last years of its existence. They are terrible indictments of Israel's failure. Their place in the prophecy of Isaiah is linked to his concern that the fate which overtook that kingdom should be a warning to Judah. Reading the will of God in history can be dangerous. But learning from the experience of the past and seeing that past in the light of the divine will are ways in which the Old Testament often points to the nature of hope.

10:1-4. *The Fate of Oppressors.* Here is a **woe** dealing especially with oppressive judgment, the manipulation of law so that it no longer offers protection to the unprotected. The coming **day** of the Lord will find those whose gains are thus ill-gotten entirely without protection. They will be among the **prisoners** waiting for exile or judgment, or among **the slain.**

The whole passage is dark, almost without relief. It needs to be read in the context not only of the prophet's whole message but also of the use and reuse of his message over the succeeding years. Such declarations of God's patience in judgment made possible the understanding and the appropriation of disaster. Thus after the Exile a community could survive which was conscious of being heir to the past and recipient of the promises of divine grace.

I. GOD AND THE INSTRUMENT OF JUDGMENT (10:5-34)

Isaiah and other prophets frequently employ the concept of an instrument of divine judgment—a nation chosen by God to bring on the people the disaster which is interpreted as the outcome of their failure. But it is a concept which it is dangerous to apply indiscriminately. As the Old Testament often indicates—and as the New Testament makes even more clear—there is not always a direct correlation between behavior and fortune. Israel was to learn a deeper significance in its own misfortunes.

The anticipation and experience of invasion by the Assyrians play an important part in Isaiah's interpretation of his own times. This can be seen in his warnings to his country to rediscover its true way of life. At the same time he could not be unaware that Assyrian policy was ruthless in the extreme. The Assyrian might be an instrument of God in the sense that the will of God could be discerned in what was done. But that he was an unwitting instrument, and was himself under judgment, was also important to recognize. The poetic and prose passages which make up this section are all concerned with aspects of this theme of the relationship between God's use of Assyria and Assyria's place in the larger working out of God's purpose.

10:5-19. *Assyria in God's Purpose.* The declaration of God's purpose in using Assyria is contrasted in the Assyrian boast of the **nations** which have been overthrown. The cities mentioned in verse 9 were all taken in about twenty years. The overthrow of these represents the overthrow of their gods, and now the overthrow of **Jerusalem** seems imminent.

10:12-19. The theme is repeated but with a new element. God will complete **work** at Jerusalem—perhaps in terms of judging the people, perhaps in terms of delivering the city from siege and destruction (cf. 1:8; 29:1-4; chapters 36–37). Then God will be ready to deal with the **arrogant** boaster.

As in 37:24-25, the prophet quotes the Assyrian boasts in language very much like the courtly style of the Assyrian royal inscriptions describing the conquests. But this boasting is out of place. The Assyrian is the instrument of divine action and must be obedient to the divine will. Thus judgment will come. God will go forth like a **fire.** The Assyrian power will be burned away like a **forest,** leaving only a handful of **trees** standing. Verse 18*c* is perhaps to be regarded as an explanatory note, applying the figure of the forest to the people.

10:20-27*b*. *Hope in Judgment.* This judgment of Assyria provides a setting for two short statements indicating the way of hope for Israel (verses 20-23, 24-27*b*). Only a **remnant** will remain. The word "remnant" picks up the comment on the Assyrian disaster in verse 19, and also links to the name of Isaiah's son in 7:3. The first word is thus of judgment (verses

20-23). But with it is linked a reassurance comparing the threat of Assyria with that of **Egypt** (verses 24-27*b*). The events of the exodus period are a message of hope, and the point is reinforced with a reference to the overthrow of **Midian** (cf. 9:4) at the hands of Gideon (Judges 7–8). Verse 25*b* should be rendered "my anger will come completely to an end." This exhortation to Jerusalem not to fear the Assyrians may be compared with Isaiah's assurances to Hezekiah in chapter 37.

10:27c-34. *The March of Assyria.* This poem, probably fragmentary, vividly depicts the Assyrian advance. Its opening line is in a badly corrupted state (see the Revised Standard Version footnote). A slightly superior alternative suggestion is "He went up from before Samaria." The advance is traced until the enemy is within sight of **Jerusalem.** Verses 33-34 provide an answer, in which again the Assyrian is depicted as a **forest,** to be **cut down** in judgment by God.

The interpretation of the section is difficult. It is clear that various elements have been combined because of their relation to the main theme of God and Assyria. What is less certain is which of these materials had a different reference before being applied to this theme. Thus the oracle in verses 33-34 is sometimes seen as an introduction to the next chapter. If this interpretation is correct, the cutting down of the forest indicates judgment on Judah and the fall of its monarchy—a theme taken up in 11:1. It is not unlikely that an oracle originally proclaiming judgment on Judah has been reapplied to Assyria. The same may be true of verses 15-19.

Such a development in interpretation would show how the message spoken by the prophet to one situation is not limited to that one meaning. It can be seen, by the prophet himself or by his followers, to speak afresh to new moments of experience. Insofar as the prophet mediates the true word of God its truth remains. Its continued significance rests, not in its being a prediction of the future, but in its revealing of truth about God. Like the whole Old Testament, it is Godward looking rather than only forward looking.

J. THE TIME OF PROMISE (11:1–12:6)

The separate elements which make up this section may well date from very different times. But as they now stand they form a unit presenting the theme of hope, partly in terms of the restoration of the Davidic monarchy and partly in terms of a gathering of the scattered members of the community. They also provide a fitting climax to the collection of oracles making up the opening part of the book (chapters 1–12).

11:1-9. *Restoration of the Davidic Kingdom.* The opening of chapter 11 links closely in thought to the end of chapter 10. Whatever the precise application of 10:33-34, the theme of a tree cut down provides the start for an oracle concerning the now fallen house of David. The theme of Davidic restoration is central, and the significance of the monarchy is seen in the breadth of conception found here.

It is likely that both this utterance and that of 9:2-7 owe much of their language and imagery to royal oracles associated with every Davidic ruler. So far as form is concerned, these can be traced back into pre-Israelite royal material. Such statements would be relevant at the outset of the reign of any new Davidic king. But their present form here seems to envisage the situation of the exilic age when the monarchy had come to an end.

11:2-5. The hopes focused on the kings were not lost. They became concentrated on a new and future figure who would restore the kingdom and completely fulfill the requirements of the true king. This is seen in the stress laid on the activity of the divine **Spirit** in the ideal king. Judgment **with righteousness** and the overthrow of evil are vital to this (in verse 4c we should probably read "violent" for **earth**). But there is a deeper aspect too. The divine Spirit is to operate in and through this ideal king not only to exercise wisdom and discernment but also to maintain true religion.

11:6-9. The right order to be established extends into the natural world. In the ideal age to which the oracle points there will be no enmity between the animals. Peace and the true religion, here expressed as **knowledge of the LORD**, will be found in the **holy mountain** of Jerusalem—and hence in the whole land, and indeed in the whole earth. In verse 6 a good suggested rendering is "calf and lion shall feed together" and in verse 7 "cow and bear shall be in amity."

11:10-16. *The Gathering of the Remnant.* The theme of the ideal Davidic king is taken further, portraying him as central to the life of all the **nations** (cf. 2:2-4). This provides a link to the statement of restoration of scattered members **of his people,** which in turn introduces a poetic utterance developing that theme. The concept of a gathering of the scattered is interwoven with that of extending the Davidic kingdom into Edom, Moab, and Ammon. It is from Assyrian exile in particular that the **remnant** will return. This theme is relevant to the period of Isaiah when Samaria fell. But it is much more significant for the period after the Babylonian exile. The language, reminiscent of later parts of the book, suggests that this is a later poem.

This would fit well too with the theme of reconciliation between **Judah** and **Ephraim.** This idea can be seen in the exilic period (cf. Ezekiel 37:15-28), and became especially important in the time of the Samaritan schism in the fourth century and later. Here again can be seen the way the material of the Isaiah tradition has been welded with later elements so that it continued to speak a message of warning and hope.

12:1-6. *A Psalm of Praise.* The prospect of a reunited people, a new Davidic kingdom, and a restored world order finds its climax here. Two short passages provide a fitting conclusion to this section and also to the whole complex of chapters 1–12. In verses 1-2 the saving power of God is stressed. Though the singular form (**my salvation**) is used, the psalm probably refers to the fortunes of the whole people. Verse 1 points to the experience of exile and acknowledges judgment and salvation.

The obscure opening of verse 3 perhaps refers to the **water** ritual of the feast of tabernacles, or booths. This feast was closely linked with the celebration of the deliverance of the Exodus (cf. Leviticus 23:43). The praise of God which follows concentrates on the greatness of divine salvation—a testimony to all **nations** of

God's nature and an invitation for all to acknowledge God. Verse 6*b* makes a verbal link back to the realization of the presence of the **Holy One** in the **midst** of Israel which Isaiah has experienced. That holiness induces awe, for it works both for judgment and for salvation.

II. ISAIAH AND THE NATIONS (13:1–23:18)

A. THE DAY OF YAHWEH FOR BABYLON (13:1–14:2)

Chapters 13–14 clearly belong closely together. The heading in 13:1, **oracle concerning Babylon,** covers them both, as may be seen from the use of the word "oracle" at the beginning of succeeding sections. But it is convenient to divide the passage into two and to make the division after 14:2 rather than at the end of chapter 13. The words of blessing to Israel in 14:1-2, though quite separate from the preceding material, form a climax. The words of judgment, directed specifically at Babylon, are answered by the assurance of divine promise.

13:1-16. *The Day of Destruction.* Chapter 13 clearly refers to Babylon (cf. verse 19). But it is less certain that this was the original purpose of verses 2-16. It has been suggested that **gates of the nobles** is intended as a play on the name Babylon ("gate of God"), but this does not seem very probable. While the imagery of these verses may be related to the day of Yahweh described in Zephaniah 1, the passage is not necessarily late. There is a close connection with the poem in chapter 2 on this theme and with the word of Amos 5. We may reasonably assume that an Isaiah utterance on the day of Yahweh has been elaborated and used to give to the judgment on Babylon in verses 17-22 a universal setting. It is not just Babylon which will fall—though to the community of the exilic period this was of immediate importance. The hostile world—indeed the whole created order—comes under the judgment of God (cf. chapters 24–27).

13:2-10. The day of Yahweh comes as God summons the divinely consecrated agents of destruction (verses 2-3). With

35

God's instruments of wrath, God prepares for the overthrow of all the **nations,** the destruction of the **whole earth.** The picture proclaims the absolute sovereignty of God. The poem continues with a vivid portrayal of the terror which God's coming brings (verses 6-8). The destruction of sinners is accompanied by cosmic evidence of God's power (verses 9-10).

13:11-16. The theme of the high ones brought low, emphasized in chapter 2, is again brought out in a series of pictures which depict the utter disaster. **Men** will become scarcer than the most precious **gold.** As the **heavens** and **earth** shake all **will flee** in the hope of finding safety. But they will be **caught** and destroyed. Knowledge of the actual conditions of warfare and of the devastation of Judah experienced in the time of Isaiah lends vividness to the pictures of this grim day.

13:17–14:2. *God's Purpose in History.* The summons to the **Medes** to bring judgment to Babylon is provided with a wider setting. The overthrow of the power which has overcome Judah is seen not just as a historic moment but as an element within God's total purpose. The relentlessness of the enemy, the shatterng of **Babylon, the glory of kingdoms,** the pictures of perpetual desolation (cf. chapter 34)—all express the kind of hostility which Babylonian power evoked. The indication of the Medes as the agent of judgment points to the exilic age. Babylon actually fell to the Medo-Persian power under the rule of Cyrus the Perisan.

14:1-2. But the meaning of the fall of Babylon is just part of a cosmic disaster. It is seen as ushering in the blessing of **Israel.** The emphasis is on a reversal of fortunes, with the subordination of Israel's oppressors. Yet there is a pointer to the entry of **aliens** into Israel's community which cuts across this otherwise narrow interpretation of God's saving purpose.

B. The Tyrant's Fall (14:3-32)

The prose introduction in verses 3-4*a* indicates that the material which follows is set in the period of the exile in

Babylon. There is the prospect of a release from servitude when Babylon falls. Together with the interpretative comment of verses 22-23 it makes the application of the intervening poem seemingly refer to the fall of Babylon. The remainder of the chapter is concerned with an earlier situation—that of the fall of Assyria and a judgment on Philistia (verses 24-31). It culminates in a final hopeful word for Zion.

14:4b-21. Oracle Against a Tyrant. This poem does not mention Babylon. There are features which suggest that it may have had a general reference, or it may have applied originally to Assyria. Whether it derives from Isaiah is difficult to say, since it contains so much that is unlike other sayings and poems of the prophet. Possibly its subject matter might account for this.

The poem is a taunt song or mocking song concerning the downfall of a tyrant. At his fall the nations rejoice and the world is released from servitude. The reference to the **cedars** in verse 8 is closely paralleled in the Assyrian boasting in 37:24. **Sheol,** the land of the dead, greets the tyrant. The **kings**—perhaps those subdued by the tyrant—deride him for being brought as low as they (verses 9-11).

14:12-15. The theme of downfall is vividly elaborated in a mythological picture. The tyrant is likened to the **Day Star.** He is pictured as rebelling and seeking to find a place enthroned in the **assembly** of the gods on the far northern mountain, to ride the **clouds,** and to be **like the Most High.** The language and allusions of this point to Canaanite mythology. A comparison may be made with similar material in Ezekiel 28.

The dwelling of the gods and the riding of the clouds are both known to us from the Ras Shamra texts found at Ugarit in northern Syria. So too is **Dawn** as a deity, of whom this figure is described as **son.** The **Most High** is Elyon, the title so often used of God in his association with Jerusalem. All these elements may be paralleled in the Old Testament, suggesting how richly Canaanite religion and mythology have influenced Old Testament thought.

14:16-21. The picture changes to that of the unburied tyrant. It has been suggested that this is a scene at his death. More probably the degradation is simply elaborated with this feature, which is frequent in taunting and judgment poems. The poem reveals a rich series of pictures concerning **Sheol,** indicating a much more varied pattern of thought than is found in the Old Testament generally. The poem closes with a general reflection on the downfall of **evildoers.**

It is clear that this poem would fit many situations. Mythological statements become metaphors. These can be applied both to wider political issues—for example, the fall of **Babylon** and to more local and individual needs. In light of the preceding chapter, where the fall of Babylon is seen as bound up with the day of Yahweh, the present immediate application can be seen as only one part of its meaning. It carries with it the sense of a world judgment on evil. This may be seen also in the way the ancient rendering of **Day Star** as Lucifer (verse 12) links the passage to ideas of a primeval fall and so to the overthrow of the whole power of evil.

14:24-27. *Oracle Against Assyria.* The application of the poem to Babylon makes for some disunity in the present form of the chapter. This judgment oracle on Assyria is not unlike that of chapter 10. It depicts the appropriateness of the Assyrian power being broken in God's own land. The oracle recalls the saving power of God expressed, as in the Exodus, in his stretched-out hand.

14:28-32. *Oracle Against Philistia.* The final section is dated **in the year that King Ahaz died.** But it is not Ahaz' death which has caused rejoicing in **Philistia,** for he was not its overlord. A small emendation of the text would give "In the year that the king died, I saw." In this context it would be reasonable to assume an allusion to the death of Sargon II of Assyria in 705. The message is a warning against premature rejoicing, and so against rebellion (cf. chapter 20). Dire judgment will come from the **north**—that is, from Assyria.

14:32. This final verse has been understood as a warning to Judah not to respond to Philistine invitations to rebel. But it can also be understood as a climax of promise, addressed perhaps to the **messengers,** or ambassadors, of more than one **nation.** The downfall of the tyrant—whether Assyria or Babylon—and the overthrow of evil by the saving power of God find a counterpart in the establishing of Zion as a **refuge** for the **afflicted**.

C. ORACLE CONCERNING MOAB (15:1–16:14)

It is difficult to reach any satisfying conclusions about these two chapters. Both are concerned with the fate of Moab, that near and often hated neighbor of Israel east of the Dead Sea. The fact that a large part of the text reappears in Jeremiah 48:29-38 in another collection of foreign-nation oracles makes genuine Isaiah material here seem improbable. The textual problems are great (cf. the Revised Standard Version footnotes). It is by no means clear whether this is a reasonably unified poem or, as is more probable, a combination of two or possibly three poetic utterances drawn together by the prose comment and application at the end (16:13-14).

15:1-9. *Lament for Moab.* This poem seems to be continued in 16:6-11 (or 12) and perhaps should include 16:2. What is in many ways most remarkable is that it contains a lament at the distressed state of Moab (15:5; 16:9). It is true that 16:6 lays the blame for Moab's downfall on its people's **pride**—a reminder of Isaiah's judgments on the proud in chapter 2. But it vividly portrays the disaster, echoing the place names within the country. In this it resembles oracles of Isaiah (10:27-32) and Micah (1:10-16). The chief places named have been identified. **Kir** (15:1) and **Kir-heres** (16:11) mean **Kir-hareseth** (16:7), a city in southern Moab. The **Brook of the Willows** (15:7) was the Zered, boundary between Moab and Edom to the south. **Dibon** in 15:9, taken from the Dead Sea manuscript, seems a doubtful correction for the unknown "Dimon" in other manuscripts, since Dibon was not on a river. **Sibmah** (16:8-9) was a few miles southwest of **Heshbon**.

16:1-5. *A Plea for Refugees.* This poem appears to depict ambassadors coming from Moab to Judah seeking refuge for fleeing Moabites. Verse 2 seems to be an intrusion and may be misplaced from chapter 15. On **lambs** cf. II Kings 3:4. **Sela** in Moab is otherwise unknown. Some who view chapters 15–16 as a single poem take it to mean the fortress in Edom (cf. II Kings 14:7). They see here a situation in which Moabites have fled south into Edom (cf. 15:7) and must seek permission from Judah to remain there because Edom is at the time subject to Judah—as, for example, in the reigns of Uzziah and Jotham.

The plea ends with the confidence that a rule of **righteousness** and **justice** will be established under a Davidic king. The implication would seem to be that even Moab will share in the final day of blessing. Perhaps such hope is to be linked with the view of Moab implied in Ruth, where David's ancestry is traced to a pious Moabite woman.

16:6-11. *Further Lament for Moab.* See above on 15:1-9.

16:12-14. *Prose Conclusion.* Verse 12 says that Moab finds no comfort in appeal to her own gods. This may be a corruption of the concluding lines of the poem. The comment in verses 13-14 indicates that the messages concerning Moab refer to the past, but now doom will soon fall relentlessly on its people.

With these uncertainties we cannot hope to discover a historical situation. The Assyrians may well have campaigned in Moab. Later disasters also undoubtedly affected that area. Even earlier events could have provoked such words. What is most significant is the presence here in the Old Testament of such poems as these. Moab, like other nations, is under the judgment of God. But that judgment is not pronounced without an expression of distress at the fate of its people. Such concern with other nations may be seen in Amos 1–2, where the unrighteousness of one nation to another brings down divine condemnation. Some scholars have thought, we have here pieces of Moabite poetry. If so, then their inclusion reveals a sympathetic understanding of the fate of a neighboring land. There must have been those in Israel who could not view with equanimity the effects of warfare. They must have expressed in poetic form the anguish which they felt and the hope which they cherished for those who were so closely bound up with their own history.

D. THE WORK OF GOD IN HISTORY (17:1–18:7)

There is no unity in this section. But it may be helpful to see in it two climaxes of thought. In 17:7-8, the first subsection is brought to a close with the hope that Israel will learn to trust fully in its holy God. In 18:7 the hope is extended to point to a day when the envoys of distant peoples will come to Zion. The remaining passages are words of judgment. They concern various peoples and belong in all probability to various situations. In the present form of the material they are subordinated to the prospect of true obedience.

17:1-11. *Oracle Concerning Damascus.* A heading, like those elsewhere in this part of the book, introduces a short oracle (verses 1-3). It proclaims doom to the Aramean kingdom of **Syria** with its capital at **Damascus.** To this is linked a word of judgment on **Israel** also. This saying belongs to the period of the Syro-Ephraimitic war, indicated more fully in chapters 7–8. Verse 3*cd* means that what is left of Syria will be no better than what is left of Israel. Verses 4-6 provide a comment on this: **the glory of Jacob will be brought low,** and in a harvest of disaster nothing will be left but the merest remnant. The **Valley of Rephaim** was near Jerusalem on the southwest.

The plea for right trust in God in verses 7-8 fits well with oracles which suggest the need for faith, which was stressed in chapter 7. Perhaps here a later interpreter has picked up various other sayings from Isaiah to make the point clear (cf. 2:20; 22:8*b*-11). **Asherim** probably refers to fertility symbols associated with the worship of the Canaanite goddess Asherah. Verses 9-11 provide a further comment, stressing both the doom which is to come and the reason for it. God has been **forgotten,** and trust has been placed in **alien** religious practices. The allusion is probably to potted **plants** representing gardens of the god Adonis.

17:12–18:7. *Judgment on Assyria and Egypt.* As so often in Isaiah, a specific word of judgment is linked with a more general statement. It is possible that the original reference of 17:12-14 was to the Assyrians, rebuked by God (as in 10:5-11) and

41

suddenly brought to disaster (as in 37:33-38). Similarly 18:1-2 alludes to the activities of Egypt, so closely involved in the political troubles of the reign of Hezekiah. **Whirring wings** probably should read "winged ships"—that is, sailboats. Egypt's Ethiopian rulers are depicted as sending **ambassadors** Perhaps this was originally intended as a reference to attempts at raising general rebellion against Assyria.

But this particular political situation is now given a wider significance. The terms used in 17:12-14 are strongly suggestive of the great final overthrow of the nations. In 18:3 the whole **world** is invited to pay heed to what God is doing. God looks down from the divine **dwelling** and doom will fall on the nations (18:4-6). Again it may be that a saying is here used which originally referred to Assyria and to Isaiah's immediate situation. But it is given a wider meaning. The great moment of judgment brings the ambassadors to **Zion,** not for political intrigue, but because it is where the name of God is revealed, where God is to be worshiped (18:7; cf. 2:2-4).

E. ORACLE CONCERNING EGYPT (19:1-25)

Three sections make up the poetic part of this chapter (verses 1-15), which has a heading like other chapters in this part of the book.

19:1-4. *Civil Disruption.* In the first section Yahweh is pictured as **riding on a swift cloud**—a portrayal derived from Canaanite thought—to the dismay of the **Egyptians** and their gods. It is as if Yahweh were again engaged in battle with Egypt as at the time of the Exodus. Indeed such a parallelism appears to underlie much of the chapter. Disaster is proclaimed in a variety of terms. There is to be civil strife, intercity warfare, and division between the two kingdoms of Egypt. There is also dismay. Egypt is led to consult her magicians, as in the plague stories of Exodus. Finally there is conquest by a **fierce** alien ruler.

19:5-10. *Natural Disaster.* In this second section the picture changes to disaster of a natural kind. The **Nile,** on which the land depends, dries up. Gone is the sustenance of **fishermen** and of those whose crafts need good crops for raw materials. **Pillars of the land** (in verse 10) probably should read "craftsmen."

19:11-15. *Failure of Wisdom.* The emphasis in this third section rests on the failure of Egypt's wisdom. This again suggests the plague stories, and is a reminder that much of ancient Near Eastern wisdom literature came from Egypt. The skill of its **wise counselors** and statesmanship of its **princes** has come to nothing. **Zoan** is believed to be a later name for the city called Rameses at the time of the Exodus (cf. Exodus 12:37).

It is difficult to decide whether these judgments on Egypt belong to the period of Isaiah. Certainly he was much concerned with the unreliability of Egypt and with the danger to Judah of Egyptian alliance (cf. chapters 20; 30-31). The language, however, is not characteristic of Isaiah. It is closely linked with that in chapters 40-66 and in Ezekiel.

19:16-25. *Conquest by Judah.* The theme of battle with Egypt is continued in this series of prose oracles. A number of them speak of what will happen **in that day.** This indicates that we are dealing, not with precise historical moments, but with a prospect of the final age. It has been suggested that these sayings are to be linked with the theme of conquest. The exodus ideas of conflict (in verses 11-15) are appropriately followed by this series about a conquest of Egypt by **Judah** which will bring Egypt to salvation.

19:16-17. Egypt is in **terror** before Judah, just as the inhabitants of Canaan were in fear (cf. Joshua 2:9; 24:12). This judgment theme provides the link with the preceding poetry.

19:18. We are told of **five cities** in Egypt where Hebrew is spoken. It is often suggested that these were places where Jews had settled during the dispersion following the destruction in Jerusalem in 586. From the period of the Exile onward increasing numbers of Jews were to be found in Egypt. In the fifth century this is attested by the Elephantine Papyri, which reveal that a small Jewish military force lived on an island opposite modern Aswan. After Alexander the Great's conquest there were substantial settlements, especially in Alexandria.

Here one of the cities is given a name, but the text is problematic. If the theme is conquest, then it may be appropriate to recall the conquest of five cities of Canaan, including Jerusalem (Joshua 10). We could then see here a promise that all Egypt will **swear allegiance** to Yahweh.

Perhaps this also explains the obscure name **City of the Sun,** which is found in some manuscripts. An alternative is "City of Righteousness," a designation of Jerusalem (cf. 1:26). If this is the original, it may mean that one of the five Egyptian cities will become the Jerusalem of Egypt. On this hypothesis the text was subsequently modified to "City of Sun," perhaps with a reference to Heliopolis, where a temple was built by a refugee high priest during the Maccabean period in the second century B.C. An even later alteration meant to deny the propriety of this shrine might then produce the third reading, "City of Destruction." But the whole question is obscure.

19:19-25. In the third saying (verses 19-22) Egypt turns to God and learns, by discipline and restoration, the way of obedience and life. In the fourth (verse 23) a still wider prospect is opened with Assyria joined to Egypt in the worship of God. In the fifth (verses 24-25) the "conquest" is complete. Egypt is **my people** and Assyria is **the work of my hands,** while Israel retains a special place as **my heritage.**

To look for a specific historical situation for such words would be inappropriate. But it may well be that in the Greek period, when Jews found themselves between the power of the Ptolemies in Egypt and the Seleucids in Syria, an interpreter of the "school of Isaiah" saw this rich promise extended even to the enemies of his people. Whatever the situation, the sayings testify to the deep concern for the outside world which can frequently be seen in this book.

F. THE PROPHETIC SIGN OF EGYPT'S DOOM (20:1-6)

It is clear that this little narrative of a symbolic action performed by Isaiah belongs with such passages as chapter 7, to the biography of the prophet. But it has been placed here because of its concern with **Egypt.** Thus it provides a further comment on the material in chapters 18–19. It is set in the reign of the Assyrian **Sargon II** (722-705), who took control of **Ashdod** in 711. The ruler placed on the throne of Ashdod by the Assyrians was deposed and a rebel put in his place. When the city later fell to Sargon, this rebel escaped to **Ethiopia** but was extradited and returned for punishment.

The prophet, **naked and barefoot**—that is, wearing only an undergarment or loincloth—portrays himself as a captive to show that the captivity of Egypt is decreed by God. Those who have relied on Egypt's help are put to shame. The people of the **coastland** of Philistia are left without hope of deliverance from Assyria.

G. THE PROPHET AS WATCHMAN (21:1-17)

The three sections of this chapter are all somewhat obscure. They contain both textual difficulties and problems of historical interpretation. The first two sections (verses 1-10 and 11-12) have probably been linked together because of the prophet's function as a **watchman.** He waits on God and is ready to proclaim the message which is revealed to him. The third passage too (verses 13-17) emphasizes the prophet's role as spokesman of God. Therefore it is convenient to treat all three together while recognizing that they were originally separate. Also to make a sharp division at the end of the chapter is probably not entirely satisfactory.

21:1-10. *The Fall of Babylon.* The heading in verse 1 is obscure, possibly because the text is corrupt. It may be that the **wilderness of the sea** refers to the area to which Babylon belongs. What is most remarkable is the expression of the prophetic experience in these verses. Just as Micah agonizes at the fate of his people (Micah 1:8), so this unknown prophet vividly expresses his **anguish** at the disaster he foresees. He portrays the complacency of those who are doomed and yet **eat**

and **drink** when they should be alert—a picture which strongly suggests a connection with the elaborate description of Belshazzar's feast in Daniel 5. The prophet, apparently in Jerusalem, foresees the coming of the message of Babylon's downfall. He is able to **announce** to his people the word which has come from God.

The most probable occasion for this prophecy is the fall of Babylon to Cyrus of Persia in 539. Some have argued that it could refer to the Assyrian conquest of Babylon in Isaiah's own time. But the situation of the prophet's own people (cf. verse 10*a*) suggests rather the hope of release from Babylonian rule. That the prophet should be in a state of anguish at such an event is perhaps to be understood as an expression of the overpowering nature of the divine word, together with the uncertainty which must attend the overthrow of one great power by another.

21:11-17. *Oracles Concerning Edom and Arabia.* The brief, probably fragmentary, oracle on **Dumah** (verses 11-12) evidently refers to Edom. Its brevity makes interpretation very uncertain. It may be an expression of the prophet's concern at the darkness of disaster in Edom and a hope that the **morning** light of deliverance will soon come. The oracle on **Arabia** (verses 13-17) consists ·first of a poetic saying apparently expressing concern for defeated **Dedanites** who have fled to the oasis of **Tema.** This is followed by a prose saying which applies the oracle to a disaster to come upon the land of **Kedar.** In both of these oracles there appears an element of sympathy for non-Judean sufferers.

H. JUDAH IN THE TIME OF HEZEKIAH (22:1-25)

It is not unreasonable to suppose that all the different elements of this chapter are related to the situation in Judah when Sennacherib invaded the country. For a time Jerusalem was threatened (cf. chapter 36–37). But this situation is clearer for some parts than for others, which seem to fit a later time better. The obscure title, **valley of vision,** is derived presumably from verse 5.

22:1b-4. *Unjustified Rejoicing.* This first part can be understood as referring to Sennacherib's withdrawal, but the detail does not altogether fit. Rejoicing at deliverance would seem appropriate to that occasion, but the loss of the **rulers** of the city appears out of place. This may be an oracle relevant to the capture of Jerusalem in 597, when those who remained might rejoice but had lost king and leaders. The prophet sees more deeply the nature of the disaster to his people.

22:5-8a. *A Day of Confusion.* This second section is also appropriate to 597. The description of the disaster in terms of the day of Yahweh fits well with the understanding of that later period, when the works of Isaiah were reapplied (see above on 2:6-4:6). The oracle could be of earlier origin and could have been reused in this new context. **Elam,** east of Babylonia, was allied with Merodach-baladan (cf. 39:1) in revolt against Assyria in the time of Hezekiah. It may have supplied troops to Nebuchadnezzar in 597. "Aram rode on horses" may be an alternate reading for **with chariots and horsemen,** perhaps referring to Arameans from the region of **Kir,** which was probably in Mesopotamia (cf. II Kings 16:9; Amos 1:5, 9:7).

22:8b-11. *Defenses of the City.* The interpretation of the preceding passages as coming from the period of Hezekiah is really due to this portion. It describes the lack of faith of those in Isaiah's own time who pay heed to the city's material defenses but not to the purposes of God. Such a comment could apply to Ahaz as well as to Hezekiah, but the reference to the **reservoir** seems to point to the latter (cf. II Kings 20:20).

22:12-14. *Revelry in the Face of Doom.* This oracle seems to indicate the same kind of situation as in verses 1-4. The people should see in their present position a summons to **mourning,** but their reaction is superficial. This would fit the period of Hezekiah, but also the days after the capture of Jerusalem in 597.

22:15-25. *Pronouncement Against Shebna.* This utterance provides the clear indication of a historical setting, and is perhaps the basis for the interpretation of the whole chapter. The section should be headed "Concerning Shebna." The officer **over the household** (literally "house," or "palace"; cf. I Kings 4:6) was one of the important royal officers. He is condemned here for wrong ambition, building himself a **tomb**, possibly on Mount Zion, and evidently having his own **chariots**. He is condemned to exile in a **wide land**—that is, a flat open country—and is to be deposed from his office.

22:20-23. Shebna's replacement by **Eliakim** seems to be borne out by 36:3, 22 and 37:2, where we find Eliakim "over the household" and Shebna "secretary." Was Shebna then simply demoted, or are there other events of which we know nothing? Perhaps behind these events there lie the complex political rivalries of a period when appeal to Egypt was in the air. The sharpness of Isaiah's attack suggests direct opposition to what he believed to be right.

22:24-25. These last verses contain yet another element—an obscure reference to the danger which threatens Eliakim. The whole section gives insight into Isaiah's concern with the political problems of his day and his judgment on the politicians who lead his people astray (cf. chapters 30–31).

III. ORACLE AGAINST PHOENICIA (23:1-18)

The poem in verses 1-12 is headed **oracle concerning Tyre,** but it is clear that it refers to the whole area of Phoenicia. Since in the Hebrew **Tyre** does not appear in verse 1c, we may see a structure in which verses 1-4 speak of **Sidon,** verses 6-9 of **Tyre,** and verses 10-12 of **Canaan** (that is, Phoenicia). The application to Tyre alone may well be due to later reinterpretation.

23:1-14. *Ruin of the Sea Trade.* The text is difficult at many points. But the judgment of Phoenicia and the lament over it are clear. The whole area is pictured as **laid waste.** The lament is attributed to the merchant **ships** on which Phoenicia depends. Verse 4 perhaps suggests the idea of the **sea** as mother of the people. Verse 10 may be emended to read: "Cultivate your land (as is done by the Nile)," suggesting the total loss of seafaring activities. The disaster is seen as resulting from God's decree; the wealth of the **merchants** avails nothing (cf. Ezekiel 27). News of the disaster reaches the seamen when they stop at **Cyprus** on the homeward voyage. The location of **Tarshish** is uncertain, but it may have been on the southwest coast of Spain. The **Shihor** was in northeastern Egypt, perhaps the eastern arm of the Nile delta.

23:13. It is likely that the poem originally referred to some event in the Assyrian period. The obscure wording of this verse most probably indicates a reinterpretation of the thirteen-year siege of Tyre by Nebuchadnezzar in the sixth century—the **Chaldeans** (Babylonians), **not Assyria,** did it. The detail of the verse makes the description more precise.

23:15-18. *The Recovery of Tyre.* Perhaps at a still later stage the poem was again reapplied—this time to Alexander the Great's destruction of Tyre and its revival in the third century. Like a forgotten **harlot** the city seeks to win back its lovers. After **seventy years** of judgment—like the period foretold by Jeremiah for Judah (Jeremiah 25:12; 29:10)—Tyre will recover. But the final word is of the dedication of its wealth to God, part of the tribute of the nations (cf. 61:6). Tyre too will have its place in God's ordering of the world. Its merchandise will be a blessing to God's people.

IV. THE LAST DAYS (24:1–27:13)

The foreign-nation oracles of chapters 13–23 are followed by a section which pictures the final age—the moment of judgment of the whole world and of the fulfillment of promise. Here an element frequently found in judgment oracles on the nations is expressed more fully. What is said about a particular people is set in the context of the expectation of total judgment and often also of final promise.

The whole world is to be brought fully under the divine will. This involves both the condemnation of failure and the expression of saving power. The establishment of Zion as central to a newly ordered world is the expression of confidence that it is God alone who will reign supreme.

We see here many of the elements subsequently developed in the apocalyptic writings of the last two centuries B.C. and the first century A.D. Examples of these writings are found in parts of Daniel and Revelation. But these chapters are not apocalyptic—that is, they do not claim to set forth hidden revelations. They contain a combination of prophetic and hymnic elements in which the final age is spoken of and the victory of God is acclaimed.

These themes run through the whole section, and it is impossible to be certain of the right method of division. One passage links to another as the unknown prophet or prophets and the psalmists combine to express the awe and the joy of anticipating God's ultimate purposes.

A. The World Judgment (24:1-20)

This passage begins and ends with the total overthrow of the earth. It is completely devastated, and verse 2 indicates that there will be no escape. No privilege or position can deliver any from the disaster.

24:4-13. *Desolation of the Earth.* The disaster is portrayed in more detail. The reason for the judgment is brought out as human failure. The **everlasting covenant** is **broken**—here not the one with Israel, but in a broader sense the covenant of right relationship between all people and God (cf. Genesis 9:17). This leads to the pronouncing of a **curse** (cf. Zechariah 5:1-4). **Mirth** and festival come to an end. **City** and land are desolate, and the desolation is as complete and final as a harvest (verse 13, cf. 17:6). There are some obscurities in the text. In verse 4 the last clause means literally "the exalted of earth's people languish" and this may be correct. But omitting "people," we may read "the heights of the earth." In verse 6 "are appalled" is possible as an alternative to **suffer for their guilt,** and for **scorched** we may substitute "weak." The reference to the **city of chaos** in verse 10 is obscure. Attempts have been made to identify the city, but perhaps it is not intended to point to a particular place. Rather, it is meant to give a general picture of the overthrow of city life, a return to anarchy and chaos. The phrase **reached its eventide** in verse 11 is very improbable. "Passed away" is a likely correction.

24:14-20. *Joy and Anguish of Final Judgment.* The moment of final judgment is one of **praise** at the **majesty** of God (verses 14-16b). Throughout the earth the faithful welcome God's glorious activity. The capital letters for **Righteous One** in verse 16 are not necessarily correct. The phrase may refer to the righteous ones who share in the new age. For the prophet, however, the moment of judgment is a moment of anguish (verses 16c-f). This ushers in a new and even more cataclysmic picture of the disaster. Three alliterative Hebrew words in verse 17a—a possible equivalent would be "panic, pit, petard"—suggest the inescapable doom. The whole universe is **shaken.** The **windows of heaven** and the **foundations of the earth**—that is, the pillars on which it was thought to stand—refer to ancient mythological notions about the created order. The picture ends in utter ruin (verses 16c-20).

B. YAHWEH'S FEAST FOR THE NATIONS (24:21–26:6)

Though the various elements in this section are not all precisely linked to the theme of the feast for the nations, this seems to be the central moment.

24:21-23. *Judgment of the Host of Heaven.* The expected judgment is extended to the heavenly sphere. The **host of heaven** itself is doomed along with the **kings of the earth.** A comparison might be made with Psalm 82, where there is the suggestion of the heavenly beings as rulers of the nations. **They will be gathered** with the kings who should maintain justice. All will be held **in a prison** until the day of punishment arrives, just as the monsters subdued by Marduk in the Babylonian creation story were kept under guard. God is established as supreme ruler on **Mount Zion.**

25:1-5. *A Psalm of Praise.* The prospect of God's victory evokes a psalm of praise. Here the references are not to particular cities or powers but to the hostile forces of the world. In verse 1 a different division improves the sense: "thou hast made wonderful counsels, faithful and sure from afar [or "of old"]." **The aliens** in verse 2 should probably be read as "the presumptuous." It is they who are brought low, and the **poor** and **needy,** the afflicted people of God, are raised and protected (cf. Luke 1:46-55). In verse 4 "winter storm" is to be preferred to **storm against a wall.**

25:6-9. *The Feast.* Like a king holding his coronation feast, **the Lord of hosts** gathers the nations on Mount Zion for a rich feast, with the **wine** fully matured. The **veil** of mourning is removed. The hostile power is overthrown—**death** here is to be understood as the power which works for weakness and destruction. **Tears** are wiped away, and the hostility expressed toward God's people is removed. To this prospect the answer **on that day** will be a confession of faith and of rejoicing at God's saving power.

25:10-12. *Doom for Moab.* Rather strangely the rejoicing is interrupted by a word of doom for Moab. However, verse 10*a* may belong with verse 9, and it has been suggested that "enemy" should be read for **Moab,** thus continuing the theme of general judgment. But the passage appears to contain some allusions to the Moab oracles of chapters 15–16. Perhaps here Moab is to be taken as a typical enemy.

The text is not altogether clear. Verse 10*c* could be read "in the waters [slime] of the dung-pit," so that the same picture is continued in verse 11. But there is no reason why two entirely different pictures should not be used—that of **straw** being trampled down and that of a man struggling **to swim.** The last phrase of verse 11 is difficult. Perhaps "the arrogance of his boasts" might be read with an allusion to 16:6.

26:1-6. *A Psalm of Confidence.* This section ends with another **song.** Like Psalm 46 it expresses confidence in the strength of

Zion, established by God. Like Psalm 24 it proclaims the opening of the **gates,** here for the **righteous nation.** The **peace** of the **righteous** who **trust** in God is contrasted with the downfall of the proud. Here as in 25:1-5 the lowly are raised in the reversal of fortunes in the final age. The confidence of the people of God is in the One who is their eternal **rock.** The assurance is significant in a passage which describes world-shattering events. To those who trust in God not even the overthrow of the world order will find them lacking in the deepest security of faith.

C. THE PRAYER OF CONFIDENCE IN GOD (26:7–27:1)

26:7-10. *The Rewards of Obedience.* The form of the prayer is close to the psalms of lamentation. It begins with reflection on obedience and its reward. The theme of obedience and disobedience continues in verses 9-10 with the reflection that even when God reveals divine **judgments** "like light" (rather than **for when**) people may **learn** but the **wicked** do not see. In verse 9 **within me** should read "in the morning."

26:11-15. *An Appeal for God's Action.* The reflection is broken by an appeal for action—for the revelation of God's will so that the wicked may now **see** (verses 11-12). The basis of this confidence in God's action is the experience of Israel's history. It is in God **alone** that Israel rests, though **other lords** have **ruled** over her. The reference may be to alien rulers. More probably it is to evil supernatural powers, which now are seen to be **dead** with no hope of restoration to life (cf. 24:21-23 and Psalm 82). It is God who has shown protection to people. God has given them increase of numbers and enlargement of territory.

26:16-19. *Hope for the Future.* The theme of **distress** and the petition for help return. The text of verse 16 is probably corrupt. Perhaps it should be emended to read: "O Lord, in distress we sought thee; we were distressed at the oppression of thy chastening." God's protection seems to have been of no avail, for the state of depression remains long with the people (verses

17-18). But God will act to give life. Unlike the alien powers which have died and will not return to life, God's people **shall live.** Just as Ezekiel 37:1-14 depicts the restoration to life of the people, dead in exile, so here the hope of the future is proclaimed. It is less likely that there is here the idea of actual resurrection for members of the community. The imperative forms of verse 19b should be read as indicatives—"shall awake and sing," with the Dead Sea Scrolls manuscript and the Septuagint.

26:20–27:1. *The Final Battle.* These verses point again to the time of waiting for the great deliverance. The day of divine judgment is at hand. The people are exhorted to wait in patience, to **hide** until the moment of **wrath** is over. Judgment will be on all the **earth,** and all **blood** will be avenged. **In that day** the whole power of evil will be overthrown. This upheaval is depicted in a final battle between God and the power of chaos, described as **Leviathan—fleeing serpent, . . .twisting serpent**—and as the sea **dragon.** Thus the prayer of confidence is justified, and the prospect of the final victory of God over evil assured.

D. GOD'S PEOPLE IN THE NEW AGE (27:2-13)

Three separate elements make up this passage. Though unrelated, they form a pattern.

27:2-6. *The Vineyard Song.* The first may be regarded as an exposition of the vineyard song of 5:1-5. God appears as the **keeper** of the people, warding off all dangers. The **thorns and briers,** which in chapter 5 were expressions of judgment on Judah, are here symbols of the hostile forces from which the people are now protected. Verse 4 would read better as: "If there were thorns and briers, in battle I would set out," and verse 5: "Or they should seek protection with me"—the enemies must acknowledge God's power. In verse 6 the new people of God spread out into all the world.

27:7-11. *Words of Judgment.* The hopeful prospect is

interrupted by sayings speaking again of judgment. Verse 7 suggests that Israel has not been judged as harshly as might be expected. Verse 8 should perhaps begin: "By scaring away, by exile." **Guilt** must be removed by the repudiation of all idolatrous practice (on **Asherim** see above on 17:1-11). The **city**—presumably Jerusalem—is judged, and the maker of Israel will show no **compassion.**

Such words of gloom contrast sadly with the passages before and after. Perhaps they were inserted later from some other context. But they have an appropriate place here, for they provide a warning such as is found in Zechariah 7–8, for example. The coming of the final age is sure, since God has decreed it. But its coming may be delayed by human failure, and the **people** of God are here in effect warned not to delay the hoped-for day of salvation.

27:12-13. *The Gathering of Israel.* The passage culminates in two short sayings concentrating on the gathering of Israel. The first (verse 12) speaks of the ideal extent of Israel's territory— from the **Euphrates** River in the north to the **Brook of Egypt,** a seasonal stream about fifty miles southwest of Gaza. In the second saying (verse 13) **Assyria** and **Egypt** are conventional expressions for the place of exile. All who belong to the community are gathered to the **holy mountain at Jerusalem.** Thus the whole section chapters 24–27 ends with the vision of a renewed and united people in the place where God reigns as supreme Lord (cf. 24:23).

V. THE SECOND COLLECTION (28:1–35:10)

A. THE WORD OF LIFE AND THE WORD OF DEATH (28:1-29)

As this chapter now stands, various elements—some earlier and some later—are woven together into a complex whole.

28:1-6. *Judgment of Samaria.* At the outset there is a reminder of the fate which overtook the drunken and arrogant leaders of Samaria in 722. This remnant of the old northern kindom consisted of little more than the city of Samaria itself. It was conquered by the Assyrians, who were seen as the instrument of divine justice. The garlanded **drunkards**, like the **glorious** city, must fall. **Of the rich valley** in verse 1*c* probably should be omitted as an intrusion from verse 4*b*. An alternate suggestion is that **of those overcome with wine** should follow verse 1*a*. In verses 5-6 a later comment speaks of the true **crown of glory** which rests in the **justice** and **strength** that God establishes. The word of judgment points to the promise of the **remnant**.

28:7-13. *Oracle Against Judah's Religious Leaders.* But just as the leaders of Samaria failed, so too do the leaders of Judah. First we are shown **priest** and **prophet** drunkenly engaged in a religious celebration, unable to deliver the true message to the people. They mock at the prophet who proclaims their doom, likening him to one who teaches the alphabet to children. But what is unintelligible to these leaders is the decree of God. And it will be an **alien tongue** that will tell it to them—that is, a foreign conqueror. They have refused to **hear** the message of well-being. This refusal turns the **word of the LORD** from blessing to doom. The word of life becomes a word of death.

28:14-22. *Failure of Political Leaders.* Next the rulers are described as mockers. It may be that this verbal link has led to the placing of this utterance here. The rulers in Jerusalem live in false security, unafraid of the threatened disaster. The prophet mockingly puts into their mouths words that describe their real position. They think themselves secure, but their **covenant** is **with death.** Their place of **refuge** is in **lies.** We cannot be sure whether this reference is to alien religious practice and trust in alien gods or to political intrigue, which links more closely with the succeeding chapters concerning false trust in Egypt.

The **overwhelming scourge,** or "flood,"—that is, Assyria (cf. 8:7-8)—will sweep them away. But again their false position is contrasted with true security. God offers freedom from fear. The **cornerstone** laid by God on **Zion** means—perhaps was actually inscribed—that the person of faith will not be "alarmed" (rather than **in haste,** verse 16; cf. 7:9). God will test human response by the standard of **justice** and **righteousness.** The **decree of destruction** in verse 22 is relentless and inescapable. The series of pictures, a proverbial expression (verse 20), an allusion to God's past intervention (verse 21), the emphasis on the strangeness of **his deed,** the reversal of God's saving activity—all point to the absoluteness of God's decision.

28:23-29. *Proverbs of the Farmer.* Two concluding passages (verses 23-26 and 27-29) use proverbial material to make the whole point again. The farmer carries through the annual cycle of work, for it is God who **teaches him.** The farmer deals rightly with the crops when they come, for it is God whose **wisdom** is **wonderful.** It may be that the prophet is here justifying the divine action. God orders the affairs of the whole world with the same wisdom as is shown in these natural procedures. Or more probably the prophet is here showing the nature of his own position. The problem of prophetic authority is raised by the mockery of his words (verses 9-10). But the wisdom which guides the farmer is also that which guides the prophet and directs his message.

B. DISASTER AND DELIVERANCE FOR JERUSALEM
(29:1-24)

The various elements of this chapter are linked together by concern for the fate of Jerusalem, both now and in the future.

29:1-4. *Jerusalem Brought Low.* The city of **David** is here described by the title **Ariel.** This possibly has original connections with the idea of the sacred mountain of God. Subsequently it came to mean an altar hearth—the part of the altar on which the fire was kindled. The title emphasizes the sacred character of this place where the cycle of religious celebrations continues (verse 1). Perhaps there is the implication that it has become nothing but empty observance (cf. verse 13). Disaster is impending. Ariel will be the altar hearth on which the victims will be its own inhabitants. The city will be besieged and brought low so that its **whisper** will be as from the grave.

29:5-8. *Overthrow and Deliverance of the City.* The exact relationship between the opening verses and this passage is difficult to determine. In part it depends on the interpretation of verse 5*ab*. The Hebrew text refers here to "strangers," and this is most often emended to **foes**—a very small change. But the Dead Sea Scrolls manuscript and the Septuagint read "proud ones," which make a good parallel to **ruthless.** This suggests that the picture of the overthrow of Jerusalem is being continued. Its leaders and then its whole life is being shattered by the onslaught of God. It is also possible, however, that verses 5-8 form a separate unit concerned with a coming miraculous deliverance. The theme of the onslaught of the nations on Jerusalem is one that often appears in prophecy (cf. Zechariah 14) and in psalmody (cf. Psalm 2). The picture is especially associated with the last days (cf. Ezekiel 38–39), and the expectation of a miraculous deliverance is bound up with it. It is possible that there is here some allusion to the siege of Jerusalem in 701 (cf. chapters 36–37). But it is most likely that the prophecy is to be taken as an elaboration of the day of Yahweh, providing a counter to the doom oracle of the opening verses.

29:9-12. *Blindness of the People.* The theme of failure returns with an emphasis on the blindness of the people (cf. 6:9-10). In verse 10 the **eyes** are interpreted as **prophets,** and the **heads** as **seers**. The theme is further elaborated in verses 11-12. A passage of prose exegesis indicates the futility of those who profess to be able to discern what will happen.

29:13-16. *Perfunctory Worship and Presumption.* Two further indications of failure follow. In verses 13-14 the disobedience is seen in worship which lacks real feeling, a reverence for God which is without sincerity. So great is the people's insensitivity that when God again acts marvelously—as God did in the Exodus (cf. Exodus 15:11)—God's people will not be able to understand. God's marvelous act will be strange to them (cf. 28:21). **Woe** is invoked on those who plan evil in secret, thinking that God does not see (verses 15-16; cf. 5:18-20).

Such is the disorder that the **clay** criticizes the **potter,** the artifact the one who made it.

29:17-24. *Restoration of Israel.* As so often in the prophetic books, failure is followed by an assurance of divine action. Eyes and ears will be opened to the reality of what takes place. Verse 17 may be a proverbial saying. The change of fortune is stressed. There is an allusion perhaps to the devastation which will precede restoration—or perhaps to the fall of Assyria and restoration of Israel, with the **Lebanon** image used as in 10:18, 33-34.

The change of fortune brings the lowly to their rightful place. The wicked are **cut off.** The theme is reiterated in verses 22-24 with an allusion to the redemption of **Abraham**—which appears as a motif in late, postbiblical literature. There is assurance of a restoring of the right relationship between people and God. **Those who err** are brought to a proper **understanding** of God's ways.

The variegated pattern within the chapter turns attention again and again to the historical situation in which Isaiah was at work and the realities of his people's failure. But it points beyond that situation. We see the continued relevance of Isaiah's message in relation both to subsequent failures and to the final triumph of God's purposes.

C. MISTRUST AND TRUST (30:1-33)

It is clear that the various oracles gathered in this chapter are not all of one period. Nor is it likely that they all derive from Isaiah. Yet from different points they converge on the one theme. There are certain ways of behaving which deny faith in God. But God is not only waiting to be gracious (verse 18); God brings into being the conditions for obedience and trust.

30:1-7. *Judah's Lack of Trust.* The theme begins within the political situation of Hezekiah's reign—especially in the period 705-701, when appeal to Egypt for help was a characteristic element in Judean policy. The rebellion of Judah is seen as lack of trust. The leaders make a **plan** and "weave a web of intrigue" (so perhaps instead of **make a league,** verse 1). They turn to Egypt for **refuge** and **shelter**—terms often used by the psalmists to express the intimacy of relationship to God.

Verse 4 is not clear. A reasonable interpretation seems to be that the Ethiopian pharaoh who united Egypt around 710 welcomes the Judean representatives through his **officials** at **Zoan** (see above on 19:11-15). He sends special **envoys** from his southern capital to meet them at **Hanes** on the border between upper and lower Egypt. Nevertheless this false trust results in **shame** rather than **help.**

30:6-7. The thought is amplified in these verses headed **oracle on the beasts of the Negeb**—the arid, sparsely settled southern part of Judah. The curious title is perhaps copied from chapters 13–23 but may be a textual corruption. "They carry through the heat of the Negeb" has been suggested. The Judean negotiators are pictured carrying gifts to Egypt through this desolate region. But the real point comes in verse 7 with its description of Egypt as **Rahab**—one of the names given to the chaos monster of Near Eastern mythology that was overcome by God in creation (cf. 51:9; Psalm 87:4). The text as it stands suggests the impotence of this monster, but it is probable that the original read "Rahab that is subdued."

The metaphor of the overthrow of chaos to indicate the overthrow of hostile powers, especially Egypt, is appropriate. But here it is given a twist to indicate that this power of Egypt is useless. It cannot resist God's power, nor can it help those who so foolishly trust an earthly nation.

30:8-17. *Vindication of the Prophet.* This oracle appears to deal with a different aspect of Judah's failure. The rebellion is described as involving **oppression** (verse 12), and the downfall is indicated as inevitable. It will be an utter destruction, leaving **fragments** so small as to be useless. But there is a relationship of thought in two features.

(1) The prophet is commanded to **write** a message which will **witness** against the disobedient. It is not clear what he is to

write. The change of content suggests that we should not look back to the preceding verses to find the answer. The thought is close to that of 8:1-4, 16. The prophet's word will prevail, and then his people will know.

(2) The prophet's position is made clear, for his contemporaries are unwilling to hear. Isaiah and those who, like him, proclaim the will of the **Holy One** are unable to gain a hearing (verse 11). But this will not prevent the carrying through of the divine purpose. There is a reminder here that Isaiah is not alone in his interpretation of the events of his time.

30:15-17. These verses return to the theme of political folly and lack of trust. Such mistrust leads to total disaster, for there is little to suggest real survival here. It is possible that the saying of verse 15*b* should be emended so as to make even clearer the political aspects of the matter: "In turning back [avoiding warfare] and keeping the treaty [of subservience to Assyria] you will be saved." The obverse of this is true **trust** in God.

30:18-33. *The Graciousness of God.* The insistence on trust leads to the recognition of God's continued willingness **to be gracious.** This theme is elaborated in this series of sayings from a later time, in poetry and prose. To the depressed community of Jerusalem—probably in the period of the Exile—the confidence of the prophet speaks afresh of the way in which God as **Teacher** will be revealed. God's people will not be permitted to **turn** aside from their true **way.** The direct contact with God will be accompanied by the complete repudiation of all idolatrous practice.

30:23-26. The whole land will be blessed in renewed prosperity. The domestic animals will have the best fodder, and there will be abundant **water** when judgment is brought on the nations. Miraculously there will come a day of brightness, a day of healing after the moment of judgment.

30:27-28. The theme of judgment of the nations, which is the other side to God's deliverance and blessing of the people, is reintroduced. These verses give a vivid picture of the **name**—that is, the person of God coming from a secret place to bring about a divine purpose.

30:29-33. The theme of judgment is applied specifically to the overthrow of the **Assyrians.** This suggests the possibility that an oracle of Isaiah, like those in chapter 10, has been elaborated into a more general statement of the fulfilling of the divine purpose among the nations. The coming of that day will be as the preparation for a great and **holy feast.** Those who oppose the divine will are to be destroyed in a fire like that which burns in the valley of Topheth on the southern side of Jerusalem (cf. Jeremiah 7:32; see comment on Jeremiah 19:1-13).

The theme of trust issues in this confidence that the divine will will prevail. As often in the prophetic books, this is in terms of destruction of the hostile nations. Yet it is clear from the use of the name Rahab for Egypt that the passage looks beyond immediate historical situations to the overthrow of all evil at the hand of God.

D. THE WAY OF DEATH AND THE WAY OF LIFE
(31:1–32:20)

Here another oracle deals with the folly of relying on Egyptian help in the period of Hezekiah (705-701). This provides, as in 30:1-5, an introduction to a series of interrelated oracles of judgment, warning, and promise. These are not all of one period. The series provides a twofold presentation of the message that faith leads to life but lack of faith leads to disaster.

31:1-3. *Impotence of Egypt.* Those who turn to Egypt are ridiculed. They do not recognize where real help lies because they fail to see that no substantial help can come from Egypt. It is God who is the truly **wise** (verse 2), and who will bring judgment. Those who turn elsewhere for assurance will soon discover that the ones in whom they trust are nothing but **men.**

The overtones of verse 3 seem to point to the folly of political alliance with Egypt. This is like the folly of trusting in other gods which have no reality, a theme taken up in verses 6-7. The false trust in **chariots** and **horses** is also reminiscent of the Assyrian taunt in 36:8, which ridicules Judah for having no riders even if horses should be given them. The whole basis of Isaiah's argument is his conviction that it is faith which counts. Without faith there is **disaster.**

31:4-5. *God's Protection of Jerusalem.* The counter to false trust in Egypt is provided here. The picture of God as a **lion** undeterred by the shouting of the **shepherds** seems a strange way of expressing the idea of divine protection. But this must be the meaning of both this simile and that of the **hovering** bird. It is conceivable that the lion picture originally referred to the futility of expecting Egyptian power to frighten away the ravaging Assyrian lion. The stress is clear now. It is God alone who can save Jerusalem.

31:6-9. *Jerusalem's Special Significance.* The above emphasis leads into this appeal and statement of assurance. Judah must repudiate its idolatry. This is the prerequisite of real trust. The judgment of God will fall on Assyria. It is not by human agency but by the very presence of God, who is as **fire** in Jerusalem, that the Assyrian will be overthrown. The thought of judgment on Assyria, which appears in chapter 10 and elsewhere, is here given a larger setting. It is recognized that Jerusalem has a special significance in God's work. It is the center of God's activity in judgment.

32:1-8. *Establishment of Righteous Rule.* Though this chapter begins a new theme, there is a link in the thought of judgment from Jerusalem. The presence of God means judgment for the nations. It means the establishment of **righteousness.** The possibility of a new and right ordering of society is set forth in terms of just rulers and judges. The language here is more reminiscent of the wisdom literature than of the royal oracles in chapters 9 and 11. In verse 1 we might render: "If a king reigns . . . , if princes rule" (cf. Ecclesiastes 10:16-17).

The condition of the people as Isaiah saw them can be changed (cf. verse 3 with 6:10—there appears to be an element of reinterpretation of the Isaiah saying). Right standards and a right ordering of society will follow from wise rule and the establishment of **justice.**

32:9-14. *Judgment of Women.* By contrast these verses take us back to the picture of the judgment. The women of the land (cf.

3:16–4:1) may rejoice now in the **harvest,** but soon there will be deprivation. Complacency will give way to lament as the land is desolate. **City** and land are destroyed. The ultimate end is a gloom as deep as that of Isaiah's temple vision (6:11).

32:15-20. *Promise of a New Age.* The section is rounded off here with a renewal of the promise of a new age. When the divine **Spirit** is **poured** out on everyone, there will be renewal of the land. **Righteousness** will bring prosperity, and there will be security. Verse 19 appears to be an odd line wrongly inserted at this point. Its text is corrupt and it may well be a fragment. It is possible that the section should end at verse 18, and that verse 20 should be regarded as the beginning of a new section.

Thus again the interaction of two aspects of the prophetic message may be seen. The words of Isaiah elaborated and reinterpreted by his successors, point to the reality of divine power and the rightness of true faith. Here is a way to life. The warnings given by Isaiah to his contemporaries serve as a continuing reminder that life is to be found where **justice** is established and that the source of that justice is the Spirit of God.

E. Distress and Deliverance (33:1-24)

The text of this chapter is often problematic. We cannot be certain about its precise meaning at many points. It is also difficult to make any entirely satisfactory decision as to how it is to be divided into sections. But just as the first Isaiah collection ends with a series of psalm passages (cf. chapters 11–12), so here the collection in chapters 28–32 is followed by what may be a group of passages linked together in a liturgical structure. Its theme is lamentation and appeal on the one hand and confidence in divine deliverance on the other.

33:1-6. *Woe to the Destroyer.* Verse 1 pronounces woe on a destroying power. It consists of a series of repetitive and punning phrases in which the themes of destruction and treachery are interwoven. It may perhaps be viewed as a counterpart to the blessing in 32:20. Or it may simply be that the woe was attached because of the previous blessing (cf. Luke 6:20-26). If the woe is Isaiah's, it may refer to Assyria. But there is no clue to such an identity in the pronouncement.

33:2-6. Verse 2 begins like a psalm, appealing to God in assurance of divine power. Verses 3-4 describe the terrors occasioned by God's presence. This in turn leads into a confident confession of faith in the establishment of **Zion** as center of **justice** and right. Though the details of the text are not clear at every point, there is a significant recognition of the place of Jerusalem in God's purpose. It is possible that this short section is a "liturgy" in itself.

33:7-16. *A Lament and an Assurance.* Verses 7-9 present a new theme of lamentation. They describe the condition of the land in terms sometimes reminiscent of the Song of Deborah (Judges 5) and sometimes of other prophetic passages. These may well be metaphors for general distress, and it would probably be wrong to look here for precise historical conditions. Verse 7 is difficult to translate. "Men of Ariel" (Jerusalem, see above on 29:1-4) has been suggested for **valiant ones. Envoys of peace** might mean "envoys of Salem" (Jerusalem). The places named in verse 9 were noted for their woodlands (cf. 35:2).

33:10-12. God gives assurance that action will be taken. Perhaps addressing the hostile nations, God speaks of the disaster to them. God will bring **fire** on them (reading "my breath" instead of "your breath" in verse 11).

33:13-16. A new element is found here, emphasizing the purification of Zion. This is a necessary preliminary to the establishment of a new and purified city (cf. chapter 1). The presence of God in judgment—a theme beloved by Isaiah and perhaps here being elaborated by his successors—brings awe to the sinners. As in Psalms 15 and 24 the conditions for dwelling with God are laid down in terms of right social action. The righteous will be established, their needs met.

33:17-24. *Restoration of Zion.* It is the purified Zion which is here portrayed. Its people look back on the **terror** of the past, the times of attack by hostile powers and alien nations (verses 18-19 and 23-24 are not so clear as the translation suggests). Jerusalem is portrayed as a place of security. There is no suggestion here of a false trust in its very existence such as seems to have existed in the time of Jeremiah (cf. Jeremiah 7; 26). Jerusalem's security rests in the presence of God. The picture of God as **judge** and **king** and savior (verse 22) is carried further in verses 23-24 with the assurance of well-being for all the people and the overcoming of all enemies.

The theme of the **rivers** of Jerusalem (cf. chapter 8) is elaborated in verse 21*cd* with what appears to be a rather literalistic statement about its invulnerability to attack by water. The same theme recurs in verse 23. Here the picture of the ship becalmed—which presumably should refer to Jerusalem's enemies—is very loosely attached to the context.

The distresses of Isaiah's period may well provide the starting point for these oracles and psalmlike sayings. But the whole structure points rather to a reinterpretation of Isaiah's message—a recognition of the wider significance of that saving power in which Isaiah's confidence always rested.

F. Judgment of the Nations (34:1-17)

In verses 5-6 there are precise references to **Edom** and its city of **Bozrah** south of the Dead Sea (on verse 9 see the Revised Standard Version footnote). However, the opening verses are directed against **all the nations** and also against the **host of heaven,** and the latter part of the chapter depicts a world returning to chaos. This suggests that an oracle against Edom has been elaborated into a message of total judgment on the nations of the world.

In chapters 13–14 there is evidence to suggest that oracles against Assyria have been reapplied to Babylon. So here too there may be material which originally had a different reference. Thus verses 9-17 need not refer to Edom but could be part of a poetic passage dealing with some other land. The whole chapter now forms a poem of vivid imagery, expressing the dire aspects of the day of Yahweh. But the variety of references and metaphors suggests that it was not originally all of one piece.

The world's opposition to God's will is here met with the outpouring of divine wrath. The attempt at frustrating God's purposes in Zion makes it necessary to reaffirm that God will act **for the cause of Zion** (verse 8). From the tone of the chapter it is not improper to see its deeper meaning in the conviction of the ultimate triumph of God in righteousness, the overthrow of the powers of evil being decreed by God.

Thus Edom becomes a symbol of the hostile world (cf. 63:1-6). No doubt the historical conditions of the exilic period contributed to this symbol. But it was based on a much earlier sense of opposition expressed in the ancient patriarchal traditions of Jacob and Esau.

34:1-8. *Call of the Nations to Judgment.* The symbolic nature of the references is made clear by the invocation to all **nations** to accept God's judgment. With them are destroyed the heavens and their **host**, symbols of forces which so often in the Old Testament came to be associated with idolatrous practice.

34:5-8. The vivid and gruesome pictures of verses 5-7 introduce a quite different element. There is no longer the thought simply of a great battleground, with the slain left unburied. Now it is judgment in a ritual of **sacrifice**—the **sword** of God **sated with blood** and fat. Probably verse 8 should be linked with this, indicating that the Edom oracle is set in the larger context of the **day** of Yahweh.

34:9-17. *Chaos and Desolation.* A new series of pictures describes the overthrow of a land, which may or may not be Edom (verses 9-12). It will return to **chaos**, the dwelling of wild birds. Their identification is not certain, but the term translated **porcupine** must denote some kind of bird. The land will lose its identity as a kingdom (verses 11-12).

34:13-14. A different picture of chaos emerges here. This refers to a number of **wild beasts**, including the **satyr**, perhaps simply the he-goat, and the **night hag**, a creature known as a storm demon but associated with the night because her name "Lilith" suggests the Hebrew word for night. It is not possible to tell where these terms are intended to describe actual creatures and where they refer to evil forces.

34:15-17. These verses return to the pictures of wild birds occupying deserted buildings. Their occupation of the land is decreed **in the book of the LORD** . We need not ask what book is meant, for the real point is that **not one** of these wild creatures is **missing** because God has brought them in and apportioned the land. It is as if the allocation of the land of Canaan to Israel were here in reverse. In fact we may wonder whether this last passage was not originally an oracle directed against Israel and its evils.

G. THE HOLY ROAD TO ZION (35:1-10)

This vision of a restored land and a revived people is in striking contrast to the gloom of the preceding chapter. All that is evil is cast out. The pilgrim exiles, redeemed from disaster, return in safety to Zion.

35:1-7. *Israel Restored and Renewed.* The land of Israel is transformed (verses 1-2). It receives all the blessings which belong to **Lebanon** and to **Carmel and Sharon**—symbols of fertility (cf. 33:9). Still more, it is the **glory** of God which is to be seen in the land. To those who lack faith there is the reassurance of God's intervention (verses 3-4). This theme is to be seen not only in the major part of chapters 40-55 but also in Haggai and Zechariah. Changed fortunes for all the distressed and still more complete change in the character of the land follow on this (verses 6-7). The allocation of the land to wild beasts in 34:13-17 is here answered by the breaking forth of water and the wild land's becoming pasture. In verse 6 we may add "shall flow" in the last phrase, following the Dead Sea Scrolls manuscript. In verse 7 **swamp** should probably read "cattle range"—that is, a pasture containing (literally) "grass with reeds and rushes."

35:8-10. *The Holy Way.* Most of all, this is the moment for the **return** of those who are scattered abroad. Plainly this refers to the situation of the Babylonian exile. But it is a theme capable of wider interpretation, for the thought of coming back to Zion formed a strong binding force in the later Jewish community.

The way to the sanctuary is open, and it is protected. The people will come rejoicing to the worship of God, as in so many of the psalms. The text of verse 8*cd* is difficult. The Revised Standard Version simply omits four words (see footnote), which perhaps should read "it shall be for his people as they journey."

The chapter provides a fitting conclusion to this collection of oracles. It belongs to a later date than Isaiah. Indeed its language and thought show such close linkages with chapters 40-55 that it may well belong to the same circle. Yet in the context in which it stands the chapter serves to draw together the various oracles of the preceding chapters which look forward to a great day of deliverance, a future of hope and blessing.

If much, perhaps most, of this material is later than Isaiah, it nevertheless stands in his tradition. He clearly saw that true life depends on faith, and that the blessings which God intends for people are real if only they will turn to God in trust and singleness of mind. At the same time this chapter points forward, beyond the historical chapters 36–39, into the next part of the book. It points to a people in exile and a prophet in the succession of Isaiah who could speak to them with confidence of the divine power to save.

VI. HEZEKIAH AND ASSYRIA (36:1–39:8)

The text of these chapters is almost identical with that of II Kings 18:13–20:19. The following points of difference and of special importance to the study of Isaiah may be noted:

36:1–37:38. *The Deliverance from Sennacherib.* This section follows closely II Kings 18:13, 17–19:37. The omission of II Kings 18:14-16, which tells of Hezekiah's submission and payment of tribute is significant. It gives the impression that Judah at this time was released from the Assyrian yoke. The omission also emphasizes the miraculous and complete deliverance of Judah. The picture of Isaiah proclaiming deliverance and condemning Assyrian pride has points in common with the previous chapters. But it is not identical. We have to recognize here an alternative tradition which emphasizes one aspect of his teaching out of its overall context of divine judgment.

38:1–39:8. *Hezekiah's Illness and Envoys from Babylon.* The narrative of the king's illness cannot be precisely dated. The visit of the ambassadors most probably belongs to the beginning of the reign of Sennacherib—that is, shortly after 705.

38:7-8. The story of the sign of the sun's **shadow** (cf. II Kings 20:8-11) has been shortened and somewhat confused. The introduction is misplaced in verses 21-22. It is significant that this narrative portrays Isaiah as a messenger of healing, even prescribing the treatment (verse 21). Some have suggested that he may have been a physician (cf. 1:5-6).

38:9-20. This psalm of thanksgiving for recovery has been added. It incorporates words of lamentation closely resembling those in the psalms and in the speeches of Job. It shows how such psalmody was understood and used. The title (verse 9) is similar to those of many psalms. **Writing** *(miktab)* may be a miscopying of "Miktam," found in the titles of Psalms 56–60. The text is at many points difficult and uncertain (see the Revised Standard Version footnotes). **Sheol** is the underworld, where the Lord's presence does not reach.

38:21-22. See above on verses 7-8.

39:1-8. The story of the Babylonian ambassadors forms here an introduction to the second part of the book, which contains prophecies from the exilic age. Thus these verses make an important link between the two major divisions of the book.

VII. THE PROPHECIES OF SECOND ISAIAH (40:1–55:13)

The prophecy of exile in Babylon brings to an end the first half of the book (39:6-7). It provides a transition point to the contrasting message of Second Isaiah (see Introduction), who stood in the succession of Isaiah. During the later years of the Babylonian exile this prophet set out his interpretation of the disaster and his understanding of restoration. It is convenient to divide his prophecies into two sections—chapters 40–48 and 49–55—though the differences between the two parts are more apparent than real. The division between Second Isaiah and what follows in chapters 56–66 is again not always clear, for there are considerable parts of the latter section closely related to chapters 40–55. But these divisions are reasonable, and the following commentary will show the recurrence of themes which bind the sections together.

A. First Collection of Second Isaiah (40:1–48:22)

40:1-11. *The Announcement of Salvation.* The first note of this opening passage of Second Isaiah is of **comfort** and deliverance. It is in sharp contrast to Isaiah's main message of judgment. In these verses the prophet picks up Isaiah's faith and confidence in the power of the holy God of Israel. The recognition of Israel's failure, however, is never far from his mind.

40:1-5. The opening words in verses 1-2 transport us, though without any description, into the heavenly council (see comment on 6:1-3). They are the equivalent of a call to prophecy. The prophet overhears the word spoken by God. The covenant promise is repeated—**my people . . . your God.** There is assurance that the "hard service" (rather than **warfare;** cf. the Revised Standard Version footnote) is over. Israel has received **double** punishment for its sin. The exile is God's judgment. It is significant for the understanding of the prophet that his message should begin with the affirmation of this alongside his confidence in God's readiness to restore.

The proceedings of the heavenly council continue as the command is given to **prepare** a processional road through the **desert** for the appearance of God. The **glory** of God will be visible to **all flesh.** The nature of that appearance becomes plain in verses 9-11.

40:6-8. This is as near as these prophecies come to a statement of prophetic call. The matter is complicated by the variances in the text. In verse 6*b* **I said** is found in the Dead Sea Scrolls manuscript and the Septuagint, but the standard Hebrew text reads "he said." There is no other direct first-person statement in the prophecy—which appears to be a sound reason for preferring the third-person form here. But the argument is not conclusive, for in other prophetic books first-person use is limited or absent. Prophetic experience may be expressed in both first- and third-person forms (cf. Hosea 1; 3). Whichever reading is preferred here, this may be regarded as the prophet's own reaction. Nor is it certain whether his response to the heavenly summons to proclaim a mesage is restricted to **What shall I cry?** Part or all of the next verses may be included, for the material here is a kind of interpretation of **all flesh** in verse 5. The revelation of God's purpose meets with human frailty. Only the **word of our God** endures.

40:9-11. Against this background the nature of the message is made clear. **Zion** is summoned to be the **herald** of good news to the surrounding **cities of Judah**—hailing the coming of God, who with mighty **arm** rescued people, caring for them as a **shepherd** cares for his **flock.** All Judah, devastated through the years of exile, will now see God come. **Reward** and **recompense** may be variously interpreted. Perhaps they are best seen as referring to the redeemed people. Possibly they refer to the offering of compensation to those who have suffered the disasters of exile.

All the essential elements of the prophet's message are here—his confidence in the presence and power of God, his recognition of human dependence on God and of the justice of God's judgment, and his vision of the declaration of God's victory to all the world. The highly poetic and rhetorical language often makes it difficult to discern the man behind the poetry. Yet there is a clear sense of his involvement in the fortunes of his people and in the message which he is required to give. He stands clearly in the prophetic line in this double sympathy.

40:12-31. *Creator and Sustainer.* Whether this passage is to be regarded as a unified poem or as originally separate units, it is clear that there is a profound unity of thought. The idea of God as creator dominates. It is God alone who controls and sustains. Only God can order the life of the world, and there is none like God. Israel's absolute allegiance to the one God is here reiterated as the basis for understanding its present position and its ground of hope.

40:12-17. Here the absoluteness of God's creating is stressed (verses 12-14; cf. Job 38–41). Only God can order the world, and none can regulate God's activities. The conception of divine counsel, which issues from God alone, is elaborated in Proverbs 8. But there is no real contrast between the denial of any associate with God here and the expression of God's own activity in creating wisdom as the agent of creation. Spirit and counsel and wisdom are all expressions of God's action. By contrast the world and its peoples **are as nothing.** The absoluteness of God's rule extends over all.

40:18-20. The Old Testament often mocks at the absurdity of images. Any kind of portrayal of God is repudiated. This is a significant theological statement, for the image as symbol very easily becomes the image as reality. Briefly here the activity of the image maker is mocked, for the image is nothing but a wooden core with a **gold** overlay. In chapter 44 an elaborate mocking passage is built on this basic thought. Verse 20*a* is very obscure. Most probably the two opening words of the Hebrew are glosses indicating the kind of wood commonly used and verse 20*ab* originally was one line: "He chooses wood that will not rot."

40:21-26. By contrast God is enthroned **above . . . the earth.** From the earth's "founding"—so perhaps rather than **foundations** in verse 21*c*—God has been known as creator and overruler of the powers of the nations. In hymnic style the attributes of God are listed in terms of activity. This leads again into the question of how God can possibly be described (verse 25). God is recognizable in creative and sustaining activity in relation to the whole world.

40:27-31. This last point—God as sustainer— forms the

natural bridge to the position of Israel. Oppressed by the experience of exile, thinking itself forgotten by God, aware of the pressures of Babylonian power and religion, Israel is fearful and lacking in trust (cf. Ezekiel 37). But God is the creator, who is never weary in creative activity, the God whose power is inexhaustible. Those who look to God (cf. 25:9) will never be lacking in **strength.**

Israel as the people of God is set in the context of God's power. Its position of distress has been a source of dismay to itself and of mockery to others who ask where is the God in whom it trusted. Now this position is seen against the background of the promise of divine action. The movement of political events is the token of the new moment which is about to come.

41:1-29. *The Nations in Court.* It seems reasonable to treat the whole of this chapter together, though it contains a number of readily distinguishable units. It is also closely linked in thought with the preceding and following chapters by its general theme of God's action and assurances. At the beginning and end the historical situation is made plain. Although the name of Cyrus the Persian is not mentioned (cf. 44:28; 45:1), there is clear reference to the victorious and speedy campaigns in which he engaged. The nations and their gods are invited to speak. Israel is encouraged to have faith and hope.

41:1-4. The nations are summoned to the **judgment** seat. They are invited to comment on the events and to indicate who is responsible for them. The court scene is clear in verse 1, though **renew their strength** appears to have the wrong sense. Perhaps some such phrase as "wait for my rebuke" should be read.

Verses 2-3 allude to events well known to the exiles. They belong within a purpose declared from ancient times. Cyrus' tremendous victories are clear (**tramples kings under foot,** verse 2*d,* should perhaps read "brings kings low") and the underlying purpose should be plain. This leads up to God's own affirmation that it is God alone who acts. The last phrase, **I am He,** is frequent in Second Isaiah. It strongly suggests an interpretation of the name Yahweh similar to that in Exodus 3:14.

41:5-7. But the events find the nations at a loss. All they can do is consult their idols and encourage one another in the belief that here the answer will be found. Verse 5c should be taken with verse 6. It thus further stresses the panic-stricken gathering. The passage anticipates verses 21-24, where the gods of the nations are directly challenged.

41:8-10. For Israel, however, the situation is to be different. The assurance that it is God who acts and who is with Israel removes all cause for fear. This is demonstrated in the historic experience of Israel—from the call of **Abraham,** whom God loved, to the choosing of **Jacob.** The relationship is that of **servant** to master. But it is deeper than that since it is the result of divine choice, and it is upheld by the assurance that God will not reject. There may be a linkage of thought to the description of Abraham as servant in Genesis 26:24. More important, in this term we begin to see something of what Second Isaiah will be saying about the place of Israel in the divine purpose.

41:11-20. The divine assurance is continued in a series of three pictures:

(1) The reversal of fortune (verses 11-13). Israel, oppressed in exile, becomes the conqueror and its enemies vanish away.

(2) The harvest (verses 14-16). Israel threshes and winnows the **mountains,** the **threshing sledge** dragged with its sharp **teeth** across the grain. There is sharp contrast between **Jacob** the **worm** (for **men** in verse 14b we should probably read "maggot" or "louse") and the strength of the mountains. But the source of Israel's new strength rests in God, **the Holy One.** God is **Redeemer**—the kinsman who protects and recovers the inheritance, as God did for Israel in the Exodus.

(3) The change from barrenness to fertility (verses 17-20; cf. chapter 35). The oppressed, seen as the **poor** looking for **water,** are promised deliverance and the barren lands are made fertile. Thus it may become known to the world what God is like. It is noteworthy that each of these pictures culminates in the affirmation that it is God who acts. All these are illustrations, side by side with the summons to Cyrus, by which Israel may know God's power—and so too can the nations, if they will pay heed.

41:21-24. The court scene is recalled with a more specific summons to the **gods** of the nations. They are commanded to **set forth your case,** to show understanding both of what has been and of **what is to come.** The test of a god's validity is the god's knowledge of events (cf. the test of a prophet in Deuteronomy 18:21-22). The ruler of **Jacob** is the controller of history and hence knows. The gods are **nothing** and bring disaster on those who look to them.

For **be dismayed and terrified** in verse 23d the reading "hear and see" of the Dead Sea Scrolls manuscript seems preferable. It seems clear that the prophet here looks to the coming of Cyrus and to the redemptive action of God as near at hand, representing the tings to come, the new things (cf. 42:9). Standing in the prophetic tradition, he looks to the past and sees how the historic experience of Israel makes sense in the light of God's revealed will.

41:25-29. As evidence for the reality of God's control of history the summons to Cyrus is repeated. It is God who **proclaimed** it, while the other gods could do nothing. God announced it first to **Zion,** who could recognize what it meant. The Hebrew of verse 27a is clearly corrupt (cf. the Revised Standard Version footnote). Perhaps it might better be emended to "First to Zion I give comfort." Cyrus is described here as one who **shall call on my name.** The Cyrus cylinder, no doubt describing the campaigns of Cyrus for the benefit of Babylonians, depicts him as acknowledging Marduk as the god who summoned him. Ezra 1:2 (II Chronicles 36:23) depicts him as acknowledging the God of the Jews as having charged him to build the Jerusalem temple. Both are propaganda statements. But the prophet here sees the whole context of the historical events as being the purpose of God. First Israel and then the nations must learn to read these aright so that they may come to the full understanding of what God is doing and to the acknowledgment of God as Lord.

42:1-18. *God's Justice for the World.* The previous chapter has appealed to the nations to recognize God. This passage goes on to show the way by which, through God's people, God's will is to be declared, God's justice is to be established, and God's light is to come to all nations.

42:1-4. This description of the agent by whom God's justice is to be established is closely similar to 41:8-10. The parallel makes clear that the identifying of the **servant** with Israel made by the Septuagint translators is the right one. **Uphold** should rather be "take hold" of Israel—to act, as was said of the true king in chapter 9, to establish justice.

Justice here—paralleled by **law** in verse 4—is wider than any narrow legalistic conception. Nevertheless, it is not satisfactory to make it mean "religion," as is sometimes done. It is clear from the following verses that the establishing of the true rights of all peoples is envisaged. In fact verse 2 may mean that because there will be no injustice "one will not cry" in distress. It has been suggested that verses 3 refers to symbolic legal practices. In any case it seems clear that the protection of the weak is in mind.

42:5-9. The initial statement of call is followed by this elaboration, where the creator God is shown stressing the nature and purpose of that calling. The message and saving action is to all **nations.** For **covenant to the people** it may well be right to read "everlasting covenant" (cf. 55:3)—the establishing of a new and permanent relationship between God and all peoples like that which exists between God and Israel.

Verses 8-9 remind the nations, as also Israel, that it is God alone who is to be praised (cf. 41:4). The gods of the nations have no power to **declare** the saving acts which are about to take place.

42:10-13. The declaration of God's sole right to be praised leads into this psalm of praise. Here the remotest and most hostile places are shown acknowledging God's glory (see comment on 21:11-17; **Sela** was the chief stronghold of Edom). The passage is much like Psalms 47; 93; and 96–97. In verse 10*c* the Hebrew text, given in the Revised Standard Version footnote, certainly seems as good as the emendation. It expresses the range of those who offer praise. In verse 11*a* "rejoice" (Septuagint) may be preferred to **lift up their voice.** As in the exodus events (cf. Exodus 15:3) God goes to battle like a great warrior.

42:14-18. The theme of battle is continued in verses 14-15, where God is vividly depicted as roused (cf. Psalm 78:65). God brings shattering action to the world, transforming it by the intensity of divine wrath. In verse 15*c* "dry places" has been suggested for **islands.**

But God's action in battle is not negative. God leads the **blind**—the nations which have not known God—whereas those who turn to idols will be **put to shame.** That **they know not** and **that they have not known** in verse 16*bc* should probably be omitted, for the emphasis is on divine guidance rather than on the newness of the **way.** Verse 18, usually regarded as the beginning of the next section, may be better linked to this. It closes the passage on a note of appeal that the nations may turn to God and find life.

42:19–43:7. *God and the Servant People.* The link between this passage and the preceding is perhaps to be seen in the repetition of words in verses 19 and 18. Here the theme of God's servant returns, but with a difference. The people called to proclaim God's word to the nations are in fact in exile. They are depressed and lacking in faith, apparently unready for the task laid on them. The whole of this passage provides comment on this situation. It is a confident statement of the action of God which brings about the transformation of Israel.

42:19-25. The **servant** of God lacks insight into God's purpose. The servant is called and **dedicated.** Nevertheless the servant is **blind.** Verse 20 should all be in the second person (cf. the Revised Standard Version footnote). It suggests a link with 6:9*b*-10.

God has acted to save—**righteousness** carries the sense of victory or salvation—but God's people are in a sorry state. There are no messengers to speak the word of renewal to them. Their lack of faith is due to their failure to **understand** that it is God—the God **against whom** Israel has **sinned**—who has brought them into this condition. The prophet never loses sight of this background to the people's position (cf. 40:2).

43:1-7. Now the new act of salvation takes place. In great poetic sweep the prophet depicts the redemptive activity of God. Verses 1-3*b* are perhaps reminiscent of the exodus events, and give marked emphasis to the presence of God with the people (cf. 7:14). These verses describe the people's triumphal progress, culminating in the renewed declaration of God's relationship to them. Israel is to be ransomed and restored. **Seba** was probably south of **Ethiopia.** Some interpreters have seen here an allusion that Cyrus' conquests are expected to extend this far. **Men** in verse 4*c* should probably be emended to "lands." Because of God's care for Israel God will give nations **in exchange** for it. God will summon the remote places of the earth to restore Israel's scattered members to their home. They will all be restored, for they belong to God and were **created** for God.

The contrast between the two parts of this section is striking, but it is a contrast frequently drawn in Second Isaiah. He sees the present condition of the people in its true perspective. He sees the coming victory of God without ever losing sight of Israel's need to learn from that condition what its true place is to be in God's purpose.

43:8–44:5. *The Chosen Witness of God.* This section follows very much the same pattern as the previous one. God's purpose for the world is declared through the chosen people, called to be witnesses to God. God has acted in the past. Now God acts again to save. The people have shown themselves to be disobedient and have come under judgment. But God nevertheless makes them into a new people, and through this there will come hope for the world.

43:8-13. The opening appears to describe a court scene, as in chapter 41. The **nations** are assembled and again challenged to produce any of their gods who can speak rightly of the meaning of history. But God has **witnesses.** If verse 8 refers to Israel, then the sense is that though its **people** are **deaf** and **blind,** yet it is now possible for them to hear and see. It may be, however, that this verse refers to the nations brought into court (cf. 42:18).

The summons to Israel in verses 10-13 is based on God's

self-declaration. God is the only God. No other exists at all, or ever could exist. Verse 12 appears to stress the establishment of relationship with Israel in its time of purity when no alien gods were worshiped. In verse 13*a* **and also henceforth** should perhaps be emended to "even from everlasting."

43:14-21. Again the prophet turns to the theme of the new Exodus, which links to the overthrow of **Babylon.** As in the past, God **makes a way in the sea** and brings to nought hostile powers. Verse 14*c-e* is obscure. The traditional Hebrew text of the last line contains the word "ships," which might be a reference to the importance of the river for Babylon. But, as written in biblical times with consonants only, the same letters pronounced with different vowels would mean **lamentations.**

The old confessions of faith spoke of the deliverance from Egypt. But now this is to be forgotten in the light of the new saving act of God (verse 18). As then, so now God will lead the people through the **wilderness** to be truly God's people, offering worship. In the Dead Sea Scrolls manuscript verse 19*d* is unclear but seems to read "paths" for **rivers.**

43:22-28. In verses 22-24 the duty of worship provides the occasion for pointing to Israel's failure. The precise meaning is not clear at every point. The implication seems to be that in the past Israel was not really worshiping its true God but some other. And instead of offering worship Israel **wearied** God with **sins.** God's prerogative of forgiveness leads into a new court scene (verses 26-28). Here the rightness of God's judgment of Israel is justified in that, from Jacob onward, those who spoke to Israel and its religious leaders were all guilty. Condemnation had to come. The disasters which have brought Israel to its present state were entirely within the divine purpose.

44:1-5. But, as in 43:1-7, God speaks further words of consolation. The chosen **servant** of God, **Jeshurun,** the true, the upright Israel (cf. Deuteronomy 32:15), is to be renewed and its descendants blessed. In verse 4 "like the green poplar" may be read for **like grass amid waters.** The outcome is seen in verse 5, which may be interpreted in two ways.

(1) It could mean that the renewed people is now found to be

totally obedient. Every member of the community acknowledging that he or she belongs to God.

(2) Or it may be that here are the people of all nations acknowledging God and taking on themselves the words which show their true allegiance. Both thoughts are entirely appropriate to the prophet.

44:6-23. *The Folly of Idolatry.* The sole reality of the one God is the theme of the opening lines (verses 6-8). Israel's **King** and **Redeemer** declares divine uniqueness. Israel's God challenges any other who claims divinity to appear and prove its claim by foretelling the things to come. It is a court scene again, as in 41:1-29 and 43:8-13. Israel provides the **witnesses** of what God has already made known. God is known to them as the only **Rock,** the one sure foundation. Verse 7c is corrupt. The Revised Standard Version offers a simple emendation (see the footnote).

44:9-20. Some interpreters arrange this middle section in lines of poetry. Certainly at many points there are clear evidence of poetic parallelism. If it is not strictly poetry, it is nevertheless highly poetic prose. Perhaps this is the most suitable description of a passage which may best be understood as a sermon, a mocking homily. It is linked with the emphatically monotheistic passages which precede and follow (verses 6-8 and 21-23). Perhaps it is based on 40:18-20 and 41:6-7.

The sermon may be by the prophet himself or by a disciple. Either way it is well placed in its present context, where its sharply ironical statements provide a foil to the hymnic framework. It is repetitive and not clear in every detail, but the overall effect is devastating.

44:9-11. These general statements emphasize the position of embarrassment into which the idol makers and their associates are put.

44:12-17. In this elaborate picture of idol manufacture the order is not logical. It moves from one part to another, as if we were looking at a composite painting in which each stage of the process may be seen simultaneously. The fashioning of metal, the marking out of wood, the cutting of a tree all run on from one to another. The workmen are weary from making a god—a curious reversal of what is right, echoed again in 46:1-2. Still more absurd, a man takes a tree and burns a part for warmth and a part to cook his food—then falls prostrate to worship an image made from the remainder.

44:18-20. The final emphasis is on the folly of a man who does this. Surely he can see the foolishness for himself, yet he goes on doing it. He is forced in the end to say **Is there not a lie in my right hand?** Yet he is unable to break away because his **mind** is so **deluded**.

44:21-23. The theme of God's redemptive power is resumed, with **these things** in verse 21 looking back to verses 6-8. The hope of Israel lies here. Sin is forgiven; restoration invites the people to **return** to their God. At the news the **heavens** and **earth** are summoned to join in the song of praise. In verse 21d **you will not be forgotten by me** is an unusual construction. We may read with the Dead Sea Scrolls manuscript "you will not disappoint me."

44:24–45:13. *God's Summons to Cyrus.* This passage is remarkable because it actually names Cyrus the Persian. Elsewhere in the prophecies there is clear allusion to his rise to power and anticipation of his conquest of the Babylonian Empire, but he is not identified. It has sometimes been thought that in 45:1 the name was added later. But there appears to be no doubt about its place in 44:28 and **his anointed** in 45:1 cannot be other than he.

The God who is creator of all things, controller of the whole universe, the Lord of history, has summoned Cyrus as a divine instrument—just as he called Assyria (10:5). The reestablishment of Jerusalem and the return of the exiles will be the sign to the world that it is God alone who acts.

44:24-28. These verses take up a theme already frequent in Second Isaiah—the creator and redeemer God. The other gods have already been shown to be worthless (cf. 44:6-23). So too are their servants, the **liars** and **diviners**. But God confirms the word which is proclaimed through the divine **servant** Israel. What prophets reveal is carried through. Thus the promise of restoration is confirmed. The God who can **dry up** the waters of **the deep**—an allusion to the great events of the Exodus —is the God who brings renewal. Verse 26*d* may be a later addition. The Hebrew text in the following line read "its ruins" instead of **their ruins.**

Cyrus is God's **shepherd,** a common ancient term for "ruler," who will carry through God's purposes. Verse 28*cd* may represent later expansion of the text, perhaps in the light of Cyrus' decree related in Ezra 1. The reference to the **temple** is a new element not found in the parallel phrases of 45:13. In any case the words introduced by **saying** are awkwardly attached. But the addition represents an appropriate understanding of the prophet's message.

45:1-8. The summons to Cyrus is described in more detail. He is God's **anointed**—the term which in its form "messiah" eventually became a technical term for the future ideal ruler. The line division might better come after this word, with **to Cyrus** beginning the next line. He is to be victorious, and the way is open to total conquest.

The **treasures** of Babylon are to belong to Cyrus. But it is not for his own sake. It is for God's **servant Israel.** Cyrus, unaware of who is calling him, is under divine compulsion. It is God alone who acts, and everything is within God's grasp. There is no room for any dualistic thought about the ordering of the universe. The characteristic hymnic outburst of verse 8 emphasizes the divine victory—the word **righteousness** carries that overtone.

45:9-13. The same declaration of God's power is reaffirmed. Here it is set against the doubts of those who see something strange in the activities of God. As the passage stands it clearly answers the objections of those who think that God should not use the foreigner Cyrus. But it is possible that there is a more general reference to the strangeness of God's ways.

The series of images for the impropriety of questioning God in verses 9-10 is clear enough despite the textual uncertainty in verse 9*b*. This might be rendered "a vessel with [that is, nothing more than] the vessels of earth." But there is more serious difficulty in verse 11*c*. The Revised Standard Version omits a

Hebrew word meaning "things to come" (see footnote). Probably it should be joined to the preceding phrase, as in the Dead Sea Scrolls manuscript, to mean "the maker of things to come." Even so, it is not clear in what sense God is being questioned about God's **children.** The creative and restoring activity of God is again brought out in verses 12-13. Cyrus acts, not as a paid mercenary, but under the authority of God. He can do no other.

45:14-25. *God the Only Savior.* The theme that there is no other God has already been made clear in the repeated statements of God's creative and saving work. Here it is taken further in sayings which concentrate on the acceptance of this truth by the nations of the world.

45:14-17. In verse 14*b* **wealth** possibly should be "toilers" and **merchandise** "merchants." The tall **Sabeans** of verse 14*c* may be inhabitants of Seba, probably south of Ethiopia (cf. 43:3), rather than the possibly related people of Saba or Sheba in southwest Arabia. The Sabeans represent the world coming to Israel as captives, as suppliants—not for Israel's own sake but because **God is with you only.**

The theme of acceptance in verses 14-15 is countered by the theme of God's absolute saving power. The **makers of idols** are in dismay. It is uncertain whether verse 15 should be regarded as a comment, as in the Revised Standard Version, or taken as the continuation of the confession made by the nations. The latter seems more likely. The text suggests that the nature of God has now been revealed in the historic events—the rise of Cyrus, the deliverance of Israel. Hence the hidden God of Israel now comes to be known to all the world. Verse 16*a* may be emended to "All who rage at him are put to shame."

45:18-19. This thought of God's self-revelation is taken further in these verses. They provide a reflection on Israel's own understanding of God. The revelation is effective in God's ordered creation. The emphasis here is on order rather than **chaos,** on revelation open rather than in **secret** or in **darkness,** leading to the affirmation that God is to be found in order. Israel is not to look for God in a world left in a state of chaos. God can be seen as God is declared in victorious and right action.

45:20-25. The **nations** can learn this too. The court scene, with the **idols** held up to scorn because they cannot reveal the secrets of history, is pictured again. Its sequel is the positive appeal that the nations may find salvation. God has **sworn** by the divine nature itself that God is to be acknowledged by all people. Only in God is victory and **strength**; so Israel's descendants shall rejoice. Verse 24 is not entirely clear, since **it shall be said of me** is an uncertain translation. We might emend to "Only in the Lord is there righteousness and strength."

46:1-13. *The Gods of Babylon.* The attacks on the impotent deities are here sharpened into a direct ridicule of the great gods of Babylon. **Bel** ("lord") is a title or synonym for Marduk. **Nebo** ("speaker") is the god of wisdom, whose name appears in those of the kings Nebuchadrezzar and Nabonidus. They are shown to be so powerless that instead of acting as gods they are carried on the backs of **weary beasts,** unable to stop themselves from being borne away to **captivity.** In sharp contrast is Israel, whose God has carried it **from birth** and will care for it to **old age.** The last phrases may be rendered "I will support, I will carry, and save."

46:5-7. The theme of God's incomparability is echoed again. The impotent deities are nothing but immovable objects, **set** in a **place** (the word might equally well be rendered "shrine"), unable to **answer** prayer or to **save.**

46:8-13. Again the contrast is drawn out in the picture of God who declares the divine will to the disobedient people. For **consider** in verse 8*a* we may suggest "be attentive," or "obedient." **From the beginning** God's **purpose** has been declared. Now the one God has chosen—**the man of my counsel** (plan) —has come, summoned like a vulture to the **prey.** What God has decreed will surely come. Those who lack faith in God will find that **salvation** is near. God will set it **in Zion,** will set Israel in splendor.

47:1-15. *The Downfall of Babylon.* In a vivid series of pictures the prophet speaks of the coming disaster to Babylon. Confident in her power and security, she imagines that she cannot be touched. Now she is to discover that the resources on which she relies are futile. The position of privilege which she enjoys is under the control of God, who hands people over to judgment for a time only.

As so often in Hebrew poetry, there are frequent changes of metaphor. Yet the whole is linked together by the use of repeated phrases. There is no precise strophic pattern, nor are there refrains. But the same phrases appear in different contexts and thus link up the various pictures. For example, **you shall no more be called tender and delicate** (verse 1) is echoed in **you shall no more be called the mistress of kingdoms** (verse 5; "mistress" is literally "great lady," the title in Israel of the queen mother). Verse 8 is echoed in verse 10, verse 9 in verse 12.

47:1-7. The opening pictures the hitherto untouched city degraded from finery to slavery, working at the **millstones**—a menial task—deprived of rich garments. **Put off your veil** probably should be rendered "uncover your tresses." But the picture changes to that of the stripped captive, and again in verse 3 to the exposure of the adulteress, or perhaps to the woman violently raped. Verse 3*d* and the opening words of verse 4*a* may be emended to "and I will not be entreated, says our Redeemer." Babylon is degraded for having shown **no mercy** to the people of God who were committed to it in punishment for their failure (verse 6) and for having imagined that its exaltation was to be **for ever** (verse 7).

47:8-11. The theme of self-confidence continues. Babylon has dared to say the words which belong to God alone: **I am, and there is no one besides me.** The **disaster** will be sudden and shattering. Babylon's love of magical practice will be of no avail to it. This stress on false security and on the suddenness of disaster is repeated. If we more correctly render "charm away" instead of **atone** in verse 11, it becomes clear that the false trust in magic is also repeated.

47:12-15. This false trust is now elaborated. Elsewhere in Second Isaiah there is frequent stress on the total incompetence of the Babylonian gods. Here the related realm of **sorceries**, magical practice, and astrology is also shown to be of no avail.

Presumably the **they** of verse 14 refers to the astrologers who, far from being able to offer protection, are themselves consumed by **fire.** This is not a fire which offers comfort; it is the fire of judgment. Nor will Babylon's trading ventures assist it (verse 15). Probably this is an allusion to attempts at winning support from allies, who wander about at random and cannot help.

The chapter is the natural consequence of what has been said in the previous sections. The gods of Babylon are useless. They cannot protect. The purpose of God is declared. It is to save people so that the world may know who God is. So Babylon, the instrument of divine judgment, must fall under sentence.

48:1-22. *The Word of Salvation to Israel.* Opinions differ as to whether this chapter can be taken as a single unit—an address delivered by the prophet to his people on some religious occasion. Some see it as a combination of various elements built around the theme of the urgency for Israel to respond, to cast off her former disobedience. The repeated stress on hearing—and by implication on obedience—may be the reason for the linking of separate elements. But whatever the true explanation, the passage now presents in a new form some elements of the prophet's teaching which have already appeared. Culminating in the summons to escape from Babylon, it provides a fitting climax to the first group of the prophecies covering chapters 40–48.

48:1-2. There is a very clear sense of relatedness, indeed of identity, between the Israel of the past and the community now addressed. Some commentators make more of a distinction. For example, by translating the verbs in these verses as past tenses they contrast the failure of the past with the hoped-for obedience of the present. But Israel is one. The covenant with the people of the exodus period is the covenant with Israel as it stands now before God. The Israel of the exile is still the disobedient people. But they are a people called to new life in the promise of a new act of salvation.

Thus these opening verses are best understood as a recognition of the continuing duplicity of the people. They gather before God to worship, invoking God's **name,** but they are not wholeheartedly God's. Verse 1*f* may perhaps better be linked with 2*a:* "It is not in complete sincerity that they are called by the name of the holy city." Even now they have not learned true faith. The polemic against idolatry is directed at Israel.

48:3-8. This point is reemphasized. Here the already familiar theme of the declaration of God's saving events is taken further in relation to Israel's stubbornness. The declaration was made so that Israel would be in no doubt of the source of these things. The temptation would be to ascribe them to the "not-gods" which are its idols (cf. Jeremiah 44). This is repeated in a different form in verses 6-8. The **new things**—the saving events—are only now declared. The people have always failed to hear. God **knew** only too well from the beginning what the people would be like.

48:9-13. Yet underlying this concern with Israel's disobedience there is the conviction of God's continuing action. The action of God stems from God's very nature and **name.** What God has done to the people, disciplining them, has been so that the divine true nature will be shown to the world. Verse 10 is not altogether clear. Perhaps the negative is out of place in the first clause and we should read: "I have refined you like silver." The declaration issues in a hymnic statement of the glory of the creator God (verses 12-13).

48:14-16. In its present context, the opening of verse 14 must refer to Israel. The people are now summoned to recognize that in the work of Cyrus, the chosen instrument, God's purpose is fulfilled. But it is possible that the original reference was to the nations, who are called to see what God has done and so to learn for themselves (cf. 45:14). But in whichever sense the phrase is interpreted, the work of Cyrus is here put in the context of a divine purpose which was declared quite openly from the beginning.

The passage is not altogether clear in its phraseology. The phrase in verse 14: **The LORD loves him; he shall perform his purpose** cuts oddly across the first-person forms. Omitting "the

LORD" (following the Septuagint) we may emend to "He whom I love will perform my purpose." Or the phrase "the LORD loves him" might be taken as a title given to Cyrus: " 'The LORD-loves-him' will perform my purpose." Verse 16*d* is also strange. Perhaps it should be taken as a declaration of the prophet's sense of his commission. This might be linked to the opening of chapter 49, where the conviction of prophetic call again seems to be strongly expressed.

48:17-19. The way of obedience is now drawn out. God's promises to the people were always promises for life (cf. Deuteronomy 30:15-20). The whole history could have been different if only the people had responded. The stress on the disobedience of the people is really the occasion for urgent appeal that Israel may be the true and obedient servant which it was always intended to be.

48:20-21. The way to this new hope lies in escape from Babylon. It is to be the declaration of the new act of salvation of God, just as the experiences of the exodus and wilderness periods testify to God's work in the past. God's **servant Jacob** is again **redeemed.**

48:22. These words appear again in 57:21, and the conclusion of the whole book in 66:24 is not dissimilar. They come like a refrain and help to bind together the separate elements in this second part of the book. They are the solemn reminder that the ways of God are blessing to those who accept them, but God's word is a word of judgment to those who turn away.

B. THE 2ND COLLECTION (49:1–55:13)

49:1-26. *Israel's Restoration and Mission.* Much of the phraseology of this chapter has close links with the preceding sections, as well as with the passages which follow. The theme of restoration and comfort echoes chapter 40. The interpretation of Israel's experience and mission to the nations echoes earlier passages and points to chapters 52–53.

The whole chapter is made up of units which may or may not

originally have stood together. There is relatedness of theme, but some difficulties in the order have suggested rearrangement. Yet to try to produce logical order does not do justice to the continual movement in Second Isaiah from one theme to another. The total impression is cumulative rather than the result of ordered argument.

49:1-4. This section begins with a reaffirmation of the call **servant** Israel's call. The description is so like that of prophetic-call experiences as to suggest that underlying it there may also be the prophet's own strong sense of vocation. From the very beginning God has chosen the people to be a firm instrument of divine purpose, the mediator of the powerful divine word. Through this people God's glory is to be declared. Yet it appears that Israel's call has been **in vain.** Again in the expression of frustration—indicative of the people's experience of failure and exile—we may sense the prophet's own insight into his people's position in the light of what he has known.

49:5-7. As so often in the prophets, especially in Jeremiah, we detect close interaction between the prophet's personal experience and his understanding of what is happening to his people. The answer to this is a double assurance. The forming of the servant was to insure that there would be a people **gathered** to God, a people **honored** and strong in God.

But this is not enough. The moment of exile, the experience of failure which seems to suggest the frustration of God's purpose, in fact ushers in a still greater hope. The **nations** are to be given the **light** (cf. 42:6). This leads to the fullest statement of reassurance in verse 7. Here it is promised that the **Redeemer** will bring the rulers of the nations to acknowledge Israel because God has **chosen** it. The very humiliation of God's people will work the greater glory.

The passage does, however, abound in difficulties—not least because the servant, here so clearly identified as Israel, appears also to have a mission to Israel. Various suggestions have been made for rearranging the material, especially in verse 5. The answer to the dilemma must be sought first in the recognition of the sense of Israel as a corporate entity which can nevertheless be symbolized by the servant concept. Israel is both the called people of God and also itself called to be the agent of creating the people of God. To the exilic age the conviction of God's choice of people must be overlaid with the recognition of its failure.

At the same time we may perhaps see in verses 5-6 something of the prophet's own experience of a call to bring a message of hope and life to his own people and his realization that this is not all that God seeks of him or of the people. The salvation of Israel is bound up with his own experience and at the same time, as in 52:13-15, with the hope of the world. The remainder of the chapter develops these themes in various ways.

49:8-13. To the people in exile these verses speak of the new establishment of a **covenant**—perhaps again an "everlasting covenant" (see above on 42:5-9). The message of comfort echoes 40:1 and ends in a shout of praise (verse 13). The preceding verses point again to

(1) the idea of a **way** through the wilderness;
(2) a restored people delivered from the bondage of exile;
(3) a new series of events like those of the wilderness wanderings in the exodus period;
(4) the reallocation of **the land** (verse 8);
(5) the gathering of the scattered members of the community (cf. chapters 35 and 40).

In verse 12 **Syene** (modern Aswan) is known from the fifth century because of the nearby Jewish military colony (see above on 19:18).

49:14-21. Zion's lack of faith (cf. 40:27-31) is answered by the assurance that God cannot forget the city which is engraved on the divine **hands** and so is ever **before** God. Jerusalem is to be rebuilt and its population will be like the jewels of a bridal diadem. The theme of a new population is taken up in verses 19-21. Here the contrast is drawn between present desolation and the future overflow of population. Zion is pictured as a mother contemplating her distress, bereaved of her **children,** and now discovering miraculously that she has new children to take their place.

49:22-26. The hope for the **nations** is echoed in their acceptance of Judah's overlordship. The reversal of fortune shows the oppressor nations bringing God's people back to their own place. They prostrate themselves to Israel because it is Israel's God who is their hope. Through the metaphors of humiliation and servitude we are to see the nations' acceptance of the worship of the true God.

As in the oracles of judgment on the nations the metaphor of God's great battle with evil is used. However much of nationalistic thought remains, the primary emphasis is on the victory of God and so on the saving of **all flesh** in the knowledge of God. The miracle lies in the release of the **captives of a tyrant.** Here is the assurance that the stronger one, even God, comes to deliver.

50:1-11. *Faithless and Faithful.* The interrelated parts of this chapter turn on a contrast. On the one hand is the failure of God's people and of those who remain obdurate. On the other is the faithful, the obedient, the true servant of God.

50:1-3. The beginning refers to doubt whether God really cares for the people (cf. 40:27 and 49:14). It looks to some as if God has totally repudiated them by irrevocable **divorce,** or has **sold** them to pay debts. But clearly the questions here expect the negative answer. No such formal divorce has been made, and the idea of God's having **creditors** is absurd. But there should not be a too easy notion of God's continuing relationship with the people. It is made clear that the selling of Israel, the divorce, are realities because of the people's **iniquities.**

As so often in these prophecies, the balance is maintained between confidence in the power of God to save and the recognition of the justice of Israel's present condition. The theme is elaborated in terms of God's failure to find response and in doubts as to God's power to save (verses 2-3). With echoes of the plagues of Egypt and the exodus experiences the power of God is proclaimed.

50:4-6. In contrast to this doubt and failure stands the figure in this passage. Together with verses 7-9 these verses are often taken to be a "servant song." The language is that of psalms of lamentation (cf. Psalm 129:3 and Lamentations 3:30), making clear that the description is metaphorical. The one who is called into God's service, through whom the divine **word** is mediated (**the tongue of those who are taught** perhaps means "a disciple's tongue" or "an expert tongue"), is continually summoned to give the message. But he finds himself faced with recalcitrance.

In verse 6*bc* the Dead Sea Scrolls manuscript has "my cheeks to the iron rods" and "turned" for **hid.** The most natural interpretation here is to understand these words as the prophet's statement of his own call. The language is much like that of Jeremiah. At the same time the overlap between the prophet's experience and that of his people is such that no sharp line should be drawn. As with other prophets—especially Jeremiah—there is a close sense of unity between prophet and faithful people.

50:7-9. Again like Jeremiah, the prophet finds himself vindicated. The legal terminology of these verses is strongly reminiscent of the style of some of the speeches of Job. The conviction that he will be protected and his opponents overthrown is one which he shares with both Jeremiah and Job.

50:10-11. In these final verses there is appeal first to those who are loyal, an exhortation to hear the words of God's messenger to them. The meaning would seem to be that the faithful can share in that vindication which has just been described. By contrast those who trust in their own strength will be brought to disaster. The precise meaning is not clear. Yet if a link is seen to the opening verses of the chapter, we may see here an allusion to the apostasy of those who, thinking that God has divorced Israel, regard themselves as free to look for other gods to protect them. Inevitably they find disappointment.

51:1–52:12. *Summons to the New Redemption.* This long section cannot be regarded as a unity, since it is clearly made up of various shorter sections. At least one of these subsections (52:3-6) appears to be in prose. Yet there is an interconnection of thought and language which makes subdivision unsatisfactory.

The repeated exhortation to hear (51:1, 4, 7, 21), the echoing of the promise of comfort (51:3, 12, 19; 52:9), the summons to awake, addressed to God (51:9) and to Jerusalem (51:17; 52:1), and the many points at which the themes of creation and redemption are drawn out—all show that here has been gathered a series of statements, exhortations, and psalm-like passages. The whole section is concentrated on the confident note of the nearness of God's great new act of redemption. It is the answer to those who lack faith. It sets the sufferings of the Exile in their true perspective. It provides the most effective foil to the passage which follows in 52:13–53:12, where the full meaning of the sufferings is drawn out.

51:1-3. The section opens with the reiteration of the promise to the people's ancestor. **Comfort** for **Zion** is seen in a right understanding of its past and of the meaning of what God did for **Abraham** and **Sarah** (cf. Genesis 17). Life will be restored in its fullness, and the desolations made into a place comparable only to the **garden of the LORD**. This confidence in the promise to Abraham was evidently a familiar thought in the exilic period. But it could be rightly or wrongly understood. Ezekiel 33:24 addresses those who put a false trust in the knowledge that Abraham, who was **one,** has become **many.** In the context of Ezekiel's emphasis on the absolute primacy of divine action such a trust would be improper. Second Isaiah sees a right understanding of the past as a proper element in true faith.

The comparison of the restored Zion with **Eden** is a pointer to understanding the nature of the Jerusalem temple. Genesis 2 indicates that Eden is the dwelling of God, committed to human beings as its guardians. Ezekiel 28 shows a similar mythological concept in relation to the king of Tyre. In the Old Testament the temple has a cosmological significance as the chosen dwelling of God from which life and blessing will flow forth. (cf. Genesis 2:10; Ezekiel 47).

51:4-6. The interpretation of these verses depends on the opening words. The standard Hebrew text makes the reference to Israel. But the context and some ancient versions favor the plural "peoples," "nations," and this form seems preferable. As so often elsewhere in Second Isaiah, the hope expressed for Israel is seen to be extended to all nations. God will **rule** over them in power (**my arms**). The present world order will pass away, but the saving power of God remains unchanging. The thought of new **heavens** and a new **earth** is not here stated, but it is clearly implied (cf. verse 16).

51:7-8. This short poetic passage forms a bridge to the next section. It probably was placed here because of the similarity of the thought of the previous verses. It makes its point in reference to Israel as the people who understand God's ways.

51:9-11. This is one of the greatest of all Old Testament statements of the meaning of redemption. It confidently affirms that the God who was the victor in the creation conflict, the victor over the power of Egypt, is here and now acting to deliver the people and to restore them in **joy** to **Zion.** The rich psalmic language is connected with the psalms of lamentation, in which the appeal to God to bestir is common. In the primeval days it was God's **arm** (strength) which overthrew **Rahab** and the **dragon** (verse 9; see above on 26:20–27:1). These two names suggest the power of chaos which features in other ancient Near Eastern cosmologies. But for Israel this victory is not a piece of mythology. It is embodied in history.

The title Rahab may be used of Egypt (see above on 30:6-7). The thought of victory over **the great deep** (chaos) is connected with the drying up of the **sea** in the exodus events. Creation mythology and past historic experience are together the ground for the confidence in God's present redemptive activity. In words which echo 35:10 the prospect of deliverance is declared.

51:12-16. Perhaps these verses should be treated as another bridge passage, not all of which appears to be poetic. Verse 13*g* looks like a gloss, and so too may be the oddly connected verse 16*c-e*. There are reminders of the themes of comfort, of lack of faith, of divine creation, of the overthrow of the **oppressor.** These suggest the hand of a later interpreter, providing a brief commentary on the central ideas of the prophet's teaching. They also show how closely his various lines of thought are bound together. On **the Pit** (Sheol) see above on 14:16-21.

51:17-23. The summons to awake is now addressed to Jerusalem. In verses 17-20 the experiences of the disaster to Judah and its capital are recalled. The **wrath** of God is pictured as a **cup** of wine reducing the judged people to impotence (cf.

Jeremiah 25:15-16). They have **none** to **comfort** and no escape from the total **devastation** which comes upon them (cf. Ezekiel 14:21). The experience of siege comes upon them again (verse 20). To this recalling and reliving of the experience of the past the answer comes in a reversal of judgment (verses 21-23). The judgment will now come upon those who brought the disaster to the people. God's cup of wrath will be theirs, for it is God who acts to vindicate.

52:1-6. Again the summons to **awake** is addressed to Zion. In contrast to the degradation of Babylon (47:1-15) Jerusalem is to be cleansed and released. A new and purified people will be there (cf. 35:8), having put on the **garments** which symbolize the new condition (cf. Zechariah 3:4). The **captive** stands up and is freed from the ropes which tie together those taken away into exile.

The promised release is commented on in verses 3-6, a passage which is almost certainly in prose and is probably a later expansion. It explains the nature of Israel's position and compares the present situation with the past—Egyptian sojourn and Assyrian oppression.

Their rulers wail appears to refer to the rulers of Israel. Perhaps, however, it should be read "their rulers [the oppressors] boast," which fits the context better. As in the psalms of lamentation, there is an appeal to the honor of God. While God remains inactive the divine **name is despised** (see above on 48:9-13).

52:7-10. The theme of good news (cf. 40:9) is resumed with the picture of the **watchmen** standing on the walls and announcing the coming of the messenger of salvation. The devastated city is restored. Jerusalem is **redeemed,** and **all the nations** see the power of God's saving act. Now God is proclaimed as King in Zion, the place where God has chosen to be revealed in royal power. The kingship of God is supreme, and it will be for the world to acknowledge it.

52:11-12. For the full acceptance of God as King in Zion it is necessary that the people march in holy procession from their place of exile to the chosen center. The priests **who bear the**

vessels are sanctified. This suggests the ceremonial procession of the ark described in II Samuel 6 and I Chronicles 13:15-16. It is like the first Exodus. But this time there will be no question of **flight** or fear. God, like the pillar of cloud and fire, goes before and behind. It is a magnificent climax to the prospect of redemption. The holy people, restored and purified, again march to Jerusalem in acknowledgment of the kingship of the God who has redeemed.

52:13–53:12. *God's Servant—Humiliated and Exalted.* This is a difficult and important passage. It will be best to consider first its contents and their meaning before making any general comment on the problems of interpretation. So far as possible the attempt must be made to consider the question of meaning without prejudging any of the issues.

52:13-15. The opening statement is in the form of a divine utterance. It points to the **servant** who **shall prosper**—or perhaps better "act wisely"—suggesting action which leads to well-being. The prospect is of exaltation in contrast to the humiliated state described in the next verses. The horror of the nations is expressed in the actions of their rulers. In the face of the servant's condition, unrecognizable as that of a man, the kings respond—they **shut their mouths.**

The interpretation is uncertain because of the difficult verb translated **startle** (verse 15*a*), which appears to mean "sprinkle." "He shall sprinkle" has been held to mean "he will act to atone," or "to purify." But the construction is strange. Perhaps **nations** is the subject: "Many nations carry out a purification ritual."

If this is correct, verse 15*ab* suggests the horror of the nations expressed in rituals designed to avoid contamination. Verse 15*cd*, in which the verbs are perfect tenses ("have seen," "have considered") would describe the unheard-of disasters which have been brought to their notice. This recalls statements of the horror produced by Judah's downfall (cf. Deuteronomy 28:37). The alternative would be to regard verse 15*cd* as alluding to the coming event of deliverance, of exaltation. But this seems to anticipate too soon what is to be said subsequently.

53:1. Just as 52:13 provides the introduction to 52:14-15, inviting attention to the exaltation of the servant in contrast to degradation, so this verse provides the introduction to verses 2-3. There, and again in the following verses, the theme of degradation is elaborated and its meaning made clear. But first there is a reminder that this is not all. There is a great act of God proclaimed. Just as elsewhere in Second Isaiah the nations are invited to come to court and consider the case (chapter 41, for example) so here there is an implicit invitation. Whether the address is to the nations or possibly to those who have failed to understand the meaning of the Exile cannot be said with certainty. These are not mutually exclusive. The revealing of the power of God is relevant to all the world and not to Israel only.

The Hebrew text has "on whom" rather than **to whom.** Perhaps this suggests the revealing of God's power against the oppressor. If so, the first clause, with its emphasis on belief, invites trust in God's action. But the point is not clear since the two prepositions are often interchanged in the Old Testament.

53:2-3. These verses imply in this context that the present condition of God's servant conceals his true nature and function. The language is highly poetic. There is the picture of a **plant** growing "straight up" (rather than **before him**) in a **dry** place. **Form . . . comeliness . . . beauty** suggest dignity; there is nothing here to suggest one who should be honored.

A group of phrases in verse 3, carried further by the language of verse 4, suggests the metaphor of leprosy. For **rejected by men** it is possible to read "withdrawing," or "aloof from men"—followed by "a man involved in pain and humiliated by sickness [see Revised Standard Version footnotes], hiding his face from us; we despised him [a rendering confirmed by the Dead Sea Scrolls manuscript] and did not esteem him." To some extent the same kind of language is used of Job. In neither case should the metaphor be taken as prosaic description—neither the servant of God nor Job was a leper. But it is difficult to imagine a more apt way to suggest the isolation, the sense of being outcast, than the language applied to such a disease (cf. the action of the kings in 52:15). Leprosy in the Old

Testament—probably not the disease now so named—involved such isolation.

53:4-6. The theme of degradation is carried further in a rich series of metaphors. These verses elaborate the ideas already suggested in verses 2-3. Thus **stricken** is an appropriate word for continuing the leprosy metaphor, though also suitable to other diseases. The earlier mention of pain and sickness is taken up again. It is developed into the statement that the servant's suffering is on account of the sin of others. The well-being which comes to them is brought about by what he has suffered. In verse 5a "pierced through" is better than **wounded.** The humiliation is willed by God (verse 6; cf. verse 10). Recalling the idea "double punishment" in 40:2, we may see here the realization that what came to the people in exile was not merely punishment but a means of bringing well-being.

53:7-9. The picture of straying **sheep** in verse 6 provides a link to a further elaboration of metaphor in verse 7. It is strongly reminiscent of Jeremiah 11:19. Both passages in fact use the kind of phraseology very familiar in psalms of lamentation. The pictures of the **lamb** (literally "sheep") **led to the slaughter** and of the **sheep** (literally "ewe") being sheared provide a further link to the legal language of verse 8a. This line is somewhat obscure because the meaning of the word translated **oppression** is not altogether clear. Perhaps we should render it "he was taken from authority and right"—that is, he was given no just trial. "Fate" would be better than **generation** in verse 8b.

The images follow one another with great rapidity—trial, sentence, death, burial. Verse 8d is again difficult. Perhaps it should be rendered "for the transgression of peoples who deserved to be stricken." Or perhaps "with transgressors he was stricken to death." Clearly the picture is of **death,** as verse 9 introduces burial. **Rich man** is odd, and perhaps the word should be rendered "rabble" or emended to "evildoers." **In his death** should perhaps be "in his tomb," as suggested by the Dead Sea Scrolls manuscript.

The obscurities of detail, however, do not prevent appreciation of the series of pictures. Perhaps most misunderstanding of the passage has occurred through failure to recognize that metaphors are used. If any one of these phrases is to be taken literally there is no good reason why they should not all be. But if all are so taken, the whole becomes absurd. As so often in Hebrew poetry the metaphors change rapidly, without explanation. We are given an impressionistic picture rather than an exact description. The application of similar metaphors to the king in Psalm 89:38-45, may be significant for our appreciation of the prophet's intention.

Is he perhaps here understanding the fortunes of his people partly in terms of the figure of their king, Jehoiachin, who suffered thirty-six years of captivity before being released and restored to some measure of honor (cf. II Kings 25:27-30)? It would be false to identify servant and king. Yet a recognition of the intimacy between the experience of people and of king may have led to the use of this kind of metaphorical language.

53:10-12. The final verses of the passage have many obscurities. But it is clear that the series of pictures leading up to death and burial (verses 8-9) finds its climax in a picture of renewed life. This becomes clearer if we use the Dead Sea Scrolls and the Septuagint reading of verse 11*a*: "after his travail he shall see light"; this phrase indicates the idea of a new coming to life. The outcome includes descendants and prosperity (verse 10*de*).

This is all set in the context of suffering and humiliation. It was God's **will** "to crush him with sickness, he himself making a sin offering" (a more satisfactory translation of verse 10*ab*). In verse 11*b* **by his knowledge** probably belongs with **be satisfied**—possibly a parallel to "see light" in verse 11*a*. But another meaning of the words may be "he shall have his fill of humiliation," and the larger context favors this (cf. verse 3). Following this, verse 11*bc* may be translated "my servant, himself righteous, will pronounce the righteousness of many"—that is, will acquit them.

53:12. It is probable that **the great** (the same Hebrew word translated **many** in verses 11*d*, 12*e*) and **the strong** (which can also refer to numbers) should be taken as direct objects of

divide. Thus God "will divide to him the many as a portion." That is, God gives reward to the servant because he humiliated himself and **bore** their **sin.** The references to **the many** and **the strong** suggest the nations.

A theme expressed elsewhere in Second Isaiah (see 49:22-26), here returns: the nations are **spoil** for God's people. This idea is perhaps not very congenial to the modern way of thinking. Yet to leave that statement without qualification would be to miss the real meaning. It is the hope and confidence that through Israel's humiliation the nations are brought to God. For this to be possible, they must be brought to Israel. Israel's humiliation is seen within the context of God's purpose as no longer punishment, but the carrying out of his will.

The interpretation of this passage inevitably leaves many problems unresolved. The vocabulary and construction are often obscure and capable of more than one interpretation. It is difficult to avoid favoring the interpretation which fits one's general approach to the problem of understanding Second Isaiah's statements about the servant of God.

Yet unless good grounds can be shown for separating out this passage and treating it independently, it is more natural to relate the thought here to other passages in Second Isaiah. The prophet uses the language of the psalms at many points. He uses hymnic phrases, ideas connected with the kingship of God, statements of the uniqueness of God. Here—though not only here—he reveals his knowledge of that more somber aspect of psalmody which is found also in the "confessions" of Jeremiah, and of which the supreme example is perhaps Psalm 22.

This point needs to be in mind when we consider the significance this passage has had for Christian theology and interpretation. Too literal reading of it has sometimes led to extravagant statements about its relationship to New Testament material. The claim that the relationship is one of prophecy to fulfillment needs to be carefully defined before it can be acceptable. The great truths of Old Testament faith are embodied in such passages as this and Psalm 22. Therefore it is not surprising that Jesus and his disciples and the early church should have found in them fit vehicles of expression for what they were saying. In so doing they were carrying further the interpretative tradition already in the Old Testament—enriching the faith of the community by the reapplication of passages rich in allusion.

54:1-17. *New Life for the Desolate City.* The theme of restoration in this chapter has two main parts. In verses 1-8 it is mainly concentrated on the renewal of Zion, pictured as a woman. Verses 11-17 turn to the idea of rebuilding the city and its future safety. The two are linked in verses 9-10 by a promise like the one made to Noah that there will be no further disaster.

54:1-3. These opening verses link back naturally to the promise of descendants to God's servant (53:10). But here the figure is of Zion as mother of her **children** (cf. 3:25-26 and 49:14). It is elaborated with details that suggest the Abraham-Sarah tradition (cf. 51:2; Genesis 11:30)—though the theme of the barren woman is common both in the patriarchal narratives and elsewhere in the Bible. The enlarging of the **tent,** joined to the promise of many children, provides a further comment on 49:19-21. It is extended into the promise of a new possessing of the land, a new conquest (verse 3). It suggests the wide extent of the Davidic kingdom.

54:4-8. The same point is made in a different form. Here there is concentration on the idea of God's forsaking the people **for a brief moment**—the moment of exile, when God's **overflowing wrath** engulfed them. Now the shame of the **wife forsaken** is to be answered in the assurance of a permanent relationship. In verse 4 there are allusions to the past life of Israel (**the shame of your youth**) and to the Exile (**the reproach of your widowhood**). Cf. the more elaborate use of this type of imagery in Ezekiel 16 and 23.

Confidence rests in the nature of God, described with a rich series of titles in verse 5. The use of **Redeemer** may be illustrated in Ruth, where Boaz is just such a redeemer, bringing new life to a family otherwise cut off. Verse 6 is not entirely clear. A suggested rendering is "when he called you, you were a woman forsaken . . . ; but who can cast off the wife of his youth?" The enduring faithfulness of God would be thus more strongly emphasized.

54:9-10. The oath to **Noah** reaffirms the absolute faithfulness of God (cf. Genesis 8:21-22 and 9:11-17). The continuance of God's **love** and **covenant** even if the **mountains** move recalls Psalm 46. It is significant to find this use of the flood narrative, which shows how the tradition is understood not just in terms of primeval history but also in terms of contemporary experience. The flood as divine judgment has been experienced by Israel in the Exile. The promise of the future includes the assurance that such judgment will not again come upon it.

Historically, of course, such an assurance did not prove to be warranted—as events in both the biblical period and after have shown. But the unshaken confidence in God's enduring love and covenant is clear both in the faithfulness of the Jewish people and in the assimilation of this promise into Christian thinking.

54:11-17. Here the desolate city is addressed. A new city is promised, built with precious stones. **Set your stones in antimony** perhaps suggests the use of mosaic. Some of the stones are difficult to identify (cf. Revelation 21:18-21). Many scholars read that "your builders" rather than **your sons** will be instructed by God (cf. the rebuilt temple and city in Ezekiel 40–46). The new city will be secure. Any attempt at overthrowing it will be frustrated by divine action.

Verses 15-16 are in part obscure. In view of their apparent intrusiveness, they may represent later elaborations of the text. Verse 17*cd* provides a link back to verse 3, the new possessing of the land and of the city by the servants of God. Thus the promise to exiled Israel is reaffirmed and the future of its life is assured.

55:1-13. *The Assurance of the Promise.* The climax of the prophet's declaration of promise is reached in this chapter. A series of utterances culminating in a renewed vision of the return of the exiles and the restoration of fertility to the land. The praise offered by the mountains and hills crowns the realization of this new life.

55:1-5. The people are summoned to return to their God, for with God is life in all its fullness. They will here find the blessings of a new promised land, the **wine and milk** which belong to the new age. The promise declared to **David** still stands. Through him, as representative of the people, there is a summons to the **nations** who will come to God. The Davidic promise here echoes especially Psalm 18:43 (cf. II Samuel 22:44). Beginning in terms of conquest, it is now understood in terms of the offer of salvation to all the world.

55:6-9. The proclaiming of the day of salvation is not without its warning note. There is promise for the people, but it demands their response. They must take advantage of the moment of opportunity. Verse 6*a* can be interpreted "while he lets himself be found." This idea, together with **while he is near,** may imply that response cannot be deferred in the expectation that God will always be there. The appeal is based on the declared will of God to forgive, and humanity must not presume on this.

55:10-13. The theme of reassurance returns in a declaration of the absolute certainty that God will fulfill the divine purposes (verses 10-11). The promise issues in the vision of returning exiles and renewed land (verses 12-13). Here is the culmination of promise. A new and restored world offers its praises to God. It is a perpetual witness to the enduring purpose of God—and a token of that mercy and comfort and blessing which form so large a part of the message of Second Isaiah.

VIII. The Oracles of Third Isaiah (56:1–66:24)

The content and style of the opening verses of this last major section of the book immediately mark a division from what precedes. Yet the division is not absolute. For example, 56:1-2 echoes the sentiment of 55:6-7, and in 56:5 there is a clear verbal link with 55:13. The Dead Sea Scrolls manuscript makes the connection by adding "for" at the beginning of 56:1.

The view that a new collection begins here has much to commend it (see Introduction). The new section belongs to the

Isaiah tradition and is conveniently ascribed to Third Isaiah. Yet the recognition that these oracles provide in some measure an interpretation of Second Isaiah often lights up the relationship. At many points there is closeness in the thought, though often variation in the use of words. There is application of the message to the new and difficult situation of a community re-establishing itself in Judah. However, it is not always possible to be certain of dating even in relation to the rebuilding of the temple at Jerusalem.

A. THE BLESSINGS OF OBEDIENCE (56:1-8)

56:1-2. *A Call to Obedience.* The nearness of divine salvation demands the response of right action. Specifically the **sabbath** is to be observed and **evil** in general to be avoided. The reference to the sabbath may point to a development of its significance in the exilic period—an ancient custom come to life because of the feasibility of observing it. It was to become one of the fundamental marks of Judaism.

56:3-8. *On Eunuchs and Foreigners.* The general demand in verses 1-2 is the occasion for two directives, perhaps in answer to a special inquiry (cf. Haggai 2:10-14 and Zechariah 7:1-3). The **foreigner** and the **eunuch,** whose place in the community is in doubt, are given reassurance. In obedience, in the keeping of the sabbath, and in the maintenance of the **covenant** there is life and blessing and the assurance of **an everlasting name** to take the place of descendants denied the eunuch. There is no clear information concerning the status of eunuchs in Israel. Deuteronomy 23:1, often quoted as evidence, does not necessarily refer to the same problem. It has sometimes been supposed that Nehemiah was a eunuch and that his "memoir" was designed to be just such a memorial and name (cf. Nehemiah 13:31).

The status of foreigners was also at times in doubt (cf. the cases in Deuteronomy 23). Here the same basic conditions apply—obedience and service. In verse 6*b* **minister,** a term used most often as a technical expression for priestly duty is perhaps intended more generally.

56:7-8. As in 2:2-4, the temple is a gathering place for all nations. The God who gathers the scattered people will bring in also those from outside. Here is the application of Second Isaiah's proclamation of salvation to the realities of a new situation. It is perhaps that of the small community of returned exiles, with their temple rebuilt (after 516), but faced with many uncertainties. The centrality of Zion, the nearness of salvation, the gathering of the scattered are all themes of hope for such a people.

B. APOSTASY, JUDGMENT, AND DELIVERANCE
(56:9–57:21)

The section begins with sayings concerned with the disobedient. It ends with reassurance to the humble. In it a number of passages, probably unconnected orignally, are drawn together.

56:9-12. *Corrupt Leaders.* At the outset the failure is connected with the inability of the people's leaders to provide right guidance. Disaster is coming (verse 9), though this should not be interpreted literally or applied to a particular political situation. It is coming because the **watchmen are blind** (cf. Ezekiel 3:16-21). The people's **shepherds** have no concern but their own profit and pleasure. The word translated **dreaming** in verse 10*e* is uncertain. Perhaps it means "panting," or perhaps "seers."

57:1-13*c*. *Corrupt Worship.* Verses 1-2 are perhaps a fragment, providing a comment on the state of disorder just described. Verses 1*e*-2 are obscure. Do they perhaps refer to the **righteous** as dead and so out of reach of danger? Or are they a wisdom saying used as a comment and offering reassurance?

57:3-10. These verses describe a judgment scene (**draw near**). They set out in detail the apostasies of the people. The passage is bitter in its condemnation. It gathers together every variety of idolatrous practice, with allusions to the evil ways of Canaan and to undesirable sexual practices which are not always clear. Verse 6 emphasizes that the people's gods are to be found in the **valley.** **Portion** and **lot** here both imply "object of worship," and are so used of Israel's God in Psalm 16:5 (cf. Numbers 18:20).

Verse 8*h* is obscure. The context suggests some kind of religious prostitution or the like, and perhaps the word translated **nakedness** indicates a phallic symbol. **Molech** (or "Melek," literally "king") in verse 9*a* probably is to be taken here as a divine title. It refers perhaps to the ruler of **Sheol,** the world of the dead. The line might be rendered "You drenched yourselves with oil for Melek."

57:11-13c. The idolatry is answered by words of condemnation. The people have neglected their God. Nothing that they do will be of any avail. Verse 12 should perhaps be read as a conditional sentence: "If I tell. . . ." Their **idols** cannot help, for the **wind** will bear them **away.**

57:13d-21. *God's Promise of Restoration.* Verse 13*de* is usually taken as belonging to the previous section. But a contrast begins here. It invites response, and verses 14-21 contain the assurance. There are allusions to the thought of Second Isaiah—especially in verse 14, which reads almost like a quotation (perhaps verse 14*a* is intended to indicate this). The assurance is given, as in 66:1-2, that the holy God is ready to help the **humble,** the righteous of 57:1 who are perishing.

Verses 16-19 echo the assurance of Second Isaiah that the judgment of the Exile is over and that the people will be restored. Verse 16 also echoes the opening of the flood narrative in Genesis 6:3 and the creation stories, though the text is not entirely clear. God is apparently affirming that what has been created will not be destroyed. The passage ends, however, with a look back at the words of judgment and a concluding phrase like that in 48:22. This marks off the section from what follows.

The specific situation for these sayings is uncertain. Such political and religious ills may have occurred in the period of the Exile, though equally well immediately after. The final verses seem to reflect the Exile, but they could quite properly be applied to words of judgment from a later date. The passage serves as a reminder that Israel did not abandon all her older ways with the Exile. Apostasy and social injustice were perpetually recurrent. The warnings and the assurances to those who remained faithful did not lose their relevance.

C. True Obedience (58:1-14)

Formal worship, no matter how correctly performed, is of no avail if it is acompanied by wrong conduct. This theme is often sounded by earlier prophets and is still emphasized in the New Testament (cf. Mark 7). The approach here is in many ways like that of Malachi with its rhetorical questions. It has less of the direct condemnation of the older prophets and more of the hortatory tone of the preacher. Yet it makes its points incisively enough. It points to the source of true blessing in the God who seeks from the people not the mere formalities of worship but the full obedience of the heart.

58:1-9b. True Fasting. The people imagine that they are making the right approach to God, as if their conduct were entirely righteous (verses 1-2). They claim to be offering a true fast, and so expect God to heed their prayers (verse 3*ab*). Fasting is regarded as an aid to prayer, making the worshiper acceptable. But their worship is denied by the outrageous conduct that goes with it (verses 3*c*-4).

Verse 3*cd* is not entirely clear. The Revised Standard Version footnote indicates a possible alternative translation of verse 3*c* that emphasizes the parallel with the following line—which, however, is also uncertain. True fasting is not to be found in the outward forms (verse 5). It is to be found in the pursuit of good in the area of social concern (verses 6-7)—a text for the portrayal of judgment in Matthew 25:31-46. The day of salvation will come to an acceptable people (verses 8-9*b*). God will respond and be revealed because the barrier which prevents contact is removed (cf. 59:2).

58:9c-12. Rewards of Right Action. This appears to be a

separate passage brought together with the preceding because the content is similar. **The pointing of the finger, and speaking wickedness**—that is, contempt and slander, or perhaps, engaging in violent attack and promoting trouble—are to be set aside and replaced by positive acts of good will. **Pour yourself out** perhaps should be "furnish bread," as in the Septuagint.

Such right ways lead into the promise of newness of life for the whole people. There will be not only the **light** of the divine presence (verse 10*c;* cf. verse 8*a*) and guidance but the rebuilding of the ruined cities (verse 12). This may point to the period of the Exile or the years immediately after, when such rebuilding was a problem and life remained economically insecure.

58:13-14. *True Sabbath Observance.* This passage presents a similar view of false and true sabbath observance. The promise is that by right action the people will recover their full **heritage.** The allusion to patriarchal promise and the use of the language of Deuteronomy 32:13—**ride upon the heights**—point to a new interpretation of the ancient giving of the land, and so the restoration of full life.

D. CONFESSION AND JUDGMENT (59:1-21)

The form of a lament psalm, with its confession of sin and its culmination in a prophetic word of assurance, is used here. It is the basis for a prophetic statement of the present condition of the people and the reasons for their distress. Basically the trouble lies in their **iniquities.** The anticipation of divine deliverance—so much the theme of Second Isaiah—is disappointed. The sins of the people hinder the effectiveness of God's action. There is no suggestion that God cannot act. It is human beings who delay the coming of the new age by what they are.

The passage is perhaps also concerned with the problem of the success of the wicked. But there is a much more general sense of the whole community's responsibility for its present condition. No too simple division into good and bad—with consequent placing of the blame on other people—is permitted here.

59:1-8. *General Indictment.* Verses 1-2 give a classic expression of the problem of sin as a barrier between the people and God. A series of more specific accusations follows in verses 3-8. As so often in earlier prophecy, the emphasis rests on injustice and failure to **know** the right way of life. In a series of vivid metaphors (verses 5-6) the consequences of evil are drawn out.

59:9-15*b*. *Confession.* This begins in general terms. The language is reminiscent of the passages in Amos 5 which describe the day of Yahweh. In verse 12 direct acknowledgment of sin is made as an expression of the community's total failure. The thought that **justice** and **righteousness** are far away runs like a refrain (verses 9, 11, 14). The meaning of **in full vigor** (verse 10*d*) is very uncertain. Transposing two letters of the Hebrew word for **oppression** (verse 13*c*) gives "deceit," which fits the context better.

59:15*c*-21. *God's Saving Action.* The failure of the people provokes God to action, for it is clear that there is no other source of salvation and right. The point of verse 16 is not that God might have expected some other to **intervene** in God's place but that salvation is God's alone. Thus God is pictured as the mighty warrior going to battle. With **his own arm** God brings judgment on all who set themselves against the divinity.

The outcome of judgment is salvation, the acknowledgment of the **name** of God by the nations (verse 19). Verse 20 adds to this hope the assurance of God as **Redeemer** of the people. Verse 21 elaborates on this point, bringing out the full significance of God's action in the establishment of an everlasting **covenant.** The answer to humanity's desperate condition, cut off from God by sin, is found in the assurance both of divine action and of the indwelling of God's word in the people.

E. The Glory of the New Zion (60:1-22)

The somewhat somber tone of chapters 56–59 gives way in chapters 60–62 to a sound of triumph and rejoicing. The last verses of chapter 59 point forward to this, picturing God coming as a warrior in triumph and assuring the people of deliverance. Now the call goes out to rejoice at the appearance of God in **glory.** God brings **light** to the people and draws the **nations** to **Zion,** which is to be restored and beautified beyond measure. Much of the language and thought of chapters 60–62 recall Second Isaiah. The recollection is so close as to raise the question whether they may be a further part of his message.

60:1-3. *The Dawn of God's Glory.* Zion is called to reflect the glory of God, who comes as the **light** of the world and draws the **nations** to this new dawn. The contrast between the **darkness** of the world and the light which God's people enjoy recalls the plague of darkness in Egypt (Exodus 10:22-23). Such an echo of the Exodus is characteristic of Second Isaiah.

60:4-9. *The Gathering of the Nations.* The nations will throng to Jerusalem, bringing back scattered Israel. They will offer their **wealth** to beautify Zion, and their **flocks** will be an acceptable sacrifice in a **glorious** temple. In verse 5*b* thrill is literally "feel awe" or "fear"—suggesting the mixture of strong emotions evoked by such an experience.

The peoples named in verses 6-7 come from various parts of Arabia. **Ephah** was a Midianite tribe (cf. Genesis 25:4). **Nebaioth,** a tribe of Ishmaelites (cf. Genesis 25:13), may be the people later known as Nabateans. During New Testament times their kingdom covered most of the territory east and south of Judea. In verse 7*c* **with acceptance** should read "for acceptance." Peoples come also from the west, across the sea (verses 8-9), bringing scattered Israel and treasures. Verse 9*a* should probably be emended to "For vessels shall gather to me." On **Tarshish** see above on 23:1-14.

60:10-18. *Restoration of Jerusalem.* The contributions of the nations serve for the rebuilding of Jerusalem. Judged in God's **wrath** at the Exile, the city is now blessed by God's **favor.** A series of pictures portrays the reversal of fortune. The wealth of the nations brings beauty of a new kind to the shrine (verse 13), and the city is renamed (verse 14*ef;* cf. verse 18*cd;* 1:26; 62:2-5). It is God the **Redeemer** who brings all this about.

60:19-22. *God as the Light of the People.* No longer will **sun**

and **moon** be needed. God is to be an eternal light for the people (cf. Revelation 21:23-26), a sun that never sets. The new age means a new possessing of **the land.** The whole people share in the salvation which God brings to them—the meaning of **righteous** in verse 21*a.* A new and purified people will increase in number under the blessing God gives.

Whether the whole chapter represents a unified poem or not is of no great importance. It reveals a unity in its stating and developing of themes connected with the new act of divine salvation—a glorified temple, a rebuilt and open city, a gathered people, the drawing in of the nations. The breadth of vision is certainly like that of Second Isaiah. Quite possibly the chapter belongs to the early years of Persian rule, whether before or after the actual rebuilding of the temple. It is an eloquent witness to the strength of faith which moved people of vision in days which were politically and economically difficult. The return from exile may not have been all that was hoped for. But there were those who could see in it the reality of God's saving power.

F. THE PROPHETIC COMMISSION (61:1-11)

61:1-3. *A Call to Preach Good News.* The opening words echo the commission of Second Isaiah in 40:9, where the summons to give **good tidings** is addressed to Zion. Conscious of the power of the **Spirit** and **anointed** by God, the prophet knows his commission to be that of release and hope for his people. **Liberty to the captives** suggests the law governing the release of slaves at the end of a six-year period (Exodus 21:1-6) rather than the more elaborate jubilee (Leviticus 25). **Proclaim the year of . . . favor** perhaps suggests a proclamation made at the beginning of such a year of release.

But the terminology may well be metaphorical. It shows a particular type of interpretation of the Exile, not unlike that in Leviticus 26:34 and II Chronicles 36:21. It is a period of slavery from which release is offered. Now the **day** of hope dawns, the day of divine "rescue" or "requital," rather than **vengeance** (verse 2*b*). The reversal of fortune is described in verse 3 in words which suggest links to chapter 60, especially 60:21.

61:4-11. *Promise of Restoration and Renewal.* The general statement of promise is followed by elaboration of the themes. The **ruins** will be rebuilt—perhaps by the nations, though this is not clearly stated. The people of God will be established as the priesthood. The nations will undertake the other activities of normal life and contribute to the upkeep of their priests (verses 5-7). The Hebrew of verse 7 is obscure. Evidently the idea of change of fortune is present. The theme of renewed **covenant** (cf. 59:21) is taken up in verses 8-9, with the characteristically prophetic emphasis on right. The new people, **blessed** by God, will be established and acknowledged by the world. This prospect evokes a psalm of praise (verses 10-11). Zion seems to be the speaker, acknowledging that it is God who has adorned her, as **bride** and **bridegroom** deck themselves. **Righteousness**—salvation—will **spring forth** before the world by the action of God.

It was the opening of this chapter that Jesus read in the synagogue at Nazareth at the beginning of his ministry (cf. Luke 4:16-21; it was probably the set portion from the Prophets for that sabbath). This shows how the prospect of release from the Exile could appropriately be a picture of the salvation declared in Christ. The presentation of the New Testament understanding of deliverance is linked not only to the exodus events, which were so much in the mind of the prophets, especially those of the exilic period. It is linked also to the experience of exile itself and to the confidence in the power of God to bring release. "Babylonian captivity" becomes a symbolic phrase to express the rule of evil. Such interpretation is found in the prophets of the exile and after, to whom the experience of disaster was so much a reality. They maintained their confidence in God's power to save even when outward circumstances seemed discouraging.

G. THE NEW JERUSALEM (62:1-12)

62:1-5. *Zion's Vindication.* The function of the prophet in the Old Testament includes intercession (cf. Genesis 20:7; Jeremiah 14:11). Here the prophet expresses his confidence in God's saving action by pledging himself to ceaseless prayer. The victory for Zion is at hand (verse 1), and the **nations** will see what God has done. The new city will be like a **crown** for God—probably an allusion to ancient representations of deities crowned with the walls of a city.

The theme of a **new name** (cf. 60:14) is taken up, but more elaborately. It is linked with the metaphor of the marriage relationship between God and the people used in Hosea, Jeremiah, and Ezekiel. The picture is extended in verse 5, suggesting the blessing of a marriage between the city and its **sons.**

62:6-9. *The Security of Zion.* It is possible that the prophet continues speaking in these verses. More probably they are intended as a divine declaration. The **watchmen** are best understood as the prophets, intercessors, those **who put the LORD in remembrance,** who bring before the Lord the promises made. This is a function often expressed in Old Testament worship. The new establishment of the city brings a confirmation of the promise of enduring peace and well-being. No further disaster will overtake God's people (cf. 54:9-10). Nor will neighboring peoples be permitted to raid the insecure land and benefit by Israel's weakness.

62:10-12. *The Way to Zion.* In a climax the summons is issued to prepare the processional way to Zion (cf. 40:3-5 and 57:14-15). God comes to the holy place bringing victory and holiness for the people. Verse 11*ef* is a quotation of 40:10*cd*. Again at the end the theme of the renaming of the city is developed. The phrases are reminiscent both of Second Isaiah and of other Old Testament promises.

For the generation of the Exile there was great concern with the reestablishment of Zion (cf. Ezekiel 40-48). The promises of

Second Isaiah point to the act of salvation by which it is to be accomplished. Perhaps we should see here a reflection of the way in which this concern expressed itself in the difficult years as the temple was rebuilt and life was being reorganized. Like Haggai and Zechariah the prophet of this passage is one who sees the essential place which Zion occupies in his people's understanding of their relationship to God. God chooses to come to them in blessing there. For the members of the community, near or far, it is the focal point.

H. THE VICTORIOUS GOD (63:1-6)

This vivid poem picks up the proclamation of 61:2 that the **day of vengeance** is at hand (verse 4). The moment is described also as the **year of redemption** (cf. "year of the LORD'S favor," 61:2). It is the moment of God's triumph over enemies, here symbolized in the reference to **Edom** (see above on 34:1-17). In question and answer the prophet—pictured perhaps as a watchman on the city wall (verse 1)—portrays the coming of the victorious God like a mighty warrior returning from the **wine press** of wrath (cf. Revelation 14:19-20), from the overthrow of God's opponents. God has been provoked to action because there is **no one** else **to help** (cf. 59:16). In verse 3*b* for **the peoples** the Dead Sea Scrolls manuscript has "my people," which appropriately suggests God's saving action on behalf of the elect. In verse 6*b* for **made them drunk** some Hebrew manuscripts read "shattered them" (cf. verse 3*d*).

The picture of God as a warrior with clothing **stained** with the **lifeblood** of enemies clearly needs careful interpretation. As an image it has certain obvious disadvantages. Yet the apocalyptic writers reveal how effectively such pictures may be used to proclaim the salvation which God brings about. That such pictures have sometimes been interpreted literally reveals a failure to understand the nature of biblical poetry.

I. THE PEOPLE'S LAMENT AND PRAYER (63:7–64:12)

This passage contains the elements characteristic of the psalms of lamentation. Many of its motifs and phrases appear, for example, in Psalm 74. Such laments were spoken on the people's behalf by a religious official—priest, prophet, singer, or possibly at an earlier date the king. Therefore this intercession may well be offered by the prophet himself (cf. 62:1). But its form suggests that it represents the lament and prayer of the whole community presented by its spokesman.

63:7-14. *God's Love for the People.* The speaker begins with hymnic statements calling to remembrance the acts of **great goodness** shown by God to the people. The reiterated expressions of verse 7 emphasize their dependence on God. In verses 8-9 the moment of being chosen by God is recalled. God was their deliverer. God brought them out, continually caring for them and sustaining them. The personal protection is probably indicated in verse 9*ab*, where the text is uncertain. A preferable rendering, based on the Septuagint, is "In all their affliction neither envoy nor messenger but his own presence saved them."

63:10-14. The divine choice did not, however, find the true response of obedience. The people **rebelled** and found in their God one who judged them. The reference may be to any or all the occasions of failure after the settlement in Canaan. The disobedience was at each stage followed by divine mercy as God called to mind the great acts of deliverance which were wrought for them through the divine **shepherds.** The continuing deliverance and guidance became, as it were, a constant reminder to God of the divine gracious nature. Thus God's people were brought again through repeated disasters to their rest in the promised land.

That verse 10 suggests the destruction of Jerusalem in 586 is clear enough. Yet it contains wider allusions to the long history of Israel. The divine actions are again described in hymnic style. Verse 11*b* is problematic, since the Hebrew reads "Moses his people."

63:15–64:5b. *Prayer for Pity.* The people in disaster turn to God. They ask God to look in **compassion** from the heavenly dwelling and show strength and jealousy for the people. Verse 16 is not entirely clear. Probably it is intended to suggest the concept of **Abraham** and **Israel,** the ancestors of the people, as their guardians. But it is God alone who is **Father** to the people. The present distress is judgment (verse 17), and it is as if God has entirely rejected the people which belong to him. Verse 18*a* appears to call the period of Solomon's temple, which was about 375 years, **a little while.** Perhaps it should be emended to read "only a little while ago they dispossessed thy holy people"—an allusion presumably to the still recent disaster of 586.

64:1-5*b*. A different kind of appeal recalls the ancient manifestations of God's power—the terrors and earthquakes evoked by the divine presence. As in Second Isaiah, the appeal is to God as the only God who alone will act **for those who wait for him.** God will be proclaimed to the nations as to those who look for salvation. Verse 5*a* may perhaps be emended to read "O that thou wouldst meet him who repents in righteousness."

64:5c-12. *Confession and Final Appeal.* The preceding appeal is supported by an acknowledgment (verses 5*c*-7) of the uncleanness of the whole people and their consequent separation from God. **There is no one** to intercede, to impress on God the distress of the people. There is nothing but total judgment. Verse 5*d* is obscure. **In our sins we have been a long time** is an attempt to interpret the literal reading "in them of old."

64:8-12. A final appeal points to the people's absolute dependence on God. The image of the **potter** and the **clay** is used as in 45:9. City and temple are desolated. But Israel is God's people. How can God **restrain** from restoration?

If an attempt is made to fit this lament into a precise historical situation, 63:18; 64:10-11 support the conclusion that the fall of the city and the destruction of the temple in 586 do not lie far in the past. The situation is not unlike that revealed in Lamentations, though conceivably there is allusion to some other event not so clearly known to us.

But we should also recognize that the language of such laments is in some degree stereotyped (cf. for example, Psalms 44, 74, and 79). Perhaps this passage should be considered an elaboration of older forms. Words which originally had specific relevance are reapplied, so that the distress of different situations might be expressed. To those who returned to Palestine to rebuild the temple such language would be deeply expressive. In other moments of need, national and personal, the recall of God's mighty acts and the acknowledgment of the people's dependence would continue to be apt.

J. THE HOPE OF A NEW AGE (65:1-25)

65:1-7. *Rebellion of the People.* As if in answer to the prayer of the previous section, this passage opens with the affirmation that it is not God who is unwilling to hear. It is God's **people** who are rebellious. The passage comes from a situation different from that of 63:7–64:12, but its position here is explained by the link of thought. The condemnation of idolatrous practices and of the unwillingness to hear God is a reminder that the people's condition arises from their own failure. In verses 1-2 it is repeatedly emphasized that God is more willing to speak than the people to hear.

65:3-7. The idolatrous practices include the making of **gardens** to alien deities (cf. 1:29; 17:10) and an unknown rite with **incense.** There are also necromantic practices involving sacrificial meals of unclean food in which the worshipers engage in rituals designed apparently to purify themselves, but not so as to approach God. These are a continual provocation. God's answer is in total judgment on them just as there was judgment on their **fathers** for similar evils (verses 6-7).

65:8-16. *The Faithful and the Faithless.* Yet the people are not wholly depraved. For the sake of the faithful **servants** God will act to bless and to restore. The faithful are like a **cluster** of good grapes holding the promise of **wine.** Some have taken the saying of verse 8b to be the beginning of a popular song of which the tune is mentioned in the titles of Psalms 57–59 and 75. From the faithful a new people will be established (verse 9). The land will be a place of blessing and safety from the Plain of **Sharon** on the western seacoast to the **Valley of Achor** near the Dead Sea. The latter suggests a new entry to the Promised Land (cf. Joshua 7:24; Hosea 2:15).

65:11-12. But again there is judgment for the apostates— those who engage in alien cults directed to Gad (**Fortune**) and Meni (**Destiny**), apparently deities of the Syrian and Phoenician area. With a pun on the second name God "destines" the faithless to disaster for their failure to respond, their evil action, and their choice of an obnoxious cult.

65:13-16. The distinction between the faithful and the faithless becomes clearer in a series of sharp contrasts between those who are God's **servants** and those addressed, who will become nothing but a **curse.** The thought is that whereas in Abraham the nations would bless themselves (Genesis 12:3), invoking on themselves God's good fortune, the **name** of these apostates will be as a curse formula to the faithful. These faithful, by contrast, will be called by a new name in token of their new nature. The somewhat obscure verse 16 pictures the faithful as blessing themselves by the **God of truth** (literally "God of Amen"), and so the former disasters are set aside.

65:17-25. *New Heavens and a New Earth.* The setting aside of the past and the condemnation of the apostates imply the purification of God's people. The setting for such a promise is a new order—a new creation like that described in Genesis 1—and a new **Jerusalem,** which will no longer lament but **rejoice.** Here will be true peace and security (cf. Zechariah 8).

None will die prematurely, but all will enjoy full life. Probably verse 20e should be rendered "and he who falls short of being a hundred shall be held in light esteem." They will enjoy the fruits of their labors and not come to an evil end. They will enjoy the closest contact with God, whose readiness to **answer** is even more vividly affirmed. Echoing 11:6-9, the prophet speaks of the restoration of peace as at the beginning (verse 25). The **serpent** as symbol of evil is kept subdued (cf. Genesis 3:14). No

hurt will be done in God's **holy mountain,** which as the center of the world's life is the token of well-being for land and world (cf. 2:2-4).

The chapter thus offers a first climax to the whole book. It picks up the themes of disobedience and judgment, with particular reference to Israel's proneness to forsake its God. It affirms the hope that God will not totally destroy, but will save and create a new people. It reveals the promise of blessing to the faithful and holds out the prospect of a new world order, a new age. There is here both warning and hope, encouragement to those who seek God and the consequence of disaster to those who turn from God. Thus the impact of the divine promise is seen as bringing both judgment and salvation.

K. The Final Word of Judgment and Promise (66:1-24)

The summarizing message here is a collection of loosely linked passages. They elaborate the themes of chapter 65 and, like that chapter, provide a reminder of the preceding prophecies. Echoes of earlier themes draw together the whole range of the thought of the book and present the reader with a last message of warning and promise.

66:1-2. *God's Dwelling Place.* An echo of I Kings 8:27 reminds us that no earthly temple can contain the God whose **throne** is **heaven** and whose **footstool** is the **earth.** Yet such is the condescension of God that God chooses to be revealed to the worshiper who comes in reverence and trust. This is no polemic against building a temple. Indeed we cannot tell whether the words belong before or after its rebuilding. It is a reminder of the freedom of God, who chooses to be revealed and to speak from the divine shrine (cf. verse 6). The temple is never to be a limiting conception. Yet like other elements of institutional religion it is a mechanism through which God chooses to be made known.

66:3-5. *Condemnation of Idolatry.* As if echoing the idea of false trust—often emphasized in earlier prophecy (cf. for example, Jeremiah 7)—a series of declarations condemns idolatrous worshipers and proclaims judgment on them. Such persons pay no heed to God. They do as they please. The precise meaning of verse 3 is not clear since the Hebrew contains no equivalent for the **like** introduced into each phrase. But comparison is the most likely sense. The point is that the worship of an unacceptable people, who have **chosen their own ways**, is as useless and indeed as dangerous as engaging in the worst of alien religious practices.

In this context **kills a man** may imply human sacrifice rather than simply murder. However, the fact that murder automatically disqualifies one from worship (cf. "your hands are full of blood," 1:15) makes this meaning also possible. Contrasted with these idolatrous worshipers are the reverent hearers of God's word (verse 5). They are treated with hostility because they are faithful, and they are mocked for their allegiance. But **shame** will be on their opponents.

66:6-14. God's Multiple Blessings. God makes divine intention known. God declares judgment from Zion on the enemies (verse 6). God expresses purpose through bringing a new people into being by miraculous and speedy **birth** (verses 7-9). To any who might doubt the reality of this promise and the assurance of its fulfillment the series of questions in verses 8-9 offers complete confidence. What God has decreed will surely come to pass speedily. So in verses 10-11 an invitation is issued to **rejoice** because of the new life which has come for Jerusalem—a fullness of life and of delight which is expressed in the metaphor of the life-giving **breasts**. In verse 11 the last phrase should be translated "from her bountiful breast."

66:12-14. The same theme is continued with a picture of new prosperity using the image of the **river** as a source of life and the coming of the **nations** with their **wealth**. The security and bliss of God's people is like that of a protected child (cf. chapter 49:22-23). There is also an echo of the message of **comfort** in chapter 40. God's work for the people offers protection for **servants** but **indignation** for his **enemies**.

66:15-17. Destruction of God's Enemies. The image of

indignation is elaborated in the picture of judgment in fire and storm, a great action against the hostile forces. Verse 17 makes more specific reference to the enemies as idolaters, indicating similar practices to those mentioned in 65:3-4. In the obscure expression **following one in the midst** the "one" may be feminine and perhaps indicates a goddess. It is possible that **their works and their thoughts** in verse 18 should be connected with **come to an end** in verse 17.

66:18-23. *The Gathering of the Nations.* Thus we are brought to the final picture—perhaps originally poetry rather than prose—of the glory of God revealed to the nations (cf. 40:5). The nations themselves bring in the scattered members of Israel as a holy **offering** to God, a sign of the faithful worship to be offered. The main part of verse 19, repetitive of verse 18, is perhaps a gloss designed to indicate more precisely the distant places involved. **Tarshish** indicates remote Spain. **Put** was evidently in northern Africa (cf. Genesis 10:13; Jeremiah 46:9; Ezekiel 30:5). Others, on the basis of Assyrian records which mention "Luddu" in Asia Minor as giving military aid to Egypt, identify it with Lydia. **Who draw the bow** should be read as Meshech, which with **Tubal** and **Javan** (Ionia) was in Asia Minor. The list traces the faraway lands from which the nations will come, places in which God's name and glory are not yet known.

The appointment of **priests** and **Levites** almost certainly refers to the returning members of the community (cf. 61:6), an enlarged priesthood to meet the needs of a larger worshiping people. For with the new creation (verses 22-23) the round of worship from sacred time to sacred time will draw in all peoples.

66:24. *A Final Warning.* The final verse introduces a last note of warning concerning the downfall of those who **have rebelled against** God, apostates who come under divine wrath. The picture of perpetual **fire** is probably taken from the burning of refuse in the Valley of Hinnom outside Jerusalem (see comment on Jeremiah 19:1-5). Perhaps, however, there is also an overtone of the final cosmic battle of the nations against God's people, in which God wins the last victory at the ushering in of the new age (cf. Ezekiel 38-39, Zechariah 14).

So at the end, with all the prospect of a glorious future in the saving power of God, there is the warning note—the reminder that the word which is a word of life is also a word of judgment. The note on which the book began is the note on which it ends. But it is a message lit up by the confidence of a great succession of prophets that salvation belongs to God and that in God all people may place absolute trust.

THE BOOK OF JEREMIAH

Stanley Brice Frost

Introduction

Jeremiah's Life and Times

The sixty years between 640 and 580 B.C. are perhaps the most important and certainly the best documented in all Israel's long history. In 641/40 Josiah became king of the southern Kingdom of Judah—just when Assyria's imperial power was beginning to falter. By his thirteenth year (627) Judah's independence from Assyria began to appear a practical proposition. At this time of political speculation a youth named Jeremiah passed through an experience which convinced him of his call to be a prophet of Yahweh (1:1-2).

However, Jeremiah did not join in the popular chorus of optimism about the nation's future. Instead, he created something of a stir by speaking repeatedly of an invasion from the North and by insisting that Judah was very far from having Yahweh's good will. Five years later (623/22) the original edition of Deuteronomy was discovered in the temple, and a national reformation was begun based on its principles. This new zeal for the covenant and the increasingly favorable political climate made Jeremiah's warning of imminent judgment appear irrelevant.

His own attitude to the reformation was ambivalent. He seems to have undertaken a preaching mission to help popularize it (cf. 11:1-8). Yet he was not wholly persuaded that this was the answer to Judah's spiritual situation (cf. 8:8-10). There were many prophets in Israel, however. Jeremiah was dismissed by those who knew him as unimportant.

During this period of obscurity Jeremiah even had his own doubts about himself (15:15-18; 20:7-10). So things continued until 612, when Nineveh fell and the Assyrian Empire became a thing of the past. This seemed to show still more clearly that Jeremiah was wrong in his interpretation of Judah's situation. We know very little about this long period of the prophet's life. It has even been suggested that Josiah's thirteenth year was actually the date of Jeremiah's birth and that he did not begin to prophesy till Jehoiakim's accession about eighteen years later. There is good reason, however, to accept the dates given in the book. It seems clear that from the age of fifteen or so until he was well over thirty Jeremiah was an obscure and unregarded prophet.

In 609 Pharaoh Neco marched north through Palestine to salvage what he could out of the wreck of the Assyrian Empire. Josiah tried to stop him at Megiddo, probably relying on divine aid as promised by optimistic prophets. But this aid was not given, and he lost his life in ignominious defeat. Neco marched on to the Euphrates, and the people crowned Josiah's son Jehoahaz. But three months later Neco on his return journey took the young king captive. He placed another son of Josiah, Jehoiakim, on the throne as his vassal, imposing a heavy tribute on the land.

Overnight the outlook for Judah changed dramatically. It was suddenly clear that it had been living in a fool's paradise. Yahweh either would not or could not save it from the political realities of the times. Jeremiah's message then became a highly relevant interpretation of Judah's situation; and the prophet himself became a figure of importance. Under the new king the reform movement ground quickly to a halt. Jeremiah's criticisms of Judah's religious practices and moral standards could no longer be so easily dismissed.

At the time of Jehoiakim's coronation, or soon afterward,

Jeremiah declared in the temple court that unless Judah changed its ways the very temple itself would be destroyed (7:1-15; 26:1-6). This prophecy caused a riot. Only the intervention of some nobles prevented his being killed by an angry mob (26:7-24).

Jeremiah continued stubbornly in the same vein, however. In 605/4 after an especially provocative outburst the temple authorities tried to silence him with a flogging and a night in the stocks (19:1–20:2). Since this had no effect, they refused to allow him to enter the temple. Jeremiah's response was to resort to what was quite a new idea. He dictated his major pieces to a friend called Baruch and sent him into the temple to read them to the pilgrims. This was an extremely important development. It meant that Jeremiah's book originated by authority of the prophet himself, whereas earlier prophetic anthologies apparently were compiled posthumously by disciples.

Jehoiakim's abortive rebellion against the Babylonians in 598 further defined Jeremiah's position. He insisted that Babylon was intended to be world ruler. It was to be Yahweh's instrument of punishment in dealings with Israel—here he was treading in the footsteps of Isaiah, who thought similarly of Assyria. Judah must submit meekly to its rule.

In 593 a group of ambassadors met in Jerusalem to plot further rebellion. Jeremiah publicly opposed Hananiah ben Azzur, who was prophesying success to the enterprise (27:1–28:16). The rebellion did not take place, and probably Jeremiah's determined opposition was at least partly responsible. But revolt, bolstered by Egyptian promises, did break out in 589. By January, 588, the Babylonians and their allies had overrun the country and were settling down to besiege Jerusalem.

Jeremiah stayed in Jerusalem throughout the siege. In its early months Zedekiah sought counsel from him (21:1-14). He told the king that surrender to the Babylonians was the only way to save himself and the city, but Zedekiah could not hope to carry such a plan with his nobles.

The Egyptian army moved up into Palestine. The Babylonians turned from besieging Jerusalem to meet it. When Jeremiah attempted to leave the city at this time to visit his family property, he was accused of deserting to the Babylonians and imprisoned (37:11-15). The Egyptian army faded away again, and the Babylonians resumed the siege. Prisoner though he was, Jeremiah still urged surrender on all in the barracks where he was held. The exasperated military leaders threw him into an empty cistern to die. But an Ethiopian—probably a slave in the king's household—rescued him. He was returned to the barracks, where he remained for the rest of the siege.

As it dragged on, a kinsman offered to sell Jeremiah a plot of family land in Anathoth. This was not an attractive proposition, since the future was so uncertain. Yet the prophet bought it and insisted on paying the regular market price. This was his testimony to his faith that Judah had a future in the purposes of God (32:1-25). The incident is particularly significant in that it shows that hope was truly a part of Jeremiah's message. After punishment would come restoration.

The city fell in 586. The Babylonians had evidently taken note of Jeremiah's advocacy of their cause, for the local commander received orders to allow him his freedom. He chose to remain with the new governor, Gedaliah, and the remnant seeking to rebuild the national life—though he had several times said that Judah's future lay with the exiles in Babylon.

When Gedaliah was assassinated and the survivors fled to Egypt, Jeremiah and Baruch went along. The last we hear of the prophet is in that country. There he protested vigorously against any belief that Egypt could provide a satisfactory home for Jewry and asserted that Nebuchadrezzar would conquer that country as he had the rest of the Fertile Crescent. It is probable that he died in the companionship of his faithful Baruch in the country he so heartily despised.

Such is the bare outline of his life. But what kind of man was he? Here there is room for a wide variety of interpretations. But since all we know of him comes from the book bearing his name, a knowledge of its character and style is necessary.

Origin and Character

Jeremiah himself took the initiative in gathering the first collection of his oracles. When this manuscript was destroyed, he encouraged his friend Baruch to produce an enlarged collection. It is important, however, to remember that the individual pieces which went into these manuscripts were not produced for posterity. They arose out of particular situations. Thus the book does not have a coherent, sequential text. Rather it consists of a collection of sayings, poems, prayers, oracles, hymns, proverbs, visions, and stories. At first sight these seem brought together quite irrationally. In fact they are often grouped in smaller collections having a rationale of their own.

The book may be divided into four major sections:

(1) the words of Jeremiah (1:4–25:14 and 25:15-38 form an independent collection of Jeremiah's sayings concerning the nations);

(2) Jeremiah's ministry (26:1–45:5);

(3) oracles against the nations (46:1–51:64);

(4) a historical appendix (52:1-34).

The temple had two focuses. First was the life of the inner court where the priests celebrated the ceremonies of the cult. Second was the life of the outer court where men congregated in "gatherings" (cf. 6:11)—that is, discussion circles or groups. Some probably met every evening, thereby serving the purposes of a club, literary association, and newsstand. Others, congregating around a teacher, probably met in the mornings for study and instruction, thus serving the purposes of a school. Still others met on the sabbath and other days of religious observance and were in fact the embryo of the synagogue. Membership was fluid and merely associative.

Jeremiah was closely attached to the life of the temple, but not to that of the inner court of the priests. His whole manner of existence was intimately bound up with the discussions, debates, studies, and public life of the outer court.

A man could rely on his gathering to provide him with an audience. Sometimes he had only gossip to relate, at other times solid news. Sometimes he had a poem to recite, a psalm expressing his feelings of joy or sorrow or hate in some particular circumstance. A prophet might produce an "oracle"—a message from Yahweh, given him to communicate to Israel. A "wise man" might produce a wisdom saying, which could be as short as a two-line proverb or as long as a psalm. A poet might produce a love song, or a wit might come up with a riddle. At times the current political situation would be discussed heatedly and anxiously. The outer court of the temple provided a home for the intellectual life of Jerusalem and Judah. Jeremiah inevitably gravitated there.

In such a gathering things were said, discussed, admired, and then—as further conversation flowed—forgotten. But some items were too striking to forget and were repeated and remembered. When Jeremiah wanted to produce a written record of what he had said, he had in addition to his own memory that of his friend Baruch, who no doubt was a companion in the same group. When, however, he set out to write a new expression of his thoughts or to recount an event which in retrospect seemed significant—that is, when he was faced with the task of written composition as distinct from oral recollection—he used the common literary style of the day. This is usually termed Deuteronomic (D) because it was first distinguished by scholars in Deuteronomy. These efforts at written composition lie behind the remarkable prose passages in the earlier part of the book (for example, 1:4–2:3; 7:1-15; 11:1-17). They are paralleled by Baruch's similar production of the later prose narratives.

Compilation

Jeremiah first produced a written record of his message in 605/4 (36:1-4). It is a reasonable guess that this consisted of 1:4–8:3—the prophet's credentials, indictment of Israel, threat from the North, temple sermon—plus a summary and conclusion in 25:1-14, which also dates itself 605/4. When the scroll was destroyed by the king (36:9-26) it was rewritten with additions (36:27-32)—probably 8:4–10:16.

Having thus begun to keep a record of his sayings, Jeremiah

continued the practice over the next twenty years. This accounts for the little collections in 11:1–24:10. Each time the summary and conclusion (25:1-14) was pushed further back by the new material. The anthology 1:1–25:14 thus includes pieces dating from 626 to 586 and may well be called "Jeremiah his book."

After Jeremiah's death in Egypt, Baruch wished to vindicate his friend and his message. He therefore wrote his own account of Jeremiah's ministry, especially the later years. He starts with the famous temple sermon (chapter 26), which he dates 609/8. He tells how the prophet further clashed with temple personnel in 593 (chapters 27–29). Then he goes straight into the events of the siege, 588-586 (chapters 32–35 and 37–39). He tells further of the tragedy of Gedaliah (chapters 40–41) and explains how he and Jeremiah came to be in Egypt (chapters 42–44). Finally he tells how he came to be writing this book (chapters 36 and 45). There has been some disturbance of Baruch's narrative, and a significant interpolation, the "Book of Comfort" (chapters 30–31). But chapters 26–45 as a whole are "Baruch his book."

The third section of the book consists of oracles against the nations (chapters 46–51 plus 25:15-38; cf. Isaiah 13–23 and Ezekiel 25–32). Not much of this material is Jeremiah's, but each piece must be judged separately. The bulk of the collection comes from the second half of the sixth century.

The fourth section (52:1-34) was added by an editor as a historical summary to the whole Jeremiah anthology. It reminds us that, in addition to Jeremiah and Baruch, other hands have been at work and that the original writings have received considerable expansions. Some scholars in fact have identified a D editor, who worked during or after the exile. He is thought to have compiled the book from three major sources of material and also composed a number of passages. However, recognition that the common literary style of the period had D characteristics seems to make such a hypothesis unnecessary.

The English versions follow the traditional Hebrew text. The Greek Septuagint omits about an eighth of the book and inserts the oracles against the nations (chapters 46–51) after 25:13 in a different order. Dead Sea Scroll fragments have shown that this version was based on a variant Hebrew recension at a time when the text of Jeremiah was fairly fluid.

The Thought of Jeremiah

Jeremiah's thinking starts from the conviction that he was a prophet. He has told us what this meant to him. It meant that God's word was given him to proclaim (1:4-10) and that he had no other commitments. It made him a man apart who must forgo family relationships (11:18-23; 16:1-4). Even though he spent his days in the gatherings of the outer court of the temple and was gregarious by nature, he knew what it was to be withdrawn in the midst of a crowd, a dedicated soul (15:15-18). As a prophet he was prepared to stand alone. Fellow prophets, priests, relatives, people, nobles, king—they all turned against him, one after the other. But he knew that with Yahweh's help he could withstand them all (1:18-19).

Jeremiah conveys the nature of the prophetic experience. He was seized with trembling and was befuddled like a drunk by the violence of the divine word coming on him (23:9). But when the pressure lifted, the message he had received had to be passed on to those to whom it was addressed. There may be medical or psychological descriptions of such a state of mind, but for Jeremiah it was the experience of divine inspiration. We may think that at such moments his subconscious thought welled to the surface of his mind, but that too may be another way of referring to inspiration.

Jeremiah was certainly in no doubt about the fact that Yahweh gave him his word and that he must declare it (20:9). To be a true prophet in Jeremiah's mind was to be a member of Yahweh's council (23:18-22). His one gripping fear, at least in the early days, was that he might be just another deluded fool (15:18*b*; 20:7-18). But with fine humility he was prepared to rest his case in the hands of God (10:23-24).

Formally Jeremiah's thought about God was not especially original. He accepted the current covenant theology. He saw Yahweh as a deity who demanded total obedience to the covenant established with Israel at Sinai (3:1-5). Jeremiah recognized Yahweh as a moral being, requiring righteousness from the people (5:1-2; 9:7-9). Yahweh was also creator of all things (10:12-16) and able even to revoke creation (4:23-26). Theologically, if not philosophically, Jeremiah was a monotheist. That is, he lived as if Yahweh was the only God in the universe—even though he would not have denied in theory the existence of other gods.

His major interest, however, was in the religious interpretation of political events. This gave a particular tone to his theology (1:10). He early realized that Assyria was doomed but could not believe that Egypt had the stamina to be its heir. The powerful forces, he believed, were those of the mysterious north—the Medes, the Scythians, the Elamites, and above all the Chaldeans.

As the Chaldeans seized power in Babylon and then led the revolt against Assyria, Jeremiah became more and more convinced that the future lay with Chaldean Babylon. Following in Isaiah's footsteps (cf. Isaiah 30:1-7; 31:1-3), he consistently discounted Egypt and saw in the northern power the chosen instrument of Yahweh's anger (27:4-7).

Basically Jeremiah's interpretation was sound. True, it led him to prophesy that Nebuchadrezzar would conquer Egypt (43:8-13), a feat which Nebuchadrezzar never accomplished. He was also led to write Egypt off as a refuge for Jewry, a view which was belied by the very lively Jewish colonies there for the next five centuries. But his main policy for Judah was undoubtedly right: loyalty to its own institutions, especially its own religion, and political submission to imperial powers it could not hope to resist. It was a lesson Jewry learned painfully in the Exile, unlearned in the time of the Maccabees, and learned afresh in the Roman disasters.

The most influential aspect of Jeremiah's thinking, however, was his experience of personal religion. A man of the outer court of the temple, he was little attracted to the cultic aspect of religion. At one time or another he questioned critically the place in the nation's life of sacrifice (6:20; 7:21-22), circumcision (4:4; 9:25-26), the written law (8:8), the temple (7:1-15), and the institutions of prophetism and priesthood (5:30-31; 23:11-15). For Jeremiah religious reality centered in his personal communion with Yahweh. Though this experience was never theologically formulated, it influenced all his thought about God.

Thus, paradoxically—though we are very doubtful that the words are Jeremiah's own—the thought of 31:31-34 sums up the positive contribution of his message more fully than any other passage in the book. The effect of his life and teaching was to give people a new understanding of the possibility and importance of a personal relationship with God. To use his own vivid phrase from another context (32:4), Jeremiah taught the world that it is possible for one to know God for oneself and to "speak with him face to face and see him eye to eye."

Jeremiah's thought may need the balance of a healthy doctrine of the church. But his own experience of the reality of God was so genuine that he stands witness over the centuries to this central fact of religion. He still recalls us to the heart of the matter.

I. JEREMIAH'S BOOK (1:1–25:14)

A. JEREMIAH'S FIRST MANUSCRIPT (1:1–8:3)

1:1-3. *Introduction.* This passage is composite. Verses 1-2 may have introduced the original first manuscript, which must have had some such identification. Verse 3 may have been added for one of the later expansions. Even so, the introduction does not cover the whole content. The present book includes considerable material relating to the period after the fall of Jerusalem. There is also much narrative apart from actual words—that is, the oracles—of Jeremiah.

1:1. The old Hebrew priesthood in the days before the monarchy was centered in Shiloh (cf. 7:14; I Samuel 1:3). Its best-known leader was Eli. After Shiloh was destroyed, the priesthood settled apparently at Nob, near **Anathoth,** two and a half miles northeast of Jerusalem. Here they incurred Saul's wrath, and he massacred the whole clan except Abiathar (I Samuel 21:1-9; 22:6-23).

Abiathar became David's priest and rose to power in newly captured Jerusalem (II Samuel 20:25). After David's death Abiathar supported Adonijah in the struggle for the kingship. When Solomon won out, he was banished to Anathoth (I Kings 2:26-27). Jeremiah was *born* a priest but *called* to be a prophet. He seems never to have served as a priest. It is one of the marks of prophetism that its adherents gave it an absolute priority over all other considerations.

1:2-3. On the dates here indicated see the Introduction.

1:4–2:3. *The Prophet's Credentials.* This section forms a single unit. It consists of a number of oracles recalled in their original poetic form together with prose "transcriptions" of others. These are set in a brief explanatory narrative. It is intended to set out Jeremiah's credentials as a prophet. When he composed his first anthology, he was debarred from the temple because of the kind of thing he had been saying (36:5), and it was implied that he was not a true prophet. Hence the need for Jeremiah to produce impeccable credentials. He cites four experiences—the original call and three other moments of inspiration whereby it was clarified and made more precise.

1:4-10. *The Call.* Of the first experience we are given only the interior account. We are not told what exterior circumstance touched off the youth's developing consciousness of the divine which exploded in this searing conviction of vocation—though we may be sure there was one. The boy feels from the very start that this is what God wants him to do. He recognizes his **youth**—he was probably about fourteen or fifteen—but feels equal to the call because of the divine resources at his disposal.

Much too much has been made of Jeremiah's reticence and sensitiveness. From the beginning he was a very tough and determined young man. Yahweh—not an intermediary (cf. Isaiah 6:6)—has put divine **words** in Jeremiah's **mouth.** Therefore the prophet can stand up to anyone. The word was thought to be very powerful. As Jeremiah pronounces doom on nations, so the divine judgment will fall on them. Where he speaks peace, there peace will follow. But we notice that he expects to have little opportunity for this (cf. 28:5-9). He would not have to travel to be a **prophet to the nations.** His word of judgment spoken in Jerusalem will determine the fate of neighboring tribes and distant empires alike.

1:11-12. *The Waker Tree.* The **almond** tree was known as the "waker" because its blossom breaks into beauty even before it has unfolded its leaves. Yahweh has appeared to be doing nothing through the long years of Manasseh's reign and the fifteen years of his successors, when Assyria was everywhere dominant. So too in the long months of winter it seems as if, as far as the tree is concerned, God has entirely ceased to operate. But now, in due season, the waker tree is being quickened into beauty once more. So too in world affairs the time is right. Yahweh will commence political activity again. Assyria is beginning to falter, and this is a sign that Yahweh is about to act. The pun on "waker" and **watching,** literally "waking," is the kind that appealed strongly to the Hebrews' love of word play (see the Revised Standard Version footnotes).

1:13-19. *The Blown Pot.* Jeremiah sees a **boiling pot, facing away from the north.** Probably he means a pot set over a fire arranged to receive a draft from the north wind. Smelters who needed intense heat arranged their furnaces thus. In Old Testament times the north was usually the direction from which disaster threatened. Yahweh is going to bring **Jerusalem** to the boil—possibly for refining purposes (cf. 6:29-30)—by bringing down invasion from the North. The sin mentioned in verse 16 is idolatry, which covers a very great deal. It is especially a failure to recognize Yahweh's unique character on the one hand and Israel's unique vocation on the other.

1:17-19. This message of doom will not make Jeremiah popular, but he is made to understand that he has the strength to stand alone. In due course the royal house, the nobility, the priesthood, his own family, and the common people—all will turn against him. Though Jeremiah stood unbending to the end, he felt his loneliness deeply, as later oracles testify (for example, 15:15-21).

2:1-3. *Israel's Original Devotion.* This is the third of the messages from Yahweh with which Jeremiah clarifies his mission. The prophetic tradition looked back on Israel's desert period as the golden age of religion—it was the priestly tradition which thought of the desert generation as apostate (cf. Psalm 95:8-11). Jeremiah pictures the Israel of that time as Yahweh's wholly devoted young **bride.** In those days no one dared lay a finger on Israel. Those eating **first fruits** instead of offering them in sacrifice were guilty of sacrilege. Similarly those attacking Israel in those golden days were despoiling Yahweh's sacred preserve and woe betide them. Now, however, Israel is disloyal and no longer **holy to the LORD.** Therefore anyone may attack it with impunity. This is the grim message which Jeremiah has been called to proclaim.

2:4–4:4. *The Indictment of Israel.* 2:4 is an introduction to the section. Jeremiah was a man with strong northern ties. Benjamin (cf. 1:1) was originally allied to the Joseph tribes, as indicated by the tradition that Joseph and Benjamin were Rachel's sons. Therefore Jeremiah often thinks of the nation under the northern terms of **Jacob** and **Israel,** and sometimes even addresses Judah thus (cf. 2:26-28). At other times he uses Israel especially for the northern kingdom (cf. 3:6-14). Here he mostly has Judah in mind.

2:5-13. *A Contention Oracle.* This oracle is modeled on law-court practice. Jeremiah makes his point by presenting the plaintiff's contention in the case "Yahweh versus Israel." The defendant is challenged to say why he has deserted Yahweh for other **gods.** There is full confidence that no sound reason can be produced.

2:7-8. Israel is perversely unmindful of its salvation history. It has **defiled** its inheritance. The **priests** do not understand their own **law** tradition. The **rulers have transgressed,** literally "rebelled," against Yahweh's guidance. The **prophets** allow themselves to be inspired by **Baal** rather than Yahweh.

2:9-13. What other **nation** has ever deserted its own **gods,** however worthless, to adopt those of another people? **Cyprus** represents the far West, while **Kedar** refers to northeast desert tribes. The two probably represent the prophet's geographical horizon. Verse 13 is an especially forceful image in a city where spring water was at a premium and the population must rely on **cisterns** and reservoirs.

2:14-25. *Israel's Apostasy.* One born a **slave** could not hope for redemption. But at least such a one was protected as property by the owner. Israel is Yahweh's servant, as close to Yahweh as a **homeborn servant.** Yet Yahweh is allowing it to be despoiled. This would not have happened if Israel had remained loyal to Yahweh as a servant should. But Israel has to learn that apostasy is **evil** in itself and **bitter** in its results.

2:16-19. This oracle must be dated soon after the summer of 609, when Pharaoh Neco's army invaded Palestine and slew King Josiah. **The crown**—scalp, not royal headdress—**of your head** may refer to Josiah. **Memphis** was the Egyptian capital and **Tahpanhes** the frontier town through which communication with Egypt flowed. Verse 18 refers to the futility of relying on political alliances with **Egypt** and the declining power of **Assyria,** which Neco was trying to raise against the Babylonians. Here Jeremiah is fulfilling his role as prophet to the nations. He can assess their motives and dependability. But his main concern is Israel's wanton behavior.

2:20-25. Israel refuses to serve Yahweh and worships the local divinities. Canaanite worship was sexual in character—hence the frequent use of the metaphor of adultery and prostitution. This image leads Jeremiah to a vivid interpretation of Israel's character. After describing it as a cultivated **vine** which has reverted to the **wild** strain and saying that its guilty **stain** is indelible, he returns to the sexual metaphor. Like an animal in **heat** Israel is in the grip of forces it cannot control. It is revolted by its own promiscuity but cannot break free from this degraded way of life.

2:26-28. *Reliance on False Gods.* Sarcasm and indignation give intensity to this outburst. In the troubled political situation people are turning to Yahweh for help as a drowning person clutches at a straw. But if they have found what they were looking for in other **gods,** why not ask them for help?

2:29-32. *Israel's Ingratitude.* This oracle is composed of several expressions of a common theme: Israel is behaving most unfairly. The people rebel and then **complain** that they do not get help. Yahweh chastens them, but they respond by slaying the **prophets** (cf. II Kings 21:16). Yahweh has been careful for Israel yet it declares itself **free** of Yahweh. A **bride** treasures her **ornaments** and **attire** as tokens of her wifely status, but Israel has been oblivious of Yahweh for long periods. The metaphors reveal not only Israel's perversity but also the prophet's angry indignation on Yahweh's behalf.

2:33-37. *Political Infidelity.* Jeremiah is against Judah's becoming entangled in foreign alliances. As junior partner, Judah always has to accept the religious domination of its ally. He uses the sexual metaphor to describe Judah's attempts to build such alliances and denounces the shifts in policy as the wantonness of a prostitute. Judah is such a born harlot that she can teach even the established practitioners! But the result is inevitable. Judah will be led into captivity in the posture which for security reasons is forced on prisoners to this day.

3:1-5. *An Irretrievable Situation.* Cf. Deuteronomy 24:1-4. Probably this law was a further definition of the Hebrew marriage code. Jeremiah uses the new strictness of interpretation to emphasize the perversity of Israel's behavior toward Yahweh. It is making their ruptured relationship irreparable. **Rain** was believed to be given or **withheld** as God was pleased or displeased with Israel. But not even drought has been effective in breaking down Israel's shamelessness. Israel talks to God and about God in aggrieved tones, as if it were the injured party (verse 4). But Israel has **done all the evil** possible.

3:6-20. *Faithless Israel, False Judah.* The original oracle is in the poetical material (verses 12*b*-14 and 19-20). It was composed in Josiah's reign. But in order to make it serve his purpose at the time of dictating his book to Baruch in the reign of Jehoiakim, Jeremiah composed verses 6-10 as a prose introduction. Later an editor inserted the prose in verses 15-18.

3:6-10. In this passage **Israel** is the former northern kingdom. The contemporary explanation of its downfall was that the northern tribes were disloyal to the covenant while Judah, at least by comparison, was faithful. But Jeremiah denies this. Judah should have learned her lesson from the punishment which fell on Israel. The dissolution of that kingdom and the subsequent disappearance of the ten tribes is expressed as a **divorce.** But Yahweh's other "wife" has not taken the lesson to heart. To continue after such a warning is to compound the crime. Judah, as yet unpunished, is more guilty than Israel, who paid the price dearly for its folly. How great a punishment must therefore be hanging over Judah!

3:11-14. The oracle itself is a feeling comment on the fortunes of the northern kingdom. Yahweh's pity will yet lead God to **gather** the scattered people **one** and **two** at a time. Yahweh will restore them to what is left of Israel—that is, to Judah with its central shrine on Mount **Zion.**

3:15-18. This is a prose insertion by an editor after the Babylonian exile. He picks up the reference to Zion, and on this he hangs a general prophecy of Israel's recovery as a nation under good rulers. Interestingly he does not specify the Davidic line. At his time of writing the loss of the **ark** in the general destruction of Jerusalem was still keenly felt. But this is to be compensated by the **presence of the LORD**—a perceptive thought—so that the symbol will not need to be replaced.

The note of universalism sounded in verse 17 is a characteristic of the postexilic period. The reunion of Israel and Judah is foretold. The insertion is a valuable witness to the hopes which upheld faith in a desperate period.

3:19-20. Yahweh has been sadly disillusioned. The intimate relationships of the family are employed, marriage and fatherhood. It is the anthropomorphism which gives the poetry its imaginative appeal.

3:21–4:4. *True Circumcision.* This appeal for repentance fittingly closes the indictment of Israel (2:4–4:4). In verses 21-23 Jeremiah imagines the people gathered **on the mountains** to weep, not for the dead god Tammuz, as was the pagan practice, but for their own wrongdoing. Verse 22*ab*, the divine call for a change of purpose, is a word play on the idea of turning.

Literally it reads "Return, sons, from your back-turnings and I will correct your mis-turnings."

3:22c-23. Jeremiah imagines that this appeal meets with the right response. Thus Israel replies: "We are disillusioned. The pagan rituals on the hilltops are an evil snare. **Salvation** is to be found in Yahweh alone. We do indeed return to him!" True penitence comes, not from fear of consequences, but from recognition of the fraudulent character of temptation.

3:24-25. Someone has added these verses as a further comment. The **shameful thing** means the pagan cult. Indulging in this has cost Israel its promised land and all that has been put into it. On prostration in lament cf. Joshua 7:6.

4:1-4. The word play on "turning" (3:22) is resumed in verses 1-2: "If you want to turn, then turn to me." The promise is held out that true repentance will bring true peace—to other nations as well as to Israel. Verses 3-4 call for inward renewal. Circumcision, a survival of tribal customs, which serves to distinguish the Jew from neighbors, is meaningless except as an indicator of inner loyalty.

4:5–6:30. *Punishment from the North.* In this section Jeremiah has gathered together a number of pieces which have a common theme—the punishment which will befall Judah if it does not respond to Yahweh's call for penitence and obedience. Much speculation has centered on the identity of the **evil from the north** (cf. 6:1, 22). However, it is probable that the descriptions given in the oracles are impressionistic, not literal. Since they were composed over the period 627-605 they may have had several models—Assyrians, Egyptians, Chaldeans, possibly Scythians, and undoubtedly nomadic raiders. The identity of the attacking forces is therefore neither a very practical nor an important matter.

The central significance is the inexorable character of the punishment which will befall Israel unless it repents. The section presents a series of vivid anticipations of the coming disaster. It contains some of Jeremiah's most striking poetry, with regard to both language and emotional intensity.

4:5-8. *A Warning.* In times of danger the peasants from the countryside took refuge in **fortified** (walled) **cities.** The oracle declares that such a time is now imminent. For the Hebrews the **north** was always ominous, partly because most invasions of Palestine were by northern powers. But also the north, in comparison with the comparatively well-known and defined south, was unknown and mysterious. Canaanite thought located the mountain of the gods in the northern ranges. The oracle is not only a call to flight but also a summons to penitence. It recognizes that the evil which is to befall is not just bad luck but Yahweh's judgment.

4:9-12. *The Great Deception.* Jeremiah here includes three thoughts. No doubt he expressed these at various times in the discussions at the temple court (see Introduction). But he has either never put them into poetic form or, having done so, has forgotten it. Two are very plain and direct. The first (verse 9) foretells universal dismay when the disaster strikes. It will not be the kind of thing with which an efficient administration may hope to cope. The third (verses 11-12) describes the disaster as being like the sirocco—the burning **wind** from the desert, too strong to be used for agriculture or to **cleanse** fetid cities. Its violence is only destructive.

4:10. The second idea is more involved. In ancient times it was thought that God had to "set up" those situations God desired to bring about. One of the methods was to entice guilty people or nations into a place or an activity or an attitude that would result in their punishment (cf. I Kings 22:20). Here Jeremiah is grudgingly congratulating Yahweh: "You have done a fine job of deception this time! Your prophets are going round saying, **It shall be well with you,** and this leaves the Jerusalemites unknowingly in the path of the most terrible danger."

But why does Jeremiah say this to Yahweh? In order that the Jerusalemites may "overhear." Thus they will wake up to the fact that prophets who allay fears and foretell prosperity are false prophets. Jeremiah, who announces the coming disaster, is a true prophet. The whole idea of the false prophet is something which we cannot accept. But it gives us a deep insight into Jeremiah's mental processes (cf. 20:7-12).

4:13-18. *Approach of the Invader.* Jeremiah foretells the kind of rumor which will run through the bazaars (verse 13). He adds an appeal for a realistic assessment of the situation (verse 14). The announcement will be made in far-northern **Dan** and taken up in the hill country of **Ephraim** and passed on **to Jerusalem:** "The enemy is coming" (verse 16) which probably should end with closing quotation marks. Verses 17-18 are Yahweh's comment that this bitter doom is punishment on Israel. **Keepers of the field** in verse 17 are those who surround it to guard the grain as it ripens, before they move in to reap. Jerusalem is ripe for reaping!

4:19-22. *Alarm in Jerusalem.* Jeremiah imagines vividly the panic which will grip Jerusalem when the invasion comes. **Anguish** is literally "bowels." People will know what it is to have their bowels **writhe**, their hearts beat **wildly**, their voices scream in terror. In desperation they ask, "How long will this go on?" They hear Yahweh's stern reply: "It is all happening because my people are morally **stupid!**"

4:23-28. *Utter Desolation.* The poet thinks of Yahweh as looking down on the land after the great disaster has occurred. Nature itself has turned against Israel with earthquake. All life has ceased. As Yahweh surveys the land turned back to primeval chaos, Yahweh comments sadly but unrelentingly: "The very heavens mourn, but as judge of all the earth I am unable to do otherwise!" (verse 28). Verse 27 is an editor's valuable comment that, powerful as the prophet's thought is, it needs balancing. God's judgments are never wholly negative. Yahweh always brings something new and creative out of every situation.

4:29-31. *The Desperate Harlot.* As the invading troops approach, all resistance melts. In panic the whole population streams out of the **city** to try to find hiding places in the hills. Jerusalem is pictured as a harlot who stays behind, relying on her power to seduce. But old and tawdry, she has no charms. Her attempts at decoration are pitiful. The prophet can already hear her gasp as she wakes up to reality when it is too late.

5:1-6. *Poor and Rich Alike.* At this time people are deriving comfort from the thought that since there are some good Israelites left, Yahweh cannot let the nation be destroyed. It would be unjust to the righteous! Even if there are only ten such people left, they will be sufficient (cf. Genesis 18:22-32). Jeremiah replies: "As in the case of Sodom, you will not find one righteous person, let alone ten!" As he reviews the perversity of the inhabitants of Jerusalem he thinks: "Perhaps this is only so with the common people. Perhaps the aristocracy are better" (verses 4-5). But he finds them just as bad. Therefore the disaster—which is pictured as the preying beast (verse 6)—will inevitably fall on them.

5:7-9. *A Brief Debate.* Jeremiah imagines the kind of reply Yahweh will make when Israel pleads for mercy. How can any righteous judge overlook such perverse crimes?

5:10-17. *Destruction of the Vineyard.* Israel was only too familiar with invaders who destroyed vineyards, olive trees, and other long-term sources of food. The vine or vineyard was often a symbol of Israel itself. In this oracle the vineyard is Israel and the command to destroy comes from Yahweh. People have tried to shrug off the prophetic warnings: "Nothing will happen. The prophets are just windbags" (verses 12-13). But the uprooted vines will be kindling, and it will be the prophetic word which will set them ablaze (verse 14; cf. Ezekiel 15:1-8).

The metaphor is dropped. The real situation is described in verses 15-17. The description does not permit exact identification, but probably Jeremiah is thinking of the Chaldeans. **But make not a full end** in verse 10*b*—or at least the word **not**—is probably a gloss. It was added by a later hand to soften the harshness of the oracle (cf. verse 18; 4:27).

5:18-19. *A Later Comment.* An editor must have added this passage. It modifies Jeremiah's unconditional threats by reminding us that it never was—it never is—God's purpose only to destroy. God's punishment of Israel is just and rational, but it is not final (cf. verse 10*b;* Isaiah 28:23-29).

5:20-29. *Creator and Judge.* Because of its history Israel was always in danger of thinking of Yahweh as a national god and a war god but not as the god of the natural order. Weather and harvests were the business of the baals, the local deities. Here Yahweh insists that God is the creator of the universe. As such Yahweh commands the **rain** and thus controls Israel's **harvest.** The fact that the rains have been withheld is due to Israel's sinfulness, exemplified by a greedy and dissolute aristocracy. Jeremiah here echoes his eighth-century predecessors (cf. Isaiah 3:13-15).

5:30-31. *Acceptance of Corruption.* The average run of the **prophets** are saying what the people want them to say. The **priests** go along with this because it leaves them in positions of authority and wealth. The common **people** know full well what is going on and like it that way. But when the moment of truth comes—as it most certainly will—what will these people do then?

6:1-8. *Invading Nomads.* Jeremiah pictures the time of judgment. He envisages Jerusalem surrounded by a horde of nomads, who settle with **their flocks** around the city to starve it out. Instead of seeking **safety** in the city his fellow Benjaminites would be better advised to get out while they can. He imagines the warning being spread south of Jerusalem. **Tekoa** was probably chosen to pun on the Hebrew word for **blow**—something like "in Bloton blow a trumpet." **Beth-haccherem,** "house of vineyards," may have been a commanding height for a **signal.** On the metaphor of a **delicately bred** lady meeting with brutal disaster cf. Isaiah 47:1-9.

6:4-5. In this snatch of conversation the nomads plan an **attack at noon,** the hour of siesta. But they are so disorganized that it is **evening** before they realize it. It doesn't matter; they can attack at midnight instead. This detail of incompetent but irresistible power reveals the invading force as naïve, brutal, elemental, horrible.

6:6-8. But there is behind the enemy an organizing mind, coordinating and planning—Yahweh. Jerusalem pumps out **wickedness** as a spring pours out **water,** endlessly. The oracle ends with an appeal for Jerusalem to repent. The invasion is yet in the future and Jerusalem can prevent its happening if it will.

6:9-15. *Scornful Hearers.* This is a summary of the divine message as Jeremiah has received it. It speaks of the rigor of the punishment to come. Even when only a **remnant** is left Israel's enemies will go over the land again, as a gleaner searches for the very last grape on a vine. This is what Jeremiah must proclaim, but his hearers are impervious to reason or threats. He has reached the point where his moral indignation cannot be contained. His **word** will become a terrible doom laid on **young** and **old** alike (on **gatherings** see Introduction). All classes of society are corrupt, especially the religious leaders. They have encouraged the complacency of Jeremiah's hearers with false messages of **peace**—the Hebrew word means well-being in general as well as freedom from war. They have not told the seriousness of the situation. The oracle betrays Jeremiah's strained relations with his colleagues and also his lack of popular support. Jehoiakim could not have banished him from the temple unless he had already become a solitary figure.

6:16-21. *Futile Sacrifices.* The oracle gives two examples of Israel's perversity. Called to walk in the good old paths of righteousness it refuses. Bid to listen for the warning note it refuses again. Yahweh calls on disinterested parties, the **nations,** the **earth** itself, to witness the justice of Yahweh's decision to punish the people. Israel thinks it can cover up its perversity with incense from **Sheba** in southwest Arabia and lavish **sacrifices.** But worship is no substitute for obedience and morality. Like other prophets Jeremiah was probably not against the cult as such. But he certainly relegated it to a very secondary place (cf. 7:21-23).

6:22-26. *Utter Panic.* Jeremiah returns to the threat of invasion and draws a vivid picture of the enemy. **Farthest parts of the earth** is poetic hyperbole and probably reflects rumors of the Chaldeans' more distant allies, the Elamites or Medes. Jeremiah pictures the news of the invasion as bringing paralyzing fear. All escape is cut off. Neither **field** nor **road** is safe. Judah will be left to indulge in futile regrets—"If only we had hearkened!"

6:27-30. *The Prophet's Function.* Jeremiah tells how he conceives of his role. He feels that Yahweh has called him to be an **assayer** of Israel. By his fierce oracles of warning and threat he is to separate out the true Israel from the larger mass of the nation. But in verses 28-30 he tells of his experience. The hotter he makes the **fire,** the more the base alloys run off, but no residue of true metal appears. There is no true Israel.

At the time he dictated his first manuscript to Baruch (605/4) this was Jeremiah's estimate of the people to whom he had been preaching for twenty years. But it is doubtful whether this strong expression of despair represented the totality of his prophetic thought. Possibly at the back of his mind a hope of renewal always lingered, for later on he expressed such a hope. However, his words are so negative that editors felt the need to gloss his oracles from time to time with words of hope.

7:1–8:3. *Israel Rejected.* This section emphasizes that Israel's sufferings are the consequences of Yahweh's condemnation of its attitudes and behavior.

7:1-15. *The Temple Sermon.* We have two accounts of the occasion to which this piece relates (cf. 26:1-6). Here the narrative is set in the context of a divine revelation (verse 1; cf. verses 16, 27-28), told from Jeremiah's first-person viewpoint. The other version is an account from Baruch's third-person viewpoint. Baruch tells us that the prophet nearly lost his life as a result of the sermon, but Jeremiah ignores this to concentrate on the message. He does not recall the actual words he used but gives a prose summary. Note that he lacks any sense of the thoughts being his own. He believes they came directly from Yahweh.

7:1-4. The occasion is one which brings **all . . . men of Judah** to the temple "in the beginning of the reign of Jehoiakim" (26:1; see comment), when the future is very unclear. The nation is numb from the shock of Josiah's death in battle, the deposition of his son Jehoahaz, and the imposition of Jehoiakim (see Introduction). The very existence of Judah is in the hands of Pharaoh Neco. At such a disastrous time people are comforting themselves with the reflection that Yahweh cannot allow Jerusalem to be destroyed, since it contains the very temple itself.

Jeremiah avails himself of the public forum of the temple's **gate,** the outer court, to attack and destroy this false confidence. The people are sheltering themselves in a pseudo-religious faith. They are piously affirming that the holiness of the Lord's shrine will safeguard the temple and the city along with it. The repetition of **the temple of the LORD** is a Hebrew idiom for a superlative—that is, "These buildings are the very temple of Yahweh."

7:5-11. On the contrary, says Jeremiah, only good living can secure Yahweh's protection. Judah's moral and religious perversions have made the temple not a place of holiness but a **den of robbers**—a cave where criminals hide and think themselves safe from capture.

7:12-15. If people think that Yahweh does not allow shrines to be destroyed, let them visit the ruins of **Shiloh.** The central shrine of the old Israelite twelve-tribe confederacy was at Shiloh, the last of its priests being Eli (I Samuel 1–4). For Jeremiah, a descendant of that family (see above on 1:1-3), the fate of Shiloh would have particular meaning. There is no biblical narrative of its destruction, but the shrine drops out of the story at the time of the Philistines' capture of the ark (I Samuel 4). Jeremiah's point is that what Yahweh has done once can very well be done again!

7:16-20. *Family Apostasy.* Probably this is not a part of the temple sermon but the prose summary of another oracle from the same general period. The corruption has eaten so deeply into the nation's life that it has perverted the very togetherness of the family (cf. 44:15-19). Even the physical environment is corrupted (verse 20). The **cakes** were crescent-shaped cookies in honor of the **queen of heaven,** the moon goddess Ashtoreth. Her name was really Ashtarath but was written "Ashtoreth" by later Hebrew editors—that is, with the vowels of the word *boseth,* "shame." Cf. comments at 11:9-13; 19:1-13; and 44:15-19. Ashtarath was known to the Babylonians as Ishtar and to the Greeks as Astarte. In southern Palestine she tended to merge with Asherah, the great Mother-goddess, who in the Old

Testament is prominent as the consort of Baal. Ashtarath was a very popular sex and fertility symbol.

Jeremiah is told not to **intercede** for these people (cf. 11:14; 14:11-12); Yahweh is now resolved on their total destruction. We need to distinguish here between the divine message of judgment and the prophet's expressions of it, to which the apparent mercilessness of God is due. God does punish, but divine mercy always responds to genuine repentance. The prophet contributed more to the message than he himself recognized.

7:21-26. *Obedience Rather than Sacrifice.* These verses are an amplification of the theme "the value of ritual." They may have been said at any time but were felt to be appropriate to this temple sermon section. **Burnt offerings** were especially holy and could be eaten only by priests. **Sacrifices** were feasts which could be shared by all. Jeremiah contemptuously urges the people to **eat the flesh** and disregard these trifling taboos. What God commands is not rituals but moral obedience.

Hebrew idiom allows the denial of one thing in order to assert another. Thus the intention here is not wholly to deny but only to relegate to second place. It is doubtful whether Jeremiah meant to deny sacrifice a place in Israel's original Mosaic religious pattern (cf. 6:20). The picture of Yahweh rising early every day to send messengers to Israel is an expression of God's continued concern over Israel's stubborness.

7:27-28. *An Unresponsive People.* Jeremiah tells how God has warned him that he will meet with no response, for **they will not listen.** Isaiah testifies to the same conviction (Isaiah 6:9-10).

7:29. *A Call to Lament.* Whatever its causes, **lamentation** was accompanied by such manifestations of grief as lying prostrate, pouring dust on the head, beating the breast, rending garments, and cutting off the **hair.** This last was still a sign of fasting in Paul's day (cf. Acts 21:24).

7:30-34. *Topheth.* Here is a compressed version of the oracle given at length in 19:1-13 (see comment). It was included here by an editor as a further oracle of rejection.

8:1-3. *A Desecrated People.* The Hebrews never conceived of existence apart from one's body. As long as at least the skeleton remained, the person remained. To revere the **bones** of the deceased was to revere the deceased. To treat a person's bones with irreverence was the ultimate insult (cf. Amos 2:1). But Israel's rejection is to be so complete that Jeremiah sees all the bones of deceased generations being emptied **out of their tombs** for mockery and desecration. And yet those still alive will be so wretched that they will long for **death.**

This probably ends Jeremiah's first manuscript, except for the coda now found in 25:1-14. What follows between 8:3 and 25:1 is expansive material, and no doubt includes the "similar words" referred to in 36:32 (see Introduction).

B. First Expansion: Indictment and Threat (8:4–10:16)

8:4-7. *Intelligence and Instinct.* It is expected that if a man falls he will get up again, or if he wanders inadvertently from the road he will turn back and find his way. But Israel has no such corrective sense. Indeed, like a **horse** with the bit between its teeth, it is running madly out of its true course. Migratory birds have the guidance of instinct to bring them back from their wanderings, but Israel's homing instinct has faded out. It has lost the instinctive patterns of the animal world, and yet it does not conform to intelligent human behavior.

8:8-13. *No Grapes on the Vine.* Barren cupboards, wells that run dry, ore lodes that have petered out—these are the modern equivalents for the metaphors of verse 13. Jeremiah is hitting hard at Israel's leadership, especially her intelligentsia. They are pinning their faith to the fact that they now have the traditional **law** in written form—the book of Deuteronomy (see Introduction). How can people be respected as mature who think that a written document—so easily tampered with or ingeniously interpreted—can really determine matters of religious truth? The oracle documents Jeremiah's disillusionment with Josiah's reform and its leadership. Note Jesus' use of this indictment for the leadership of his own day (Mark 11:13). With verses 11-12 cf. 6:14-15; Jeremiah was not above reusing lines from earlier oracles.

8:14-15. *Futile Flight.* With bitter sarcasm Jeremiah imagines a group planning to leave their village and its dried-up well in order to go to the **cities**, where the problem will be worse. The result will be to **perish** there rather than here! The oracle must come from some time of drought which Jeremiah interprets as a sign of Yahweh's displeasure (cf. 3:3; 14:1-6). He is calling for a more realistic attitude: "Don't run away; face up to the cause—your sinfulness toward Yahweh."

8:16-17. *An Invasion Threat.* This oracle warns of Yahweh's punishment to come. The enemy is already at **Dan**, the most northern area of Israel. The **snorting** of the war horse was to the ancient world what the rumble of the tank is to ours. The foe is implacable—as impossible to deal with as an **adder** is impervious to the snake charmer's wiles. It was thought impossible to charm adders because they were deaf.

8:18-21. *Disaster Dialogue.* The prophet laments his distress at Israel's suffering. He imagines the desperate cry: "Where is Yahweh? Will he not help us?" **King** refers to Yahweh, not the Davidic ruler. Yahweh's only reply is to ask why the people provoke Yahweh by their disloyalty. They are left to face a stark future. The time of **harvest** is over, and they have no food for the year ahead.

8:22–9:1. *Balm in Gilead.* Gilead, east of Jordan, produced a resinous gum from its trees which was much used as an ointment for wounds. But Israel is seriously wounded. It is no good calling for all the balm Gilead ever produced—no salve can cure this wound.

9:2-9. *Social Comment.* These verses should probably be regarded as a unit. Because of the moral corruption Jeremiah longs to get away from the city to the clean loneliness of the **desert**. In the city **neighbor** can no longer trust neighbor. "**What else can I do**," asks Yahweh, "but punish them?" People live in cities for mutual support and encouragement. But a city where everyone is trying to cheat their neighbor defeats its own purpose. A wise person will leave, and a moral God will destroy, such a city.

9:10-11. *Lament for a Forsaken Land.* This is another oracle of warning. If Israel will not repent, the land will be so devastated by war that it will be forsaken even by the **birds.** In the **ruins** of Jerusalem only **jackals** will remain.

9:12-16. *Question and Answer.* Probably verse 12 is an original saying of Jeremiah, a rhetorical question implying the same ideas as the foregoing oracle. But a later editor did not like leaving the question unanswered. He supplied the appropriate response in verses 13-16 along very orthodox lines.

9:17-22. *Two Oracles of Lament.* The first oracle (verses 17-19) calls for the professional **mourning women** to come and lead a lament over fallen Jerusalem. The second urges these women to make sure their guild is well supplied with practitioners because their services are going to be much in demand.

9:23-26. *True Worth.* Two editorial comments are found here. The first is a somewhat moralistic but thoroughly sound statement of what is really worthwhile—not shrewdness in affairs, or physical strength, or wealth, but a true understanding of the nature of God. The editor gives a very attractive summary of this nature. Paul found these verses very significant (cf. I Corinthians 1:26-31 and II Corinthians 10:17).

The second is directed at some of Israel's neighbors who also practice circumcision but without the meaning it should have. That they also use other distinguishing marks shows them up as aliens. This comment reflects an attempt to claim circumcision as a peculiarly Jewish custom. But another editor who had read 4:4 added his own comment that Israel also was not properly circumcised (verse 26d). This thought was much in the air in the seventh century. Israel was learning to distinguish between symbol and reality.

10:1-16. *Psalm on the True God.* It was common to conclude a small prophetic collection with an appropriate psalm. The collection 8:4–9:26 is rounded off with this psalm. The ideas are fairly commonplace. Probably it is not Jeremiah's work but comes from about the fifth century.

Verse 1 is an editorial introduction. Verses 2-5 form a cultic oracle. The sentiments are the usual Jewish polemic against idol worship expressed with biting sarcasm.

In verses 12-16 the relationship to Psalm 135 is so close that there must have been borrowing one way or the other. Since Psalm 135 has a more liturgical structure, the chances are that this passage was borrowed and polished for use in worship. Verse 11 is an editorial comment jotted down in Aramaic by a reader and inadvertently taken into the text by a later copyist.

C. EDITORIAL INSERTION: PROPHETIC FRAGMENTS (10:17-25)

These are a number of separate pieces, most of them probably from Jeremiah. They survived in the collective memory of the prophetic traditionists of the postexilic period. Verses 17-18 are a warning of judgment to come expressed in the form of an admonition: "Get packed—you're going to be deported!" Verse 19 is a lament fragment (cf. 8:18) which says that Israel must recognize its woes as divine punishment. Verses 20-21 are another lament fragment, depicting Israel as a bedouin widow whose camp has been ravaged and who has no one to help it reconstruct its **tent** or its life.

Verse 22 is a vivid forecast of the threatened invasion as the punishment from Yahweh. Verses 23 and 24 are two wisdom sayings (cf. Proverbs 20:24). Verse 25 is a call for vengeance on the **nations,** a frequent element in postexilic prophecy.

D. SECOND EXPANSION: JEREMIAH'S WORDS AND DEEDS (11:1–24:1)

This collection of Jeremiah's sayings was probably collected by him with Baruch's assistance (see Introduction) sometime between the burning of his first manuscript (604) and the

Babylonians' first capture of Jerusalem (597). It is a miscellaneous anthology and lacks the planned structure of the earlier collection (1:4–8:3).

11:1-17. *Jeremiah and the Reformation.* After an initial enthusiasm for the Deuteronomic reformation Jeremiah became disillusioned with it (cf. 8:8-13; see Introduction). It seemed to him that it led the people to place faith in external authorities, whereas he believed that nothing short of a changed heart could meet the demands of a moral God.

In this passage he tells of his initial conviction that he should **proclaim all these words** on a preaching tour in support of the reform. The key words and ideas of Deuteronomy—the **covenant,** the deliverance from Egypt, the ideal of God and people as one sacral society, the promise of prosperity in return for obedience—these are the theme of his message.

11:7-8. As the Deuteronomic school understood it, the covenant was a two-edged sword. It brought prosperity to the faithful, but it also brought fearful punishments on those who were disloyal. Israel's troubles—the divided kingdom, the loss of the ten tribes, and more recently Josiah's death and the Babylonian oppression—are interpreted as Yahweh's punishments for its faithlessness.

11:9-13. The charge of disloyalty to the covenant is stated more clearly. With verse 13*a* cf. 2:28. **Shame** in verse 13*b* probably hides the name of a god or goddess—most likely Ashtarath (see above on 7:16-20). This was so abhorrent that scribes were unwilling to copy it.

11:14-17. Jeremiah's indignation over Judah's idolatry is so strong that it blots out his sense of God's infinite patience. In verse 15 we should probably retain the words of both the Hebrew text and the Septuagint (see the Revised Standard Version footnote) and translate: "Can many vows and sacrificial flesh . . ." Jeremiah was convinced of the secondary nature of ritual in religion (cf. 6:20; 7:22).

11:18-23. *Assassination Plot.* This passage is an oracle in poetry plus an explanatory comment in prose. It was called forth by the profound shock of Jeremiah's discovery that his relatives

153

were plotting to murder him. At the time of original delivery the circle of hearers no doubt knew the circumstances and understood the poem. But when it came to be written down years later some explanation was needed.

What roused the relatives' anger we can only guess. But the inclusion of this oracle immediately after the account of Jeremiah's reformation activities may give the clue. The law of the single sanctuary urged by the Deuteronomic reformers must have aroused the bitterest opposition of the priests of Anathoth. When they heard that one of their own clan members was actually advocating the reform—perhaps even had come to Anathoth and preached on the virtues of closing the family shrine—their resentment against him may well have flared up to the point of murder. Jeremiah narrowly escaped death, and a wave of revulsion swept him into an intense cry for **vengeance** (see below on 12:1-4).

Repeated years afterward, the curse is in no way weakened—the **men of Anathoth** must bear a fearful **punishment**. Jeremiah was a man of fierce and intense emotions (cf. 12:5-6; 20:10-12).

12:1-4. *A Psalm of Perturbation.* Why do the **wicked prosper?** Jeremiah sets the problem out in a wisdom psalm (cf. Psalm 73) but leaves it unanswered. All he can do is say "How long, Yahweh, how long?" (cf. Psalms 6:3 and 74:9). In the final analysis we have to recognize that there is no answer except that of faith (cf. Psalm 37:9). Verse 3 seems misplaced and probably belongs after 11:19. Verse 4 envisages the **land**, aghast at the **wickedness** within it, refusing to nurture such evildoers and perferring to become a sterile wilderness. The ultimate wickedness, however, is the notion that Yahweh is morally indifferent.

12:5-6. *Stark Realities.* The debate going on in Jeremiah's mind turns into an interrogation by God. His experience with the people of Anathoth has jolted him out of an unrealistic assessment of his situation. He now realizes that he has taken on far more than he previously understood.

He thought he had to race only **with men;** he now finds he must run against **horses.** He thought he had only to cross open country; he now finds he must plunge through the **jungle** on the banks of the **Jordan.** Yet he is already feeling exhausted by his previous efforts. Moreover he cannot turn to anyone for help, least of all to his own family, his **brothers** and the **house** of his **father.** What will he do now? Yahweh asks challengingly. Will he weakly give up? No answer is given, but in fact Jeremiah never failed to conquer his fears and continue in his vocation.

12:7-13. *Abandoned Heritage.* Farming in most of Palestine is precarious. What one generation sweats to bring into production another will in disgust allow to go back to bush. Yahweh, says the prophet, has reached that point with Israel. He invites **wild beasts** to infest it. The vineyards have already been well **trampled** by nomads and their flocks anyway—possibly a reference to the marauding bands noted in II Kings 24:2. **Harvests** are so miserable that farmers blush for them and let the land go back to nature. The hurtful thing is that no one **lays it to heart.**

Yahweh's **house** (verse 7a), though usually the temple, is here synonymous with **heritage.** In verse 8 the figure changes and the land becomes an attacking **lion.** In verse 9a **bird of prey** is probably a mistaken repetition of the same word in the next line. Restore in its place the normal Hebrew word for "bird" and read verse 9ab as: "Is my heritage to me like a speckled bird, with the birds of prey against her roundabout?" Discovery of seals inscribed with roosters proves that chickens were known in Jeremiah's day, though never clearly mentioned in the Old Testament. The picture here may be of a hen with hawks wheeling above her. Possibly verses 8 and 9ab are misplaced fragments.

12:14-17. *Universal Repatriation.* This postexilic passage neutralizes the foregoing threat oracle. It promises that not only Judah will be restored but also every other **nation** which learns Yahwism from the Jews, as previously the Jews learned Baalism from them. The editor glimpses the truth that a negative is never God's last word and that the word must be to all people.

13:1-11. *A Dramatized Threat of Exile.* Babylon became the suzerain power as a result of the victory at Carchemish in 605. It was probably not long after this that Jeremiah recognized the likelihood that Judah would eventually provoke the Chaldeans and would be driven off into exile as a result. This disaster could be averted only by God. But if Judah continued to be disloyal to Yahweh, Yahweh would work to bring it about.

To bring this understanding home to his compatriots Jeremiah here engages in an "acted oracle"—a symbolic action whereby Yahweh's word is expressed. He attracts a crowd—the nucleus no doubt is his own circle in the temple court. He calls some nearby spot the **Euphrates** for the purpose of his mime, and then carries out the sequence of actions. Judah is intended to **cling** to Yahweh as closely as a **waistcloth** to a **man.** But if it becomes estranged from Yahweh and is driven into exile on the Euphrates, it will be a **spoiled** nation and **good for nothing.** The somewhat grostesque imagery should not distract us from the earnestness of Jeremiah's intention. In verse 11 **Israel** was probably substituted for "Jerusalem" (cf. verse 9) to suit the pan-Hebraism of the postexilic period.

13:12-14. *A Riddle.* A favorite pastime in Hebrew society was posing riddles (cf. Judges 14:10-20). Jeremiah's proposition is on the surface so trite as to be meaningless. The pottery **jar,** about two feet high and holding around ten gallons, was specifically made for storage of **wine.** "Of course jars get filled with wine," his listeners reply. Then the prophet discloses the hidden meaning. The wine is going to be the divine intoxication which blinds people to danger and lures them on to their fate (cf. 25:15; Isaiah 29:9; 63:6 and the Greek saying "Whom the gods would destroy they first make mad").

13:15-17. *A Warning Against Pride.* The imagery of disaster used here is that of someone caught on the **mountains** at nightfall.

13:18-19. *Political Comment.* This oracle concerns an attack on the **Negeb,** the arid southern region of Judah. Presumably the attack is from the south. Therefore it probably refers to the threat posed by Pharaoh Neco's northern march in 609 at the beginning of the expedition which resulted in the death of Josiah (see Introduction).

Jeremiah was more critical of Josiah than were most of his contemporaries, with whom the king was generally popular. Here he evidently holds Josiah and Jedidah (II Kings 22:1), the **queen mother,** in some degree responsible. Jeremiah's attitude is: "You asked for trouble, and now you have it!"

Some interpreters see this oracle as coming instead from the three-month reign of Jehoiachin (Jeconiah, 598-597). This ended in deportation of the young king and his mother Nehushta to Babylon (29:2; cf. II Kings 24:8-15). On this assumption verse 19 would predict Babylonian conquest of **all Judah,** even the southernmost region. But the oracle would then be very out of place chronologically.

13:20-27. *Violation of Judah.* Here is another political comment, this time on invasion **from the north**—probably by Nebuchadrezzar following his victory over Neco in 605 (see above on verses 1-11). Again it is directed in part against the king, now Jehoiakim. Verse 21 is obscure but probably means that Jehoiakim's foreign policy is going to boomerang: the very Babylonians he has secretly courted while a vassal of Neco will be the commanders of the new occupying forces.

13:22-27. The violation of Judah is likened to the rape of a woman—a feature of invasion which occurred often enough to suggest the metaphor. It fits in with the frequent use of the image of adultery to describe Judah's participation in pagan cults. For example, in verse 27 **neighings** compares Judah to a mare in heat—and thus presents its punishment as "poetic justice." Verse 23*ab* has become a proverb in the English language. Verse 23*cd* shows how concerned Jeremiah was with his country's propensity for evil.

14:1–15:21. *A Little Psalter.* Here are three corporate laments, in which the whole community expresses distress. Later comments have been added. This suggests that when Jeremiah first produced them, they provoked such unfavorable criticism that he came back later with rejoinders. We cannot date the drought which gave rise to the first two psalms—14:2-9

157

and 17-22—but presumably it was between 604 and 586. The third piece (15:5-9) deals with invasion and might come out of any of those troubled years. A fourth psalm (15:15-21) is an individual lament. Jeremiah is appealing for God's help in his increasingly difficult vocation.

14:1-16. *In Time of Drought.* The psalm in verses 2-9 is a genuine cry for help. The imagery shows Jeremiah at his poetical best. The confused **servants,** the dumbfounded **farmers,** the wretched **hind** forsaking her fawn, the **wild asses,** panting as they wait for death to come—these are unforgettable pictures.

14:7-9. The appeal to Yahweh is in equally vivid terms. Does Yahweh care for the people no more than does a **stranger,** a passing tourist? Or has Yahweh in fact lost control of nature, so that God is as **confused** as the people? This last piece of rhetoric shows that the appeal to Yahweh is genuine and sincere. Only later was Jeremiah convinced that there would indeed be no merciful intervention.

14:10-16. Jeremiah later attached an oracle to the psalm (verse 10). This represents Yahweh as replying that the drought is a thoroughly deserved punishment. Did Jeremiah represent truly the mind of God in this matter? This question also arose among his contemporaries. Other **prophets** were interpreting Yahweh's will quite differently.

As justification Jeremiah attached to his psalm and oracle an assertion that his attitude toward the people of Judah was dictated by Yahweh (verses 11-12) and that Yahweh had pronounced violently against the false prophets (verses 13-16). The structure of the passage thus enables us to see Jeremiah at work in the cut and thrust of the violent debate which he constantly provoked.

14:17–15:4. *Appeal and Rejection.* The psalm of corporate lament in 14:17-22 contains a description of the disaster (verses 17-18) and an appeal to Yahweh for help (verses 19-22). That he can help is shown by the fact that in the past he has given his people **rain**—a reminder of the prime importance of rainfall in Jeremiah's country.

15:1-4. As in the preceding passage (14:1-16) there is an added oracle: "Yahweh will not save you" (15:1-3). Even if **Moses and Samuel**—famed as interceders—pleaded for them, it would make no difference. They will be destroyed. The symbolism of the **four kinds of destroyers** is later to be seen in the four horsemen of Revelation 6:1-8. Verse 4 is an editorial gloss laying the blame for Judah's misfortunes on **Manasseh**—a belief of the Deuteronomists to which Jeremiah would not subscribe (cf. 31:29).

15:5-14. *Yahweh's Lament for Jerusalem.* The third psalm (see above on 14:1–15:21) is verses 5-9. It is a lament ascribed for poetic effect to Yahweh, who is depicted as having run out of patience. He describes Israel's sufferings. But because there is no penitence he warns that the disaster will run its full course.

15:10-11. Such a message to a city struggling to survive could only result in anger and enmity. Jeremiah therefore follows the psalm with a half-humorous address to his **mother,** by way of comment. Why was he ever born to be such a contentious fellow? But—and here he becomes fully serious—God knows how he has prayed for these people! Clearly 14:11 and 15:1-3 do not represent the prophet's only mood. Verse 11 presents textual difficulties. Probably **on behalf of the enemy** should read "with respect to the enemy."

15:12-14. Verse 12 is obscure. Possibly it is part of Jeremiah's prayer, as paragraphed in the Revised Standard Version, and refers to the stubbornness of the Judeans. More probably, however, it is the beginning of the grim divine answer: you cannot **break iron, iron from the north,** and that is what the invasion will be—an iron weapon stabbing deep into Judah's entrails. It will result in Judah's destruction and exile, for Yahweh's anger is unrelenting. With verses 13-14 cf. 17:3-4.

15:15-21. *The Prophet's Lament.* The fourth psalm (see above on 14:1–15:21) is an individual lament. The prophet is the butt of ridicule and the object of hatred. He has found great **joy** and **delight** in his ministry, though it has often led to self-imposed ostracism. But is there no answer to his deepest questioning, except the one he cannot contemplate—the utter rejection of

Israel? Is Yahweh going to let him down, becoming to him **like waters that fail?**

15:19-21. The answer comes straightway: Jeremiah must be faithful to his message, whether it pleases him or displeases him, whether it brings him honor or persecution. If he is true to his message, he will prevail in the face of all opposition. It may be at fearful cost but he will prevail, as God will prevail.

We have to recognize that Jeremiah had limited horizons. He had no hope of an afterlife, nor could he see hope in the historical future. The one thing he could clearly see was that he must cling to his intellectual integrity and speak the truth as he knew it. Only thus could he hope to emerge—in ways unknowable to him—intact. We ourselves know at least the human sequel. Jeremiah has stood at the bar of history and has emerged honorably acquitted. Indeed he won the highest esteem, while his detractors have long since been forgotten.

16:1-21. *Impending Doom and Undying Hope.* Looking back, perhaps soon after Nebuchadrezzar first deported part of the population in 597, Jeremiah sees his own unmarried state as a sign from Yahweh which points to the impending disaster (verse 2). The literary development of this thought is a written composition, as distinct from an oral recollection (see Introduction). Thus it is in the Deuteronomic prose style which was the characteristic literary style of the period. This, however, is an elevated example which verges at times on the poetic (verses 3-4, for example).

16:1-4. *Jeremiah's Single State.* Jeremiah moved from Anathoth to Jerusalem, away from his family, while still a youth (cf. 1:6). No doubt one result was that the family was not able, or perhaps was not concerned, to arrange a marriage for him. And since he was never sufficiently driven to seek a wife for himself, he remained single.

He now sees in his bachelorhood—a quite unusual status in the ancient Near East—a divine warning that the family life of the nation is going to be cruelly disrupted. Yahweh, knowing what disasters are to befall the population—disasters which will destroy family life—has prevented him from becoming involved.

16:5-9. *Futility of Mourning.* At a time of death the rituals, the visits of sympathetic friends, and the family affairs that must be attended to soften the pain. But in the coming disaster these consolatory patterns will be disrupted—as will also the joys of family life.

16:10-13. *The Disaster Questioned.* People will ask desperately: "But why has **all this great evil** happened?" Jeremiah can only give the traditional answer: "It is punishment for your sins." Because Israel was forearmed with this explanation, however, its faith in Yahweh survived the overwhelming shock of the disappearance of the Judean kingdom.

16:14-15. *An Editorial Comment.* This later insertion is a reminder that doom is never God's last word. It is largely repeated in 23:7-8. In Jeremiah's day Judah faced the horror of the Exile. But the day was to come when return from exile would rank with the Exodus itself as evidence of Yahweh's care and concern for the chosen people.

16:16-21. *No Refuge.* When Yahweh brings down doom, there will be no place to hide. The **hunters** will search the land, their **fishers** will search the rivers and lakes. If Israel has not realized before the serious purpose of Yahweh, it will certainly learn it then (verse 21)! Into this sequence of thought the later editor has inserted an interesting scrap of poetry (verses 19-20). However, it is not as suitable as he presumably thought. The promise is that the **nations** themselves will awake to the worthlessness of their own religious traditions and turn to Yahweh as the one true God.

17:1-4. *Indelible Evil.* In the temple expiation rituals the sacrificial blood was daubed on the **horns** of the **altar**—the four corner projections of the altar. Thus the horns of the altar were the primary place of expiation—and just there Judah's **sin** is indelibly **engraved!** But while this metaphor is telling and vivid, the other thought is even more pregnant: it is written **on the tablet of their heart.** The time will come when the prophetic insight will look for this indelible writing to be erased and for a new message to be written there (cf. 31:33). **Asherim** were wooden poles or images of the fertility goddess Asherah. With verses 3-4 cf. 15:13-14.

17:5-18. *Four Words and a Psalm.* This section is a little collection of Jeremiah's incidental remarks which are in the wisdom tradition of Israel (cf. the book of Proverbs). In the discussions in the temple court he often produced notable sayings—many no doubt extemporaneously, and some he believed worthy of preservation. There seems to be an underlying common theme—permanence.

17:5-8. *The Humanist and the Religious.* There is a profound difference between one **who trusts in man,** whose resources are wholly humanistic, and one **who trusts in the LORD.** The one has an ephemeral character, the other an enduring. This thought has often been expressed and Psalm 1 is closely related to this passage.

17:9-10. *Proverb and Comment.* Verse 9 is a version of the proverb "There's no accounting for human nature." Jeremiah has capped it with the rejoinder that Yahweh audits every life. The balance God strikes has to be settled.

17:11. *Fugitive Wealth.* This is a vivid picture of a sterile **partridge** hen enticing other birds' chicks—but there is no natural tie, and they do not stay. Easy wealth is as quick to go as to come.

17:12-13. *Permanence of True Religion.* Yahweh is abiding reality, and the temple is the visible expression of that reality. One who has roots in its worship is a solid character. One who neglects it is as transient as a message **written in the earth**—that is, the dust.

17:14-18. *Yahweh, Jeremiah's Trust.* This is an individual lament psalm. It begins with the assertion that Jeremiah has looked up to Yahweh—one can tell a person's worth by what they praise. Jeremiah is presently being criticized as a false prophet. People are saying that his warnings are never justified by events (verse 15). But God knows he never wanted these disasters to happen (verse 16*a-c*). It is just that in the fierce light of Yahweh's truth he knows they must happen (verse 16*de*). "Yahweh, don't go back on me. Don't let me down. Don't turn out to have been an illusion. Let my critics find that what they trusted in is false, but do not let me." The little psalm deeply reveals Jeremiah's innermost thought. He is so sure he is right about God and the truth of his vocation, but then the abyss appears at his very feet.

Suppose he *is* mistaken? It is a cry of horror we are hearing: "O God, let it not be so!" True religious faith is balanced precariously on doubt. Jeremiah has the spiritual insight to recognize this and go on believing. Cf. 20:7-13.

17:19-27. *Sabbath Observance.* This is the kind of thing Jeremiah said when he went on his preaching mission on behalf of the reform party (cf. 11:1-8). The oracle promises prosperity and a stable monarchy if the **sabbath day** is respected. Probably until Josiah's reform the sabbath was little observed. It was the recently discovered book of Deuteronomy which made the sabbath a meaningful institution.

The passage shows a respect for the ordered patterns of life and a readiness to find significance in the cult (verse 26) which many scholars find foreign to Jeremiah's thought. But his mind was characterized by remarkable breadth. Elsewhere he contemptuously dismisses insincere worship, yet he might well in another mood recognize the very real value of sincere practices. Verse 26 names the several regions of Judah: the **land of Benjamin,** the territory north of Jerusalem; the **Shephelah,** the western foothills bordering on the Philistine coastland; the **hill country,** the central backbone from Jerusalem to Hebron; the **Negeb,** the arid region to the south.

18:1-12. *Parable of the Potter.* Jeremiah wanders through Potters Street. There the thought strikes him that as the potter shapes and reshapes the clay, so Yahweh, who made **Israel,** can unmake it and remake it. If Israel will not cooperate with Yahweh, God will bring about the collapse of the nation. Jeremiah does not add "in order to remake it," but that is going to emerge in his preaching a little later. Verse 12 is probably an editorial comment. Like the addict, Israel knows its plight, but also knows it cannot reform. The comment puts its finger on the weakness of the prophetic preaching—it lacked a gospel. That was to come later.

18:13-17. *Israel's Perversity.* This is a typical threat oracle. The point of the comparisons was not clear to early editors, and the passage has suffered in transmission. The emendations of the Revised Standard Version make good sense. For Israel to forsake Yahweh is as contrary to nature as that **snow** should forsake **Sirion,** a peak in the perennially snow-clad Hermon range, or that the snow-fed streams should **run dry.** Therefore Yahweh will punish Israel to the degree that those who behold it will be profoundly shocked.

18:18-23. *Opposition.* Jeremiah is no longer blind to the extent of the resentment he is arousing (cf. 11:18-20). He has been attacking priests, prophets, and wise men, Israel's traditional teachers. Naturally they hit back. In gathering his pieces to preserve them Jeremiah tells us this (verse 18) in order to introduce a psalm of cursing (verses 19-23; cf. Psalm 109). In the battle of words bitter things are said. Both sides feel keenly, as has generally been the case in religious disputes.

19:1-13. *The Smashed Flask.* The third-person narrative in verses 1-2, 10—20:6 appears to be a prose contribution by Baruch. However, he was probably writing under Jeremiah's close guidance and so reporting faithfully. Because of its nearness to Potters Street (cf. 18:1) and the consequent dumping of a lot of potters' rubbish just outside it, one gate of Jerusalem was known as **Potsherd Gate.** This gate led to a valley known either as the **valley of the son of Hinnom,** after a previous owner, or as **Topheth.** This second name may originally have had other vowels, making it perhaps Tephath. "Tephath" may have had a particular significance which is now lost, or it may have been just a place name.

Because of its previous association with child-sacrifice cults, Josiah made this valley into a garbage dump for the city (II Kings 23:10). It smoldered continually with rubbish fires. When the doctrine of an afterlife with rewards and punishments became widespread among the Jews—during the second and first centuries B.C.—*Ge* ("valley of") *Hinnom* was corrupted into Gehenna, the New Testament term for hell.

These facts led Jeremiah to perform another acted oracle (see above on 13:1-11). He gathered a very respectable group and led them to the Potsherd Gate. On the way he bought an **earthern flask.** In that place of shards he asserted that Yahweh would **break** Jerusalem irreparably, and then he threw the **vessel** on the ground. The seriousness of this lay in the fact that such symbolic actions by the prophets were held not merely to illustrate the divine activity. Indeed, they were meant to set it in motion, to trigger it, as it were. Hence Pashhur's strong reaction in 20:1-6.

19:3-9. Into the story an editor has inserted this comment. In the catastrophe of the Exile Israel's faith in God was preserved by strong insistence that the disaster was his judgment on guilty Israel, who had indeed often been warned. Verse 2 provided an opening into which a typically Deuteronomic summary of the divine indictment and judgment could be inserted, and the editor took advantage of this.

19:14–20:6. *Official Intervention.* In the outer court of the temple, Jeremiah repeats his message of doom against the city. As a result **Pashhur,** the executive priest, tries to silence him by having him flogged and put in the stocks. When he is released the next day Jeremiah lets loose a mighty curse on Pashhur. Whether it was fulfilled is not specifically recorded, but the mention of another man in the same position in 29:25-26 suggests that Pashhur was one of the officials taken into captivity to Babylon in 597.

Though no date is given for this incident, it seems probable that Jeremiah's acted prophecy was inspired by the Babylonian victory over the Egyptians at Carchemish in the late summer of 605. The incident resulted in his being debarred from the temple, which in turn caused him to begin dictating his first manuscript to Baruch (36:1-3; see Introduction).

20:7-13. *Self-Questioning.* This psalm ranks with the next piece (verses 14-18) and with 15:15-21 and 17:14-18 as the best of Jeremiah's self-disclosures. The clash with Pashhur which precedes it is useful only as supplying the general circumstances. The psalm was not necessarily provoked by that incident but arose out of Jeremiah's situation as a prophet of doom to his generation.

He loved people and was a sociable man. No doubt he spent his whole time in the temple court—talking, arguing, withdrawing to be silent and to compose, breaking back into the conversation with his latest piece. But his participation in the group and the general tone of his pieces were by no means always well received. Prophets of doom are not popular. Yet Jeremiah needed encouragement, response, praise. It was this tension which set up the conflict within him (cf. 17:14-18).

At the beginning of this psalm he feels that he may possibly be one of those poor fools whom Yahweh for inscrutable purposes lures on to be a false prophet (cf. I Kings 22:19-23). Yahweh has **deceived** him, and how readily he was taken in! He has gone around proclaiming **Violence and destruction!** These have not come, and he is reduced to a **laughingstock.** And yet there is the divine compulsion. If he resolves to be silent, there is **burning fire** in his **heart,** and the urge to communicate becomes uncontrollable.

On the other hand—his mind is swinging from one side of the interior debate to the other—he is in very real danger. There are men in the outer court of the temple who are only waiting for one clear instance of false prophecy to get rid of him. But it won't happen! He is not a false prophet; Yahweh is on his side and will soon intervene on his behalf. His enemies will be thoroughly discredited while he will be vindicated.

Verse 13 is an anticipatory thanksgiving for this vindication. Laments were generally ended like this in order to assert in the strongest possible manner that the longed-for salvation would indeed come (cf. Psalm 22:22-31). Thus the psalm ends with Jeremiah's confidence in himself and his mission thoroughly renewed—at least for the present. He was a man of faith who had to wrestle with doubt daily.

20:14-18. *A Birthday Curse.* The mood of this second complaint is despondent. Jeremiah is convinced that he will not be vindicated (verse 18). He wishes he had never come into existence. He expresses this thought in the form of a curse on the **day** of his birth. This is a fine example of what was a widely esteemed art form. Cf. Psalm 109:6-19 and Job 3:1-26, which have the same theme. The birthday curse was probably widely used by contemporary poets.

This is the last of the self-revelations or "confessions" of Jeremiah. After this we have only his comments on public affairs and narratives about him. It is fitting that the last confession should show him despondent, bitter, self-distrustful. This was his inner burden. Outwardly he never faltered in his vocation. Jeremiah fulfilled his mission at a total cost of himself.

21:1–23:8. *Comments on Kings.* This small collection brings together some of Jeremiah's comments on the kings through whose reigns he lived—Josiah, Jehoahaz, Jehoiakim, Jehoiachin, and Zedekiah (see Introduction). The comments are arranged in no discernible order.

21:1-10. *Counsel for Zedekiah.* An editor inserted the first piece to summarize Jeremiah's attitude to the Babylonian siege of Jerusalem in 588-586. It is unlikely that Jeremiah said in effect: "Whether you surrender or do not surrender, you yourself will die" (verse 7). It would have weakened his case, and it contrasts with 38:17-18, which comes from Baruch. This story was part of the massive effort by Israel's teachers during the exile to show that the catastrophe had been long planned by Yahweh and long merited by Israel. **Pashhur the son of Malchiah** is not the priest of 20:1-6 but a courtier opposed to Jeremiah's policies (cf. 38:1-6). **Zephaniah** was "second priest" at the fall of Jerusalem (52:24; cf. II Kings 25:18). Apparently he succeeded to Pashhur the son of Immer's position (cf. 29:25-26; see above on 19:14–20:6).

21:11-12. *Warning to a King.* The king should not neglect his highest function, the dispensing of **justice.** The first part of the king's day was regularly given over to this (cf. II Samuel 15:1-3). Probably the king addressed is Jehoiakim, who preferred the fruits to the labors of kingship (cf. 22:15-17).

21:13-14. *Rebuke to Royal Arrogance.* Verse 13a may be translated: "Behold, I am against you who reign over the valley, perched on the projecting cliff." Jehoiakim had built a new palace (cf. 22:13-14). Since Jerusalem had been spared capture for nearly two hundred years, he felt very secure. Jeremiah warns that the blaze of Yahweh's anger will set fire to the forest—that is, the wooden pillars of the palaces—and destroy all the city.

22:1-9. Call for Good Government. If the king performs faithfully he will continue in power undisturbed. But verses 6-7 show the other side of the coin (cf. Isaiah 1:19-20). The royal house is the palace—the word means also "dynasty." It is prized as if it were Gilead, the forest-rich district across the Jordan, or the summit of Lebanon, famed for its cedars. Even so, if the king and his subjects are disobedient, it will be utterly destroyed.

22:10-12. Lament for Jehoahaz. This little oracle is almost unique in the Old Testament. It is a contemporary comment on the event which proved the turning point of Hebrew history—the death of King Josiah at Megiddo. This disaster was such a profound contradiction of the belief that the good prosper and the wicked are cut down that no one knew what to say. It is for the most part shrouded in an embarrassed silence. Even though Jeremiah was neutral toward the king, this is his only reference to the incomprehensible event. II Chronicles 35:25 mentions a lament for Josiah by Jeremiah and other elegies. But if they ever existed, none have survived. The Chronicler often records what ought to have been rather than what was.

Even here Jeremiah's allusion to the tragedy is very much in passing: "Don't weep for Josiah! He is dead and out of it all, happy man! But weep for his sucessor Jehoahaz [Shallum was his preregnal name], who has been carried off to Egypt and will never come back." There will be no divine intervention, no miraculous salvation. Judah will be swept inescapably forward to the political doom and spiritual anguish which its way of life has brought on. This oracle was no doubt uttered in the year 609, immediately after the event. It implies that Jeremiah was faithful to the end of his ministry.

22:13-19. Jehoiakim's Luxury. Neutral to Josiah, contemptuous of Zedekiah, Jeremiah harbored only constant enmity for

Jehoiakim. Throughout his reign of eleven years this king refused to recognize the new facts of the political situation—that Judah's independence had died at Megiddo with Josiah and that he himself was only a vassal, first of Egypt and then of Babylonia. Jehoiakim was so insensitive to the urgency of the times that he spent most of his reign building himself a **great house** of remarkable richness (see above on 21:13-14). He was required by his overlords to tax his subjects to the utmost to raise a huge annual tribute (II Kings 23:33-35). Therefore he carried out his building project by reviving the practice of forced labor which had led to the division of the kingdom at the death of Solomon (verse 13).

22:15-19. Jeremiah contrasts Jehoiakim's recklessness with Josiah's conscientious and prosperous rule and prophesies a catastrophic end to the reign. Jehoiakim may live luxuriously, but he will die disastrously. His burial will be like that of a dead donkey tossed on a rubbish heap. As far as we know, he died and was buried normally (cf. II Kings 24:6; see below on 36:30).

Some scholars have conjectured that he may have been assassinated by courtiers who recognized the folly of his rebellion against Nebuchadrezzar. In any case he certainly died facing disaster, for the Chaldeans were at the gates of the city in irresistible force.

22:20-23. *A Call to Lament.* Since Jehoiakim's reign is to end so disastrously, Jeremiah calls Jerusalem to bewail its fate. **Lebanon** is north, **Bashan** northeast, and the **Abarim** mountains east. At all these points of the compass Jerusalem will seek its military allies—its **lovers**—and find no help. What good then will it be that Jerusalem has been enriched with cedar-paneled palaces (cf. verse 14)?

22:24-30. *Jehoiachin, the Last of the Line.* Jehoiakim's son Jehoiachin is called here by his preregnal name **Coniah,** a shortening of Jeconiah. He reigned only three months and was deposed by **Nebuchadrezzar.** He was imprisoned in Babylon for thirty-seven years before the turning wheel of political fortune gave him an easier old age (52:31-34). But he never returned to Palestine. Though his uncle, Zedekiah, did in fact occupy the throne for another eleven years, Jehoiachin was the last generation of the royal line to rule in Jerusalem. From David to Jehoiachin there had been four centuries and twenty generations. On the king's **mother** see above on 13:18-19.

22:28-30. Jeremiah has announced the inevitability of Jehoiachin's captivity. Now he expresses also in this second oracle its tragedy. The royal house is like a great, fine vase which has held noble wines. Now, cracked and useless, **a vessel no one cares for,** it is fit only to be smashed. The three-fold **land** in verse 29 is an idiom of intensity underlining the seriousness of the proclamation (cf. 7:4). The eighteen-year-old king probably already has **children** (cf. I Chronicles 3:17, which lists seven sons). But he will be **childless** in that none of them will occupy the **throne of David.**

23:1-8. *Messiah Promised.* A promise of a future scion of the old stock who will reascend the throne of David and restore peace and prosperity to Judah is found in this oracle. He is no heavenly being, nor is there any promise of a new age to come. These are later concepts, as yet unthought of. The promise here is simply of a "good time" under an ideal king. The last king's name is Zedekiah, meaning "Yahweh is my righteousness." Correspondingly the new king's name will be **The LORD is our righteousness**—which should be taken here as "vindication," with the emphasis on vindication for the nation as a whole. This word play on the name makes it probable that at least this part of the oracle was nearly contemporary with Zedekiah's reign.

Thus Jeremiah—if the oracle is his—was one of the earliest exponents of messianism. It was at that time a very simple and undeveloped idea. The future prince is called simply the **Branch,** as he is often in the Old Testament. Since verses 3-4 and 7-8 (cf. 16:14-15) view the Jews as dispersed in **all the countries,** they are probably editorial insertions from a later time.

23:9-40. *Comments on Prophets.* This collection of sayings about prophets, parallel to the collection of sayings about kings, is significant in that it tells us much about Jeremiah's understanding of prophecy and also of his relations with his fellow prophets. Unknown to himself, Jeremiah was in fact preparing the way for the end of prophecy as a functioning institution in Israel, and indeed in all mature religion. The essence of prophecy was ecstatic intuition—that is, the message "given" in a parapsychological experience, not arrived at as the result of rational thought processes. However, when the great crisis of Israel's life arrived, the prophets were fiercely divided. Each side condemned the other's interpretation and advice (cf. 28:1-16; 29:8-9, 29-32). Thus the undependability of the institution was revealed for all to see.

Other prophets had differed sharply with their colleagues (cf. Isaiah 28:7-8), but never before had the issue been so critical. Deuteronomy 18:21-22 was an honest but naïve attempt to deal with the general problem. But when a generation later Second Isaiah's glowing prophecies were not fulfilled, prophecy as an institution was finished (cf. Zechariah 13:2-6). Jeremiah by his controversies undoubtedly contributed a great deal to its decease.

23:9-12. *Ungodly Prophet and Priest.* The title for the whole little collection is **Concerning the prophets.** The first oracle begins with a description of the effect of Yahweh's word on the prophet—he is cast into a disordered state of mind and appears befuddled and **drunken.** This reference is intended to authenticate the message which follows. The whole **land** wilts because of the **wickedness** of the spiritual leaders, both **priest** and **prophet**. It is apparent in the temple itself. Jeremiah does not specify the charges (cf. 5:30-31) but declares that such wickedness will be specifically punished.

23:13-15. *Comparison with Samaritan Prophets.* Yahweh says that the prophets of Samaria were bad enough—they worshiped **Baal** and **led . . . Israel astray,** and everybody knows their punishment. But the **prophets of Jerusalem** are worse. They are as bad as the men of **Sodom** and **Gomorrah** (cf. Genesis 18:20; 19:24-25). Yahweh therefore announces his intention to punish them with bitter and deadly experiences.

23:16-20. *The Issue.* Here the fundamental issue is made clear. The other prophets are optimistic regarding the future and reassure the people as to Yahweh's intentions. Jeremiah sees that disaster lies ahead, and that this is Yahweh's punitive purpose. He hates his own message but nevertheless has to proclaim it. His indignation against those prophets who give way to the temptation to please the people rather than to declare the truth is all the more intense because his own inner battles are won at great cost. These others have never been in Yahweh's **council.** They do not know God's purpose—one of **wrath** and destruction. When the time comes they will **understand it clearly** enough!

23:21-22. *Uncalled Prophets.* Jeremiah's opponents have no true vocation and no authentic message. If they had been present at Yahweh's decision-making sessions, they would turn Israel back from its present evil course. That they encourage it reveals their lack of true insight. This and the preceding oracle imply that Jeremiah has been a member of Yahweh's council. He knows Yahweh's secrets.

23:23-32. *Lying Dreams and the Word.* In this important passage Jeremiah gives (see Introduction) a warning against counterfeit revelation. It is composed as written prose (see Introduction). Some prophets evidently rely on their dreams as their source of inspiration. The possibilities for self-deceit are too obvious. Jeremiah dismisses their ramblings scornfully— mere **straw** in comparison with the **wheat** of the authentic word, which is like a **fire** to burn, a **hammer** to smash. Evidently there is also a good deal of borrowing of ideas (verse 30), but Jeremiah rejects such secondhand revelation contemptuously.

23:33-40. *Rebuke for a Phrase.* In English the word "burden" used to mean the chorus of a song and still can refer to the gist of a message. But its basic sense is something carried physically. This extension of meaning parallels a similar extension of the corresponding Hebrew word (cf. Isaiah 13:1 and 15:1, where "oracle" is literally "burden"). The prophets' use of this double meaning in the phrase **the burden of the LORD** has become thoroughly undesirable to Jeremiah—a "burden" which Yahweh will **cast . . . off.**

24:1-10. *Parable of the Figs.* This account of an oracle concerning the Jews deported to Babylon in 597 with **Jeconiah** (Jehoiachin, see above on 22:24-30) obviously must come from Zedekiah's reign. It is thus one of the last pieces to get into "Jeremiah's book" (see Introduction). It illustrates the way everyday incidents could supply the metaphor in which the divine word expressed itself.

Two worshipers have placed in the temple "first fruits" consisting of **baskets of figs.** One has had a **good** crop, the other a **very bad** one—or has chosen a poor selection for the offering. The contrast strikes Jeremiah forcibly. He has been brooding over the poor quality of leadership remaining in Judah and remembering the worthy Israelites now in Babylon. The two baskets immediately become for him a parable, an expression of the divine word. By it he states a judgment which history has substantiated: the future of Israel lies with the exiles in Babylon.

E. CONCLUDING WORDS (25:1-14)

This is probably the end of Jeremiah's original anthology (1:4–8:3; see Introduction). It has been worked over by postexilic hands.

25:1-10. *Summary of a Ministry.* Dating in the Old Testament is by the regnal year of the king, counted in Jeremiah's time from the first new year following his accession. Scholars are not agreed on whether Judah observed the new year in the autumn or the spring during this period. If we assume that an autumnal new year was continued until the Exile, Jehoiakim's first regnal year began in the fall of 608, nearly a full year after Pharaoh Neco placed him on the throne. His **fourth year** extended from the fall of 605 to the fall of 604. The Babylonian new year, on the other hand, came in the spring. The **first year of Nebuchadrezzar,** who succeeded his father in September 605, began in the spring of 604.

The synchronism in verse 1 may be correct—the words in parentheses are missing from the Septuagint and may be a gloss. If so, the date indicated, which is probably that of the dictation of Jeremiah's first manuscript (cf. 36:1), is narrowed to the six months between the Babylonian spring and Judean fall new years of 604. Counting back **twenty-three years,** Jeremiah's ministry began in 627, which until September was the **thirteenth year of Josiah.**

25:5-10. This is the heart of Jeremiah's message—an appeal to repent and be saved. The Christian gospel stands essentially in the prophetic tradition.

25:11-14. *Punishment of Babylon.* Jeremiah looked forward to a final restoration of Israel (cf. 32:9-15). He believed the time of its captivity would be about **seventy years** (cf. 29:10). But these verses dwell on the punishment which Babylon is to receive after seventy years, and it is probable that they owe much to someone directly interested in seeing Babylon suffer, someone writing in the later years of the Exile. Probably the collection for which Jeremiah himself was responsible (see Introduction) ended with the words **this book.**

F. UNIVERSAL JUDGMENT (25:15-38)

In the Septuagint the collection of oracles against the nations (46:1–51:64) is inserted after **book** in 25:13, and this passage is used as the closing summary of that collection. The passage is itself composite. Verses 15-16 and 27-29 record in prose an oracle of Jeremiah against the **nations** generally. Into this has been inserted a roll call of the nations (verses 17-26) to show that none has been overlooked or can hope to escape. Then follow three small oracles on the same general theme (verses 30-31, 32-33, and 34-38).

Thus the passage as a whole must be regarded as a little collection of Jeremiah's sayings against the nations which was later overshadowed by the larger collection in 46:1–51:46. In one tradition, represented by the standard Hebrew text, the passage remained independent as it appears here. In the other tradition, represented by the Septuagint and some Dead Sea

Scroll fragments, it came to be attached to the larger collection as a summary (see Introduction).

25:15-16. *The Cup of Wrath.* Jeremiah has already used this metaphor of drunkenness against Israel (13:12-14). Now he uses it against **all the nations** to foretell universal war as universal judgment. The passage is continued in verses 27-29.

25:17-26. *Roll Call for Judgment.* This list of the nations to be punished comes from the period after the fall of Jerusalem. It could be from Jeremiah himself. **Jerusalem** lies **waste,** and the dominant power is **Babylon.** Uz was probably in the desert to the east or southeast beyond Edom (cf. Job 1:1-3). **Dedan, Tema, Buz** were Arab desert tribes whose foreign customs aroused strong Israelite dislike (cf. 9:26). The list reveals considerable geographic knowledge in that it places in order the lands and peoples from Egypt through to Persia.

Finally the judgment is to fall on **Babylon also.** This may be a later addition, for it uses the "athbash" ciper for "Babylon," a device popular late in the Exile. The cipher substituted the first letter of the Hebrew alphabet for the last, the second letter for the next to last, etc., and with only consonants involved always produced an apparent word. Thus BBL, "Babylon," became SSK, "Sheshach."

25:27-29. See above on verses 15-16.

25:30-31. *The Lion of Judgment.* This metaphor is used also in Amos 1:2. All people are within Yahweh's **fold**—only now God has become the lion which attacks it.

25:32-33. *Universal Plight.* Disaster will move from one **nation** to another like a storm sweeping across the weather-map. Someone has added the gruesome detail that the dead will be too many to bury.

25:34-38. *No Escape for Shepherds or Sheep.* These verses gather together many of the preceding ideas and metaphors. To refer to rulers as **shepherds** was quite usual. Jeremiah uses the image to emphasize the dismay—not only the **flock** but also its keepers are being butchered. The **lion** metaphor is also resumed. The whole piece is a vigorous warning of the divine judgment to come.

II. BARUCH'S BOOK (26:1–45:5)

Baruch's book has more structure than at first appears. Chapters 30–31, the "Book of Comfort," require separate consideration and are omitted here (see below on 30:1–31:4). Otherwise, the narratives and the probable dates to which they refer are as follows:

Jeremiah			
26	Temple Sermon	Accession Jehoiakim	609-8
27-28	Clash with Hananiah	4 Zedekiah	593
29	Correspondence with Babylon	Mid-period Zedekiah	593?
32	Purchase of Field	10 Zedekiah	587
33	Further Prophesying	10 Zedekiah	587
34	Freeing of slaves	10 Zedekiah	588
35	Rechabites	10 Jehoiakim	598
36	Writing of scroll	4 Jehoiakim	604
37-38	The siege	10-11 Zedekiah	588-6
40-43	The aftermath	Post fall of Jerusalem	583?
44	Ministry in Egypt	Early Exile	582?
45	Oracle to Baruch	4 Jehoiakim	604

Note that some of the narratives are not in chronological order. Moreover each one has its own little introduction, often repetitive, giving the impression that at one time it circulated separately. A possible explanation is that after the death of Jeremiah, Baruch felt that he should continue to exert his master's influence on the current situation. The question of the day was whether Israel's faith in Yahweh and in its own distinctive future was a delusion. The destruction of the Judean state seemed to imply this. Yet it was possible to interpret that disaster in such a way that it could be recognized as Yahweh's deed—a severe disciplining in order to purify Israel for its renewed role in the days to come. This last was the prophetic interpretation of Israel's experience.

Baruch wanted to impress this prophetic interpretation upon the exiles in Egypt, many of whom were surrendering both their faith and their national identity (cf. 44:1-30). He therefore wrote up a number of incidents in the life of his master to show that Jeremiah not only foretold the disaster, but also persisted in the prophetic interpretation of it. Baruch at first circulated these narratives separately among the scattered groups of exile. Later he gathered them together to produce what is here called "Baruch's Book."

The order in which Baruch assembled his narratives was roughly chronological. Only two dates, chapters 35 and 36, are seriously out of line. The incident concerning the Rechabites is dated in the text as taking place during the tenth year of Jehoiakim, which was 599/98. If this date is correct, it was probably intended to relate the incident to the first capture of Jerusalem by Nebuchadrezzar in 597. If, however, Jehoiakim should be viewed as an error for Zedekiah (see below on 35:1-19) the narrative would be in place in the sequential order.

The other misplaced story is that of the writing of the scroll. This should either follow the temple sermon in chapter 26 or precede the personal story of Baruch in chapter 45. In this latter position it would authenticate what has gone before. It may have been written especially to round off the series when the pieces were collected into a book. A later scribe, realizing that it was not in its chronological position, moved it to follow the other "Jehoiakim" story (which was already wrongly assigned to that reign), and so the present disorder was reached.

It should be noted that Baruch did not put the events during the siege in the reign of Zedekiah in strict order. The purchase of the field (chapters 32–33) took place after Jeremiah's imprisonment. The incidents relating to the freeing of the slaves and to the Rechabites (chapters 34 and 35) took place while he was still free to come and go. But Hebrew writers frequently put the important incident first, even though it was chronologically later. Chapters 32–33 should thus in strict chronology follow chapter 37 or perhaps chapter 38.

A. EVENTS BEFORE THE SIEGE (26:1–29:32)

26:1-24. *The Temple Sermon.* The phrase translated **beginning of the reign** was apparently a technical term for "accession year"—that is, the part of a year between a new king's actual accession and the following new year, which began his first regnal year (see above on 25:1-10). Thus Baruch's account dates the temple sermon in 609/8. It is instructive to compare his version with that of Jeremiah in 7:1-15. There Jeremiah is intent on the message and gives it with some fullness. Here Baruch gives its main thrust and then hurries on to tell what the consequences were—a part of the story which Jeremiah ignores. The prophet disregards himself in his message. The disciple conveys the message only to explain how his master was in danger for his life.

26:7-9. The message is so unpalatable that it causes something of a riot. The spark that sets it off comes from Jeremiah's colleagues, the **priests and prophets.** Jeremiah is in a minority—though not wholly alone (cf. verses 20-24). His message is so contrary to the popular line that he appears to be an "enemy of the people." The nation, it is recalled, is in a state of shock following the death of Josiah and its vassalage to Pharaoh Neco.

26:10-15. The **princes**—the civic rulers—intervene to stop the riot and hear a charge. Jeremiah's defense is that his message is a true word of Yahweh. If need be, he must die rather than withhold this word. If they condemn him, the magistrates will be guilty of **innocent blood.**

26:16-19. The magistrates wish to avoid decisive action and cite the parallel case of **Micah** (cf. Micah 3:9-12). They urge the people to reform their behavior—this would make their task easier and ought to satisfy the prophet. The magistrates see the riot as an "incident" which can be handled by skillful administration.

26:20-24. Baruch shows how the situation might have developed quite differently. Prophets did sometimes lose their lives for their plain speech. He draws attention to the case of

Uriah, who was even brought back **from Egypt** to be put to death by **Jehoiakim.** Presumably this took place later in Jehoiakim's reign, and Baruch cites it as an example of what might have happened to Jeremiah. **Ahikam** and his father, **Shaphan,** were prominent under Josiah (cf. II Kings 22:3, 12). Ahikam's son Gedaliah was appointed governor of Judah after the fall of Jerusalem (cf. 40:5–41:3). He is therefore an important person, whose protection counts for much.

27:1–28:17. *Clash with Hananiah.* The story is dated **in the beginning of the reign of Zedekiah.** Some manuscripts read "Jehoiakim." The phrase has been mechanically copied from 26:1. The date is actually the fourth year of Zedekiah (593), as in 28:1*b*. Baruch did not find anything in the intervening period to distract him from his main purpose—which was to expound Jeremiah's interpretation of Babylon's role.

27:2-7. During Zedekiah's reign there is an attempt to form an anti-Babylonian alliance. **Envoys** come to Jerusalem from **Edom . . . Moab . . . Ammon . . . Tyre . . . Sidon.** As an acted oracle (see above on 13:1-11) Jeremiah puts on a porter's **thongs and yoke-bars** to urge submission to **Nebuchadnezzar,** who is world ruler by divine decision (cf. Isaiah 20). Nebuchadnezzar, which should be Nebuchadrezzar, is mistakenly spelled in chapters 27–28 and elsewhere in the Old Testament. Babylon's day of punishment will come, he says, but until then all peoples should **serve** him. **My servant** in verse 6 means "my instrument."

There is an unequivocal statement of monotheism in verse 5. In verse 7 the Chaldean power is limited to three generations—Babylon fell in 539. These two verses suggest that the wording has been touched up by a later hand. But the general policy is quite in line with Isaiah's warnings against such alliances (cf. Isaiah 30:1-7) and the attribution of this attitude to Jeremiah is undoubtedly correct.

27:8-15. Each king represented at the conference has his own spiritual advisers, ranging from magicians to **prophets.** They are unanimous in support of the alliance. But Jeremiah dismisses them as dishonest time servers (cf. I Kings 22:1-28 for a close parallel). He especially includes prophets of Yahweh—they too can be false (cf. 23:21-32).

27:16-22. Jeremiah carries his message to the **people.** Some popularity-seeking prophets have been telling them that a quick reversal of fortunes may be expected—and especially that the sacred **vessels** looted from the temple when **Jeconiah** (Jehoia-chin, see above on 22:24-30) was deported will speedily be returned. Jeremiah says that if they are true prophets they will worry about preventing the rest of the temple treasure from going the same way. For himself he is convinced that the point of no return has already been reached. Judah will now go forward steadily to disaster.

28:1-4. Jeremiah's attitude arouses direct contradiction by one particular prophet, **Hananiah the son of Azzur,** who promises a return of both captives and temple paraphernalia **within two years.** The erroneous date **at the beginning of the reign** is repeated from 27:1 (see above on 27:1-28:17). But now the correct date also appears—the **fifth month of the fourth year** of Zedekiah (July-August 593; see below on verse 17).

28:5-9. Jeremiah's reaction is not swift denial. He replies that he hopes Hananiah's prophecy will **come true.** However, the tradition of Yahweh's prophets has always been one of punishment and doom.

28:10-11. Hananiah is so sure he is right that he counters Jeremiah's acted oracle (see above on verses 2-7) with one of his own. He steps up to Jeremiah, takes the yoke-bars from him, and smashes them. So will Yahweh break Babylon's power. Jeremiah does not protest, but goes off quietly to think about it.

28:12-16. Jeremiah is sure that he is right and Hananiah wrong. Later he reappears with an oracle repeating the divine intention to sustain Nebuchadrezzar as world ruler. A **wooden** yoke can be broken, but this is one of **iron.** As for Hananiah, Jeremiah is now convinced that he is a false prophet, and that Yahweh will remove him speedily.

28:17. Two months later Hananiah dies. Jeremiah naturally sees in this fact divine authentication of his message. Throughout the period of the divided monarchy months seem to have been identified by numbers, rather than names, beginning in the spring. The usage no doubt grew out of international commerce. Apparently it did not affect the Judean religious and regnal new year observance, which occurred in the fall, and those at the beginning of the **seventh month** (September-October).

If by **same year** Baruch means Zedekiah's fourth year (cf. verse 1), it would indicate that this and other dates in his book are based on regnal years beginning in the spring. On the other hand he may well mean merely the next seventh month without regard to the fact that technically it began Zedekiah's fifth year. His usage in 25:1-3 and 36:1, 9 (see comments) seems to support the latter interpretation. However, the evidence is inconclusive and exact equivalents of his dates cannot be determined.

29:1-32. *Jeremiah's Letter.* Zedekiah has reason to send envoys to Babylon, and Jeremiah asks them to carry a **letter** to the Jews now living there in **exile** as a result of the first deportation in 597 (see above on 22:24-30). In the letter he urges the exiles to settle down and build a new life for themselves. They are to be there for a long time. They are to be good citizens of their new country, for in its **welfare** lies their own. But they are not to cease to be Yahweh's people, even in a strange land. Jeremiah can say this because his religion is free of all limitation, either geographical or cultic.

29:10-14. This passage is probably a later insertion. It may come from an editor who knew that from the battle of Carchemish in 605 to the Persian capture of Babylon in 539 was roughly **seventy years.** The intention is to encourage restoration hopes.

29:15-19. Similarly the postexilic editor has inserted threats to the royal house to show that the disaster was foretold (verses 16-19). Read verse 15 with verses 20-23.

29:20-23. There are **prophets** among the exiles (verse 15), including some true prophets—for example, Ezekiel and Second Isaiah. But **Ahab** and **Zedekiah** are false prophets according to Jeremiah. No doubt a great deal of what they said was subversive from the Babylonian point of view. Death by burning was a regular Babylonian method of execution (verse 22; cf. Daniel 3). Jeremiah warns that these foolish men will surely end in the **fire.** Whether the charge of immorality (verse 23) is seriously leveled we cannot be sure, but Jeremiah is clearly quite well informed on affairs in Babylon.

29:24-32. A prophet in Babylon called **Shemaiah** objects to the letter. He writes angrily to the priest **Zephaniah** in Jerusalem—successor to Pashhur, who earlier put Jeremiah in the **stocks** (cf. 20:1-6; 52:24)—telling him to use his authority to silence Jeremiah. The priest, however, reads the letter to Jeremiah. We cannot be sure of his motive, whether by way of admonition or by way of friendship and warning. Jeremiah's reaction is characteristically violent. He sends back the rejoinder that neither Shemaiah nor **his descendants** will live to see the good which is coming for Yahweh's people. The quarrel between Jeremiah and those who differed from him was bitter and intense (cf. 23:16-20). Both sides felt that the future of the nation depended on the prevalence of their point of view.

B. The Book of Comfort (30:1–31:40)

In the early postexilic period the urgent need was to restore Israel's hope in its future. Therefore the fact that many of the great prophets had left behind them oracles of doom, prophesying Israel's utter destruction, was a very real embarrassment. Jeremiah did not intend to say that Israel would be completely eradicated. He did in fact utter oracles of hope and restoration (cf. chapter 32), but many of his most memorable pieces were oracles of doom.

An editor in the prophetic tradition undertook to put the matter in the right light. He took some characteristic sayings of Jeremiah and counterbalanced them—almost, one might say, reversed them—by words of promise. His purpose was to produce a little collection of "Jeremiah's" teaching which would be encouraging to the battered nation. The result is this little "Book of Comfort." The amount of material in it coming directly from Jeremiah is probably fairly small. The group to which the editor belonged was profoundly influenced by Second Isaiah and many of the pieces are reminiscent of his teaching.

30:1-3. *Introduction.* The editor knows of Jeremiah's writing activity (chapter 36). He uses that knowledge to give an air of authenticity to his own **book.**

30:4-8. *Reversal of Doom.* Verses 5-7 are probably an oracle from Jeremiah himself. They are a typical oracle of doom. Whether verse 7*d* is original is difficult to decide, but it provides the transition to the comforting promise of verses 8-9. National independence and the restoration of the Davidic monarchy are the two promises made. In the early postexilic period the restoration of the Davidic line was often more stressed than the hope of the emergence of a particular prince of that house—that is, the coming of the "Branch" (23:5).

30:10-11. *The Return of Jacob.* The compiler has an encouraging little fragment which is more in the tradition of Second Isaiah than of Jeremiah—particularly in its use of **Jacob** for the whole Hebrew people (cf. Isaiah 41:8, 43:1, 44:1). The last line perhaps should be read "but I will not punish you utterly" (literally "exact utter vengeance"). This piece is used again for a similar purpose in 46:27-28.

30:12-17. *The Healing of Israel's Wounds.* Verses 12-15 look very much like a genuine Jeremiah oracle. Judah has suffered terrible **punishment** (cf. Isaiah 1:5-9 for the same metaphor) and has deserved it. The compiler adds to this oracle of doom a "happy ending" (verses 16-17). Again this is from the Second Isaiah tradition.

30:18-22. *The New Jerusalem.* This oracle envisages Jerusalem rebuilt, filled with many people, ruled by a Jewish **prince** genuinely respectful of Yahweh, with the covenant of God and people firmly renewed.

30:23–31:1. *Yahweh's Storm.* Again a little saying of Jeremiah's, threatening the approach of Yahweh's relentless anger. The compiler has seized on the last line and added his own remark: "Yes, what Israel will understand is that Yahweh is their God and Israel is Yahweh's people." He has cleverly made his point: after punishment comes forgiveness and restoration.

31:2-6. *Yahweh's Everlasting Love.* This beautiful little oracle is very much in the style of Second Isaiah. The patience of God is inexhaustible. As a result northern Israel and Judah will be restored, and **Zion** will be the happy center of Yahweh's worship.

31:7-9. *The Exiles' Return.* This oracle offers a picture of all the scattered Israelites coming back amid universal joy (cf. Isaiah 49:8-13).

31:10-14. *A Watered Garden.* The restored nation is pictured in idyllic terms. Again the style is strongly like Second Isaiah.

31:15-17. *No More Weeping.* A fragment of Jeremiah (verse 15) provides the text for this piece. He imagines **Rachel,** the mother of the Joseph (Ephraim and Manasseh) and Benjamin tribes, weeping from her tomb in **Ramah** over her slaughtered **children.** Jeremiah was himself in a camp for deportees in Ramah (40:1). But the editor takes the imagery further and pictures Yahweh as bidding her weep no more. **There is hope for your future,** he says—an expression of the editor's grand theme.

31:18-20. *The Prodigal's Awakening.* Here **Ephraim,** a common name for northern Israel, is envisaged as coming to repentance. Smiting on the **thigh** appears to be a gesture of grief. This time the editor adds his fragment from Jeremiah at the end—a proclamation of Yahweh's undying love for Ephraim. He thus makes his point that human penitence will always be met by God's love.

31:21-22. *The New Development.* Israel is bidden to establish **waymarks** in the desert so that its people may find their way back. Israel is not to hesitate, thinking this may be dangerous, for Yahweh has introduced a new factor into the situation which has transformed Israel's whole position. The enigma is in the last line. What is the new move of Yahweh which has so radically changed the whole picture? The translation **a woman protects a man** would seem to mean that **virgin Israel** protects Yahweh, which does not seem appropriate, if only because the new move is of Yahweh's making. Several emendations have been suggested—for example, "a woman becomes a man," but this does not link with any other biblical, or indeed ancient Near Eastern, cultic or mythological idea.

The verb is a form of the root "go around" and thus can mean "encompass." This suggests a woman carrying a man-child in her womb. If this is the meaning, the promised **new thing** is the birth of the Messiah, and the enigmatic character of the oracle is due to its dangerous political implications. Haggai, Zechariah, and Zerubbabel probably all fell foul of the Persian authorities because of messianism. The oracle then ranks with Isaiah 9:2-7 as a prophecy of hope based on an expectation of a deliverer to be born to the royal house.

31:23-25. *Zion a Blessing.* In the day of its restoration Zion will be so pleasant and lovely that people will confidently call down a blessing on it.

31:26. *Apocalyptic Framework.* Some of the material the editor is using may have come from a work of apocalyptic character—a revelation of hidden secrets. In this type of literature revelations were often represented as being received in dreams. Part of the apocalyptic framework seems to have been inadvertently retained.

31:27-28. *Yahweh the Farmer.* Yahweh's **seed** is Israel, and Yahweh will cultivate Israel's holding with very great care. The passage echoes Jeremiah's own words in 1:10.

31:29-30. *Individual Responsibility.* The proverb means: "The generation of Manasseh sinned, but we are bearing the punishment." It implies that Yahweh is unjust. The reply says nothing about the past but promises that in the golden age to come each person will bear the responsibility **for his own sin** only. The oracle testifies to the emerging importance of the individual.

31:31-34. *The New Covenant.* This oracle is of such importance in the Bible as a whole that scholars have been reluctant to admit that it may not be Jeremiah's. It certainly complements his somewhat negative teaching. Circumcision, the ark, the temple, the city, the state, prophet, priest, king can all go, he says, since they are not essential. But what *is* essential? This great oracle declares it: **I will put my law within them, and I will write it upon their hearts.** When the time of restoration comes, people will do what is right from inner conviction and desire. In this way the **covenant** of Yahweh and Israel will be finally and permanently renewed. Ezekiel sets the same idea in different imagery (cf. Ezekiel 36:24-28).

Jesus made the phrase **a new covenant** his own at the Last Supper. The organization of scripture into two covenants—that is, testaments—follows from this. Here the talk is of an old covenant renewed—the covenant of Yahweh and Israel. It is not accompanied by any new obligations, for the old are well known. Jesus used the phrase to speak of a truly new covenant, with all people rather than with Israel, and with new obligations, those of the law of love. Whether Jeremiah voiced this prophecy or not, it certainly is in keeping with his teaching. The profound insight it displays is fully worthy of the prophetic tradition at its best.

31:35-37. *The Immutable Covenant.* The Hebrews early grasped the notion of the patterned and stable functioning of nature, a notion on which all modern science is based. Here that idea of imperturbable nature is used to illustrate the immutable character of Yahweh's covenant with Israel—it is as unshakable as a natural law.

31:38-40. *The New City Plan.* This oracle foresees Jerusalem as not merely restored but enlarged. Beginning in the northeast at the tower of **Hananel** (cf. Nehemiah 3:1; Zechariah 14:10) the new boundary is traced to the **Corner Gate** (cf. II Kings 14:13), probably on the northwest. It goes on around through the unknown **Gareb** and **Goah** to the **Horse Gate** (cf. Nehemiah 3:28) so as to take in the Hinnom (verse 40*a;* see above on 19:1-13) and **Kidron** valleys. All this territory, though now polluted, is to become part of the city **sacred to the LORD**. The idea of the renewed covenant is to be embodied in a renewed Jerusalem. So ends a little work which is one of the most striking in all scripture.

C. EVENTS DURING THE SIEGE (32:1–35:19)

32:1-25. *The Field at Anathoth.* Possibly the **tenth year of Zedekiah** ended in the fall of 587 (see above on 25:1-10 and 28:17). If so, the synchronism with the **eighteenth year of Nebuchadrezzar,** which began in the spring of that year, dates this incident within the six-month period between the equinoxes. Jeremiah's arrest, confinement in a prison, and transfer, after an appeal to Zedekiah, to the **court of the guard** are related in 37:11-21. Chronologically, therefore, this chapter should come after chapter 37, possibly after chapter 38. The introductory summary in verses 2-5 suggests that the various narratives in Baruch's book originally circulated independently. In verse 5 **until I visit** him means here "until I punish him"—that is, with death.

32:6-8. When a man was forced by need for money to sell part of his land, he was required to offer it first to the members of the family, who had the **right of redemption** (cf. Ruth 4:1-6). **Hanamel** wants to sell a field at **Anathoth.** But it is a highly speculative proposition in which he is trying to interest Jeremiah since the city is under siege and the future is very insecure. Money could be easily carried by escaping refugees, but it would be foolish to acquire land at such a time. Notice that prophets firmly believed that they received premonitions; Elisha was disconcerted by not having had a premonition of a significant event (II Kings 4:27).

32:9-14. Jeremiah buys the land, and we have an interesting description of the legal formalities. **Silver** money in Jeremiah's day consisted of bars or rings which had to be **weighed** at each transaction. A **shekel** was a little less than half an ounce. Many deeds of sale dated in the next two centuries have come down to us from the Jewish colony on the Nile island of Elephantine.

To guard against alteration this deed is prepared in duplicate and one copy is **sealed.** Sealing means that it is rolled and tied and the ties are fastened with clay into which is impressed a signet ring or stamp. The documents are placed for safekeeping in an **earthenware vessel** or jar. In verse 12 **Baruch** naturally draws attention to his role as Jeremiah's confidant.

32:15. Jeremiah discloses that his actions are symbolic. The purchase of the field is an acted oracle intended to foretell that Israel will one day be restored. There is little reason to doubt that this message of hope after doom was part of Jeremiah's thought. But before the blow fell it attracted little attention. People were more concerned with the possibility that the disaster could be averted. When Jerusalem had fallen, it became all-important to accept and live by this hope.

32:16-25. Baruch recalls that Jeremiah prayed aloud after the ceremony. Here he gives us his version of that prayer—a version which owes probably more to him than to Jeremiah. The theological standpoint is thoroughly in accord with Deuteronomic orthodoxy. The prayer ends abruptly. Perhaps the expansions which follow are substitutes for some phrase like "for thou wilt yet show favor to Jerusalem."

32:26-44. *Deuteronomic Expansions.* At this point in Baruch's narrative later editors saw an opportunity to reinforce their interpretation of the great disaster. In verses 26-35 they show why Yahweh punished Judah so severely. Then in verses 36-44 they stress the message of restoration. On verse 35 see above on 19:1-13. On verse 44 see on 17:19-27.

Everything is contained within the bounds of Deuteronomic thought, but the notion of the renewed heart is very much to the fore. This passage, especially verses 38-40, ranks with 31:33 and Ezekiel 36:26 as the great Old Testament anticipations of the first summary of Jesus' teaching: "Repent, and believe in the gospel" (Mark 1:15). That is, "Change your mind and believe the good news!"

33:1-9. The expansions of Jeremiah's message of hope (cf. 32:15) are continued. Verse 4, which is textually obscure, seems to refer to desperate but not uncommon practices for the defense of a besieged city. But Jerusalem's lot is going to be so changed that its **prosperity** under very evident divine favor will win the respect of its neighbors. Indeed its present persecutors will have reason to **fear** its renewed strength and vitality. This last thought is not followed up. In later, apocalyptic works it was to become a dominating theme.

33:10-13. The social joy of a happy people, and the liturgical joy of a worshiping people both find their place in the renewed city (cf. Psalm 136:1). On verse 13 see above on 17:19-27.

33:14-26. This expansion is very late and was not included in the Septuagint (see Introduction). It is of special interest because it is a messianic prophecy, looking for the divinely chosen descendant of **David** to come and restore the Judean kingdom. His reign is to be characterized by **justice** (cf. Isaiah 11:3-4). Not everyone longed for the Messiah, the **Branch** of the old tree of David. The priesthood was generally neutral or even hostile to the idea. In this passage the references to the priesthood alongside the Messiah may well be placatory in character.

The claim that the divine **covenant** with the house of David and with the **Levitical priests** is as immutable as the physical laws of the universe must be recognized as hyperbole. While Davidic messianism may be held to have come to fulfillment in Jesus, the Zadokite priesthood—the Levitical group which controlled the temple—came to an end in the first century A.D. The writers behind these additions were thus wrong in some of their forecasts, but they were right in their optimism and their faith.

34:1-7. *A Warning and a Promise.* Baruch's narrative, interrupted since 32:26, continues with this message to **Zedekiah.** It testifies to his accuracy, for verses 4-5 record an oracle personally reassuring to the king which was not fulfilled (cf. 52:9-11). Yet Baruch honestly includes it (see below on verses 21-22). The fear which a tyrant like Nebuchadrezzar could instill in the little princedoms of Palestine is well caught in **you shall see the king of Babylon eye to eye and speak with him face to face.** Baruch's purpose is to place on record the consistency of Jeremiah's message: "This is Yahweh's will; surrender to it."

The incident took place in the early months of the siege. The reference to **Lachish and Azekah,** cities in the foothill region southwest of Jerusalem, has received much illumination from the discovery at the site of Lachish of a number of letters written on potsherds during the reign of Zedekiah. One of them, dated in his ninth year (589/88), is the report of a Judean captain to his superior: "We are watching for the smoke signals of Lachish, . . . because we do not see Azekah." No doubt Azekah was already overrun, and Lachish must have fallen soon after. Jerusalem was left to stand the siege alone.

34:8-22. *Treachery to Freed Slaves.* When the Babylonians first approached Jerusalem there was a great need for national unity. Thus it was proposed that all **Hebrew slaves** be given their freedom. Jeremiah refers to the old law that a fellow Hebrew could be enslaved for only **six years** and must then be released (Exodus 21:2; Deuteronomy 15:12). This custom had fallen into disuse, but with the Babylonian threat it was revived. Now the Egyptians have made a show of strength and the Babylonians have had to raise the siege (verse 21; cf. 37:6-15). Thinking that this is permanent relief, the slaveowners have promptly reenslaved those who were recently liberated.

34:17-20. Evidently the ceremony of liberation was a solemn and public one. It was accompanied by an ancient **covenant** ritual in which the sacrificial beast was cut into **two . . . parts** and the parties to the covenant **passed between** them (cf. Genesis 15:7-10, 17-18). By some legal device the rich have found a way around this covenant, and are reenslaving poverty-stricken Hebrews. This cynicism shocks Jeremiah deeply. Yahweh, he says, will give the Jewish leaders freedom—freedom from divine service and freedom to die by war, hunger, and disease!

34:21-22. Verse 21 may be meant specifically to revoke the oracle of personal reassurance to **Zedekiah** recorded in verse 4. The Egyptians soon pulled back and the siege was resumed without further interruption to the tragic end. This incident of the slaves evidently impressed Jeremiah deeply. It revealed how far-reaching was the decay of Judean public and private morality. Only **fire** could purge such corruption!

35:1-19. *The Rechabites.* This incident is dated in the days of

Jehoiakim at a time when the Rechabites have come into Jerusalem for safety because of attack by Nebuchadrezzar. But Nebuchadrezzar did not bring his army against Judah until the time of Jehoiakim's death in December 598. The occasion has therefore been taken by some to be the earlier attack by marauding bands of **Chaldeans** and **Syrians** (cf. II Kings 24:2).

But the Rechabites were strongly opposed to city life (see below on verses 2-11). It seems doubtful that the situation ever became desperate enough to drive them into Jerusalem during the reign of Jehoiakim. If instead we recognize Jehoiakim as a mistake for Zedekiah and the time as the siege, this narrative falls into place chronologically.

35:2-11. The **Rechabites** were a clan who, in protest against civilization, maintained a semi-nomadic existence despite the progressive urbanization of Israel. Rather like the modern gypsies, they avoided houses, agriculture, or anything that would tie them to one locality. Since growing grapes is a long and restrictive process, a prohibition against **wine** was outstanding among their taboos. Jeremiah gathers a group of Rechabites in one of the cloister alcoves of the temple and publicly offers them wine, which as anticipated they refuse.

35:12-19. The loyalty of the Rechabites to their principles provides Jeremiah with the basis for his prophetic declaration: The members of this clan have an abnormal way of life in which they persist wholeheartedly. Israel has a wholesome way of life and a more pervasive obligation, arising out of a covenant with Yahweh, and yet cannot keep to it. There is a future for a disciplined group such as the Rechabites. But for the Israelites there can be only the punishment they have brought on their own heads.

D. The Writing of the Scroll (36:1-32)

The mistaken attribution of the foregoing piece (35:1-19; see comment) to Jehoiakim's reign suggested to an editor that he bring this other Jehoiakim story to stand with it. Its proper place is probably at the end of Baruch's book, just before the oracle to Baruch in 45:1-4 (see above on 26:1–45:55). Chronologically, however, the events belong following chapter 26. See also comment on 19:14–20:6.

The dictation of the scroll is dated the **fourth year of Jehoiakim** and its public reading the **fifth year . . . ninth month**—that is, December 604. If Baruch counted the fifth year as beginning in the fall (see above on 25:1-10) the writing may have occurred as late as September 604, about three months before the reading. But if he reckoned on a spring new year (see above on 28:17) the interval was at least nine months and the scroll was prepared in the winter of 605/4.

36:2-8. *Jeremiah's Exclusion from the Temple.* Jeremiah was a man of the outer courts of the temple (see Introduction). There he warned for many years of a foe from the north, an idea which seemed irrelevant and harmless. When, however, Egypt fell back in 605 before Nebuchadrezzar's advance Jeremiah's preaching suddenly became relevant and dangerous. He was meddling in high affairs of state and must be stopped. The way to do this, it appeared, was to deny him the forum of the outer courts. But if Jeremiah could not speak one way, he would find another. He took the revolutionary step of writing out some of his most striking pieces. Jeremiah was not thinking of his teaching's survival—Jesus never wrote a book—but was intent solely on its communication.

36:9-10. *The Cloister Reading.* On a **fast** day, an occasion which Jeremiah hopes will put the crowds in a mood to accept his message, he sends Baruch into the temple with his scroll. If it consisted of 1:1–8:3 plus 25:1-14 (see Introduction) it could easily be read three times in one day. The circle which customarily gathered in the cloister of **Gemariah** was one that had access to the officials. Doubtless it was chosen with this in mind. **Shaphan** was **secretary** under Josiah (cf. II Kings 22:3-10; see above on 26:20-24).

36:11-19. *The Secretarial Office Reading.* Gemariah's son, probably a youth, hears the cloister reading. He hurries to tell his father, whom he finds in the palace in the office of the present **secretary.** With them are the other **princes**—that is, officials of the government—including **Elnathan,** who brought back the prophet Uriah from Egypt (cf. 26:22). After summoning Baruch and hearing the scroll, they particularly inquire if the sayings were actually dictated by Jeremiah—literally "Were these words from his mouth?"

Why Baruch should add the detail **with ink** is not clear, especially as the word occurs only here. Possibly it is an error for a phrase like "on his behalf" or "as much as he would." The fact that this document comes directly from a prophet gives it an authority which otherwise it would not have. But the officials recall the king's character and warn Baruch and Jeremiah to **hide.** The case of Uriah (26:20-23) shows this to be a wise precaution.

36:20-26. *The Palace Reading.* When the officials report to the king, he insists on hearing the scroll read. But the oracles of doom leave him unmoved. Even though two or three of those present risk the royal displeasure by protesting, he shows his disdain by burning the scroll piecemeal.

It is sometimes suggested that the scroll must have been made of papyrus imported from Egypt because the burning of one made of skin would have created a stench. The evidence of the Dead Sea Scrolls suggests that leather was the usual material for the Palestinian scribe. The sheets of a scroll were stuck or stitched together, and Jehoiakim evidently cuts them off one after another. After the last one he orders the arrest of Jeremiah and Baruch, but they have already disappeared. Baruch feels their survival is providential: **the LORD hid them.**

36:27-32. *The New Scroll.* Jeremiah and Baruch use their enforced leisure to prepare a second scroll—the former one with additions. This second scroll is probably the groundwork of 1:1–25:14 (see Introduction). Jeremiah pronounces a curse on Jehoiakim (cf. 22:19), which was not fulfilled (cf. II Kings 24:6). It seems that Baruch was not disturbed by unfulfilled details so long as events bore out the main thrust of his master's prophecy. This he could fully claim.

E. FURTHER EVENTS DURING THE SIEGE (37:1–39:18)

This narrative is concerned with the part played by Jeremiah during the siege. Baruch refers to other matters only as they are necessary to this purpose.

37:1-2. A Recapitulation. This summary clearly indicates that Baruch's book was issued in separate parts. On **Coniah** see above on 22:24-30.

37:3-5. A Royal Plea. Prayer under these circumstances is considered a highly important matter. The **priest** who is "dean" of the temple (cf. 29:25-26; 52:24) and another important courtier seek out Jeremiah and ask him to **pray** for the city. **Jehucal** appears again in a slightly different spelling in 38:1, where he is one of those who take the lead against Jeremiah. The occasion is the brief period during the siege when an Egyptian show of strength temporarily draws off the attacking Babylonian forces. Jeremiah at this time is still at liberty. Up to this point the narrative is not very coherent because Baruch is still linking this particular story with the general course of events.

37:6-10. Consistent Warning. There is general rejoicing at the Babylonian withdrawal but Jeremiah remains unimpressed. He is sure they will return.

37:11-15. Jeremiah's Arrest. Jeremiah is among the refugees who stream out of the city to return to their own homes. Probably he wants to reestablish connection with his family lands. He may have drawn some small income from the land, which enabled him to live in Jerusalem these many years without, so far as we know, secular occupation. After the Babylonian withdrawal there is no doubt a general move against known sympathizers with their cause. Jeremiah is not such a one, but that is what he appears to be. He is arrested, flogged, and imprisoned.

37:16-21. Royal Inquiry Renewed. After some time in the cellars of Jonathan's house Jeremiah is brought out to appear before Zedekiah. The return of the Babylonians and the resumption of the siege make it seem possible that he is right after all. Zedekiah wants to know his version of Yahweh's intentions. Jeremiah gives the answer sternly and uncompromisingly: the Babylonians will take the city. The king is sufficiently impressed to make things a little easier for the prophet. But he does not take his advice and surrender the city.

38:1-6. *Jeremiah in the Pit.* Jeremiah continues to expound his view of the political situation to the anger of the Jewish leaders. In their view he is destroying the morale of their **soldiers,** with whom he is in direct contact in the guardhouse. The king bitterly states his own weakness and his complete loss of control of events. He cannot prevent his courtiers from doing what they want. Yet they are not prepared to execute Jeremiah out of hand. He still seems to have divine protection. They throw him into an old **cistern,** now empty of **water** but feet deep in mud and debris. Jeremiah cannot last long there.

38:7-13. *The Rescue.* An **Ethiopian** slave, **Ebedmelech,** proves indeed a "good Samaritan." Baruch gives us remarkable detail at this point, as if perhaps he was himself involved.

38:14-23. *A Question Repeated.* The king is a pitiable figure, constantly asking for the truth and yet, when he finds it unpalatable, seeking to evade it. Jeremiah has consistently urged **surrender** in the past, and does so now. Even at this time the king can save the **city** from utter destruction and his own miserable **life** if he will surrender to the Babylonians. Otherwise what Jeremiah has already seen in **vision** will become a reality—the harem **women** being **led out** to the conquerors wailing a proverb, "You trusted in false friends." The reference is to Egypt, against whom the prophets have warned for so long (cf. Isaiah 20:1-6; 30:1-7; 31:1-3), and on whom the resistance party still pins its last hopes.

Zedekiah's reply shows how tragic is Judah's position. There are such animosities among the Jews that he fears, not the attacking enemy, but his own people who have gone over to that enemy. Judah is indeed a sick nation.

39:24-28. *A Miserable Subterfuge.* To finish this unhappy scene the king begs his prisoner to tell a lie. Jeremiah agrees to do so. He will not compromise on the divine word, but in lesser matters he is more accommodating.

39:1-10. *The Fall of the City.* After a lengthy siege a **breach** is made in the wall and Jerusalem is taken. The names in verse 3 have become muddled. Probably only two junior generals are intended—**Sarsechim the Rabsaris** (lord high chamberlain?) and **Nergal-sharezer the Rabmag** (head of the cabinet?). It is probable this whole paragraph was adapted from II Kings 25:1-12 by an editor who felt that some account of the fall of Jerusalem should be included. If it is omitted the story of Jeremiah flows smoothly from 38:28 to verse 11.

39:11-14. *Jeremiah's Release.* The Babylonian intelligence has evidently sent back favorable reports on Jeremiah. He appears to them as a sympathizer and a spy on their behalf. They therefore free him from prison and turn him over to the new governor, **Gedaliah** (see below on 40:7-12).

39:15-18. *A Belated Oracle.* Baruch now remembers **Ebed-melech** (cf. 38:7-13). Somewhat belatedly he tells us that Jeremiah sent a message of personal reassurance to his rescuer. Baruch records the same phrase used of himself (45:5; cf. 21:9). He probably intends us to understand that Ebed-melech was also one of those who survived the butchery and the subsequent fire.

F. THE AFTERMATH (40:1–43:44)

40:1-6. *Jeremiah's Decision.* Here is another introduction suggesting a unit designed for independent circulation. It picks up the incident told already in 39:11-14 and retells it in greater detail. At first Jeremiah is included in the group of survivors who are to be marched off to Babylon. He is already at **Ramah,** five miles north of Jerusalem, where the exiles are being gathered. Baruch puts into the mouth of **Nebuzaradan** a remarkably orthodox speech. But the outcome is the same as in the previous chapter. Jeremiah chooses to stay in his beloved homeland. He can tell the exiles in Mesopotamia that Israel's future lies with them (24:4), but he is not himself the stuff of which emigrants are made.

Archaeologists are divided between two proposed locations of

Mizpah, where the new governor has his headquarters. One about two miles north of Ramah is favored by many. But the other, about four miles southwest of Ramah and a mile and a half south of Gibeon, fits the account in 41:10-12 better (see below on 41:11-18).

40:7-12. *Gedaliah's Attempts at Salvage.* The Babylonians decide to incorporate Judah into their imperial system. Gedaliah, a member of a prominent family, is appointed **governor** (see above on 26:20-24). Gedaliah tries to rally the remaining Jews. He succeeds in attracting some who have escaped to other lands to return to Judah.

40:13-16. *Gedaliah's Danger.* In the disorganized country-side there is still much unrest. To some Gedaliah looks simply like a collaborationist. To others—for example, the Ammonite sheikh in the desert—he looks disturbingly like a man who may yet put Judah on its feet again. To yet others he is someone of whom to be jealous. Into this last category falls **Ishmael,** himself a member of the royal house (41:1). **Johanan** warns Gedaliah of his danger, but he misreads the situation and is overconfident.

41:1-3. *The Murder of Gedaliah.* Ishmael kills Gedaliah and many of his supporters, together with the few Babylonian **soldiers** left to represent the imperial power. He also kills a number of **Jews** who have accepted Gedaliah's leadership. **All** in verse 10 is an exaggeration.

41:4-10. *Murder of the Pilgrims.* Whether these men were normally resident in the towns mentioned we do not know. But the time of the feast has arrived and, though the shrine has been destroyed, they value the act of worship so greatly that they undertake the perilous journey. Jeremiah is being proved right. The temple may be destroyed, but the religion of Yahweh goes on.

The disheveled state of dress of these pilgrims and their somewhat pagan demonstration of grief by inflicting on themselves superficial wounds point to their sincerity. Why Ishmael murders them is not clear, unless it is to keep secret his murder of Gedaliah. Yet he spares **ten** who bribe their way to survival.

41:9-10. As a fortress **Mizpah** has a large **cistern** for water supplies in time of siege, which is traced back to the time of **King**

Asa in the ninth century. This serves as a common grave. Ishmael rounds up the rest of the Mizpah community—mostly women, but including Jeremiah, and presumably Baruch—and sets off to hide in the desert among the **Ammonites.** This story surely comes from an eyewitness.

The women and children can be sold as slaves. The **king's daughters** can hardly be daughters of Zedekiah, for the Babylonians would not leave persons so politically valuable behind. Usurpers often legitimatized their claims by marrying into the family they were displacing. Perhaps they are Gedaliah's daughters.

41:11-18. *Johanan's Retaliation.* Ishmael doubtless goes to **Gibeon** for water from the **great pool**—that is, the cistern, which was rediscovered in 1956-57 and excavated. If Mizpah were north of Ramah (see above on 40:1-6) Gibeon would be to the southwest and therefore the opposite direction from Ammon. This account therefore favors the location of Mizpah southwest of Ramah and about a mile and a half south of Gibeon. Johanan's attack frees the captives, though Ishmael and some of his men escape. Johanan and the survivors camp near **Bethlehem.** They know the Babylonians will seek to punish someone for this outrage and fear that they will not be too careful in their choice.

42:1-22. *The Oracle of Jeremiah.* The people are seeking, not Jeremiah's opinion, but a direct communication from Yahweh. **Good or evil** in verse 6 means simply "pleasing or displeasing." The prophets' ecstatic states could not be brought on at will, though they could be encouraged (cf. II Kings 3:15). On this occasion they have to wait **ten days** before Jeremiah can deliver the oracle. In verse 10 **repent of the evil** is a phrase used very much from the sufferer's point of view. Here it implies only that Yahweh's purpose is changing.

As it turned out, **Egypt** was to provide a home for generations of Jews, especially at Alexandria, right on into the second century A.D. Some of the best Jewish literature and the best Jewish scholarship was to come from Egypt—for example, the Septuagint, Wisdom of Solomon, and the writings of Philo. But Jeremiah and Baruch can see no good thing in Egypt. At the end of the chapter Baruch allows his knowledge of subsequent events to appear in the oracle. The people are scolded for a choice they have not yet made.

43:1-7. *Counsel Refused.* The refugees do not trust Jeremiah's advice. They say that it is colored by his own prejudices and those of Baruch. This last addition (verse 3) suggests that **Baruch** had more influence with the prophet than the rest of the book would lead us to believe. Jeremiah and Baruch apparently have no choice but to go along with the general decision. **Tahpanhes** was the first town in Egypt which a refugee from Palestine would reach.

43:8-13. *Babylonian Conquest Foretold.* Probably **Pharaoh's palace** means simply a government building rather than a royal residence. The symbolic act of hiding the stones **in the mortar in the pavement** may have taken place in the roadway outside. A little knot of people busy with a small hole would not arouse much curiosity.

The oracle, if understood by the Egyptians, would most certainly interest them. The Hebrew text of verse 12c reads: "He shall array himself with the land of Egypt as a shepherd putteth on his garment" (King James Version), which suggests Nebuchadrezzar carelessly walking off with the country's wealth. The Revised Standard Version, following the Septuagint, has a grimmer thought. As a **shepherd** periodically delouses his **cloak,** so Nebuchadrezzar will systematically eradicate all life from Egypt. Nebuchadrezzar may have raided Egypt—an inscription claims a victory over Pharaoh Amasis in his thirty-seventh year—but there was never any such sweeping conquest as Jeremiah foretells. **Heliopolis** was a center of worship of the sun god.

G. Ministry in Egypt (44:1-30)

In this narrative Baruch gives an account of Jeremiah's general message during his Egyptian exile. One particular incident is given wherein he clashes with his fellow refugees.

44:1-14. *Appeal and Warning.* Jeremiah has settled in

Tahpanhes on the frontier (43:7). **Migdol** was fairly close by. **Memphis** was the ancient capital of Lower Egypt and **Pathros** was an old name for Upper Egypt. The Jews were already widely dispersed. Verses 2-10 are an appeal to learn the lesson of their experience. Verses 11-14 warn that if they are disloyal to Yahweh in Egypt as they were in Palestine, the same punishment will befall them.

44:15-19. *A Different Reading.* In verse 15 **Pathros** should be omitted as a gloss. The disloyal Jews to whom Jeremiah is talking here have observed the same events as he has. But they draw very different conclusions. As they see it, during Manasseh's reign their **fathers** worshiped the **queen of heaven** and all went well with them. Then Jeremiah and his friends carried through the Deuteronomic reformation, and since then nothing has gone right. Thus they are now returning to Asherah-Ashtarath, the Great Mother (see 7:16-20)—and all will be well.

It was a justifiable interpretation of the facts, and yet those who accepted it had no future. The future lay, as events have shown, with the prophetic interpretation of Israel's history. Therein was Jeremiah's genuine inspiration from God.

44:20-30. *Reiterated Warning.* Jeremiah repeats his warning at length. He ends by declaring that punishment will befall **Pharaoh Hophra.** His eyes then are not on distant centuries, but on the immediate future. Hophra was in fact dethroned and murdered—but as a result of internal rebellion, not foreign invasion.

H. Consolation to Baruch (45:1-5)

Baruch has so far remained very much in the background. Here he allows himself to take a small bow at the close. The oracle to Baruch is sometimes read as a rebuke to him, but it is a sincerely meant "well done, thou good and faithful servant." In the general disaster he cannot help being involved, but at least his own **life** will be preserved as a **prize of war,** something snatched thankfully out of the conflict. Baruch introduces the oracle here simply to say: "This is who I am, and this is what authenticates for you the foregoing manuscript." He leaves us with the impression that he is a very modest, a very reliable, and indeed a very remarkable person.

III. ORACLES AGAINST THE NATIONS (46:1–51:64)

One of the subjects of a prophetic ministry was Yahweh's judgment on foreign **nations.** This was especially true of Jeremiah (1:10). Often the disciples of a prophet gathered together the things he had said about other peoples, and such collections now appear in various places in the prophetic anthologies—for example, Isaiah 13–23. In Jeremiah the collection is found here in the Hebrew text. It comes after 25:13 in the Septuagint, which also has the contents in a different order.

A. CONCERNING EGYPT (46:2-28)

46:2-12. *The Battle of Carchemish.* The introduction is in verse 2. Then we have two pieces (verses 3-6 and 7-12) which relate to the battle between the forces of Egypt, pushing north in an attempt to gain Syria-Palestine, and those of the Babylonians, pushing south in an attempt to overrun all the western provinces of the former Assyrian Empire.

46:2. The two armies met at **Carchemish** on the upper **Euphrates.** Jeremiah consistently sees **Nebuchadrezzar** as the instrument of Yahweh's purpose. Babylonian records show that the battle occurred in the summer of 605. The dating **in the fourth year of Jehoiakim** is correct only if his regnal years are counted from a spring new year (see above on 25:1-10; 28:17; and 36:1-32). However, this verse may well have been inserted by an editor at a time when the Babylonian calendar was universally observed.

46:3-6. This first piece is decidedly satirical. It describes the

Egyptians' careful preparation for the battle as if these are the actions of determined men, ready to do or die. But what's this? They're running away! The moment of revelation comes in the line **terror on every side!** The panic is supernaturally inspired. The Egyptians discover that they are fighting, not against men, but against Yahweh.

46:7-9. Similarly these verses picture the Egyptian army rising as irresistibly as the **Nile** and spreading relentlessly over the land. The **warriors** of verse 9 may be mercenaries (cf. verse 21; on **Put** and **Lud** see comment on Isaiah 66:18-23). Again there is the moment of dreadful revelation (verse 10). The Egyptians discover that the purpose of Yahweh is to hold a holocaust **in the north country** and that they are the destined victims.

46:11-12. The tone changes to that of a taunt song: **Go up to Gilead** and see if you can get anything to cure a wound such as this! On Gilead's medical reputation see above on 8:22–9:1.

Whether Jeremiah produced these pieces before or after the battle, they are by way of comment on current affairs. Their effect is to warn Judah against throwing in its lot with Egypt.

46:13-26. *Conquest Foretold.* Here there are five separate pieces with a common theme. They have often been assumed to come from the period immediately following Nebuchadrezzar's victory at Carchemish. However, the time of Jeremiah's final years in Egypt seems more likely (cf. chapters 43–44).

46:14-17. The eastern border towns, and even **Memphis,** the capital, are warned to **stand ready** for attack. **Apis** was the **bull** worshiped at Memphis as a reincarnation of the god Ptah, later called Osiris. The question is, "Why did your god flee and leave you defenseless?" The answer is, "because Yahweh butted him"—the word is used in Ezekiel 34:21 of animals shoving weaker ones aside.

Verse 16 may refer to deserting mercenaries (cf. verses 9, 21), or it may refer to Jewish refugees. If the latter, Jeremiah's point is to say to the Jews that Egypt will be overrun. In dismay they will ask why they ever went there for protection (see above on 42:1-22; 43:8-13). He finishes with an accusation against

Pharaoh as the braggart who never acts. Possibly this involves a word play which can no longer be recognized.

46:18-19. Egypt is warned that "a mountain of a man" will invade it and it must get ready **for exile.** But the oracle is of course really directed to Jews—either the pro-Egyptian party in Jerusalem or, more probably, the exiles who fled to Egypt with Jeremiah. This is seen by the comparison with **Tabor** and **Carmel,** mountains in northern Palestine which would mean nothing to the Egyptians.

46:20-21. Egypt's coming distress is foretold. The **beautiful heifer** will run amok, tormented by a **gadfly from the north**—that is, Nebuchadrezzar. **Her hired soldiers** (cf. verse 9), on the other hand, will become as docile as **fatted calves.**

46:22-24. Egypt is pictured as slithering away like a snake through the riverside scrub. Its attackers are like the peasants who swarm to cut the brush down and so deprive it of its last hiding place. Again the enemy is **from the north.**

46:25-26. The theme is repeated in plainest terms in prose. **Thebes** was the chief center of worship of the god **Amon.** The closing promise of restoration is probably a later insertion by a Jew living in Egypt and concerned for its welfare.

46:27-28. *Editorial Addition.* An editor, wanting to round off this Egypt collection, found a small, reassuring piece in the style of Second Isaiah and added it here. It has been used for the same purpose in 30:10-11 (see comment).

B. CONCERNING PHILISTIA (47:1-7)

This oracle envisages the destruction of the coastal cities of Palestine, both Phoenician (verse 4c) and Philistine. Since the **waters are rising out of the north** the oracle is clearly connected with the foe-from-the-north oracles of 4:5–6:30 and dates from the same general period of Josiah's reign. It is part of the general warning to Judah to repent before the disaster falls. However, an editor knew that Philistia succumbed first, not to the Babylonians, but to the Egyptians when Pharaoh Neco captured

Gaza on his return from his northern march in 609. This editor has added an introduction erroneously linking the oracle to the Egyptian attack (verse 1).

47:4-7. The **Philistines** were remnants of the old Aegean civilization which was dominated by **Caphtor,** or Crete. They were also said to be the descendants by intermarriage of the **Anakim,** the legendary mighty men of pre-Hebrew Palestine. Both references emphasize the present disaster by contrasting it with past glories. **Tyre and Sidon,** Phoenician cities, are considered along with Philistine **Gaza** and **Ashkelon** because they are coastal cities lying in the path of a northern invader. How can Yahweh's **sword** hold back when Yahweh has given it a commission against all the **seacoast?**

C. CONCERNING MOAB (48:1-47)

Here are some twelve pieces concerned with Moab. Probably the first two (verses 1*b*-2 and 3-8) and possibly the third (verse 9) are Jeremiah's own work. They envisage Moab as invaded and exhort it to **flee.** This is in line with Jeremiah's general message that Palestine will be overrun by the foe from the north, and that all the little kingdoms must be warned beforehand in order that at least the Jews will know that it is Yahweh's doing.

The other pieces reflect the age-old rivalry of Israel and Moab. They are jingoistic saber-rattlings in which Moab is told that Yahweh is now going to punish it so that it will never recover. These pieces rely heavily on two literary forms, the lament and the taunt song.

In the lament the prophet foresees the death of the enemy by uttering a dirge over it as already dead. He expresses himself as if the enemy's downfall has broken his heart, though in reality he will rejoice over it. This air of authenticity gives his writing the power to unnerve the enemy and convince him of defeat before the battle begins. In the taunt song the psychology is less complicated. The prophet simply hurls taunts at his enemy and exults over his downfall.

A marked characteristic in both these forms is the use of geographical names to achieve parellelism and poetic intensity. Some place names in this passage are known from other contexts, but some are now unidentifiable. Some of these oracles make puns on the place names, and some of the phrases were in fairly common use and occur elsewhere in similar collections (cf. verses 4-5 with Isaiah 15:5).

48:1*b*-2. *Moab Silenced.* The names **Nebo . . . Kiriathaim . . . Heshbon** refer to known Moabite towns. **Madmen** may be a name distorted to make a pun. The victim of the planning in verse 2 is presumably Israel. Jeremiah is saying that the forthcoming destruction of Moab is only, after all, poetic justice.

48:3-8. *Moab's Destruction.* This oracle has suffered in transmission (see the Revised Standard Version footnotes) but the Revised Standard Version is probably not far from the original intent. The three places named were probably all near the southern end of the Dead Sea; on **Zoar** cf. Genesis 19:20-22. The **wild ass** typifies the unapproachable desert dweller. **Chemosh,** the national god of Moab, must bow to Yahweh's plan for history. The implied monotheism is getting to be almost explicit.

48:9. *A Fragment.* This verse is a victory chant to be sung over and over again by the girls who greet the returning Hebrew warriors as they enter the city with their booty (cf. Exodus 15:20-21; I Samuel 18:6).

48:10. *A Slogan.* This is probably a recruiting slogan, brought out every time a raid on Moab was planned.

48:11-13. *The Decanting of Moab.* This jingoistic piece is redeemed only by the interesting metaphor. Moab's time for being poured **from vessel to vessel** has come, and indeed his very **jars** will be broken. It is also interesting to see that the worship of Yahweh at **Bethel** (cf. I Kings 12:26-33) is considered as pagan and false as the worship of **Chemosh.**

48:14-20. *The Destroyer of Moab.* Here are two pieces—verses 14-17 and 18-20—which "lament" the approaching downfall of Moab. **Dibon** and **Aroer** were Moabite cities near the **Arnon** River.

48:21-27. *Recital of Cities.* This list of cities aims to say that all
Moab will be destroyed. Most of the places are unknown. On
the image of drunkenness see above on 13:12-14. Verse 27
means "Did you deride Israel, as helpless as one who has fallen
into the hands of bandits? But now it is your turn to be derided."
Wagged your head was a sign of scorn.

48:28-33. *Shouts of Mourning.* Isaiah 15:4, 8-10 uses many of
these same phrases. **Kir-heres** is a variant of Kir-hareseth (cf. II
Kings 3:25-27). **Sibmah**, between Nebo and Heshbon, was in a
vine-growing area. **Jazer** was in Ammonite territory north of
Moab. It may have been a center for the Tammuz cult, in which
weeping for the dead god was a prominent feature. The author
declares that the weeping for Sibmah will exceed even that at
Jazer (verse 32*ab*). The original text of verse 32*d* may have read
simply "reached as far as the sea (see the Revised Standard
Version footnote). If so, the meaning may be that Sibmah's wine
crosses the Dead Sea (verse 32*c*) and even has markets on the
Mediterranean Sea.

48:34-39. *Lament for Moab.* The places named in verse 34 are
at the northern and southern borders of Moab. Discovery of
what is believed to be a mouthpiece of the musical instrument
translated **flute** indicates that it was actually a primitive clarinet.
Its reed tone would be especially suited to mourning. Verses
37-38 give a vivid picture of an ancient Near Eastern population
at a time of public lament. Cf. Isaiah 15:2-3.

48:40-44. *Threefold Terror.* With verses 40-41 cf. 49:22. The
image of the triple peril in verses 43-44 occurs in Amos 5:19-20
and even more closely in Isaiah 24:17-18.

48:45-47. *Woe and Hope for Moab.* Verses 45-46 are very
much what we have now become accustomed to. Verse 47*ab* is
something new. When the golden age comes, Moab will be
there, like Israel, chastened and pardoned. This promise and
those in 49:6, 39 suggest that an editor has worked through the
collection marking those nations who may be restored. Such
promises do much to redeem otherwise unattractive material.
Verse 47*c* comes from the compiler of the little collection.

D. CONCERNING AMMON (49:1-6)

Ammon was a seminomadic people on Israel's eastern border, where the high plateau of Transjordan slopes gently into the Arabian Desert. The first piece (verses 1-2) comments that the Gadites have lost their territory, but even so there are other Israelite tribes ready to inherit it. **Milcom,** the Ammonite god, has certainly no right to possess it. **Rabbah,** modern Amman, was the Ammonite capital. In verses 3-5 we have the lament-style invective using stock phrases (cf. verse 3*ef* with 48:7*cd*). On verse 6 see above on 48:45-47.

E. CONCERNING EDOM (49:7-22)

This is a literary unit put together out of a number of oral pieces. After the fall of Jerusalem in 586 the Edomites looted Judah. Thus they became the most hated of all Israel's neighbors. Much of what is here is not Jeremiah's and reflects this later feeling.

49:7-11. *Edom Stripped Bare.* The inquiry as to whether Edom has run out of wise advice, for which it earlier had a reputation, is sarcastic. Eliphaz the friend of Job came from **Teman,** a city and district of Edom. **Dedan** was an Arab people living southeast of Edom. Beginning in the sixth century invasions by Arab tribes drove the Edomites out of their homeland and into southern Judah. The reference here may be to a colony of Dedanites already settled in Edom. **Esau** was considered the ancestor of the Edomites (cf. Genesis 36). Verse 11 is probably more ironical than kindly.

49:12-13. *Yahweh's Cup.* The metaphor is Jeremiah's (cf. 25:15-29). But the suggestion that guilty Edom should be made to **drink** because guiltless Israel has been forced to is foreign to his thought. **Bozrah** was one of the most important of the Edomite cities.

49:14-16. *Mountain Heights No Refuge.* Edom was noted for its cliffs, its rock dwellings, and its mountain forts. But even though its refuge is built as high as an **eagle's** nest, Yahweh will bring it down. **Rock,** Hebrew *sela,* may allude to the Edomite cliff fortress Sela (cf. II Kings 14:7).

49:17-22. *Edom a Horror.* Edom will become a complete ruin like **Sodom and Gomorrah** (cf. Genesis 19:24-25). Passers-by will **hiss,** the biblical gesture of astonishment. Verses 19-21 are used again in 50:44-46. Verse 22 uses phrases from 48:40 and is reminiscent of 30:6. It is significant that there is no prophecy that Edom will ever be restored (see above on 48:45-47).

F. Concerning Damascus (49:23-27)

The sentiments and often the phrases are like those we have several times encountered. **Hamath and Arpad** were two towns well to the north of the city. If they have fallen there is nothing left to protect Damascus from a northern enemy. Verse 26 is repeated in 50:30. Verse 27 is adapted from Amos 1:4.

G. Concerning Kedar (49:28-33)

Hazor was a center for the nomadic or semi-nomadic Arabian tribes known rather vaguely as **Kedar,** the "dwellers in black tents" (cf. Song of Solomon 1:5). It is not the famous Hazor of northern Galilee but probably an unidentified settlement east of Palestine. There are two pieces here—verses 28-30 and 31-33. Both are probably from Jeremiah. The oracles further emphasize the futility of Judah's attempting to resist the Babylonian manifest destiny. The nomads were especially known by, and despised for, their tonsorial habits (cf. 9:26; Leviticus 19:27).

H. Concerning Elam (49:34-39)

Elam was renowned for its archers (cf. Isaiah 22:6). The Elamites were a people to the east of Mesopotamia. Probably they were first known to the Judeans as part of Nebuchadrezzar's forces in 597, the time of the first deportation. Thus the oracle is probably correctly dated (on **beginning of the reign** see above on 26:1-24). It could come from Jeremiah—though why he should have singled out the Elamites from the rest of the Babylonian soldiery is not clear. To set up one's **throne** in a territory is formally to annex it (cf. 1:15; 43:10). A comment adds that after the day of Yahweh the Elamites will be restored to their former affluence (see above on 48:45-47).

I. CONCERNING BABYLON (50:1–51:64)

The oracles devoted to Babylon display a bitter animosity toward that city which is not characteristic of Jeremiah. They rejoice in the fall of Babylon as something which is soon to take place. They borrow pieces from other collections, adapting them perfunctorily to Babylon. This collection was probably compiled during the Exile since it predicts the violent destruction of Babylon. Actually its fall to the Persian Cyrus in 539 occurred without a battle and with no damage to the city.

50:2-5. *Bel Dismayed.* The original saying is in verse 2 and comments on the falsity of Mesopotamian religion as revealed by the fall of Babylon. To this verse 3, with the characteristic phrase **out of the north**, has been attached to make it conformable to Jeremiah's teaching. **Bel** and **Merodach,** or Marduk, were alternate names of the great Babylonian deity. Verses 4-5 depict the national repentance for which the compiler fervently longed.

50:6-7. *Israel's Plight.* The theological interpretation of the fall of Jerusalem as due to sin saved Israel's faith in God and its own future. But it deprived Israel, at least in part, of the opportunity to blame its enemies. This thought is used here to underline Israel's plight—its enemies can destroy it and justify their actions. We can detect an unspoken indignation: "This is not just!"

50:8-10. *Flight from Babylon.* As the threat to Babylon grows more ominous, a Jewish prophet calls on his people to flee from the doomed nation.

50:11-16. *Yahweh's Vengeance.* Though Babylon is the instrument of Yahweh's anger, nevertheless in due time God will punish it for its arrogance. Cf. Isaiah 10:5-12. That time has now come, and a Jewish prophet rejoices in the thought.

50:17-20. *Israel's Story.* This remarkable little piece puts the whole biblical interpretation of Israel's history in four verses. But before the blessed golden age should come, many more conquerors and epochs were to intervene. Prophets always tend to foreshorten their perspectives. The places named in verse 19 were all in the territory of the former northern kingdom.

50:21-27. *Invitation to Plunder.* A prophet in Yahweh's name invites all who will to join in the plundering of Babylon, who richly deserves what it will get. **Merathaim,** which means "double rebellion" in Hebrew, is a word play on a name for southern Babylonia. **Pekod,** Hebrew for "punishment," is a similar word play on the name of an eastern Babylonian tribe. "Double rebellion" will get its deserts and "Punishment" will live up to its name.

50:28. *Jewish Escape.* A prophet envisages the exiles set free at last, getting back to **Zion** to announce that Yahweh has exacted **vengeance** on the Babylonians for the destruction of **his temple.**

50:29-30. *Further Invitation.* Yahweh is thought of as inviting Babylon's enemies to attack it. Verse 30 repeats 49:26.

50:31-32. *Day of Reckoning.* Yahweh announces that Babylon's **time** of punishment has come.

50:33-34. *Israel's Redeemer.* Because Yahweh is **strong,** the present situation will be reversed—**rest** for Israel, but **unrest** for Babylon.

50:35-38. *Incantation.* Its literary quality lifts this example of solemn cursing out of the secondariness of this chapter. The sentiment may be regrettable but the style is splendid—especially in the last scornful phrase.

50:39-46. *Borrowed Pieces.* Verse 39 is composed of stock phrases (cf. Isaiah 13:19-20). Verse 40 repeats 49:18. Verses

41-43 are taken from 6:22-24, except that the original "O daughter of Zion" has been altered to **O daughter of Babylon.** Verses 44-46 are applied to Edom in 49:19-21.

51:1-5. *Chaldea's Guilt.* This is probably typical of the oracles which circulated widely among the exiles as the Persian threat to Babylon grew more ominous. It is characterized by a spirit of revenge toward Babylon and of reassurance to Israel. **Chaldea** is written in the athbash cipher (see above on 25:17-26) as LBQMY (see the Revised Standard Version footnote) for KSDYM, Chasdim, Hebrew name for the Chaldeans. But since **Babylon** is written plain the use of the cipher is just an affectation.

51:6-10. *Flight from Babylon.* Here is another oracle reflecting the growing threat to Babylon. On verse 7 cf. 25:15-29. Verse 8 adopts the lament technique for gloating over a foe (see above on 48:1-47). Verse 9 with hypocrisy says that the speakers wanted to heal Babylon but its wound was too grievous (cf. the same gibe at Egypt, 46:11). The note of patriotic reassurance comes in at the end.

51:11-14. *A Siege of Babylon.* This is another oracle from the period of Babylonian decline. The **Medes** to the northeast presented the first threat to the Babylonian Empire. They became part of the Medo-Persian coalition headed by Cyrus which was eventually to bring Babylon down.

51:15-19. *The Creator.* Here is a very different type of production. These verses are quoted from 10:12-16 (for their relation to Psalm 135 see comment on 10:1-16). In this context they have a particular significance. Vengeance and patriotism have been left far behind, and the question is the contrast between the Hebrew concept of God the Creator and the Mesopotamian notion of an image. The dignity of Israel as the people of God is expressed at the close—a very different sentiment from the rather tawdry chauvinism of the earlier pieces.

51:20-23. *The Hammer of Yahweh.* This is in the style of 50:35-38, though the repetitions are considerably less effective. The question is, who is being addressed? Formally it is no doubt Cyrus (cf. Isaiah 45:1-7). But the real audience is the exiled

Jews, who are being encouraged by the news that Cyrus will **break** Babylon and free them from oppression.

51:24-26. *The Burnt Mountain.* These assorted threats against Babylon reflect the years prior to Cyrus' capture of the city. **Destroying mountain** for the flat plain of Babylon refers probably to the city's artificial religious mountain, the ziggurat, a huge many-storied temple. In the future it will be known as **burnt mountain** because of the fierce fire which will pass over it.

Babylon is not even to be a source of reusable building materials. This very ancient practice was deprecated by Kheti III of Egypt as early as 2070 B.C., and is deplored to this day by archaeologists. It is still current in lands where building materials are scarce.

51:27-33. *Babylon Ripe for Harvest.* **Ararat** was roughly modern Armenia. The **Minni** were a people living south of Lake Urmiah on the borders of Media. **Ashkenaz** probably refers to a Scythian tribe. The Jews of the Middle Ages identified Ashkenaz with Germany; hence today Central European Jews are Ashkenazim whereas Spanish Jews are Sephardim.

The oracle pictures the Babylonian soldiery as completely unnerved, while the **king** receives one message after another telling of positions lost, **fords . . . seized,** and **bulwarks . . . burned.** Though this oracle is unfulfilled, since Babylon fell without a fight, it is a fine piece of imaginative composition.

51:34-37. *Yahweh's Vengeance.* Jerusalem pleads its plight before Yahweh, pointing out what Babylon has done to it. Yahweh promises vengeance.

51:38-44. *Babylon's Overthrow.* Though the Babylonian soldiers **roar . . . like lions,** Yahweh will send a drunken stupor on them, so that they will be led **like lambs to the slaughter.** Babylon will thus be captured, engulfed by the **sea,** and left an utter **desert.** The prophet is mixing his images somewhat violently, but his purpose is to say that the forces of nature will also be ranged against the city.

The sea is a constant image of the forces of evil in the Old Testament. It is an echo of the myth in which the Creator battled with the primeval sea monster of chaos. **Bel,** the great god of

Mesopotamia, here represents Babylon. He will be forced to disgorge **what he has swallowed**—that is, Israel. Babylon in verse 41a is again written in athbash cipher (see above on 25:17-26).

51:45-46. *A Warning.* This is a warning to the Jews to get out of doomed Babylon while they can.

51:47-53. *Judgment on Images.* The downfall of Babylon is prophesied. It is to pay for Israel's dead, as multitudes have died for Babylon. The exiles are to recall Jerusalem (cf. Psalm 137:5-6). They are to rejoice that the evil powers which the images of Babylon represent are to be overthrown.

51:54-57. *Destruction of Babylon.* The attacking army is again likened to the sea. The metaphor of divinely inspired drunkenness is also employed (cf. 25:15-29).

51:58. *Summary.* This little oracle sums up all that has gone before. The last two lines occur again in Habakkuk 2:13 and probably were fairly common currency. The meaning is that all the effort which has gone into building Babylon has only been preparing what is to go up in flames.

51:59-64. *Symbolic Action.* It is unlikely that this is a historical incident, yet it is an action which Jeremiah might well have conceived. All the foregoing words, 50:1–51:58, are to be written down—an instruction which shows incidentally that written collections of prophetic words were being made at this time. **Seraiah** is to remind Yahweh of the divine determination to destroy Babylon and then cast the weighted scroll into the **Euphrates.** Its sinking will symbolize the sinking of Babylon. This is a good instance of an acted oracle (see above on 13:1-11).

We have no other evidence that **Zedekiah** made such a journey in his **fourth year**—that is, 594/93—but there is nothing improbable in the idea. But the strong anti-Babylonian sentiments of chapters 50–51 are not characteristic of Jeremiah. It is unlikely that he would have set in motion the symbolic actions here narrated. The story probably grew up among the Jews of the Exile who hated their Babylonian masters. In verse 64b the editor of this little collection marks its end.

IV. HISTORICAL APPENDIX (52:1-34)

A final editor wanted to give the whole Jeremiah complex a suitable historical reference. He therefore took from the great "History of the Kingdoms" the portion which told of Zedekiah's reign, the capture of Jerusalem, the destruction of the temple, and the deportation of the Jewish population (II Kings 24:18–25:30). Because the story of Gedaliah is told at length by Baruch in 40:1-16, however, he omitted the shorter account of it found in II Kings 25:22-26. The fact that certain details appearing in verses 10-11 and 18-23 are omitted from II Kings is probably to be explained by later editing of II Kings. The **tenth day of the month** (verse 12) is given as the seventh day in II Kings 25:8. There is no way to tell which is correct.

52:28-30. *Statistics of the Captivity.* These verses do not appear in the Septuagint. They come not from II Kings but from an entirely different source, perhaps a Babylonian record. The date in Nebuchadrezzar's **seventh year** is borne out by the Babylonian Chronicle, which records that he captured Jerusalem on the second of Adar—that is, the twelfth month—of his seventh year (March 16, 597).

The date of the second deportation, the **eighteenth year,** in verse 29 conflicts with the **nineteenth year** in verse 12 (cf. II Kings 25:8). No satisfactory explanation for the discrepancy has been found. Verse 29 presents a chief reason that many scholars date the destruction of Jerusalem 587 rather than 586. The **twenty-third year** (582/81, verse 30) probably refers to the time of the troubles following Gedaliah's assassination.

The figures for the number of captives are so sober that they sound genuine. What then became of the rest of the population? The answer is that most of them were the **poorest of the land** (verse 16). They were left to till their little plots and struggle as best they could. Many chose to emigrate—to Egypt and other nearby lands or to Mesopotamia as voluntary exiles. The idea of forced mass deportation is historically as well as practically unsound.

52:31-34. *A Concluding Hopeful Note.* The value of the

appendix was not only that it substantiated the main thrust of Jeremiah's interpretation of Judah's situation. It also allowed the book to end, as all scripture must, on a positive and hopeful note. These last verses record how, even in Jehoiachin's lifetime, the tide began to turn. The changed political situation after the death of Nebuchadrezzar in 562, when Babylon began to feel the need of friends, saw Jehoiachin's status transformed the following year from that of prisoner to royal guest. This was the first faint light of dawn. Sunrise was to be delayed twenty-three years. But in 538 a return to Jerusalem was to be permitted, and after another twenty-three years the temple would stand once more as the house of God.

THE BOOK OF LAMENTATIONS

Harvey H. Guthrie, Jr.

INTRODUCTION

Name and Place in the Bible

In the Hebrew Bible the book of Lamentations takes its name from its opening word, **How**—the characteristic beginning of a funeral dirge. The rabbinic tradition designates it "Lamentations," and this title is used in the Greek Septuagint, Latin, and English. In the Hebrew canon Lamentations is included in the Writings—one of the major divisions along with the Law and the Prophets. It is read in the synagogue on the ninth of Ab (July-August), the day on which the destruction of the temple in A.D. 70 is bewailed. The Septuagint is responsible for Lamentations's position after Jeremiah in the Christian canon. The rationale for this move was provided by the tradition that it was written by Jeremiah (see below).

Form

The book consists of five poems, each of which constitutes a chapter. The first four are acrostics, whose twenty-two short stanzas begin successively with the letters of the Hebrew alphabet in order. There are two exceptions. In chapter 3 each couplet within a stanza begins with that stanza's letter. And in chapters 2–4 for some unknown reason the order of the letters *ayin* and *pe* is reversed.

Although chapter 5 is not an acrostic, it conforms to the pattern by consisting of twenty-two couplets. The purpose of the acrostic form may be to provide a memory aid as well as to achieve completeness by running the course of the entire alphabet.

The poems employ literary forms known elsewhere in the Old Testament as well as in the ancient Near Eastern culture of which Israel was a part. Chapters 1, 2, and 4 are basically funeral dirges. Chapter 3 is an individual lament, combined with expressions of thanksgiving and trust. Chapter 5 is a communal lament.

Origin

The poems are all concerned with what happened to Jerusalem and Judah in the Babylonian invasions of the early sixth century B.C. A misreading of II Chronicles 35:25 and the Septuagint preface to Lamentations are the basis of the very ancient tradition that the author of the poems was Jeremiah. There is no concrete evidence for the validity of this tradition. The Hebrew canon (see above) does not associate the book with the prophet.

The consensus of scholarly opinion is that the poems originated in Palestine among those remaining after Jerusalem's fall in 586 B.C. Some have held chapters 3 and 5 to be much later than the other poems, but the present tendency is to doubt this. Indeed, the order of the poems may reflect the order of their composition. Chapter 1 may possibly have originated after the first Babylonian siege of 597. Chapter 5 may have come from a time somewhat removed from the disaster of 586.

The poems may very well come from one author, although there is no way of knowing. They certainly were written on different occasions. Some think that they were used in cultic rites on an annual day of mourning over the destruction of Jerusalem and the temple.

Significance

Lamentations is an eloquent statement of Israel's response to its downfall. This response includes the prophetic insistence that God's purpose is the ultimate source of meaning for that disaster just as it was for Israel's origins. Chapter 3 explicitly seeks to invest catastrophe with meaning, and prefigures the servant songs in Isaiah 40–55. Thus the book has had significance for Christians as well as Jews. Traditionally it is used in many churches during Holy Week.

I. A LONELY CITY (1:1-22)

Hermann Gunkel, whose work on Hebrew poetry was epochal, characterized this poem, and those in chapters 2 and 4, as "political funeral dirge." This is a form for mourning used to bewail Jerusalem's fall. While the poet may not be strictly bound by forms (the latter part of this poem is individual lament), this points to something important.

In Lamentations, as in other Hebrew poetry, modern questions of authorship and of the individual experience of the poet can miss the point. Israel's poetry is based on forms arising out of the life of a worshiping community. This is more important for an understanding of that poetry than modern conjecture about the poet's sentiments. So here ancient forms are used to express a people's reaction to the fall of their holy city, the place that had signified the presence of their God.

1:1-11. *Jerusalem's Widowhood Described.* **How** is a formal characteristic of the funeral dirge (cf. 2:1; 4:1, 2; Isaiah 1:21; Jeremiah 48:17). Jerusalem is pictured as a widow with no companion to accompany her, as was the custom, in her lament over her loss. This uncomforted aloneness is a theme of chapter 1 (cf. verses 9, 16, 17, 21). It is theologically important. The real situation of Jerusalem is thoroughly faced, and this must come before anything else.

1:3. The reference could be to the deportation of the people in 597 or of 586. **Resting place** denotes Yahweh's gift to Israel of the land that was the sign of divine presence. **Her distress** can also be translated "her narrow defiles."

1:4. The reference is to the end of the worship of Yahweh. **Maidens** in this context refers to cultic functionaries (cf. Psalm 68:25; Jeremiah 31:13).

1:5-7. The funeral dirge here gives way to an element common in laments over individual distress—concentration on **enemies.** Verse 5 implies a question of whether the gods of the enemies may have prevailed, but then goes on to make the point of the classic prophets. It is precisely the sovereignty of Israel's righteous God that has brought it disaster. Verse 6 refers to Jerusalem's rulers, Yahweh's surrogates. It expresses the problem posed for a faith such as Israel's, based on concrete events and situations, by the catastrophe of 597-586. Verse 7 has too many lines. Either the second or third couplet must be an addition.

1:8-9. The terms here are reminiscent of Hosea, Jeremiah, and Ezekiel. They express the prophetic interpretation of Jerusalem's fall. Verse 9c is a lament cry, presupposing that God's reputation is bound up with the fortunes of the people.

1:10-11 carries out the theme of the last lines of verse 9. Since the talk is not of the actual destruction of the temple, some cite these verses as evidence that chapter 1 comes from the period between 597 and 586.

1:12-16. *Jerusalem's First Lament.* The viewpoint changes from a lament *over* Zion to a lament *by* Zion. This could indicate that the poem had a cultic usage with different voices taking different parts. **Is it nothing to you** is only a guess at what an obscure text means. One scholar translates, "Now then!"

Verses 12-16 explicitly state that Yahweh is responsible for Jerusalem's affliction. Verse 12 calls the world outside Israel to look upon this as a manifestation of Yahweh's righteous sovereignty. Verse 13a then uses language traditionally associated with a deity's visit to earth to picture Yahweh's activity in Jerusalem's fall. The picture of the hunter (verse 13b) is often used of enemies, and thus is a strong one to use of Israel's God.

1:14 indicates once again that lamenting Israel has understood the prophetic message.

1:15 contains two colorful pictures—Yahweh commanding the forces that ruin Jerusalem's finest men and Yahweh treading on Jerusalem as in a winepress (cf. Isaiah 63:1; Joel 3:13). **Assembly** has sacral overtones, and may imply more than earthly powers.

1:16 with its picture of weeping Zion reverts to the theme of there being no comforter for her.

1:17-22. *Jerusalem's Second Lament.* Verse 17 is a transition, taking up themes present in the earlier stanzas.

1:18-20 begins like Jeremiah 12:1. There the words may be sarcastic, but not here. Underlying them may be a custom seen in Joshua 7:19-21. According to this, one in the wrong praised the righteousness of God. At any rate, the lament of Jerusalem, unlike other laments from the same culture, locates its problem in the facts of divine righteousness and human sin. The prophetic lesson has been learned. Verses 19-20 recount, as laments always do, the items in the distress.

1:21-22 closes the poem on a note hard for modern readers to understand—calling down evil upon one's enemies. Two things lie behind this recurrent element in laments: the empirical, this-worldly theology of Israel and its conviction of the involvement of God's own reputation in the fortunes of the people.

II. THE LORD HAS DESTROYED (2:1-22)

Like the first poem, this is based on a funeral dirge, with the characteristic **How** at its beginning. However, attention here is focused on the terrible wrath of God manifested in the catastrophe which has overtaken Jerusalem. The poem falls into two parts—the poet's own lament in verses 1-19 and a lament by Jerusalem itself in verses 20-22. The description of what has happened is so vivid that many have taken this poem to be an eyewitness account of the destruction wrought in Jerusalem by the Babylonians in 586. Some hold that transitions such as those at verses 11 and 18-20 are due to liturgical use of the poem.

2:1-19. *The Poet's Lament.* The theme of the poem is set down in verse 1. The cloud imagery comes from the cult, and is connected with manifestations of deity. It turns a lament into a hymn celebrating God's sacral act, now an act of wrath in which the previous blessing of Zion is reversed. The holy city's divine election holds even in its sin. It remains a witness to the righteousness of God which now manifests itself as wrath. Thus what might merit sheer wailing is here celebrated in hymnic language. Again the prophetic interpretation of Jerusalem's fall has been understood.

Couplet 1*b* applies an astral image, used elsewhere of foreign rulers (Isaiah 14:12; Ezekiel 28:17), to the sacred city itself. Couplet 1*c* asserts that Yahweh has deserted the temple. So the day is a **day of his anger.** To see how radical this is, cf. what Psalms 46, 48, and 132 claim for Jerusalem.

2:2-10 describes what has happened in **the day of his anger,** just as a hymn to God's majesty recounts Yahweh's mighty deeds. Verses 2-5 recall the devastation of the land that led to the siege of Jerusalem itself, first by the Assyrians (730-680) and then by the Babylonians (600-586). In this Yahweh, seen by cheap piety to be an ally, is the real **enemy** (verses 4-5). What verses 6-7 assert about God's destruction of sacred things and places verges on blasphemy, or would to a faith that did not locate God's activity in empirical events—even tragic events.

Verses 8-9 insist that what has happened is the result not of meaningless fate but of the righteous purpose of a righteous God. God is the destroyer of all the institutions through which God was sought (verse 9). The conclusion to this section in verse 10 describes the only reaction now appropriate to the reality of how God's righteous sovereignty has manifested itself.

2:11-12 is a transition in which the poet himself reacts to the situation by lamenting. These verses give a graphic description of the effect of famine on children in the besieged and fallen city.

2:13-17 takes up a central theme of this poem. The disaster by which Jerusalem has been overtaken is **vast as the sea.** Like the day of Yahweh's wrath, it is incomparable. There is no parallel to it. Therefore no one is qualified to comfort Zion. In the light of this theme, verses 14-17 look to possible comforters.

In verse 14 the poet explicitly sides with the minority prophets against those in the majority who maintained themselves by prophesying the peace and security Israel wanted to hear. Such prophets have been disqualified by events. Reality has voided their credentials, and they can say nothing to comfort Jerusalem now. The poet makes explicit what has been implicit all along—his acceptance of the interpretation given to Jerusalem's downfall by prophets such as Jeremiah and Ezekiel.

2:15-17. Given what verse 14 has said, is there any possibility of help from outside Israel? Not at all. Both neutral passers-by (verse 15) and Israel's enemies (verse 16) rejoice in Jerusalem's catastrophe. They see it as what it deserved. So, can God be Jerusalem's comforter (verse 17)? No, for the point of the whole poem is that the disaster is precisely God's doing. Given what Israel had become, Yahweh's day for it had to be a day of wrath.

2:18-19 moves from the lament of the poet to introduce that of Jerusalem itself. With no comforter, Zion can only pour out its grief constantly to God. In hymns praising God's activity the characteristic beginning is an imperative "call to worship" (cf. Psalms 29:1; 47:1; 103:1). Here, in the manner of the poet himself (see above on verse 1), Jerusalem is called on to recite the deeds of Yahweh in the only way it now can, to be a witness to God even in its present condition.

2:20-22. *Jerusalem's Lament.* The poet has the city speak as a grief-stricken mother. The horrors catalogued speak for themselves. The pervading theme is stated at the beginning, **"Look, O LORD, and see! With whom has thou dealt thus?"** This is a central thesis of the poem: no precedent exists anywhere for what has happened to Jerusalem. Thus the siege and fall of city and temple are not just tragic disaster. They plunge Israel into a crisis of faith. God seems to have acted in this day of wrath in a way contrary to the divine character and purpose. Though the poems of Lamentations probably originated separately, even if from a common author, the crisis of faith expressed at the end of this poem leads naturally into the one in the following chapter.

III. AN INDIVIDUAL LAMENT AND SONG OF CONFIDENCE
(3:1-66)

Unlike chapters 1 and 2, this poem is not modeled on a funeral dirge. Its problems have resulted in much debate. Puzzling changes in pronouns occur. An "I" speaks in verses 1-20 and 48-66, while in verses 40-47 "we" is the subject. Also baffling are the various forms used. Verses 1-20 are an individual lament, while verses 21-24 combine elements of the individual thanksgiving and song of trust. Verses 43-47, where the subject is "we," are a communal lament. Verses 25-42 combine didactic and hortatory moods, reminiscent of the wisdom literature.

To the problem of finding an interpretation accounting for all this must be added the question of the poem's relation to the rest of Lamentations. Solutions have varied widely. Noting its differences from the rest of the book and its mixtures of pronouns and forms, many have held this poem to be a composite and the latest part of the book. More recently others have accounted for the various voices and elements with the theory that behind it lies cultic usage in which different persons and groups played their parts. It has also been held that the alternation between "I" and "we" is no problem, the "I" being collective.

Recent interpreters have tended to date the poem close to the disaster of 586 or in the period of the Exile. They have seen the author as a comforter of Israel on the basis of tragic experience. He brings meaning to Israel's suffering by a figure not unlike the suffering servant of Isaiah 53. There are diverse elements in the poem, but its acrostic form indicates a unity of authorship. The following interpretation seeks to do justice to both.

The poem is not a lament over Jerusalem's fall. It addresses itself to the tragic problem posed for Israel by the situation so eloquently described in the poem in chapter 2. This argues for

common authorship. The poem bases the comfort it offers to
Israel on the experience of tragedy and deliverance described in
many psalms in which lament, confession of confidence, and
thanksgiving are combined (for example, Psalm 27). Thus verses
1-24 are the poet's presentation of what will speak to Jerusalem
in her disaster. Verses 25-39 then point to the lesson the poet
believes to come from what is presented in verses 1-24. Verses
40-51 exhort Israel to act on the basis of the lesson, giving voice
to the lament of Israel and of the poet himself. Finally verses
52-66 are the poet's song of confidence (firm enough that he can
use the perfect tense) that Yahweh will act in redemption as
Yahweh has acted in judgment.

To assign to the poem a definite time of composition or author
is very difficult. It could come from almost any time after 586. If
the other poems originated in Palestine, this would come from
there too.

3:1-24. *The Basis of Hope.* The question of chapter 2 was,
Who can comfort Jerusalem in its unprecedented disaster? The
answer is given here. Whatever the particular tragedy
presented in a lament might be, the basic point was always that
in it chaos was threatening order, death swallowing up life (cf.
Psalm 88). This poem holds that in the suffering and disaster that
call forth the lament there is a basis for speaking to the Jerusalem
which has known the bitter wrath of God.

3:4-18. The heart of a lament is always a compelling and
graphic recitation of the suffering being undergone. Three
things occupy attention: the lamenter's own suffering, the
enemies who plague him (verse 14), and God, who is
withholding the divine life-giving and saving presence.

Here, while everything is permeated with the sufferer's
plight, there is remarkable concentration on God's responsibility for the situation—**He has . . . He has . . . He has. . . .**
Indeed, as in Job, the utter despair of the sufferer is made plain
as the figures usually used for evil and demonic enemies are
applied to God (verses 10-12). The point is that things have come
to where it is possible to cry out to God only that order has been

overwhelmed by chaos, life by death (cf. such classic laments as Psalms 22, 88, and 143).

3:19-23. But all this is cried out *to God.* Implied in every lament is what is called "the certainty of a hearing." This certainty is itself the subject of Old Testament poetry (cf. Psalms 27:1-3 and 23). So here, after verses 19-21 have turned from description of distress to direct calling on God, verses 22-24 express the confidence that God will hear.

The basis of the certainty is the important Old Testament concept of *hesed,* usually rendered **steadfast love** in the Revised Standard Version. The basic connotations of the word have to do with committed, loving loyalty to a covenant obligation. The concrete character of Hebrew thinking is shown by the word's being used here in the plural. It refers to specific events and actions, not an abstract concept. Its meaning is indicated by its being parallel to **faithfulness** (verses 22-23).

3:24. The phrase **says my soul** means "I say to myself." Israelites who take the covenant seriously can be reminded that Yahweh is their **portion**—the possession measured out to them in life. And Yahweh's record is such that even in deepest distress hopeful waiting is justified. When a lament was recited in a time of distress in the sanctuary, it was answered after a time of vigil by an oracle pronouncing salvation. Thus **I will hope in him** has very concrete overtones.

3:25-39. *The Lesson to Be Learned.* Verses 25-26 provide a transition to the next section of the poem by alluding to the cultic setting of a lament. To seek Yahweh originally meant to go to the sanctuary. The word for **wait** may originally have referred to the period of vigil preceding the oracle of salvation (cf. Psalm 27:14; Isaiah 40:31). But the sanctuary is now gone. The poet begins to insist that its procedures provide a lesson in the principles by which God works at any time. So verse 27 is a typical wisdom maxim. It may indicate that the poet is chiefly concerned with the younger generation with whom Israel's future lies.

3:28-30. In line with what has been implied in the preceding laments, particularly chapter 2, the poet insists that the first step to salvation is an acceptance of the situation for what it is. Note the reticent realism of verse 29*b*. Verse 30 is certainly support for the contention that Isaiah 53 shows a kinship with Lamentations.

3:31-33. Out of acceptance of judgment can come knowledge of the basically good purpose of God which undergirds judgment. What looks like two opposing things are to God one thing. God's **steadfast love** (see above on verse 22) is always the same. It is the source of what to sinful humans seems to be wrath. But to one who accepts and repents (verses 28-30) it is the basis of hope.

3:34-37 develops explicitly what underlies the confidence of verses 31-33. The will of Israel's God is not meaningless injustice but righteousness (verses 34-36). And Israel's God is the sovereign Lord. Thus even the tragic disaster through which Israel has passed is something filled with meaning.

This is the prophetic insight which redeemed catastrophe from meaninglessness for Israelites who, like this poet, understood the prophetic message. The lesson was proclaimed by the prophets and typically enunciated in Israel's ancient faith. Now it is that to which the poet points Israel. The rhetorical questions of verses 37-39 provide a transition to the two final parts of the poem.

3:40-51. *The People's and the Poet's Lament.* Given the theology underlying verses 34-39, the cause for lament inevitably shifted in Israel from what it was elsewhere. For Israel the fundamental human problem was not that creaturely finitude was assailed by meaningless and amoral forces from which salvation was desperately sought. For Israel the fundamental problem was human unrighteousness, creaturely rebellion against the sovereign righteousness of God.

Disaster such as that by which Jerusalem had been overtaken was a secondary and understandable by-product of this basic problem. Meaning was to be found for those who would seek it in ruthless honesty about themselves (verses 40-41). And the search would lead to fruitful lament, lament over what was really wrong in life (verse 42).

3:43-51. The description of Israel's present condition in verses 43-45 is as graphic as anything in chapters 1 and 2. Yet the communal lament to which the poet calls the survivors of Jerusalem moves in hopeful trust to its conclusion in verses 49-51. This whole chapter may be understood as a unity. This section would be the poet's rhetorical summons to Israel (with which he identifies himself) to lament. Therefore the switch from plural to singular pronouns in verses 48-51 would be no problem. It is only a sign of the extent to which the poet is himself involved in the situation.

3:52-66. *The Poet's Song of Confidence.* In Israel's sacred poetry the counterpart of the lament was the song of thanksgiving. In this the poet, after a cry for deliverance, recited how God had saved him. This form underlies the conclusion to the present poem. Verses 52-54 describe a desperate situation in traditional lament language. The poet then uses prolepsis—the figure in which one anticipates coming events as if they have already occurred—to describe how God will answer the cry of Israel (verses 55-66).

The **Do not fear!** of verse 57 may be a direct quotation of what was said in the oracle of reassurance that followed a lament in the sanctuary. Emphasis on **enemies** arises out of the derision to which Israel was subjected following its downfall (cf. Psalm 137). It is also in line with the concrete character of Israel's faith, in which God's purposes and the forces opposing them were seen in terms of the events and persons in real life. If the sentiments of verses 64-66 are neither understandable nor acceptable to the modern reader, they arise from the point of view just described. They occur many times in the psalms. They come from a faith which could not conceive of God's salvation and blessing in other than visible, historical terms.

IV. THROUGH TRAGEDY TO VINDICATION (4:1-22)

Here there is a return to the funeral lament form of chapters 1 and 2. The typical **How** (see above on 1:1) is the beginning. This poem is another acrostic. Here the three-couplet stanzas of chapters 1–3 give way to stanzas of two couplets.

In content this poem returns from the themes of chapter 3 to the kind of thing found in chapters 1 and 2. It vividly describes the results of the Babylonian siege and destruction of Jerusalem. Its conclusion looks through tragedy to vindication. The realism of its reference to the city's troubles has caused some to assert that the poem was written by an eye-witness of the siege. However, the denunciation of Edom at the end may indicate a later time in the exilic period when Edom's encroachment on former Judean territory resulted in a good deal of animosity.

4:1-2 refers to the destruction of the temple, the chief tragedy of Jerusalem's downfall for the pious Israelite. Verse 2 leads into what is to occupy attention in most of this lament—the suffering of the people in Jerusalem. **The precious sons of Zion** is evidence of the meaning to Israel of its election as God's people.

4:3-5 describes the famine that accompanied the siege, concentrating on the terrible results of it for the children of the city. On the ostrich and its treatment of its young cf. Job 39:13-18.

4:6 is one of a series of stanzas coming at regular intervals in this poem (verses 6, 11, 16). These punctuate the recitation of the disaster with proclamations of it as God's wrath on a rebellious people. Here the proverbial wickedness of Sodom (cf. Genesis 19) serves as a model of the condition of Jerusalem.

An insight into the Hebrew view of life is provided in the double meaning of **chastisement** and **punishment**. Each word can denote both evil and the consequences of it in a world ruled by a righteous God. Unlike chapters 2 and 3 this poem simply alludes to Israel's sin in a vivid description of the siege and destruction of Jerusalem. It does not dwell on the point, but takes the prophetic interpretation of the dreadful events for granted.

4:7-8 describes in vivid terms the change produced in even the most handsome and healthy of Jerusalem's youth (**princes** may not be correct) by the famine.

4:9-10 asserts that death in the famine was worse than falling in battle. Hunger drove even the most compassionate of mothers to kill and eat their children.

4:11 again explicitly connects what the poem laments with God's judgmental wrath (cf. verses 6, 16). Unlike 2:20, in which verse 10 is paralleled, verse 11 does not question Yahweh's involvement in the disaster.

4:12 provides a transition to a new section by underlining verse 11. What Yahweh has done in judgment was beyond the imagination even of those not themselves involved in feeling for Jerusalem. This verse brings to mind the advantageous location of Jerusalem (II Samuel 5:6). It also points to Israel's conviction about its invulnerability. Jeremiah had to warn against this (Jeremiah 7; 26).

4:13-15 locates the cause of the judgment of Jerusalem in the sin of prophets and priests. Some have interpreted **The blood of the righteous** as an allusion to some specific wrong of the religious leaders. More probably it refers to their responsibility for what has happened to the innocent in the siege and destruction. Verses 14-15 probably describe the prophets and priests (cf. verse 16), though a number of interpreters have applied them to the **righteous** of verse 13.

In line with what all the classic prophets had insisted, this poem asserts that those whose responsibility it was to declare God's will to the people had not done so. Because of the perversions of prophet and priest, Israel's view of its God had become perverted. Therefore God, without compromising the divine character, could act toward Israel only in judgment. So the blood of the righteous is on the hands of the leaders.

4:16 is a counterpart to verses 6 and 11. It explicitly states that the defiling of the sacral persons from their ritual cleanness and their exile into foreign lands is the work of Yahweh.

4:17-20 concludes the lament's account of Jerusalem's terrible fall. It describes how nothing could be relied on to avert the disaster.

Verses 17-18 indicate that the poet understood what the prophets had continually insisted—that no foreign alliance could thwart Yahweh's judgment on his people (cf. Isaiah 30–31;

Jeremiah 2:18, 36). Verse 20, contrary to the claims so often made for the Davidic monarchy (II Samuel 7; Psalms 2; 110), recounts how Yahweh's own king could not stop the fall of Jerusalem, but experienced its consequences himself.

4:21-22. Unlike the poems in chapters 2 and 3, this poem does not question the ultimately redemptive purpose of Yahweh even in divine wrathful judgment. Thus it ends with words of comfort to Israel. Some interpreters believe that cultic usage underlies the poem, and that these final verses were an oracle of reassurance addressed to the lamenting community.

In line with Israel's concrete view of things (see above on 3:58-66), God's comforting of Israel is pictured as a very visible punishment of Edom, a major enemy. Edom had apparently taken advantage of Israel after the Babylonian invasion and therefore came in for much castigation during the exilic and postexilic periods.

V. A COMMUNAL LAMENT AND PRAYER (5:1-22)

This poem differs from the others in two ways. First, although the number of couplets is the same as the twenty-two letters in the Hebrew alphabet, it is not an acrostic. On the one hand, this fact has been used to argue for its basic unity and for its having come from the same writer as the other poems. On the other hand, some have held this to be an artificial device imposed by other writers. Current critical opinion tends toward the former view.

Second, this poem is a pure example of the communal lament (cf. Psalms 44; 74; 79; 80; 83). It begins with a cry to God, recites the causes of the lament in the first person plural, and concludes with a petition to God for relief. Various hints are given about the use of such poems (Joshua 7:6-9; Judges 20:23, 26; I Kings 8:33-34; Jeremiah 14:2; Joel 1:13-14). They make it seem possible that this one was written for some public occasion of lamentation after the fall of Jerusalem in 586 B.C.

5:1-18. *The Lament.* Verse 1 begins in the manner of the lament, either communal or individual. There is a direct call on God and an imperative request that God **remember** (better, "direct his attention to") the condition of the lamenter or act.

5:2 is descriptive of more than a political and economic disaster. The word for **inheritance** is central to Israel's theology. The concrete sign of its relation to God was God's provision for Israel of a land of its own. The loss of that land to other peoples presented a crisis for faith, and that crisis is the central subject of Lamentations.

5:3-5. Verse 3 can be interpreted as a description of the situation when many people had been killed. More likely, in line with verse 2, it is a tragic assertion that Israel has been abandoned by its God. Verse 4 carries on the same line of thought, the point being that the rights to the resources of the land now belong to others. Verse 5 provides a climax with its declaration of the loss of personal freedom.

5:6-8 forms a unit. It refers to pacts made in the two centuries before Jerusalem's fall as expansion of various imperial powers began to spell Israel's doom. As the prophets had consistently insisted, the compromise involved in such pacts was apostasy from Yahweh's claim to absolute sovereignty. It had to be characterized as sin and iniquity.

Verse 7 must precede the doctrine advanced in Ezekiel 18. Verse 8 asserts the bitter irony that a people whose relation to their God originated in emancipation from slavery are now subject to peoples whose gods are oppressors rather than redeemers.

5:9-15, typical of the lament form, recounts the difficulties being undergone by those who have survived the fall of Jerusalem. Harvesting of crops is made dangerous by bedouin marauders from the desert (verse 9). Famine has produced illness (verse 10). All elements of society suffer the results of chaotic lawlessness (verses 11-14). Joy is entirely turned to sadness (verse 15).

5:16. The hardest fact of all is the voiding of Israel's choice as God's blessed people. The lamenting community accepts the prophetic assessment of the reason for the catastrophe.

5:17-18 provides both the climax of the lament proper and the transition to the petition. The central tragedy of it all for Israel is the cessation of its life as the community whose worship on Zion is the earthly, visible locus of the sovereignty of God. In the most profound sense chaos has replaced order—yet not entirely for the people whose prophets have made possible the confession of verse 16*b*. If tragedy has meaning, God can still be turned to in prayer for the future.

5:19-22. *The Petition.* What was implied in the above is made explicit in the hymnic introduction (verse 19). It is not Yahweh's sovereignty but Israel's previous status that has collapsed. So the lamenting **Why** (verse 20) and a petition for restoration (verse 21) can be addressed to Yahweh. And, if the central fact of life is God's sovereignty, then the tragic situation of Israel may even be faced as unalterable. The last verse of Lamentations sums up the evidence of all its poetry that there were those in Israel who could accept the prophetic interpretation of its downfall.

THE BOOK OF EZEKIEL

William Hugh Brownlee

INTRODUCTION

According to the superscription (1:1-3) and scattered notes (3:15; 11:24-25; 40:1-2) Ezekiel was among the first body of exiles taken to Babylon along with King Jehoiachin in the spring of 597 (cf. II Kings 24:10-17; on the historical background see Introduction to Jeremiah). It is thus from "Chaldea,"—that is, Babylonia—that he is represented as predicting ruin for Judah until the fall of Jerusalem in 586 (chapters 1–24). He then predicts the doom of Judah's neighbors (chapters 25–32) and the restoration of Israel (chapters 34–48).

Problems of Place and Unity

At first glance the book appears more of a unity than most other prophetic books. But the traditional assumption that it is the work of a prophet living among the Babylonian exiles offers a number of difficulties:

(1) Ezekiel's prophetic mission is to warn the "house of Israel" of coming ruin (3:16-21). This term as used in the book refers to the southern kingdom of Judah—except where it means the northern kingdom as distinguished from the southern (for example, 4:4-5). It is limited to the people remaining in

Palestine. When the exiles are included it is changed to the "whole house of Israel" (11:15; 37:11).

(2) Ezekiel's sermons are addressed to Judah and Jerusalem. Repeatedly he is told to "make known to Jerusalem her abominations" (16:2; 22:2). Such addresses are found throughout chapters 1–24 and are usually worded in the second person. He is said to "dwell in the midst of a rebellious house" (12:2), to which he acts out warnings of exile and captivity. His appeals for repentance are motivated by the plea to avoid ruin and death. The only judgment predicted is that which will befall Judah. In contrast, after the fall of Jerusalem and Judah the messages of comfort in chapters 34–48 are addressed to Jews scattered all over the world rather than specifically to those exiled in Babylonia.

(3) A number of passages are most naturally understood as involving Ezekiel's presence in Palestine (5:5; chapters 8–11; 21:2-7; 24:25-27; 33:24; see comments.) To fit the traditional assumption that he was in Babylonia they must be interpreted as visions or the like. The account of Pelatiah's death while Ezekiel is prophesying (11:1-13) especially seems to require an actual confrontation at the gate to the temple (see below on 11:13). Elsewhere he is told to face in certain directions and see different parts of Palestine (6:1-7; 20:45–21:5; see comments).

(4) Ezekiel shows intimate acquaintance with conditions in Palestine but tells us nothing of conditions among the exiles. There was a Jewish colony near the river Chebar at a place called Tel-abib (1:1-3; 3:15, 23), but this tradition could have been known to a late editor. Aside from this, one can gain little information about the exiles from the book. Contrast Jeremiah 29:4-23, a letter written to the exiles from Jerusalem, which gives more information about them than this entire book. Also see Isaiah 40–55, written among the exiles at a later time.

(5) The statements which place Ezekiel among the exiles appear to be editorial additions. No sermon is concerned explicitly with the Jews in Babylonia. Rather such references occur mainly in headings and brief notations. The materials written from an exilic point of view in the visions may also have

been later embellishments designed to identify Ezekiel with the exiles.

(6) Materials in the book supporting the exilic locale tend to distort Ezekiel's personality. The portrayal of the prophet as being in Babylonia yet completely absorbed in the affairs of Judah makes him appear given to semi-mystical daydreaming, as if suffering from a split personality or similar psychopathic condition.

Certain exilic passages suggest other abnormal traits. For example, the stupor in which he is said to remain after going to the exiles (3:10-15) seems cataleptic (cf. 4:4-8). Before he has even started to preach he is allegedly told to go home and keep quiet, his powers of speech paralyzed (3:22-27). He supposedly stays there till Jerusalem's fall (33:21-22). According to these passages he never carries out his mission of summoning the nation to repentance. Nor does he obey the continual commands to speak.

In facing these and other problems of the book scholars convinced of its essential unity and Babylonian locale have generally taken for granted the prophet's psychic abnormality. This is offered in explanation of many of the difficulties. But such an approach is superficial and does not deal adequately with all the problems.

Some have followed the lead of the ancient Jewish historian Josephus (first century A.D.), who theorized that Ezekiel wrote letters to the Judeans from Babylonia. Since there is no evidence for written correspondence by Ezekiel himself, the scholars place the burden of it on disciples and others who communicated with Judah. Travelers between the countries, it is assumed, would carry oral reports. Thus the book's sermons calling Judah to repentance would be spoken in Babylonia in the hope that report of them would reach the intended audience. While recognizing that there was communication between the exiles and the homeland (cf. Jeremiah 29), we may question whether reliance on such means would be adequate for a prophet called to confront the Judeans with the threat of ruin.

A number of scholars have proposed a double ministry for

Ezekiel partly in Palestine and partly in Babylonia. They have suggested rearrangements of the materials to fit the two stages. Some see him as going into exile in 597 but returning to Jerusalem after his call. There he preached doom until the destruction of the city in 586. After this he was again taken captive to Babylonia and became a herald of hope to his fellow exiles. Others place him in Palestine throughout the first part of his career. They assume he was exiled in 586—or probably a few years later (cf. Jeremiah 52:30), since 33:23-29 implies his being in Judah after its devastation.

In either form this theory is attractive as a solution to the book's problems. Once we recognize, however, that Ezekiel's oracles of doom were spoken in person to the Judeans for whom they were intended and reflect fully life in the homeland, we come to expect the same intimacy concerning life in Babylonia. Failing to find this, one cannot attribute with confidence any oracles to the prophet himself in an exilic setting. In recent decades, therefore, some perceptive scholars have concluded that Ezekiel's ministry was entirely Palestinian and that all the exilic material comes from editors of later times. This view seems to solve more of the book's problems than any other.

The Prophet and His Message

The reform introduced by King Josiah (II Kings 23) called for the centralization of worship in the Jerusalem temple. Worship at the "high places" was outlawed. After Josiah's death worship at these hilltop shrines came into vogue again. Ezekiel condemned the rulers of the nation for letting this happen (cf. 6:1-7; see below on 34:1-10). The Deuteronomic law (Deuteronomy 12–26), on which Josiah's reform was based, included new formulations of old laws that were distinctive of Israel. Ezekiel upheld these as a safeguard against religious syncretism (11:12; 20:32).

As a priest (1:3) Ezekiel revered the temple (7:22; 24:19-21) and was concerned for the "holy things" of the sanctuary (22:8, 26). He insisted that offerings should be presented to Yahweh alone (16:18-19; cf. 24:1-14) and urged obedience to the priestly traditions. Yet much of the priestly material in the book is from later hands. Most of the sins which he himself condemns are ethical.

He gives the fullest of the prophetic statements of what constitutes righteous living (18:5-9; cf. Isaiah 33:15; Micah 6:8). His primary interest was in the ethical principles expressed in the Deuteronomic law. His invectives against idolatry were quite as much for ethical as for cultic reasons. His equating of idolatry with adultery was not wholly allegorical (16:24-25; 18:15; 22:9). He especially condemned crimes against children (16:20-21, 44-45; 20:25-27).

Ezekiel is well known as a prophet of individualism. He was also a herald of divine love for each person. His message was that God loves sinners and for this reason warns them through the prophet. It is God's displeasure at the prospect of death for the wicked that moves God to throw open the door of repentance and life to all who will enter (18:23, 31-32; 33:10-11).

Ezekiel was a younger contemporary of Jeremiah and lived and preached for a time in the same city, Jerusalem. It is evident that he at least heard Jeremiah preach and was influenced by the older prophet's thought. See for example:

EZEKIEL	JEREMIAH
7:26	18:18
12:2	5:21
13:16	6:14
20:4-31	7:21-26; 11:1-8; 16:10-13
22:17-22	6:27-30
33:1-9	6:17

The ancient rabbis recorded the tradition that Ezekiel was the "son of Jeremiah," meaning a disciple.

Most of Ezekiel's own material in the book is poetry, though some of his writing is prose. Some of the poetry has been preserved in essentially its original form (for example, chapter 19) but much has been masked by later editing (34:1-10) and interpolating (chapter 1). The following commentary translates a number of the oracles in their presumed original poetic form.

Like all great poets Ezekiel excelled in a vivid and colorful imagination. This is especially characteristic of his allegories (chapters 15; 16; 17; 23). His symbolic imagery is developed most beautifully in his dirges (chapters 19; 27). People listened to him out of appreciation for aesthetic beauty, even though their minds were too engrossed with selfish passions to heed his teaching (33:30-32). Rarely have truth and beauty been combined more effectively in Hebrew literature.

Far from being a recluse living in a remote, imaginary world, Ezekiel was a man who mingled freely with the people and felt their every mood. He is constantly addressed as "son of man"—that is, an ordinary person despite his priestly descent. His intimacy with the social, economic, political, and religious aspects of Judah's life is seen continuously. This knowledge was not a divine gift, but the result of living among the people of Judah. His divine inspiration lay in his addressing their situation with a word of God.

The genuine text contains four visions:
(1) the glory in the storm cloud (reconstructed from chapters 1–3);
(2) the eating of a scroll (2:8–3:3) held in Yahweh's hand, who appeared to him as in 8:1*b*-2;
(3) the coming destruction of Jerusalem (chapter 9);
(4) the resurrection of the nation (37:7-10).
In none of these is it stated that he was transported miraculously from Babylonia to Palestine, or that he saw events from afar. However, he does speak of making ecstatic trips to various spots in terms of being "lifted up" and "brought" by Yahweh or his Spirit—like Elijah (I Kings 18:12, 46; cf. Acts 8:39-40). Such language was later understood as describing miraculous transport and was used to explain his physical presence in Jerusalem in chapters 8–11.

The Editors and Revisers

The earliest of the additions to Ezekiel's work are no doubt those which promise return of the Jews from the many lands to which they were scattered. The principal themes of these hopeful passages are:

(1) The dispersion will bring the Jews to repentance (6:8-10; 12:15-16) and will purify the nation (13:9; 20:37-38).

(2) Yahweh will gather them home (34:12-16).

(3) This will lead them to know Yahweh (20:38, 42; 34:27) and move them to repentance (20:42-43).

(4) They will recognize Yahweh's unmerited kindness (16:54, 61; 20:44; 36:31-32), which will be solely for the sake of Yahweh's own holiness and glory (36:17-23).

(5) Restoration will involve the spiritual gifts of cleansing and regeneration (36:24-26) and the material gifts of productivity (34:25-31) and security (36:8-13, 28-30).

(6) The Davidic kingdom will be restored (17:22-24; 34:16, 23-24) and the temple will be rebuilt (37:26-28).

(7) Once more Yahweh will accept their worship there (20:40).

(8) Thus Yahweh's name will be vindicated before the nations (36:36).

The fact that these passages sometimes misinterpret the earlier passages to which they are attached is evidence that they do not come from Ezekiel himself.

The description of the new temple, the new law, and the new land in chapters 40–48 involves a priestly program. The late editors of the book were much interested in this, and their hand is evident in this section. Yet it is clear that not all this material is from the same hands. The late editors probably identified the new temple with that standing in Jerusalem in their day, which had been built by the returning exiles under Zerubbabel in 520-515. But underlying their material is an earlier prose work which antedates the rebuilding. Some of this may have been written by an exiled disciple of Ezekiel, and may have inspired the first unsuccessful efforts at rebuilding in 537.

Two passages seem to reflect the situation described by Nehemiah at the beginning of his governorship (23:36-49; 34:17-22; see comments). Therefore these probaby date from his time or shortly before. The oracles against foreign nations (21:28-32; chapters 25–32; 35) contain some supplements from later hands. For example, some of the additions to the three oracles against Tyre in chapters 26–28 may have been inspired by the conquest of the city by Alexander the Great in 332.

The apocalyptic description of the invasion of Gog (in chapters 38–39 is a late addition. This is seen by its presupposition that a long time has elapsed since the recognized prophets lived (38:17; 39:8). Possibly this material reflects the conquest of Palestine by Alexander the Great.

The latest major editing of the book radically rearranged it, including the assembling of material into two parts—chapters 1–24 which threaten and chapters 25–48 which promise. Rich and tedious elaborations were added which intensified its priestly concerns and focused on its assumed origin in the Exile.

The idea that Ezekiel was a prophet of the Exile may have arisen as a misunderstanding of the method of dating certain of his oracles, which may be his own or may have come from a disciple. All the dates are in years of the "exile of King Jehoiachin" (1:2; cf. II Kings 25:27)—apparently calculated from the spring of 597—rather than in regnal years of Zedekiah. The thirtieth year in 1:1 is probably an exception. This dating rests on the authentic legal fact that Jehoiachin remained king of Judah while in exile and Zedekiah was merely appointed regent or acting ruler. In the ruins of ancient Babylon tablets have been found which refer to Jehiachin as king, and seals and seal impressions on jars found in Palestine show that crown property in Judah was still kept in his name.

No doubt many in Jerusalem preferred to ignore this fact. They wanted to write off Jehoiachin and seek freedom under Zedekiah—a view reflected in the references to Zedekiah as king and the dating by his regnal years in II Kings 24:17–25:2 and in Jeremiah. Thus it would be easy for those of a later time to misinterpret the dating by Jehoiachin as evidence that Ezekiel accompanied the exiled king to Babylonia. Ezekiel's peculiar method of referring to the divine motivation of his travels in the vicinity of Jerusalem would then contribute to the misunderstanding by suggesting that he was supernaturally transported back to Palestine to deliver his sermons.

Once Ezekiel was taken to be an exilic prophet, later editors seized on this assumption and emphasized it. It became an important basis for the arguments implicit in their work. In their hands the book was shaped into an effective weapon with which to counter attacks on the legitimacy of the Jewish temple and its priesthood.

To certain minds the fact that the temple in Jerusalem was destroyed by the Babylonians proved that it had not been built at the only place which Yahweh had chosen to be worshiped with sacrifices. The fact that its most prominent priests were exiled seemed to show that Yahweh had repudiated the priesthood of Jerusalem. Those advancing such arguments were probably the Samaritans, who supported a rival temple on Mt. Gerizim, near the ancient city of Sechem.

The interpretation of Ezekiel as a prophet among the exiles provided an effective answer to such challenges. Yahweh's manifestation in such overwhelming fashion by the river Chebar (chapter 1) proved that Yahweh did not abandon the exiles. Yahweh's calling of the exiled priest Ezekiel to be a prophet proved that Yahweh did not reject the exiled priests of Jerusalem.

The theme of divine glory provided an argument for continuity between the destroyed temple of Solomon and the rebuilt temple of Zerubbabel. It was only because of sin that the glory departed from the first temple—an event which Ezekiel witnessed some years before the fall of the city (8:4; 9:3; 10:1-22; 11:22-23), and which made possible the destruction of the building (43:3). Meanwhile the glory that had resided in the temple from the time of the dedication by Solomon took up its abode among the exiles, where it was seen by Ezekiel, and where it constituted "for a while" a sanctuary there (11:16).

The vision of the restored temple at Jerusalem in chapters 40–48 is attributed to Ezekiel. This gave his authority to the rebuilding under Zerubbabel and authenticated the new temple's priesthood and rites. This vision promised that the glory which had taken up its abode with the exiles would return to Jerusalem (43:1-7; 44:1-4). Thus it gave assurance of the divine presence in the temple of the editor's day. Later Jews referred to God's luminous presence as the "glory of the *shekinah*," literally "[divine] abode," or simply as the shekinah. Ezekiel's work as edited made possible the tracing of the shekinah succession through the Exile.

The Samaritan rivalry seems to have reached its height in the period following the conquest of Alexander the Great, who according to Josephus gave the Samaritans permission to build their temple on Mt. Gerizim. Thus a reasonable estimate for the date of this editing is around 300 B.C.

The late editors did such a thorough job both of rearranging and of elaborating that a superficial study of the book gives a false sense of literary unity. Fortunately they left some traces of their methods—especially in chapters 1–3; 8–11 and 43:1-5—by which much of their work can be recognized.

I. Judah's Doom (1:1–24:27)

A. Ezekiel's Prophetic Call (1:1–3:27)

1:1-3. *The Dates and Place.* The reference of the **thirtieth year** has been the subject of much debate. Some scholars have taken it to be based, like the other dates of the book, on the **exile of King Jehoiachin.** On the significance of this basis see the Introduction. These scholars therefore think that it identifies the year, 568, when the book was compiled and published. Poetic criteria, however, indicate that this date in verse 1*a* was a part of the original poem that underlies the vision of verses 4–28*b* and therefore refers to the beginning of Ezekiel's prophetic ministry. The date of verse 2 does not fit these criteria. It probably belongs to a prose superscription which an early editor prefixed to the poem.

It may have read: "The word of Yahweh which came to Ezekiel the son of Buzi, the priest, on the fifth day of the (fourth?) month. It was the fifth year of the exile of King Jehoiachin." If so, the date of verse 2 was intended to refer to the same event as that of verse 1*a*. It simply located it on a more commonly used basis of time.

Scholars generally reckon the numbering of months in the Old Testament as counted from the spring equinox, in accordance with the Babylonian system. In this book the years also seem to be counted from a spring new year. Hence the date denoted is July 31, 593. The Targum, which is the Aramaic version, explains the thirtieth year as counted from King Josiah's reform. Starting from the passover of Josiah's eighteenth year which climaxed the reform (II Kings 23:21-23) July 31, 593, falls in the thirtieth year. Some scholars today accept this explanation.

The thirtieth birthday was very important to one of priestly descent (cf. Numbers 4:2-3, 46-47). Therefore a number of scholars believe that the reference is to Ezekiel's age at the time of his call. Having become old enough to serve in the temple as a **priest,** Ezekiel contemplates his future. He goes forth into the plain (see below on 3:22-27), perhaps to pray. The relapse of Josiah's reform is a serious concern. The time seems to be drawing near when the curses of the covenant must be fulfilled (cf. Deuteronomy 27:14-26; 28:15-68). When a sudden electrical storm comes up—an unusual occurrence at this season—Ezekiel is ready to see in it a vision of Yahweh's glory and to hear a call to become a prophet.

The **river Chebar** was a navigable canal connected to the Euphrates southeast of Babylon in the **land of the Chaldeans**— that is, Babylonia. **King Jehoiachin** and his retinue were kept in the capital, as Babylonian records show (cf. II Kings 25:27-30). The other Judean exiles are here said to have been resettled by the Chebar.

1:4-28b. *The Vision in the Storm.* Yahweh's **glory** (verse 28*b*) rides on a **throne** (verse 26). This surmounts a most intricate chariot whose locomotive power consists of **four living creatures,** or cherubs (cf. 10:15). These were winged creatures, usually with human heads and animal bodies. Each has **four faces**—the cherubs of 41:18-19 have only two—which may be symbols of the four leading deities of Babylon: Nabu, the human-faced revealer; Nergal, the lion-faced god of the underworld and of plague; Marduk, the leading Babylonian deity, who was represented by a winged bull; and Ninib, the eagle-faced god of hunting and war.

Pagan deities were essentially personifications of the powers of nature. Only Yahweh was conceived of as a power distinct from and yet over nature. Yahweh's throne is only the **likeness of a throne** and Yahweh's figure is only a **likeness as it were of a human form** because the Lord is spirit. Only in visions does Yahweh appear otherwise. His description in verse 27 is probably adapted from 8:2.

The chariot's perfect mobility is indicated by the three-fold means of locomotion: **feet, wings,** and **wheels.** The wheels are **full of eyes**—(cf. 10:12) suggesting omniscience. Underlying this vision as we now have it was undoubtedly a simpler original in which Ezekiel told of seeing Yahweh's glory in a storm cloud. Fortunately the priestly editors have left many tracks behind where they went about enlarging on it.

One of their habits is to insert literary echoes of passages which they have separated from their earlier connections. Thus the original setting of Ezekiel's vision in a plain (3:22-23) can be recognized by the duplication in 3:22a of **the hand of the Lord was upon him there** (verse 3b). There is a duplication in 3:23b of **behold** (verse 4a), there translated "and lo," which is followed by a summary reference to the vision in its expanded form.

Ezekiel's vision involves a storm **cloud,** which contains the **likeness of . . . living creatures.** Verses 5b-12 are an interpolated description of these. They are introduced again in verse 13, which gives the original description of them in terms of the storm. Verses 14-28a are further late elaboration.

It is clear that Ezekiel was a poet (see Introduction). If we apply poetic criteria to the vision, we get a further refining of his message by deleting small portions of the text which mar the rhythm. In Hebrew poetry the rhythmic pattern does not consist of alternating stressed and unstressed syllables, as in English. There are regular numbers of emphasized syllables per line, with occasional variations to reflect various moods.

Following is a restoration and translation of the original poem describing the vision, with its continuation in verse 28c–2:5; 3:12-14. Here some indication of the Hebrew rhythm is given by the English phrasing and by the indention of lines with only two accents. Others have three, except for 2:1b-2, where three lines (or stichs) take four stresses each.

1:1	It happened in the thirtieth year,
	in the fourth month, on the fifth of the month,
3b	the hand of Yahweh was upon me.
3:22	Then he said to me, [Ezekiel,]
	"Arise, go forth into the plain,
	and there will I speak with you."
23	So I arose and went forth into the plain.
	And behold!
1:4	A wind of a storm was coming;
	Out of the north, an enormous cloud!
	Around it appeared a radiance,
5a	and within it a semblance of beasts!
	Thus their appearance:
13	as coals of fire aglow.
	The fire had a radiance,
	and from the fire came forth lightning!
28	This was a view of Yahweh's glory.
	When I saw it, I fell on my face,
	and I heard the voice of one speaking.
2:1	And he said to me: "Son of man,
	Stand on your feet that I may speak with you."
2	The Spirit then entered me and set me on my feet,
	and I heard him again speaking to me:
3	"You I now send forth
	to the house of Israel.
	who have engaged in rebellion against me,
	both they and their fathers!
4b	So say to them,
	'Thus says Yahweh'—
5a	whether they will listen,
	or whether they will forbear."
3:12a,	Then the wind caught me up and took me away;
14	and I went in the wrath of my spirit;
	and with power was Yahweh's hand upon me.

As Ezekiel described his experience, then, he felt a divine impulse to go forth into the plain. There he saw, not an imaginary scene, but a real storm approaching. Its dark cloud flashed with lightning and perhaps glowed on the edges from the setting sun. Amid the turbulence Ezekiel made out the shapes of animals that suggested to him the cherubs thought to bear up Yahweh (cf. Psalm 18:9-12). Others who saw the storm may have been simply frightened. Only Ezekiel was aware of the glory of Yahweh in it.

1:28c–2:5. *The Prophetic Commission.* Overawed, Ezekiel falls down. The divine voice commands him to **stand upon** his **feet.** When Yahweh commands, Yahweh also empowers. Therefore **the Spirit . . . set** him **upon** his **feet** (cf. 37:10). Then again he **heard** Yahweh **speaking,** to **send** him on his mission. In the power of the wind he feels the might of Yahweh's hand, which is to sustain him throughout his whole ministry. As the text now stands his message is to be the word of Yahweh (2:4*b*). The content is not specified. A change of person in 2:5*a* would yield "If only you will listen, if only you will stop," which would become the message introduced by **Thus says the Lord GOD**.

2:6-7. *Sitting upon Scorpions.* Verse 6 is a self-contained unit. It is not a part of the visions which precede and follow. After Ezekiel begins his ministry he finds that his fears of those to whom he must preach are justified. To sit and talk with them is to **sit upon scorpions.** The hostility suggests actual confrontation of the Judeans whom Ezekiel is condemning (see Introduction); preachers who talk about the sins of those at a distance are not generally unpopular. In verse 7 an editor has repeated parts of verses 4-5 to tie verse 6 into the context.

2:8–3:3. *The Scroll.* What was only a metaphor for Jeremiah (Jeremiah 15:16) becomes a vision to Ezekiel. To **eat** symbolizes acceptance of the divine commission. The filling of the **stomach** means that it has been fully assimilated into his own person. The sweetness like **honey** indicates the satisfaction that comes from proclaiming the word of Yahweh. This is not a sequel to the vision of 1:4-28. In the storm there was no human figure with a **hand.** Even in the expanded version the human figure mounted on the celestial chariot is too remote to extend a hand. Perhaps the original setting is to be found in 8:1*b*-2. If so, 2:9 is the continuation of 8:2, verse 8 being an editorial transition.

3:4-9. *Courage for the Task.* This is the continuation of the preceding scroll vision. Ezekiel is not sent out as a missionary to foreigners. Such people **would listen** and repent. He must preach to the **house of Israel,** who **will not listen.** Yet this is no time for him to sit in his house and dread a hostile public. He must go out and face his opponents. No matter how grim they may be, Yahweh will make him even more hardheaded and bravehearted. **Hard** here plays upon the name Ezekiel, which means "Yahweh makes **hard,**"—that is, gives strength and courage.

3:10-15. *Commission to the Exiles.* This is a later addition. In contrast to the preceding instruction to preach to the house of Israel, it sends the prophet to the **exiles** in Babylonia at **Tel-abib** on the **river Chebar** (see above on 1:1-3). Verses 12*a* and 14 were probably adapted from the original conclusion of the storm vision (see above on 1:4-28*b*). Ezekiel's saying that the wind or the divine **Spirit** —the same word in Hebrew—**lifted** him and **took** him to another place was no doubt mere metaphor. But the late reviser interpreted it as a miraculous mode of transport (cf. 8:3).

3:16-21. *Appointment as a Watchman.* See below on 33:1-9, where this passage is more fully preserved.

3:22-27. *Vision and Dumbness.* On verses 22-23 as the probable original setting of the storm vision see above on 1:4-28*b*. The **plain** of the vision has often been equated with the "plain in the land of Shinar" (Genesis 11:2)—that is, Babylonia—because the same Hebrew word, **biqah,** is used. But the word means either valley or plain. In either case it is suitable to Palestine. The Genesis Apocryphon, among the Dead Sea Scrolls, identifies the Valley of Shaveh or King's Valley (Genesis 14:17) as the *biqah* of Bethhaccherem and locates it in the vicinity of Jerusalem. Such a place is also mentioned in the Mishnah (third century A.D.). An area of modern Jerusalem south of the old city known in Arabic as el-Baqa, "The Plain," may be this site. Since Beth-haccherem means "house of the vineyard," the conjecture that Ezekiel's home and vineyard were near this "plain" is appealing (see below on 19:10-14). Another suitable location, however, is the Valley of Gibeon (cf. Isaiah 28:21). Excavations have disclosed a considerable wine industry at Gibeon. Both these valleys as military approaches to Jerusalem would be suitable locations for the vision of 37:1-14. Near each are lookout points from which different parts of the country could be viewed (cf. 6:2; 20:46; 21:2).

3:24-27. These verses are likewise editorially displaced. Obviously Ezekiel was not **shut** in his **house,** stricken **dumb,** and **bound** perhaps with paralysis or catalepsy (cf. 4:8) from the beginning of his ministry till the promised release came with the fall of Jerusalem (33:21-22). For the probable original context and form of this passage see below on 24:25-27.

B. SYMBOLIC PANTOMIMES (4:1–5:17)

4:1-3. *Mimic Siege of Jerusalem.* Verses 1-2 are in poetic rhythm:

> Now you,
>> O son of man, take a soft brick
>> and lay it down before you.
>> Then engrave upon it a city,
>> and place against it a siege wall.
>> Then build against it a tower,
>> and heap up against it a mound;
>> and set armed camps against it,
>> and with battering rams invest it.

The words "Now you" are introductory and stand outside the rhythm. Only two omissions are needed: the explanation **even Jerusalem** and **against it** after **battering rams.** The fact that even the instructions for a symbolic pantomime should come in poetic form justifies a search for possible underlying poetry in presumably prose passages.

4:3. This verse adds further details concerning the siege. It contains no poetry, however, and is probably a later embellishment. The **iron wall** is not the wall of Jerusalem, for the engraving of a city must have included the wall. It probably represents the Exile, which supposedly separates the prophet from Jerusalem.

4:4-8. *Exile Symbolized.* Here the **house of Israel** and the **house of Judah** distinguish the former northern and the still existing southern kingdoms of Israel. On **days** standing for **years** cf. Numbers 14:34.

The Septuagint reads only 190 years for the duration of Israel's exile (verse 5). This figure subtracted from the date of the first deportations, 734-732 (II Kings 15:29), gives 544-542 for the expected return of the northern kingdom. **Forty** years (verse 6) from the second exile of Judah, 586, brings us down to 546. Thus the two exiles would end about the same time. It is questionable, however, whether they are to be understood as concurrent.

The number **three hundred and ninety** is more difficult to interpret but probably correct. Its explanation may be that 390 + 40 = 430, the duration of the Egyptian sojourn (Exodus 12:40). If the intent was to depict the combined exiles as being 430 years, then Judah must remain in exile 40 years after the return of Israel. Counting 390 years from the fall of Samaria (722) brings us to 332, the time of the conquest of Palestine by Alexander the Great. At that time Shechem, the first capital of Israel, was rebuilt.

Presumably the author of this late passage wrote during the 40 years following that event and predicted a restoration of Judah in 292. It was probably during this period that the book received its last major editing (see Introduction).

4:9-17. *Food Scarcity and Defilement.* Two quite different concerns are represented here: scarce food under siege and impure food in exile. Features of the two are mixed up in the symbolic interpretations (verses 13-15, 16-17). Either two independent symbolic actions have been telescoped into a single narrative or one has been overlaid with the other. The material about scarcity in verses 9-11, 16 can be restored to poetic form and is probably Ezekiel's. Originally it may have read somewhat as follows:

> Now you, take barley,
> and put it in a vessel,
> and make bread of it.
> Your food shall you eat by weight;
> from time to time shall you eat it.
> And water by measure shall you drink;
> from time to time shall you drink it.
> And he said to me, "O son of man,
> lo, the staff of bread I am breaking,
> that bread they may eat by weight
> and water they may drink by measure!"

It is not certain which grain was mentioned in the original poem, but **barley** seems most likely. With **staff of bread** cf. our saying that bread is the "staff of life." In verses 16-17 **with fearfulness** and **in dismay** are echoes indicating the 12:17-19*a* at one time followed this poem (see above on 1:4-28*b*). Verse 17 is probably an expansion of the conclusion that originally was part of 12:19 (see below on 12:17-20). **I will do this** was supplied by the Revised Standard Version to make the present connection of verse 17 smoother.

The rest of the passage cannot be restored to a poetic form and is probably from another hand. The mixture of grains in verse 9 signifies impure food (cf. Deuteronomy 22:9-11), as does the use of **human dung** as fuel for cooking. In the Middle East even today small girls gather animal droppings and pat them into discs, which are then dried on the roof and used for cooking.

5:1-17. *The Threefold Fate of Jerusalem.* As in Isaiah 7:20, shaving symbolizes devastation. The **third** of **hair** to be burned **in the city** is interpreted as death by pestilence and famine (verse 12). The third to be struck **round about** is to suggest the doom of the city's defenders. The final third is to be scattered **to the wind** as a symbol of dispersement. The introduction to the interpretation is to be found in verse 11, where **I will cut you down** could also be rendered "I too will hold a shearing."

Later additions by an early hopeful editor (see Introduction) specify that a **small number** of hairs is to be bound in Ezekiel's **skirts**. They are to come from the last third and the binding represents their preservation. One could hardly recover hair thrown to the wind, but God can recover the scattered people. Reference to them is added to the interpretation in 6:8-10 and 12:15-16, which probably belong immediately after verse 12. The **fire** which will **come forth** from some of this preserved hair (verse 4) may reflect the events after the fall of Jerusalem described in Jeremiah 40:11–41:10.

5:5-10. *Jerusalem in the Midst of the Nations.* This passage is independent of the preceding symbolic pantomimes. In verses 5-6 the indictment may be restored as follows:

> This is Jerusalem!
> Amid the nations I put her;
> Around her are the lands!
> But she rebelled against my judgments
> more wickedly than the nations,
> and against my laws, than the lands!

This is Jerusalem refers to the place where Ezekiel is standing. The city at the **center of the nations** is still unfit to be their spiritual capital (Isaiah 2:2-4). Because it has not kept God's **ordinances,** literally "judgments," it must know God's punitive **judgments** (verses 8-10).

5:13-17. These verses are an editorial expansion on the judgments of verses 8-10 and a conclusion to chapters 4–5. In verse 15 **you shall be** instead of the King James translation "it shall be," is supported by one of the Dead Sea Scrolls.

C. ANNOUNCEMENTS OF DOOM (6:1–7:27)

6:1-14. *A Threat to High Places.* Verses 1-7 and 13-14 form a unit which no doubt originally stood before 20:45. The high places were local sanctuaries on hilltops. In accordance with

Deuteronomy 12:1-14 these were outlawed by King Josiah (II Kings 23:8, 13-14, 19-20) but were revived after his death. Yahweh was sometimes worshiped at these shrines, but the danger of idolatry was greater at such centers.

When the attack comes, the idolaters will flee to the high places for sanctuary. They will be cut down there by the ruthless foe. The destruction will extend throughout the land, from the arid **wilderness** in the south to **Riblah** in Syria, the northern-most boundary of David's empire. Verses 8-10 were added by an early hopeful editor to follow 5:12, but later editing interrupted this connection.

6:11-12. This brief unit describes a dance of doom in which Ezekiel beats time with his **hands** and **foot** as he chants the coming destruction. **Far off** and **near** clearly refer to distance from Jerusalem.

7:1-27. *The Coming of the End.* Such language as **Now the end is upon you** and **Now I will soon pour out my wrath** strongly suggests that Ezekiel may be speaking directly to inhabitants of Jerusalem (see Introduction). It is a time of crisis, probably when news of Nebuchadrezzar's approach with his army has been received. Yahweh is a God of justice, Yahweh's mercy has spared the people in the past (cf. 20:17) the **day** of reckoning has come (verses 4, 9; cf. 8:18; 9:10). According to the Septuagint it is the "day of the LORD" (verse 10*a*). This idea of a catastrophic day of divine action was older than Amos and Isaiah, and was emphasized by Zephaniah. It became especially popular in postexilic times.

Though the idea is not unknown to Ezekiel (cf. 13:5; 30:2-3) it is doubtful that here he means anything more than a day of doom for Judah. Thus we may suspect that the statement that the end involves the **four corners of the land**—that is, the earth, as the phrase is translated elsewhere (Isaiah 11:12)—is an interpolation.

7:10*b*-11. This passage is textually corrupt and obscure. With the Septuagint we may omit **violence** and translate: "Pride has budded, has grown up into a rod of wickedness." The last phrase may mean either a rod used for wicked purposes, referring to

Jerusalem, or a rod for punishing wickedness, referring to Nebuchadrezzar. Perhaps both meanings are intended.

7:12-19. The imminence of war leads to falling prices in real estate. But **let not the buyer rejoice, nor the seller mourn,** for both will suffer loss. When Jerusalem is besieged, those who are prospering will soon find nothing to buy. **Silver and gold . . . cannot satisfy their hunger.** At all times there are needs greater than money, but only in times of disaster do we fully realize this.

7:20-27. Such an impasse has come because the people have misused their wealth (verse 20) and have oppressed their fellows (verse 23*b*). People in all stations will be impotent (verses 26-27). Those who do not recognize God's lordship over life and wealth in times of peace must learn God's lordship in a time of judgment.

D. Visits to the Temple (8:1–11:13)

8:1-3b. *The Journey to the Temple.* Part of this passage may belong elsewhere as the introduction to the scroll vision (see above on 2:8–3:3). The original beginning of the present narrative may be extracted as follows: "In the sixth year, in the sixth month, on the fifth day of the month, the elders of Judah were sitting before me; and the Spirit lifted me up and brought me to Jerusalem." **Elders of Judah** would most naturally refer to those active in Palestine rather than to exiles in Babylonia (see Introduction). Here they consult Ezekiel on a date, September 18, 592, a little more than a year since his call (see above on 1:1-3). This indicates that in a short time Ezekiel has achieved considerable reputation as a prophet.

Later editors assumed that Ezekiel was in Babylonia. They have inserted two alternate explanations for his report of visiting the temple in Jerusalem: a miraculous flight **between earth and heaven,** and inspired **visions.** Without these verse 3*b* is in line with 11:1 and 37:1. It is a way of describing what was probably a trip into the city from some outlying village in or near the plain of 3:22. For the idea of miraculous transport of a prophet the editor may have been indebted to Elisha's vision of Elijah's departure into heaven (II Kings 2:11-12, 16).

8:3c-6. ***The Image by the Northern Gate.*** The words **of the inner court** are apparently an error for **north,** for that court is not reached until verse 16. Read rather: "to the entrance of the **north** gate that faces north." Cf. 11:1. The word translated **image** here is used in II Chronicles 33:7 as a substitute for the name Asherah (cf. II Kings 21:7). On the worship of this Canaanite fertility goddess cf. Jeremiah 7:18 and 44:17-19, 25.

8:7-12. ***The Secret Chamber of Images.*** This is a gate chamber of the outer court of the temple like that portrayed for the inner court in 40:38. The entrance from the vestibule has been closed off, but the users of this secret chamber have another way of getting in. In the hastily plastered-over doorway Ezekiel notes a hole caused by fallen plaster. He proceeds to enlarge it and enter. On the wall are portrayed divine beings in animal form, as was common in Egyptian temples.

The presence of **seventy . . . elders** suggests a meeting of a pro-Egyptian party which sealed its conspiracy with Egypt in occult practices. In 592 such a party would need to hide. Later it became strong enough to force the puppet King Zedekiah to revolt against his Babylonian overlord—which resulted in the final siege and destruction of Jerusalem.

8:14-15. ***Women Weeping for Tammuz.*** This scene takes place at the northern entrance to the inner court. Tammuz was originally a Sumerian vegetation deity. In Syria he came to be identified with Hadad or Baal as a god who died in the summer at the beginning of the dry season and revived with the coming of the rain in the fall.

8:16-18. ***The Sun Worshipers.*** Ezekiel moves ever deeper into the temple precincts. Yahweh brings him into the inner court, where only priests should enter. Solomon's temple was so placed by its Phoenician architect that on the days of the equinox the rising sun would penetrate the open doors of the **porch** and pass through the "holy place" to shine into the "most holy place" at the back. To the orthodox this may have served as a practical means of dating spring and fall festivals or as a symbol of Yahweh's entrance into the sanctuary.

Others, however, are here finding an occasion for religious syncretism. To them Yahweh's being a "sun and a shield" (Psalm 84:11) is more than a poetic metaphor. By facing the rising sun these worshipers turn **their backs to the temple,** the place of God's spiritual presence.

9:1-11. *A Vision of Slaughter.* Grief and vexation at the sacrilege in the temple now give way to mystic vision. Yahweh summons seven heavenly messengers. One of them, a scribe with a **writing case,** marks the **foreheads** of those **who sigh and groan over all the abominations.** This will protect them from the death to be administered by the other six angels. The **mark** is literally a letter, tau, which in the older script had the form of a cross. As today, such a mark was sometimes used as a signature and is so translated in Job 31:35. Here it represents God's signature (cf. Revelation 7:2-3; 14:1).

Judgment begins in the temple, for those closest to God are the most accountable. The idea of individual responsibility and individual punishment in this vision (cf. chapter 18) is contradicted by the declaration in verses 9-10 that none will be spared. These displaced verses evidently should follow 11:13 (see comment). We see this indicated by their poetic form and by their introduction in verse 8, which is an adaptation of 11:13*b*—a literary echo characteristic of the late editors responsible for the rearrangement (see above on 1:4-28*b*).

10:1-22. *Yahweh's Departure from the Temple.* It is possible that the preceding vision was originally followed by another which portrayed the burning of the buildings of Jerusalem. If so, only its beginning remains. The rest has been replaced by an extensive interpolation with a different theme, Yahweh's abandonment of the temple. The divine **glory** must leave the temple and the city to make possible their destruction.

Small insertions about the glory have prepared for this (8:4; 9:3). The description of the departure of the glory in verses 18-19 is concluded in 11:22-23. The burning is never carried out (cf. verse 7) and nothing is said of how the righteous escape. On the imagery of the chariot, the **cherubim,** and the **wheels** see above on 1:4-28*b.*

11:1-12. *Another Visit to the Temple.* The language of verse 1*a* indicates a new beginning (cf. 37:1) and introduces a different visit from that of chapter 8. The concern this time is not with cultic sins but with evil counselors of the king. In the **east gate,** probably that of the inner court, **twenty-five men** who are **princes of the people,** or officials, are gathered to confer. They declare that the people in Jerusalem are like meat in a kettle about to be cooked. Under such circumstances their whole effort should be directed toward defense. They should not try to **build**—that is, repair **houses.** It is their **wicked counsel** in the past which has brought the city to its present dilemma.

This incident originally must have come later than Ezekiel's allegory of the pot (24:1-5), which is dated at the beginning of the final siege. Thus on this occasion Ezekiel must have come to the gate from some place inside the city.

11:7-12. Unfortunately this passage has suffered some editorial additions which have confused its original meaning. As it now stands the **caldron** seems to symbolize the city's protecting walls and the **flesh** its most distinguished citizens. The prophet's indictment then denies that they are so distinguished. He declares rather that the victims of their assassination are the real meat of the city.

These counselors will be removed from the kettle and judged **at the border of Israel,** at Riblah (see above on 6:1-14). There, after the destruction of Jerusalem, a number of leading citizens were taken before Nebuchadrezzar and executed (II Kings 25:18-21). Riblah was of course far north of the actual border of Judah at that time. But as the point of greatest expansion under David and Solomon it was ideally regarded as the proper border by the later contributors to the book (cf. 48:1).

The original meaning of Ezekiel's reply was probably: "This is indeed a kettle filled with the flesh of men you have killed; therefore many of you will be slain and become flesh in the kettle" (verses 6-7). **Your slain** in verse 7 means "those of you who will be slain." **Whom you have laid in the midst of it** is a misleading insertion.

11:13. *The Death of Pelatiah.* There can be no doubt that this verse, which is in poetic form, comes from Ezekiel himself and reports an incident in his experience. It is strong evidence for the view that Ezekiel was a Palestinian prophet (see Introduction) and confronted in person the people of Judah and Jerusalem with his sermons. During one of the sermons Pelatiah collapsed and died. Defenders of the Babylonian locale have offered various explanations—for example, that Ezekiel learned of Pelatiah's death later. But none of these provide for the interaction described in the text.

11:13b. The **remnant of Israel** may mean either Judah, which was left after the northern kingdom was destroyed, or Jerusalem (cf. Isaiah 1:8-9). Does the death of Pelatiah foreshadow a destruction of this remnant? The original answer is to be found in 9:9-10, which is also poetic, and which is clearly out of place (see above on 9:1-11). This answer is an unqualified "yes, the remnant will be destroyed." In place of this the later editors have substituted an originally unrelated passage (verses 14-20). This more agreeable answer indicates that a remnant will be preserved in the Exile.

11:14-25. *Dispossession of the Exiles.* Verses 14-16 originally had nothing to do with what now precedes them. Rather they come from a later time, after the destruction of Jerusalem. They deal with the situation that arose when the poor left behind by the Chaldeans were **given** fields left vacant by the exiles (cf. 33:23-29; Jeremiah 39:10). This distribution included property belonging to exiled relatives of Ezekiel.

Your fellow exiles is a substitution from the Septuagint for the Hebrew "men of your redemption"—that is, kinsmen whose property one is obligated to redeem when it is lost through debt or otherwise (cf. Leviticus 25:25; Ruth 4:3-6; Jeremiah 32:6-12). The property vacated by Ezekiel's relatives should be held in trust by him until their return.

More important, Ezekiel insists that they have not **gone far from the Lord.** Yahweh will be with them and will be their

sanctuary in the lands to which they have gone (verse 16). This declaration became an important building stone for the late editors in the development of their theory of the shekinah-glory succession as an authentication of the rebuilt temple (see Introduction).

11:17-25. An early addition of hopeful material is to be found in verses 17-20 (on verse 19 cf. 36:26-27). In substituting verses 14-20 for 9:9-10 (see above on 9:1-11) the late editors added verse 21 as a characteristic literary echo of 9:10*b* (see above on 1:4-28*b*). Verses 22-23 are the conclusion of the account of the departure of Yahweh's **glory** from the temple and city (chapter 10). When last seen the glory is atop the Mt. of Olives. Finally verses 24-25 bring the combined temple vision to a conclusion by taking Ezekiel back to **Chaldea**—Babylonia—by the same method or methods by which he is said to have left (see above on 8:1-3*b*).

E. ORACLES AND ALLEGORIES (12:1–17:24)

12:1-16. *Pantomime of Coming Exile.* Ezekiel reflects on his frustration in preaching to those who seem willfully blind and deaf. His thoughts come to him as a **word** from Yahweh. The **rebellious house** is the **house of Israel,** to whom he has been sent as prophet (cf. 2:3-7; 3:17). This passage offers strong evidence that Ezekiel's ministry was in Palestine to the people of Judah rather than in Babylonia (see Introduction). Acting out the threat of exile would be highly effective for impressing on Judeans the risk of their present course. Such dramatization would hardly be needed for those already in exile.

That Ezekiel **dug through the wall** suggests a structure of sun-dried clay bricks. This has been noted as favoring a Babylonian locale because the rarity of stone there made such construction common. On the other hand building with this material in Palestine was not uncommon. For example, at the site of Shechem excavators have turned up walls of this kind from all periods of its history.

12:3b-7. One going into exile would be able to rescue only a few valuables. These, together with the necessities of the journey, would form his **baggage.** This would perhaps be carried in a sack over his shoulder. The **wall** dug through depicts a breached city wall. However, in the enactment it was probably the wall of a courtyard, perhaps in Ezekiel's home village. On verse 6b see below on verses 8-16.

12:8-16. An editor has added certain details to the passage (cf. especially verses 6b and 12-13). These make it a prediction of the flight of the **prince,** Zedekiah, and his capture and blinding at Riblah (cf. II Kings 25:5-7, see above on 11:7-12). On verse 14 see below on verses 17-20. On verses 15-16 see above on 5:1-17.

12:17-20. *Pantomime of Eating in Fear.* The action of this passage was probably not mere stage acting. Rather it was a real experience of Ezekiel to which he attached a symbolic meaning (cf. 21:6-7). The Hebrew of verse 19a probably means "and say *to* the people of the land." If, as seems probable, this term means rural citizens whom Ezekiel is informing of the coming exile, the passage is evidently to be dated before the siege. Thereafter the people of the surrounding countryside were gathered within the walls (cf. 22:17-22). The poetic form of the oracle in verse 19 may be restored as follows:

> They shall eat their bread with fearfulness,
> and they shall drink their water in dismay,
> that they may waste away under their punishment,
> and look at one another in dismay.

The result described in the last two lines comes from 4:17b (cf. 24:23), where this brief pantomime evidently once stood (see above on 4:9-17). In rearranging the material the late editors substituted a result that would not logically follow. The Hebrew should be translated "*that* their land may be stripped . . . ." This must have been the original conclusion of verse 14.

12:21-28. *Skepticism About True Prophecy.* In verses 21-25 the validity of prophetic prediction is questioned by skeptics. They point to the **long** time that has elapsed without the threatened doom. Ezekiel has been predicting it for several years, and no doubt the same persons have been hearing Jeremiah even longer, yet the end has not come. On the other hand in verses 26-28 only the immediate relevance of prophecy is questioned, on the assumption that it concerns **times far off.** The answer to both attitudes is that the fulfillment is **at hand.**

13:1-16. *False Prophets.* Those who prophesy **peace**—Hebrew "peace" means not merely freedom from attack but also prosperity and general well-being. These false prophets should be warning of the coming doom. They are **like foxes among ruins,** indifferent to the destruction of the nation. Or, if the reference is to jackals (the same Hebrew word is used in Psalm 63:10 and Lamentations 5:18), they are scavengers looking for gain from it. Instead of standing in the **breaches** as defenders or helping to repair the **wall** (cf. 22:30)—that is, the moral defenses of society—they cover its cracks with **whitewash** and leave it to collapse when a hard rainstorm hits.

13:17-23. *False Prophetesses.* This oracle deals with two different subjects. Possibly it represents a combining of two originally separate oracles:

(1) a condemnation of female practitioners who, like the men of verses 1-16, prophesy **out of their own minds** for a small fee (verse 19a), telling **lies,** indifferent to moral values (verse 22);

(2) a condemnation of sorceresses who claim power to slay their clients' enemies by use of **magic bands** and **veils.** The sin of sorcery lies, not in any supposed effectiveness of black magic, or even in its malice, but rather in its presumption in invading the sphere of the supernatural. Thus white magic is also to be condemned. Nothing in the Scriptures justifies hunting witches to blame for our troubles, but much condemns the attempted exercise of occult powers.

14:1-11. *Idols in the Heart.* A group of **elders of Israel** come to Ezekiel seeking an oracle (cf. 20:1). It is uncertain whether this designation is to be distinguished from "elders of Judah" (8:1; cf. 8:11-12). Possibly it refers to leaders from the territory of the former northern kingdom. If so, their coming to Ezekiel may indicate that he lived north of Jerusalem (see above on 3:22-27).

The northern people came under King Josiah's rule and reform (II Kings 23:15-20). However, after his death, they were separated from Judah and relapsed into their former syncretistic religion which included use of idols (cf. II Kings 17:41). Whether from north or south—or even from the exiles in Babylonia, where of course there was great temptation to syncretism—the idolatrous elders are to be given no oracle by the prophet. Yahweh will **answer** them with acts of judgment.

14:12-23. *Survival of the Righteous.* From four punishments which might befall a land it is repeated that the **righteousness** of even **Noah, Daniel, and Job** would save only themselves but **neither sons nor daughters** (cf. chapter 18; Genesis 18:22-32). Noah is well known for having saved his sons and their families by his righteousness (cf. Genesis 7:1). Ezekiel may have known a version of the Job story in which the sons and daughters of Job 42:13 were the same as those of Job 1:2 (cf. Job 1:5).

Daniel, in this book spelled Danel in the Hebrew, cannot refer to Ezekiel's supposed fellow exile (cf. Daniel 1:1-7). As early as 1900 it was suggested that this Daniel must be an ancient sage from the tradition of some neighboring people (cf. 28:3). Such a figure has since been discovered in the tablets dating back to the fifteenth century dug up at Ras Shamra in northern Syria, site of the ancient Canaanite city of Ugarit.

According to the story told in the tablets Daniel was a good and wise king who beseeched heaven with sacrifice and prayer for a son. At length Baal was moved to intercede for him before the supreme god El, and his petition was granted. When the son, Aqhat, reached young manhood, he was presented with a magic bow by Kothar, the god of craftmanship. Anath, the war goddess, tried to buy it from him. On his refusal to sell she brought about his death. The conclusion of the story is not fully preserved. But there are indications that through the prayers of Daniel, the pious father, Aqhat was restored to life.

14:21-23. The repeated insistence that only righteous individuals will be saved, applied specifically to Jerusalem (verse 21), is contradicted by the statement in verses 22-23. This says that the **survivors** of the city's destruction going into exile will be typical Jerusalemites who, by their manifest wickedness, will prove to those already in exile that Yahweh was justified in such punishment. Poetic criteria show that underlying this editorial conclusion is the original ending of Ezekiel's oracle:

> How much more when I send upon Jerusalem my judgments,
> to cut off from it both man and beast!
> Yet will there be left in it some survivors;
> [They by their righteousness will deliver their lives.]

The final line or something similar, presumably suppressed by the editors, is implied by **How much more**—what has been true of lands generally is even more true of Jerusalem. Addressing the contradiction to the exiles is quite exceptional, but cf. the intrusion of "sons and daughters" in 24:21, 25.

15:1-8. *Parable of the Vine Wood.* This oracle evidently was spoken soon after the fall of Jerusalem. It refers to the **fire** by which the city was burned (cf. II Kings 25:8-9). Before its burning Jerusalem was like vine wood, which is low-grade lumber. How much less valuable it is now! The parable proper (verses 1-5) is poetic. It was followed originally by only verse 6, in which the last clause probably should be translated "so have I given up the inhabitants of Jerusalem." Verses 7-8 seem to be a later addition in which the experience of the city is traced down to the debacle which occurred at Mizpah (II Kings 25:25-26; Jeremiah 40:13–41:18). Thus those who escape from the fire of Jerusalem are to go forth to another fiery doom (cf. 5:4; 19:14a).

16:1-43c. *Jerusalem the Unfaithful Wife.* Here is a long poem on the history of Jerusalem, presented in allegorical form. For Jerusalem really to perceive the nature of her sins she must see them against the background of all the wonderful things God has done for her in the past.

16:1-5. Jerusalem was originally a Canaanite city, with **Amorite** and **Hittite** inhabitants. In allegorical terms she is described as born of an Amorite **father** and a Hittite **mother** who, rather than give her the care proper for a newly born infant, abandon her in an **open field.** Unwanted infants in pagan society were usually so exposed in a public place, where someone else might take pity on them—cf. Moses left in the bulrushes.

16:6-7. Seeing the infant Jerusalem in her helpless and impure state, Yahweh says: **Live, and grow up like a plant of the field.** This refers to the sparing of the city during the conquest under Joshua. It was allowed to survive as a Jebusite stronghold in Hebrew territory. The child's being **naked** signifies the poverty of the city.

16:8-14. Yahweh sees that the young lady is now grown and enters into a marriage **covenant** with her. The marriage stands for David's capture of the city by stratagem to make it the capital of his kingdom (II Samuel 5:6-9). He spared the inhabitants and even married some of the Jebusite girls (II Samuel 5:13-16). The spreading of Yahweh's **skirt** over the lady may allude to the pitching of the sacred tent in Jerusalem to house the ark (II Samuel 6:12-19). The adornment, **beauty,** and **renown** of the city reached a climax in the time of Solomon.

16:15-34. As a wife Jerusalem turns to adultery and becomes a **harlot** (cf. Jeremiah 3; Hosea 1–3). She uses her God-given wealth for the erection of pagan **shrines** and **images,** idols whose service is infidelity to Yahweh (verses 15-19). She practices child sacrifice (verses 20-21) and temple prostitution (verses 23-25). Even international alliances are cited as infidelity (verses 26-29; cf. Jeremiah 2:18-19; Hosea 8:9). These not only showed lack of trust in Yahweh alone for national security but often involved ceremonies recognizing the gods of other nations (see above on 8:7-12). In times of weakness this opened the way to pagan influences in religion (cf. II Kings 16:10-15).

Tucked away here is a reference to a reprimand which went unheeded (verse 27). In the annals of Sennacherib reference is made to his attack on Judah in 701. He **diminished** the territory of Hezekiah, turning over certain towns to the kings of cities of the **Philistines.** The degeneracy of Jerusalem reaches its worst when she has to hire her lovers by annual payments of tribute (verses 30-34).

16:35-43. None of Jerusalem's jealous lovers among the

nations can count on her fidelity. She has played off one against the other. Hence they will at last assemble against her and strip her of her **clothes**—that is, her wealth. They will leave her **naked and bare** as she was at first. The first Chaldean invasion may be envisioned in verses 37-39 and the second in verses 40-41. Ungrateful Jerusalem has forgotten her past, from which Yahweh saved her (verse 43; cf. verse 22). Her execution is to be a lesson to **many women,** meaning nations.

16:43d-63. *Jerusalem and Her Sisters.* Verses 44-52 are an independent indictment which has been supplemented with a message of hope (verses 53-63). This is united to the preceding allegory by a transitional statement (verse 43d), *by the insertions of* her husband and and **their husbands and** (verse 45), and by the allusion to the **covenant . . . in the days of your youth** (verses 59-60). The great sin of the Amorites and Hittites was the exposing and sacrifice of their **children** (verses 3-5, 20-21). It is this sin which makes Jerusalem more wicked than **Samaria** and **Sodom.** Samaria was guilty of **abominations**—idolatry—but not this! Sodom's sin was **pride,** self-sufficiency, and neglect of the **poor.** The story in Genesis 19:4-11 was told to illustrate the degeneracy of the city of Sodom after an "outcry" against it arose (Genesis 18:20). This outcry came from the throats of the oppressed poor. Ezekiel is like Jesus in regarding offenses against children as the gravest. That Jerusalem is judged worse than Samaria (verses 47, 51; cf. 23:11) may owe something to Jeremiah 3:11.

16:53-63. The promise of the restoration of Sodom and Samaria is probably from the early hopeful editor (see Introduction). If divine love can restore Jerusalem, how much more Sodom and Samaria, who were less sinful. Restoration will precede repentance and will be the ground of shame and penitence (cf. 20:42-43 and 36:31-32).

17:1-21. *The Eagle, Cedar, and Vine.* This **allegory** takes the form of a fable in which eagles engage in horticulture. The narrative in verses 3-10 has received an exilic supplement in verses 22-24. Intervening is an interpretation which leaves no doubt of the story's meaning (verses 11-21).

17:3-6. An **eagle,** the king of Babylon, comes to **Lebanon**—that is, Jerusalem, whose temple and palaces were built of cedars of Lebanon. He takes the **top of the cedar,** Jehoiachin, along with other **topmost . . . twigs,** high officials, and puts them in the **land of trade,** Babylon. Then he takes the **seed of the land,** Zedekiah, and places it **in fertile soil . . . beside abundant waters**—that is, in a relationship of dependence on the great power of the Euphrates, or Babylon. There it becomes a **low spreading vine,** a subservient vassal. It directs its **branches,** its international ties, toward this eagle alone.

17:7-10. Then another **eagle,** the king of Egypt, appears in the sky. The **vine,** Zedekiah, redirects its **branches** toward the new eagle so that he may **water it**—give it military aid. This eagle moves the vine to **good soil by abundant waters,**—that is, makes it tributary to the Nile. Can the newly transplanted vine **thrive?** To this question two negative answers are given:

(1) **He,** apparently meaning the first eagle, will root it out (verse 9).

(2) The **east wind,** Babylonia (cf. 19:12; 27:26), will blast it (verse 10). The verse is probably an interpolation by one concerned that the allegory should indicate precisely that Zedekiah was exiled to Babylon and died there (cf. verses 16, 20). **Ezekiel's** original prediction was spoken before the event (verse 10). It foresaw only that when struck by the hot wind blowing in from the desert, a Chaldean invasion, the vine should **wither away on the bed where it grew**—that is, suffer military defeat (cf. verse 21).

17:11-21. Ezekiel's allegory was propaganda against the policies of Zedekiah. He did not dare express himself in plain language lest he be accused of treason. He did not have the close friends in high station that Jeremiah had. Therefore he needed to be more subtle in his criticism of the king or he might suffer the fate of the prophet Uriah (Jeremiah 26). Thus it seems certain that Ezekiel did not provide this explanation of his allegory but left it to his listeners to interpret as best they could.

17:22-24. *The Messianic Tree.* According to this supplemental allegory a **sprig from the lofty top of the cedar,** meaning a

265

descendant of Jehoiachin, will be planted on a **lofty mountain,** Jerusalem. There it will grow into a **noble cedar,** a mighty ruler, whose **branches** will shelter **beasts** and **birds,** other countries. As a consequence **all the trees of the field,** all other kings, will **know** that Yahweh is the Lord of nations. This early hopeful addition (see Introduction) may have in mind Jehoiachin's grandson Zerubbabel. Some hoped he might be the one to restore the Davidic monarchy. Matthew 1:12-13 and Luke 3:27 trace the ancestry of Jesus through Zerubbabel, whose name means "sprout of Babylon."

F. INDIVIDUAL RESPONSIBILITY (18:1-32)

Here is a thesis for which Ezekiel is justly famous. The occasion must have been one of pessimism, when the predicted doom appeared inevitable. Instead of taking personal responsibility for what was happening, people were blaming their ancestors. Ezekiel himself had preached that the people were guilty of the sins of their fathers (2:3; chapter 20) and that Jerusalem had inherited certain sins from its Amorite and Hittite ancestors (16:3, 44-45). This inheritance of sin, however, was only sociological and environmental. Sins of their fathers may be inherited, but only because their children fail to hear or heed the call to repentance.

The popular **proverb** that Ezekiel denies was known to Jeremiah also (Jerimiah 31:29). Ezekiel's denial is based on his faith in Yahweh's sovereign claim over every **soul.** Every person must make his or her own answer to God. If people are **righteous** Yahweh will not surrender them to suffer for the sins of their ancestors. Only **the soul that sins shall die.**

The death of which Ezekiel speaks is not the natural one which each person must face. Nor is it the death of the soul as we use the term. The **soul** here means the "person," as often in the Bible. The threat to life envisaged here is the Chaldean invasion (cf. 33:1-6). Apart from a miracle, Ezekiel's message could not have been literally fulfilled. There must have been many examples of the wicked escaping and of the righteous being slain. Yet back of this is a sound faith that God is **just** and deals with people as persons. Ultimately this faith was to be vindicated, but it called for a doctrine of immortality which had not yet been revealed to the Hebrews. Jeremiah did right in transferring faith's fulfillment to the future (Jeremiah 31:27-30).

The final plea (verses 30-32) is for repentance based on the love of God, who will punish the unrepentant but is grieved to do so (verses 30-32). Each generation, in the light of new insights, is called on to forsake the sins of its **fathers.** To denounce traditional sin calls for courage. To renounce it calls for equal courage, for it pits the individual against the rest of society with its inherited way of life. Christ died to save people from unworthy tradition (I Peter 1:18-19).

G. THE FATE OF JERUSALEM (19:1–24:27)

19:1-9. *The Lioness and the Young Lions.* In verse 2 the reference of the pronoun **your,** which is singular, is a question to which a number of answers have been given. The most likely is that the poem is to be understood as spoken by Yahweh to Ezekiel (cf. 12:1-3*a*). Thus his **mother,** who is compared to a **lioness,** represents the nation of Judah (cf. Genesis 49:9). In the Hebrew the poem is in 3/2 rhythm—that is, with three stresses in the first part of each line and only two in the second part. In the Revised Standard Version each Hebrew line is rendered by a full line representing the three-stress part followed by an indented line representing the two-stress part. This is the rhythm commonly used in a **lamentation** or dirge, seen predominantly in Lamentations.

In the poem as we have it there are two exceptions to the regular dirge rhythm. Verse 4*cd* is in 2/2 rather than 3/2 rhythm. It identifies the first **young lion** with King Jehoahaz, the son and immediate successor of Josiah, who after a reign of only three months was taken captive to **Egypt** (II Kings 23:31-34). To be parallel with Jehoahaz the second young lion should be

Jehoiachin, who also reigned only three months before being taken into exile by Nebuchadrezzar (II Kings 24:8-16). The second young lion is identified in verse 9*a-c*, which is the other exception to the rhythm. It has an extra part line, 3/3/2.

If we eliminate the two irregularities, by omitting verse 4*cd* entirely and removing from verse 9*bc* the words **to the king of Babylon; they brought him,** the explicit references to both Egypt and Babylon disappear and the usual identifications of the two young lions with Jehoahaz and Jehoiachin may be reconsidered.

Without verse 4*cd* the first young lion is simply **taken in their pit** but not exiled. Thus he may well represent King Jehoiakim, whose eleven-year reign ended with his death late in 598 while Nebuchadrezzar was beginning to lay siege to Jerusalem. The natural parallel to Jehoiakim is Zedekiah, who also ruled eleven years and also by rebelling against Nebuchadrezzar brought on a Babylonian invasion and exile. Even with the interpolation verse 9 fits Zedekiah better than Jehoiachin, for Nebechadrezzar came to Jerusalem and took Jehoiachin, but Zedekiah was **brought** to Nebuchadrezzar at Riblah. Instead of **into custody** (verse 9*c*) the Hebrew text reads literally "into strongholds," evidently referring to those of Riblah.

Because Jehoiachin ruled only three months and inherited a hopeless situation from his father, he could accomplish little. He might legitimately be skipped in this poem. A possible reference to him, however, appears in verse 5*a*. In the Hebrew text this reads "when she saw that she had waited." This could refer to the brief reign of Jehoiachin, who never had a chance to become a young lion.

Each young lion is said to have met his doom when he **learned to catch prey** and **devoured men.** This is a subtle attack on Judean nationalism. The greatness of Judah was to be obtained in other ways (cf. Revelation 5:5-6).

19:10-14. *The Vine and Its Strongest Stem.* Here Judah is compared to a grapevine. This poem does not continue the previous allegory but is another on the same theme. Verse 10*a* probably should read: "Your mother was like a vine of *your* vineyard," as in two Hebrew manuscripts. The last phrase in all other manuscripts includes "your." These words are apparently addressed by Yahweh to the prophet (see above on verses 1-9). This suggests that Ezekiel had a vineyard and that an experience with one of his vines underlies this allegory. On the location of his vineyard see above on 3:22-27.

19:10-12. The first three pairs of lines (verses 10-11*b*) are in the 3/2 dirge rhythm (see above on verses 1-9). They describe Judah in its prosperity. The **strongest stem** has often been taken to mean Zedekiah. However, it more probably represents not so much a particular ruler as the Davidic dynasty. The ruin of the vine is brought about by the arrogance of this main stem. A translation of the unamended Hebrew text of 11*c*-12 is as follows:

> Its height towered
>   among the clouds.
> It was seen in its height
>   with the mass of is branches.
> But plucked up in fury,
>   she was cast down to the ground.
> The wind from the east
>   dried up her fruit—
>   now stripped off and withered.
> Her strong main stem,
>   the fire consumed it.

"It" and "its" here refer to the strongest stem, and "she" and "her" refer to the vine, which is also "mother."

In contrast with the rest of the poem this portion is in 2/2 rhythm—that is, each half line has only two stresses. The Revised Standard Version follows most analysts in repunctuating verses 12*c-f* as 3/2. Since verses 11*c*-12*b* can be handled only as 2/2, they are often assumed to be a later addition. Yet it is these very lines that unlock the meaning. From them we may recognize that this allegory makes use of a popular myth in which a plant grew so tall that it reached heaven and because of such arrogance met its downfall (cf. Genesis 11:1-9; Daniel

4:10-37). Thus the word translated **thick boughs** in verse 11*d* should rather be understood to mean "clouds" as in 31:3, 10, 14.

In the grape culture of Palestine vines were severely pruned. They were made to lie close to the ground so that they would not be scorched by the sirocco during the dry summer months. The arrogance of the Davidic dynasty, as represented in Jehoiakim and Zedekiah, has exposed the vine of Judah to the **east wind**, meaning Chaldea (cf. 17:10; 27:26).

19:13-14. The conclusion concerns the aftermath of Jerusalem's fall. **Transplanted in the wilderness** refers to the impoverished circumstances of those remaining in the land. The vine has already suffered from **fire** in verse 12*f*. Therefore the repetition in verse 14*a* apparently refers to Ishmael, who as a scion of the Davidic **stem** brought further suffering to the nation (see above on 5:1-17; 15:1-8).

20:1-3. *An Inquiry from Israel's Elders.* On August 14, 591 Ezekiel is visited by elders of Israel (see above on 14:1-11). They have come to **inquire of the LORD**—that is, to secure an oracle from God. Yahweh's refusal to answer is itself an answer. **Is it to inquire of me that you come?** has a double meaning. The Hebrew could also be translated "Is it to seek me that you come?"

20:4-32. *The History of Israel's Rebellion.* Since they were in Egypt the people of Israel have repeatedly **rebelled**. Yahweh has spared them, but Yahweh's patience is running out. In each period of history the recurrent pattern is:

(*a*) revelation of the covenant, or a plea to obey it,

(*b*) violation of the covenant,

(*c*) threatened punishment,

(*d*) deferred anger.

In the second cycle (verses 10-17) elements *c* and *d* (verses 13*d*, 14) are repeated in a sort of poetic parallelism (verses 15-16, 17). The same repetition was intended in the latter half of the third cycle (verses 21*b*-24) but is incomplete. Instead of the expected repetition of element *d* we find Yahweh giving **statutes that were not good** and **making them offer** child sacrifices (verses 25-26). Obviously the text is not intact.

After verse 24 there originally must have come a variation of verse 17 as the conclusion of the third cycle. Next should follow the beginning of the fourth cycle in verse 28, of which the opening words should be translated "So I brought them" (cf. verse 10). The original introduction to verses 25-26 is now found in verse 27. This identifies the ascription to Yahweh of bad laws and the institution of child sacrifice as a blasphemy uttered by the people. Their accusation ends with **first-born,** the remainder of verse 26 being editorial. Thus the logical original order is verses 28-29, 27, 25-26*a*, 30-32.

The joining of verse 27 to verse 25 calls for the following translation: "In this, moreover, your fathers blasphemed me, while dealing treacherously with me [saying that] it was I who had also given them statutes that were not good . . ." The restoration fits with the denunciation of child sacrifice in verse 31.

20:33-39. *The Purging of Gathered Israel.* Those dispersed will be gathered once more into the wilderness. But instead of being in the **wilderness of the land of Egypt,** Sinai, they will be in the **wilderness of the peoples,** possibly meaning the desert region of northern Arabia. Hosea 2:14-15 also speaks of a new wilderness experience but in the Judean wilderness (cf. 47:1-12).

Only those willing to observe God's covenant will be brought from the wilderness into the land of promise—like sheep entering the fold under the counting shepherd's **rod.** The doctrine of individualism expressed here is in accord with Ezekiel's theology, but the concern with the dispersion is characteristic of early hopeful editors (see Introduction).

20:39-44. *The Accepted Worshipers.* Verse 39 is probably the conclusion to verses 4-32. If the people are so obstinate, let them **go** ahead **and serve** their **idols.** But the impending doom will soon bring this profaning of Yahweh's name to an end! In the new setting, however, verse 39 is transitional to verses 40-44. Verse 39*b* seems to refer to the abandonment of idolatry by the dispersed people as a condition for their acceptable worship in the Holy Land. Those brought home from the dispersion will again worship on Mount Zion. There alone will they present sacrifices. When Yahweh shows acceptance of them by blessings, they will loathe themselves for their past sins (cf. 16:63; 36:31). This is another early hopeful addition (see Introduction).

20:45–21:5. *Doom for the Whole Land.* Three oracles belong in this series. The first, however, is misplaced (see above on 6:1-14). Standing where he can see the different sections of the land, Ezekiel threatens first the "mountains of Israel" (6:1-7), those to the north. He then turns to the **south** (20:45-48), and finally to Jerusalem (21:1-5). His vantage point would be some place where the northern and southern areas could be seen from the city—possibly the Mount of Olives. The threat to each area becomes an ill omen for the whole land (6:14; 20:47; 21:4).

20:45-48. The name **Negeb**, literally "parched," is applied to the desert country south of Beer-sheba. But this was not **forest land,** or even brush land. So frequently was the name used to refer to the south that here apparently Ezekiel applies it to the wooded area between Jerusalem and Hebron.

20:49. Some of Ezekiel's listeners are inclined to dismiss his messages as **allegories.** No doubt their reaction is to the messages of chapters 16–17 rather than those of chapters 15 and 19, which were spoken after the destruction of Jerusalem.

21:1-5. Ezekiel declares that Jerusalem itself is doomed. **Sanctuaries** is evidently a plural used of the temple (cf. Leviticus 21:23; 26:31). The cutting off of **both righteous and wicked** evidently antedates the developed individualism of chapters 9 and 18. Thus these oracles are fairly early.

21:6-7. *Sighing with a Broken Heart.* This is no mere symbolic pantomime. As in 12:17-20 (see comment) Ezekiel interprets his own emotion as a message from God. The verses come from before the siege of Jerusalem and an editor not unnaturally linked them to the preceding passage with a **therefore.** In verse 7 **all knees will be weak as water** may also be translated "all knees will flow with water." The Septuagint reads "all knees will be defiled with water," that is, urine. In times of fright one may lose bladder control (cf. 7:17).

21:8-17. *The Song of the Sword.* This is more than a song, for symbolic actions accompany it. This is sword dancing, a more elaborate version of the dance of doom in 6:11-12. Such a performance must have been rhythmical and poetic (cf. 33:30-33). Verses 10*b* and 13 contain interpolations from wisdom literature (cf. Proverbs 13:24; 15:32; 29:15).

21:18-23. *The Sword at the Crossroads.* Judah has rebelled against the Babylonian overlordship. Its yoke has been felt since 605, when Nebuchadrezzar drove the Egyptians from Syria and Palestine. It has been especially heavy since 597, when an earlier revolt ended in the exile of King Jehoiachin and the installing of Zedekiah as puppet ruler (see Introduction). During that revolt the **Ammonites** of Transjordan aided Nebuchadrezzar against Judah (II Kings 24:1-2). Now they have revolted. So too has Zedekiah, under pressure from prominent Judeans who prefer a return to Egyptian vassalage (see above on 8:7-12).

Ezekiel selects a fork in the road to represent the **parting of the way,** the crossing of the caravan routes. Nebuchadrezzar must decide whether to move first against **Rabbah,** the capital of Ammon, or Jerusalem. Ezekiel even sets up a **signpost** to mark the ways to the two cities. He acts out the part of Nebuchadrezzar using **divination** to determine the will of his gods about which place to attack first. On the **arrows** cf. II Kings 13:14-19. On the **teraphim** cf. Judges 17:5 and Zechariah 10:2. Complex instructions for reading oracles from the **liver** of a sacrificed animal, as well as marked clay models of livers, have been dug up in Mesopotamia.

21:23. This verse is strong evidence for Ezekiel's presentation of the oracle before an audience in or near Jerusalem rather than in Babylonia (see Introduction). Not only does he perceive the reaction of those present to his acting out the processes of divination. He is also aware that some of them have made **solemn oaths,** evidently with the Egyptians who have been encouraging the rebellion against Babylonia.

21:24-27. *Indictment of Zedekiah.* This passage contains no mention of the sword but is attached to the preceding by its

therefore. The poetic indictment of Zedekiah (in verses 25-27) may be restored as follows:

> And you, O prince of Israel,
> Unhallowed one, whose day has come,
> the time of your final punishment—
> Thus says Yahweh:
> "Remove the turban, and take off the crown!
> Exalt the low, and abase the high.
> A ruin, ruin, ruin I will make it,
> Till he comes whose right it is and I give it to him."

Zedekiah is only a **prince** (cf. 12:10, 12) since he is the regent for the exiled King Jehoiachim rather than rightful king (see Introduction). Thus he is **unhallowed** because he does not participate in the sacredness of the royal office. This situation was not understood by the later editor. He inserted **wicked** in an attempt to explain "unhallowed" and thus upset the rhythm. **Things shall not remain as they are** is a paraphrase of the Hebrew, which reads literally "this, not this." **There shall not be even a trace** involves an emendation of the Hebrew "this too was not." Evidently these are marginal notes that were copied into the text. "This, not this" may mean that the preceding prediction was fulfilled but not the following. If so, "this too was not" means that the prediction following it was not fulfilled. Alternatively these may be notes of a scribe about the text, indicating that one clause was well attested but others were not found in all manuscripts. The final line would be more intelligible if it could follow verse 26b and thus refer to the crown.

This is the only passage in which Ezekiel faces Zedekiah in person. The occasion probably was a public appearance just before or during the siege of Jerusalem. To give morale to the war effort Zedekiah dons royal apparel. The wearing of the **turban** and **crown** is a claim to be king. It is thus a symbol of his revolt against Babylonia, since the Babylonians reserve the title king for Jehoiachin. Verse 27c maintains that the crown must be saved for Jehoiachin, who is expected to return someday.

21:28-32. *The Doom of Ammon.* The sword which was to fall on Jerusalem (verses 18-23) will finally attack Ammon as well (cf. 25:1-7). Note the numerous parallels in language with other passages declaring the doom of Jerusalem and Judah:

with verse 28*cd* cf. verses 9-10;

with verse 29*a* cf. 22:28;

with verse 29*b* cf. verse 25;

with verse 31*b* cf. 22:21*a*;

with verse 32*a* cf. 15:4*a*;

with verse 32*b* cf. 24:7.

If this says anything, it means that Ammon is to suffer the same doom as Judah. There is one exception. Instead of being exiled Ammon is to be punished on its own soil (verse 30*b*). On the **origin** of Ammon cf. Genesis 19:30-38.

22:1-16. *The Defiled City.* Here Jerusalem is informed of **all** its crimes. Foremost are murder and idolatry. Oppression of the **sojourner**—the resident alien—and of widows and orphans goes hand in hand with contempt for the **holy things** of the sanctuary and with disdain for the **sabbaths.** Dishonesty and bloodshed have so corroded the city that its lack of morals will mean also lack of morale (verse 14). Its end will be dispersion **among the nations.**

22:17-22. *The Smelting Furnace.* As Nebuchadrezzar's army approaches the people flee from the small villages into Jerusalem. Ezekiel seems to be there. He greets them with this message comparing them to materials thrown into a smelting furnace. **So I will gather you** employs a participle which may be best interpreted here as meaning "so I am gathering you." The analogy implies that there will be a purified product emerging from the flame (cf. verse 15; Isaiah 1:24-26).

22:23-31. *The Need for a Deliverer.* Here the people are still in their rural villages, where the lack of rain spells disaster in agriculture. This has come as a punishment for decadence in society. All are affected, from top to bottom. **Princes** in verse 25 probably means the kings of Judah. In verse 27 it translates a different Hebrew word referring to high officials. Verses 25-27 expand on Zephaniah 3:3-4. On verse 28 cf. 13:1-16. On **people**

of the land see above on 12:17-20. Into the breached **wall** some heroic figure must step, not only to repair it, but to ward off a hostile foe. The broken wall is the moral bulwark of society. The breach is sin. The enemy who opposes is Yahweh.

23:1-35. *Oholah and Oholibah.* With this allegory of Yahweh's two unfaithful wives cf. chapter 16 and Hosea 1; 3. Marriage with sisters, both living, was forbidden by the later Priestly legislation (cf. Leviticus 18:18). **Oholah** means "her tabernacle" and **Oholibah** means "my tabernacle is in her." The former symbolizes **Samaria,** whose temples are considered illegitimate. The latter is **Jerusalem,** which contains the true temple. Ezekiel accepts the Deuteronomic principle of only one legitimate sanctuary (Deuteronomy 12:1-14).

Samaria and Jerusalem are here viewed as the nations Israel and Judah, and so their marriage could take place in **Egypt.** Their **harlotry** consists of making alliances with foreign nations instead of relying on Yahweh alone for protection. On Oholah's infidelity and punishment cf. 16:15-43. On Oholibah's infidelity cf. 16:15-29, especially verses 26-29. On Jerusalem's being **worse** than Samaria cf. 16:46-47, 51 and Jeremiah 3:11.

23:22-35. Oholibah's punishment is to be administered by Babylonia and its Assyrian subjects. **Pekod** is named in Assyrian records as a Babylonian tribe. Proposed similar identifications of **Shoa and Koa** are doubtful. The cruel deeds mentioned in verses 25-26 represent indignities suffered by captives. The root meaning of the verb for "go into exile" in Hebrew is "go naked" (cf. Isaiah 20). In verses 32-34 a drinking song has been adapted as a taunt song.

23:36-49. *Judgment of Oholah and Oholibah.* This passage uses the symbolism of verses 1-35 but applies it to an entirely different situation. Here the infidelity consists of cultic and moral sins. Since the passage portrays the doom of both sisters as future, it must refer to the postexilic cities of Samaria and Jerusalem. Since both together have **defiled** the temple at Jerusalem it antedates the Samaritan schism and thus is prior to the final editing (see Introduction).

The situation described seems similar to that with which

Nehemiah had to contend. His foes from territory of the former northern kingdom had allies in Jerusalem (Nehemiah 2:19-20; 4:7; 6). These were connected by marriage with the Jerusalem priesthood (Nehemiah 6:18; 13:28). One of them was even allowed to use a chamber of the temple (Nehemiah 13:4-9). That idolatry and child sacrifice (verses 37-39) should be problems in postexilic Jerusalem is surprising, but cf. Isaiah 57:5, 9.

23:45-49. The judgment is to be administered, not by the Chaldeans, the "wicked of the earth" (cf. 7:21, 24), but by **righteous men**—that is, faithful Jews. A violent reform like that of Josiah is prescribed (cf. Deuteronomy 13:12-16; II Kings 23:15-20). The reforms of Nehemiah and Ezra saved the country from the upheaval proposed here.

24:1-14. *The Corroded Cooking Pot.* On the very day that Nebuchadrezzar **laid siege to Jerusalem,** January 15, 588, Ezekiel seized a rusty cooking **pot.** He proceeded to cook with it until all its contents were burned to a crisp. While cooking meat, he seems to sing a familiar work song, but he adapts it to portray the imminent disaster of Jerusalem. His action became proverbial (cf. 11:1-12). Ordinary people used pottery cooking vessels. Since Ezekiel was a priest (1:3) and the **pot** he used was **copper** (or bronze), as was usual for temple cooking vessels, this appears to be a castoff utensil from the temple. It had been declared unfit because of its deeply embedded **rust.** This view seems to be confirmed by the words **without making any choice,** which is literally "for **her** no lot has fallen." The feminine pronoun refers to the feminine noun **pot,** not to the masculine noun **piece** of the preceding clause. The casting of lots was a common priestly practice. But no lot was cast for this vessel because of its ritual impurity. (For cooking in the temple, cf. 46:19-24, and for sacrifices on the eve of battle, cf. Psalm 20).

The original oracle about the pot, its contents, and the fire has been elaborated. Editorial interpretation is introduced prematurely in verse 6*ab*. By weaving interpretation into the text earlier, it converts literal details of the cooking into instant allegory. Thus **Take out of it piece after piece** after mention of **the bloody city** suggests exiles rather than pieces of meat (cf.

11:7-12). The words "for her no lot has fallen" were transferred to the end to refer to these worthless exiles. The imperatives of verses 3-5 and 6c-f which belong to the cooking song were probably continued by those of verse 11.

The original sequence of connections may have been somewhat as follows:

> 5c Boil its pieces, [boil them,]
> d yea seethe its bones within it—
> 6c *in a pot whose rust is in it,*
> d whose rust departs not from it,
> f for which no lot has fallen.
> e Take out of it piece after piece,
> 11a then set it empty upon the coals . . .

Ezekiel's interpretation appears in verses 9-10 and 12-14. It emphasized the catastrophe of Jerusalem due to its deeply ingrained moral corrosion. Its **filthiness** in verse 13 refers to all the wrongs that King Josiah's reform (cf. II Kings 23) had vainly **cleansed** away. Jerusalem was too corrupt for reformation. Therefore it must face the scorching flames of the Babylonian siege.

24:6a-b, 7-8. Jerusalem's blood-guilt was the subject of an independent oracle. Like 22:1-16 (cf. 24:9) this was addressed to **the bloody city.** It was inserted into the cooking song in order to explain the city's **rust** as **the blood she has shed.** But since Ezekiel's pot was **copper** (verse 11) rather than iron, it would have green rust. The sole point concerning the blood is that like the blood of righteous Abel (Genesis 4:10-11) it cannot **be covered.** Always open to Yahweh's gaze, it invokes his **wrath.**

24:15-24. *The Death of Ezekiel's Wife.* When it is apparent that his wife is to die, Ezekiel is told how to behave so that her death will symbolize the impending destruction of the temple. He is to make no outward show of **mourning,** accepting God's judgment as just. As she is the **delight** of his **eyes,** so the temple is to the people. An editor has tried to turn the emphasis from the temple to the **sons and daughters** of the exiles (verse 21c; cf.

14:22-23). This is most obvious in verse 25*b*, where the Hebrew contains no **and also.** On the date of this event see below on verses 25-27.

24:25-27. *Ezekiel's Dumbness.* This continuation of the preceding narrative seems to have been broken up by later editors, who placed its beginning in 3:24*b*-26 and its ending in 33:21-22. The beginning may be restored and translated:

> And he spoke with me and said:
> "And you, O son of man, behold,
> Cords will they place upon you,
>   and bind you with them.
> Go, shut yourself in your house,
>   and go not out among the people.
> Your tongue I will stick to your palate,
>   that no longer you may be their reprover,
>   for they are a rebellious house.

The editors moved **Go, shut yourself within your house** (3:24*c*) to the beginning of the divine speech in order to have Ezekiel return home at the end of his vision. But originally it must have followed the warning that he might be **bound** (3:25)—not by a divinely imposed paralysis as in 4:8 but, as the active verbs in the Hebrew suggest, by human hands. Ezekiel is in danger of being imprisoned because of the furor aroused by his prediction that the temple will be destroyed.

Ezekiel is to know of the destruction only by **report** of a **fugitive** (cf. 33:21-22). Therefore the house in which he shuts himself must be outside Jerusalem and presumably is his village home. Early in the siege an Egyptian force drew off the Chaldeans for a time so that it was possible to leave the city (cf. Jeremiah 37:11-15). Perhaps Ezekiel's departure occurred during that period. Several oracles against Egypt, however, are dated between that time and the fall of the city (29:1; 30:20; 31:1; 32:17). More probably, therefore, this incident took place soon after the breaching of the city wall and the flight of Zedekiah.

If so, Ezekiel's withdrawal to silence was ended in less than a month by the fulfillment of his prophecy. At the coming of the fugitive, Ezekiel will be released from his dumbness. The fulfillment of this expectation is 33:21-22. Hence the present passage probably records the experience of **the evening before the fugitive came** (33:22*a*).

II. Judah's Restoration (25:1–48:35)

The material in this book has been arranged into two parts, with the natural division between chapters 24 and 25 (see Introduction). Part I speaks primarily of doom for Israel. Part II is concerned almost entirely with hope—the doom of neighboring nations being viewed as an element of Israel's hope (see below on 28:24-26). In chapters 25–32, seven nations are doomed: Ammon, Moab, Edom, Philistia, Tyre, Sidon, and Egypt. Since the number seven symbolizes completeness, this result may have been achieved editorially. See below on 28:20-23.

A. The Doom of Neighboring Nations (25:1–32:32)

25:1-17. *Oracles Against Closest Neighbors.* In 21:28-32 the **Ammonites** are threatened with attack from the Chaldeans. Here a later foe threatens, the **people of the east**—that is, the tribes of northern Arabia east of Transjordan. These people are also to take over **Moab** and **Edom**. On **Teman** and **Dedan**—here apparently an Edomite town rather than the Arabian oasis mentioned in 27:20 and 38:13—see comment on Jeremiah 49:7-11. The Arab encroachments may have been somewhat gradual, beginning perhaps during the Exile and increasing during the following century. As a result the Edomites were driven entirely out of their ancient homeland and settled in southern Judah. They eventually took over the region—so that by the time of Alexander's conquest (32) most of Judah's former territory was called Idumea.

Meanwhile the encroaching Arabs founded the Nabatean Kingdom with its capital at Petra, where they hewed out many beautiful tombs in the cliffs. In their heyday their power extended around the southern and eastern sides of Palestine from Egypt to Mesopotamia. The foe who is to sudue the **Philistines** is not specified. Gaza, a chief Philistine city, was conquered by Alexander after a two-month siege. **Cherethites,** here apparently used as an alternate name for the Philistines, probably designated a Philistine tribe in the southern part of the country.

26:1-21. *The Rock of Tyre Laid Bare.* Tyre, whose very name meant "rock," was an important Phoenician port on an island half a mile out in the Mediterranean. On Israel's relations with Tyre see I Kings 5; 7:13-45; 9:11-14, 26-28; and 16:31.

26:1-2. The incomplete date in the **eleventh year**—that is, 587/86—seems to set the oracle before the fall of Jerusalem (see below on 33:21-22). But verse 2 describes Tyre's reaction to this disaster as the reason for its coming doom. It is uncertain whether the date has been incorrectly transmitted or whether verse 2 is a late addition. Tyre rejoices over the collapse of Jerusalem, the **gate of the peoples.** It thinks its own riches will be increased because it will not need to deal with Judean middlemen or pay for the right of passage in commerce by land.

26:3-14. The doom of Tyre is presented first figuratively (verses 3-5a). The island city will be destroyed by **many nations** like **waves** of the **sea.** Next its fate is explained historically (verses 7-14). Verses 5b-6 bridge the two sections. Weapons of land siege are to be brought to bear against the city. Its **daughters on the mainland** are its suburbs on the shore.

Nebuchadrezzar had to spend thirteen years in his siege of the city according to the Jewish historian Josephus (cf. 29:18-19). This must have been largely a naval engagement in which he was at a disadvantage. Alexander the Great, however, in 332 captured the "daughters" of Tyre and used their demolished buildings to construct a causeway about 200 feet wide extending out to the island. He was then able to use siege weapons, and took Tyre after seven months. This causeway was broadened still more with the demolished walls and buildings from the island itself, which he threw into the sea (verse 12). Thus from then on Tyre was a peninsula rather than an island. It is possible that verses 1-5a come from Ezekiel and anticipate Nebuchadrezzar's attack. The rest seems to reflect a knowledge of the siege of Alexander the Great and must derive from a later poet.

26:15-21. The coastal cities lament Tyre's downfall in one supplement (verses 15-18; cf. 27:28-36). Another (verses 19-21) foretells Tyre's descent into the **Pit**—that is, Sheol, the **nether world** of the dead beneath the **deep** (cf. 31:15-18; 32:17-32).

27:1-36. *The Shipwreck of Tyre.* The poem of this chapter is a beautiful dirge over the anticipated fall of Tyre, compared with the wreck of a ship. **O Tyre, you have said, "I am perfect in beauty"** may originally have read "O Tyre, you are a ship, perfect in beauty." The ship's construction is described as the best that international trade can provide (verses 4-7). **Senir** is an alternate name for Mount Hermon and **Bashan** was in northern Transjordan. **Cyprus,** literally Kittim, is probably the city-state Citium on the island of **Cyprus,** then known as **Elishah.** The ship's crew are **skilled** seamen from all the chief cities of Phoenicia.

27:9c-25a. In this passage Tyre is not a ship but a harbor and center of trade. It is an interpolation into the poem. Verses 9c-11 provide a transition to an amazing catalog of Tyre's commerce. On **Lud and Put** see comment on Isaiah 66:18-23. **Helech** and **Gamad** may have been in nothern Syria or Cilicia. **Tarshish** may have been on the southwest coast of Spain. **Javan** is related to Ionia and designates Greece. **Tubal** and **Meshech** were in Asia Minor. **Beth-togarmah** was probably in Armenia. **Helbon** was near Damascus. The places of verses 19-22 were in Arabia and those of verse 23 probably all in upper Mesopotamia—though **Canneh** and **Eden** may have been in southern Arabia.

27:25b-36. The ship poem of verses 3b-9b is now resumed. The heavy cargo presages a wreck (verses 25b-26). Tyre's wealth is coveted by Chaldea, symbolized by the **east wind.** The **pilots** have brought it into stormy seas by rebelling against the

Babylonian overlordship (cf. Jeremiah 27:1-11). Universal **lamentation** follows the sinking of the ship, but the dirge seems to end in taunt.

28:1-10. *The Presumptuous King of Tyre.* The word translated **prince** here is not the one that Ezekiel uses of Zedekiah (see above on 21:24-27) but an equivalent of "king" (cf. verse 12). Thinking himself secure on his island **in the heart of the seas,** the ruler acts as if he were a **god**—and may even claim to be so. In prophetic thought this is blasphemous. It can lead only to dethronement and descent **into the Pit** (see above on 26:15-21). Verses 3-5 attribute the pride of the Tyrian ruler to his **wisdom,** which made him rich. They are a later addition, requiring a resumptive review in verse 6. They share, however, with the rest of the chapter in mythological colorings. On **Daniel** see above on 14:12-23.

28:11-19. *Expulsion from Eden.* The **king of Tyre** in Ezekiel's time was Ithbaal II. In the traditional Hebrew text he is compared with a cherub who sinned in the garden of Eden and was expelled (verses 14, 16 King James Version). Thus the king's self-deification is interpreted as an angelic being grasping after divinity. A different vocalization of the same Hebrew consonants yields the interpretation of the Septuagint adopted in the Revised Standard Version, that the king was **with the guardian cherub,** who **drove** him **out** (cf. Genesis 3:24).

On the king as a **signet** ring cf. Jeremiah 22:24 and Haggai 2:23. The **perfection** of the king at creation consisted in **wisdom** and **beauty.** This first man was not naked but clothed with precious gems. These represent not only the splendor of paradise but his special qualifications as a priest-king (cf. Exodus 28:4, 17-21). The Septuagint text ascribes to him all twelve precious gems of the high-priestly breastplate (cf. Exodus 39:10-13). This Eden is a **holy mountain of God,** a temple site (cf. 20:40), and the king is accused of profaning his sanctuary (verse 18). On the plural **sanctuaries** see above on 21:1-5.

Tyre's dishonesty in business breeds **violence.** As a port with worldwide trade relations Tyre could have mediated like a priest great spiritual blessings. But preoccupation with the material led to the corruption of its wisdom and to its experience of "paradise lost."

28:20-23. *The Doom of Sidon.* Sidon was another Phoenician city about twenty-five miles north of Tyre. Though it was less important than Tyre in the days of Ezekiel, there were times both earlier and later when it was more important. This oracle, in which divine **holiness** is the ground of **judgments** on Sidon, is very brief and non-circumstantial. It was probably added editorially in order to give a total of seven nations that are doomed. See above on 25:1–48:35.

28:24-26. *God's Purpose in Judgment.* Like the preceding passage, this appears to be a later addition. Here the judgment on other nations is seen as enabling Judah to arise as a nation once more, unmenaced by bad **neighbors**. This widely held view explains the placing of the oracles against foreign nations (chapters 25–32) at the beginning of the second half of the book, in which hope for Israel dominates. Thus God's **holiness** will become **manifest** both in judgments on the neighbors and in salvation for Isarel (cf. 20:41; 36:23).

29:1-32:32. *The Dragon of the Nile.* This poem, dated January 7, 587, is directed against **Pharaoh** Hophra (588-569). The **dragon** was a mythological foe, thought to be subdued in the Creation but ever and again threatening to undo the work of God. The dragon is variously called Leviathan or Rahab.

During the Babylonian siege of Jerusalem, evidently sometime in 588, Hophra led an army into Palestine to assist his allies who were in revolt against Nebuchadrezzar. He was soon driven back into Egypt. **Draw you up out of the midst of your streams** may allude to his expedition and **cast you forth into the wilderness** to his defeat. The **fish** that **stick** to his **scales** may represent his subjects—or perhaps the mercenaries which made up a large part of the Egyptian army.

29:6-16. Like the Tyrian ruler (28:2) the pharaoh is guilty of self-deification. But after having stirred up revolt against the Babylonians he has proved to be only a flimsy **reed** on which to lean. His land is to be laid **waste** from **Migdol** in the Delta region to **Syene,** modern Aswan, at the southern frontier with

Ethiopia. A dispersement for **forty years** will be followed by restoration to **Pathros**—that is, Upper Egypt, the territory upstream from the Delta, the traditional original homeland of the Egyptians. This is a later amplification. Egypt was not subdued until 525, when the Persian army of Cambyses conquered the country. It did not lie waste forty years, but as a Persian province it was a **lowly kingdom.**

29:17-21. *A Prey for Nebuchadrezzar.* This passage is dated April 26, 571. It indicates that Nebuchadrezzar was not enriched by his siege of **Tyre.** A Tyrian contract found at the site of Babylon, dated in his forty-first year (564/63) and attested by a Babylonian "keeper of the seal," implies that Tyre became his vassal in return for lifting the siege.

His soldiers had no opportunity for looting. They did not receive the expected reward of their **labor**—for their heads **made bald** by constant wearing of the helmet and their shoulders **rubbed bare** by burdens. With the end of the siege of Tyre, however, they were set free to attack and loot Egypt. A fragmentary Babylonian record indicates that in Nebuchadrezzar's thirty-seventh year (568/67) they undertook this. How far they advanced is unknown. In the situation of **that day** of attack on Egypt the **horn**—that is, the power—of Israel is expected to grow up again. The prophet's message will be vindicated. His mouth need not be shut because of shame (cf. 16:63).

30:1-19. *The Day of Egypt's Doom.* This passage portrays Egypt's doom first as the work of Yahweh (verses 1-9; cf. 26:1-6), then as the work of **Nebuchadrezzar** (verses 10-12; cf. 26:7-14). Unlike the other Egyptian oracles it is undated. Also unusual is the theme of the **day** of Yahweh (see above on 7:1-27).

30:5-12. The prose interpolation in verse 5 lists among Egypt's supporters some from the **land that is in league,** which may also be translated "covenant land," or Palestine (cf. 20:5-6). Jewish soldiers were serving in the Egyptian army. A colony of these was at the southern border on the island of Yeb, where they had a temple (see comment on Isaiah 19:18). On **Migdol to Syene** see above on 29:6-16. On the second prose interpolation (verse 9) cf. Isaiah 18.

30:13-19. The cities named encompass all Egypt from north to south. On **Pathros** see above on 29:6-16. **Tehaphnehes** is an alternate spelling of Tahpanhes.

30:20-26. *Pharaoh's Broken Arm.* On April 29, 587, the people are still hoping that Pharaoh Hophra will bring his army back to permanently relieve the Babylonian siege. They suppose he has recovered from his **broken . . . arm**—that is, his defeat the year before (see above on 29:1-16)—and is ready to try again. But the next time both his **arms** will be broken.

31:1-18. *Pharaoh as a Towering Tree.* This passage is dated June 21, 587, less than two months after the preceding. It heaps scorn on the pro-Egyptian propaganda by picturing Pharaoh Hophra as a tall and beautiful tree, which, however, is nothing but overweening pride that spells doom (cf. 19:11-12; 29:3-5). The tree's extravagant growth exceeds that of other trees in the garden of Eden and so it is cut down (cf. chaper 28 and Daniel 4:4-33, where Nebuchadnezzar's arrogance is like that of Hophra). The myth has been amplified with later material (verses 14c-18). This consigns the tree to the **nether world**, where it is to be placed among other trees (kings) which have been similarly felled.

32:1-16. *A Dirge for the Dragon.* This funeral **lamentation** and prophecy of doom for Egypt is dated March 3, 585. Thus it follows the fall of Jerusalem. Pharaoh Hophra is flexing his military muscles. He thinks he is a **lion**. Instead he is a **dragon** who muddies the **rivers**—the Nile branches of the Delta. He will be caught in a **net** and slain by Yahweh (cf. 29:3-5). A later expansion (verses 9-15) applies the doom to Egypt's **multitude**. The rivers will be **clear . . . like oil** because no one will be left to muddy them.

32:17-32. *Sheol the End of Worldly Glory.* The date of this passage is incomplete in the Hebrew. The date given in the Septuagint, April 27, 586, is earlier than that of verses 1-16, but the passage was placed here by the editors as an appropriate conclusion to the series of oracles against foreign nations. **Sheol** in the Old Testament is simply a **Pit** in the **nether world**—the land under the earth, where all the dead go. The idea that it contained a place of punishment, a hell, arose later, under Persian influence. In the Old Testament threats that the wicked will be sent to Sheol mean merely that they will suffer an untimely death.

This passage is distinctive in that it implies that there is some sort of differentiation in Sheol for the **uncircumcised** and those **slain by the sword.** It eventually contributed to the idea of Sheol as a prison for the wicked, from which they would be resurrected for judgment.

B. The Revival of Israel (33:1–37:28)

In their arrangement of the materials of the book into two divisions—the first pronouncing doom and the second proclaiming hope for Israel—the late editors placed the anti-foreign messages (chapters 25–32) at the beginning of the second half. Now they present the messages of comfort for Israel. Chapter 33 has been skillfully edited not only to provide an introduction to them but also to point up the overall parallelism between the two halves by a series of passages with parallels in the first half.

33:1-9. *The Parable of the Watchman.* Here verses 7-9 repeat 3:17-19. The whole passage really belongs in the earlier context, soon after Ezekiel's call. But verses 2-6 are essential if we are to see this as a parable showing how Ezekiel came to understand his mission. Just as in time of national peril a negligent watchman is court-martialed, so Ezekiel will forfeit his right to live if he does not **warn the wicked.** The coming death is that to be inflicted by the Chaldean army. Ezekiel does not expect to save the entire nation but he hopes to rescue individuals. His own salvation depends on his being a personal soul winner, one who reclaims sinners for true life in the society of God's people.

33:10-11. *A Plea for Repentance.* As in chapter 18, the quotation of a saying of the people is answered by a call to repent (cf. 18:23, 30-32). The earlier saying concerned shirking responsibility (18:2). This saying expresses acceptance of responsibility but with a note of despair—it is too late. The answer is that it is never too late for the **wicked** to **turn from his way and live.** The passage is as suitable for a period after the destruction of Jerusalem as before.

33:12-20. *Personal Responsibility.* This is largely a repetition of earlier material. With verses 12-16 cf. 18:1-20. With verses 17-20 cf. 18:25-29.

33:21-22. *Release from Dumbness.* Here is the continuation of 3:24b-27 and 24:25-27. In the present arrangement Ezekiel's dumbness is traced back to the very beginning of his ministry (3:24b-27). In the view of the late editors this ministry consisted of warning of doom before the destruction of Jerusalem and proclaiming hope afterward. Thus each of these divisions of his ministry is made to start with a relationship to his dumbness. At the beginning of the first he becomes dumb. At the beginning of the second he is released from dumbness. Actually Ezekiel's dumbness involved only a brief period before the destruction of the temple (see above on 24:25-27).

The **fugitive** messenger is to come on the day the temple is destroyed (24:25-27). The date given in verse 21—January 8, 585—does not fit with the record in II Kings 25:8-10 and Jeremiah 52:12-14. The Septuagint and Syriac versions and eight Hebrew manuscripts read "eleventh year," which would be evidence for a date of 587 rather than 586 for the fall of Jerusalem. But at best there is an interval of nearly five months between the fall of the temple and the arrival of the messenger. Even according to the traditional view that Ezekiel was an exile in Babylonia this is too long for word of the event to reach him. Ezra was able to lead a whole caravan from Babylonia to Jerusalem in only 108 days (Ezra 7:9; 8:31).

Clearly there is an error in the date. The most plausible correction is a reversal of the figures for month and day to read "in the fifth month, on the tenth day of the month"—that is, August 17, 586. The mistake may have been either editorial, to harmonize with the editor's idea that Ezekiel was in Babylonia, or accidental, helping to give rise to this story.

The wall of Jerusalem was breached in the fourth month. But the Chaldean army which pursued Zedekiah to the vicinity of

Jericho did not return to demolish the temple and the rest of the city until the fifth month. The exact date was the tenth of that month according to Jeremiah 52:12-14. According to II Kings 25:8-10 it was the seventh. Some manuscripts and versions read the ninth day. This last date fits perfectly with the assumption that verse 21 originally read fifth month, tenth day.

On the **evening before** Ezekiel has a premonition. As a result of this his **mouth** is **opened** before the arrival of the fugitive **in the morning** with the news. This premonition is meaningful only if it coincides with the destruction of the temple in Jerusalem. Thus the date in verse 21 is intended to identify the day after the destruction of the temple. Even if the seventh is correct in II Kings 25:8, we may assume that the process of demolition occupied several days and that the destruction of the temple itself took place on the ninth.

Thus the passage may be most logically understood on the basis that Ezekiel was not in Babylonia—where one who had **escaped** the Babylonians at Jerusalem would certainly never seek refuge—but at his village home (see above on 3:22-27; 24:25-27). This would have been near enough for a messenger who slipped out of the doomed city under cover of darkness to arrive in the morning.

The opening of Ezekiel's mouth sounds like deliverance from real dumbness, brought on by the severe emotional stress of his wife's death and his own narrow escape from being imprisoned. For a possible figurative meaning, however, cf. 29:21; Psalms 22:15; 38:13-14; 39:9; and Lamentations 4:4.

33:23-29. *The Land Grabbers.* After the fall of Jerusalem the poor were given vacated estates of the exiles (cf. Jeremiah 39:10). They are now fighting among themselves for even larger holdings. This is the same situation which prompted 11:14-21, which was placed earlier to provide a parallel in the first half of the book (see above on 33:1–37:28). It is addressed to the same people before they started fighting. **These waste places** and the use of the second person indicate that Ezekiel is preaching directly to the guilty persons, thus creating difficulties for the suggestion of some scholars that Ezekiel had a preexilic ministry in Palestine but was taken to Babylonia with those exiled at the time of the fall of Jerusalem (see Introduction). It is possible but unnecessary to suppose that Ezekiel was exiled later, several years after the fall of Jerusalem.

33:30-33. *Ezekiel as a Singer of Love Songs.* Ezekiel's **voice** is so attractive that people listen to his preaching as if he were a popular singer. Yet they give no heed to his message. In a way they were right in being reminded of **love songs,** for it was divine love as well as justice which he preached (cf. verses 10-11).

In the context of the following chapters Ezekiel's songs become also promises of hope in the view of the editors. Verses 33 harks back to 2:5. The doom of the nation still lies ahead in this passage, which could date from almost any time after Ezekiel became known for his eloquence. As placed by the editors—with only one oracle intervening since his release from the dumbness—it suggests a meteoric soaring to popular fame.

34:1-10. *Doom for False Shepherds.* This beautiful poem (verses 2-5a, 6a, 8b-10) comes from early in Ezekiel's ministry. It condemns the leaders of the nation for their selfishness and their failure to enforce the Deuteronomic reform after King Josiah's death. They are especially condemned for allowing the resumption of worship at the "high places" (see above on 6:1-14).

Unfortunately several prose interpolations have obscured not only the poetry but also the meaning. The straying of the sheep on the **mountains**—that is, to the local hilltop shrines—is interpreted as wandering over the world in a farflung dispersion (verse 6b). As a result many analysts have denied any part of the chapter to Ezekiel and supposed it to be dependent on the postexilic material in Jeremiah 23:1-3. A closer parallel to Ezekiel's original idea is found in Jeremiah 50:6-7, which refers to worship at the high places. But this is later than Ezekiel's poem.

34:11-31. *Hope for the Scattered Flock.* Ezekiel's idea inspired several supplements, mostly from the early hopeful editors (see Introduction). Verses 11-16 declare that Yahweh will do what the rulers of Judah failed to do as shepherds. Verses

17-21 seem to reflect the troubled situation of the mid-fifth century. They portray Yahweh as sternly condemning the selfishness of certain members of the flock (cf. Nehemiah 5:1-5). Verses 23-24 speak of **David**—that is, the future messianic king who is to be the true **shepherd.** Verses 25-31 promise that Yahweh will renew the **covenant** and give every material **blessing.**

35:1-15. *Doom for Mount Seir.* This is another oracle against Edom (cf. 25:12-14). It is evidently a product of the early hopeful editors (see below on 36:1-15). **Mount Seir** refers, not to a single peak, but to the whole highland range south of the Dead Sea. This covered most of the land occupied by the Edomites from the time of the Exodus until the Exile. Some of the Edomites pillaged the ruins of Judean cities left by Nebuchadrezzar's army (verse 5). They are described as wanting to **take possession** of **two countries,** meaning the territory of both Israel and Judah in Palestine. But the prediction is that their own homeland will be made **a desolation and a waste.**

Archaeological evidence shows that in fact the **cities** and villages of the Seir region were **not . . . inhabited** during the fifth century. The Edomites were pushed out of their land by nomadic Arabs, who left few traces till later centuries. But any Jewish rejoicing over this was premature, for the Edomites settled in southern Palestine and in time took possession of most of the former territory of Judah (see above on 25:1-7). Eventually an Idumean, or Edomite, Herod the Great, became ruler of all Palestine.

36:1-15. *Renewal for Israel's Mountains.* As the Seir range is to Edom the mountains of Palestine are to Israel. In this continuation of chapter 35 the early hopeful editors say that the desolation predicted for Seir has already befallen the land of Israel. But its fertility will soon support a large population of returned people.

36:16-38. *Spiritual and Material Blessings.* Yahweh's people have suffered exile and dispersion because of their sins. But Yahweh will restore them, say the early hopeful editors, to **vindicate Yahweh's holy name** (cf. 20:9). It is no more materialistic to predict abundance than to predict deprivation, provided the spiritual aspects of life are properly stressed. Here spiritual renewal (verses 25-28) apparently precedes the bounties of nature. At least the spiritual and material blessings belong together.

37:1-14. *The Vision of Dry Bones.* The language of verse 1 refers to a physical journey in a state of spiritual compulsion (see above on 8:1-3*b*). Ezekiel is in the **valley** when he sees the dry bones of soldiers slain in one of the battles against the Chaldeans. This could be the same valley, or plain, where he received his call (see above on 3:22-27). Or it could be the plain of Jericho (cf. Deuteronomy 34:3; II Kings 25:5). In the bones he sees a symbol of his deceased nation. **Can these bones live?** Contemplation gives way to ecstasy and he hears the divine command: **Prophesy to these bones.** When he does, he sees them reassembled. He is then commanded: **Prophesy to the breath**—the wind. Thereupon life comes into the bones.

37:11-14. The original conclusion is verse 11 alone, which speaks to the mood of the day and identifies the bones as the **whole house of Israel.** For those who heard Ezekiel speak no more was needed, for they would find there the meaning. It is through prophetic preaching that the nation is to be reunited and have spiritual life breathed into it once more. This will be a work of new creation. An addition (verses 12-14) overlooks the four-fold stress on prophesying and states rather that Yahweh will reassemble Jews residing in foreign lands. Thence they will emerge as from **graves.** In the original vision the bones are only **upon the valley**—that is, on the surface.

37:15-28. *Pantomime of Two Sticks.* This symbolic action is reminiscent of others that portray coming doom (chapters 4–5). Ezekiel writes **Judah** on one stick and **Joseph,** ancestor of the two largest northern tribes, on the other. Then he fits them together in his hands as a single stick. When asked what this means, he explains that the southern and the northern tribes of Israel will be reunited as **one nation.** This hope of reconciliation is further developed by a later author in verses 20-28. The citizens of the two former kingdoms are reunited in the homeland under a Davidic king and the temple is rebuilt. On the **covenant of peace**—that is, promise of well-being—cf. 34:25-31.

Ezekiel's theme of reconciliation was shared by some (cf. Isaiah 56:3-8) but ignored by many of the returning exiles (cf. Ezra 4:1-3). A complete reversal of his pantomime of the sticks is found in Zechariah 11:7-14, where the "brotherhood between Judah and Israel" is annulled.

C. ORACLES AGAINST GOG OF MAGOG (38:1–39:29)

38:1-23. *The Invasion and Doom of Gog.* This is apocalyptic material—material dealing with hidden revelations and future events. It is concerned with a foe of the last days. The name **Gog** has been variously explained. Some derive it from Gyges, who founded around 670 a great kingdom in Asia Minor, of which Croesus was the last ruler. Others derive it from the name of the Sumerian god of darkness, Gashga or Gaga. More likely it is simply an invention to go with Magog, which is taken, like all other geographical names in the chapter except **Persia,** from Genesis 10:2-7 (see above on 27:9*c*-25*a*).

Though most of the nations represented by these names have been identified, Magog is otherwise unknown. The historian Josephus may have been correct in connecting the name with the Scythians, the foe believed to have been threatening from the north during the early part of Jeremiah's ministry. Gog's forces, however, are drawn from all directions, as these names indicate. Revelation 20:8 locates Gog and Magog "at the four corners of the earth."

The prototype of Gog is the Assyrian ruler Sennacherib; cf. "I will put my hook in your nose, . . . and I will turn you back on the way by which you came" (Isaiah 37:29). But while Sennacherib is to be led away from the Holy Land, however, Gog is to be brought into it (verse 4). Verses 2-9 represent Gog as directed against Israel by Yahweh. Verses 10-13 view him as motivated by his own lust for plunder—a different perspective that suggests a different hand. In Revelation 20:7-8 it is Satan who raises up the hordes of Gog.

The language of this chapter is full of allusions to other parts of the Old Testament—Isaiah and Jeremiah, for example. It presupposes a return of the Jews from many lands to which they have been scattered—not simply in the first difficult times of resettlement, but after they have long been settled and have become prosperous (verses 8, 12-14). Description of the land as consisting of **unwalled villages** probably applies rather generally to postexilic times. Only Jerusalem and a few other places were fortified before the time of the Maccabean revolt. Another indication of late composition is the idea that the great invasion of Gog will fulfill the words of God's **servants the prophets.**

Therefore it seems most likely that the historical figure behind Gog is Alexander the Great, whose homeland, Macedonia, has been identified with the Magog of Genesis 10:2. Having conquered Palestine (332) and moved on to the East, he is here represented as about to return to his doom. Some Jews may have welcomed Alexander as a liberator, but this view did not last. The passage expresses the faith that no matter how powerful the foe that assails God's people, or how successful its invasion of their territory, God's almighty hand can give victory.

39:1-16. *Another Account of Gog.* This passage is more a parallel to chapter 38 than a continuation. Verses 1-2 are a condensation of 38:2-9, agreeing that Gog is brought against Israel by Yahweh. The concern for Yahweh's **holy name** in verses 7-8 is also similar to the reason given in 38:16. On the other hand the doom of Gog described here (verses 3-6, 9-16) is quite different from that in 38:17-23. With different vowel points the Hebrew for **Valley of the Travelers** may be read as "valley of the Abarim" and thus refer to a mountainous region **east of the sea,** meaning the Dead Sea.

39:17-20. *Yahweh's Sacrificial Feast.* Verse 4b prepares for this passage which gives an appropriately gory conclusion to the picture of Gog (cf. Revelation 19:17-18). On the other hand its literary quality so excels the preceding material that it may have been composed by Ezekiel himself for a different setting. If so, it is probably a parody on some cult song inviting the Judeans to sacrifice at the high places, where Ezekiel predicts there will be a different sort of slaughter (cf. 6:2-7).

39:21-29. *God's Vindication in History.* This is the conclusion not simply of chapters 38–39 but of chapters 1–39. A theme of which the editors never tire is that people will **know** Yahweh through divine acts and that Yahweh's **holiness** will be manifest to **all the nations.**

Verses 21-22 apply to the judgment of God (cf. 38:23; 39:7). But they apply equally to the oracles against foreign nations. In the perspective of history the nations will see that Yahweh is holy and sovereign. This explains the judgments they have suffered and also those the Jews have suffered (verses 23-24). The supreme manifestation of Yahweh's holiness, however, will be redemption of Israel (verses 25-29; cf. 20:44; 36:36; 37:28). On **pour out my Spirit** cf. Joel 2:28-29.

D. Design for the Future (40:1–48:35)

The plans of this section for the future temple, its sacrifices, and the allotment of land are presented in the form of a vision. But they are worked out with a mathematical precision that is more the product of study than of vision. The architectural details probably reflect memories of Solomon's temple—as demonstrated by their help in interpreting its description in I Kings 6–7. This points to a mid-sixth century date for the basic material. Yet the concern for such technicalities, as well as other differences in outlook and style from the original material in chapters 1–39, suggest a disciple rather than Ezekiel himself as author of chapters 40–48.

40:1. *The Date.* Though composition around the time indicated is not unlikely, the precise date is symbolic rather than actual. The **twenty-fifth year** has begun, a quarter of a century, and the **fourteenth year** is two times seven. By the ancient method of counting, the year in which the **city was conquered** is taken as the first year. Therefore the first ten days of the twenty-fifth year have begun the fourteenth year since that event. The **beginning of the year** suggests new year's day. In rabbinic calculation, which may be that of pre-exilic Judah, this would be the first day of the seventh month, in the fall. Here, however, the **tenth day** is specified and the phrase may refer rather to the first month. The tenth of the seventh month is the day of atonement (Leviticus 16; 23:26-32).

Another mode of calculation, apparently followed in the dates of chapters 1–39, puts the new year in the spring. The tenth of the first month was said to be the day on which Israel entered the Promised Land (Joshua 4:19; cf. Exodus 12:1-13).

40:2-4. *Introduction to the Vision.* The author uses some of the language of 8:1-3*b* (see comment) to describe his transportation. But here the situation is quite different in that the temple he visits is entirely visionary. The **very high mountain** is the hill on which the former temple stood. Its height is exaggerated (cf. Isaiah 2:2). The building on it is a **structure like a city** because it is surrounded by walls and gates. The angelic guide instructs the author to use his **eyes,** to see the vision, his **ears,** to catch the words, and his **mind,** to understand the whole.

40:5. *The Outside Wall.* The guide's **measuring reed** measures **six long cubits.** The cubit, based on the length of the forearm to the fingertip, was variously calculated. Here the long cubit is defined as containing an extra **handbreadth.** It would measure about twenty and a half inches. Thus the reed is about ten feet three inches long. This is the height and thickness of the temple's outer wall.

40:6-47. *The Gates and Courts.* The gates described here are admirably suited to defensive purposes, for guards can occupy the **side rooms.** Their purpose is to keep out the unfit (cf. 44:4-15). There are three gates leading from the outside to the **outer court,** on the east (verses 6-16), north (verses 20-23), and south (verses 24-27). Corresponding to each of these is an inner gate leading from the outer court to the **inner court** (verses 28-37). All six are identical except that the inner gates are reversed—that is, the **vestibule,** the largest room, is toward the outside. They also have extra rooms attached (verses 38-43).

The **barrier** before the side rooms (verse 12) probably refers to their raised level. Apparently the first side rooms—those farthest from the vestibules—are set back one and half cubits to give the enlarged **breadth** of **thirteen cubits** (verse 11) to make room for swinging doors.

40:17-19. The **outer court** is the area two hundred cubits wide—a **hundred cubits** between the gates (verse 19) plus **fifty cubits** for each gate (verse 15). It lies between the outer walls and the temple proper with its inner court. Fronting on this court, with their backs to the outer wall, are **thirty chambers** for the use of the laity. They serve as a place to eat the sacrificial feasts and to obtain shelter when coming from a distance as pilgrims. In front of the chambers is a **pavement,** probably mosaic, which extends out as far as the ends of the outer gates on three sides and reaches the priests' chambers on the western side (42:3). In good weather the laity could congregate or feast there as well.

40:20-37. The northern and southern outer gates and the southern, eastern, and northern inner gates are repetitiously described as like the eastern outer gate (verses 6-16). **Seven steps** lead to the northern and southern outer gates, and presumably to the eastern outer gate. **Eight steps** lead to the inner gates.

40:38-43. The gate referred to in verse 38 is presumably the northern gate to the inner court (cf. verse 35). If so, **tables** are set up in front of it and inside for use in preparing **sacrifices.** A chamber for washing the sacrifices adjoins the vestibule. Since the eastern gate is also used for sacrifices (46:1-8) it presumably has the same equipment, including the chamber off the vestibule.

40:44-47. The **inner court** is the **foursquare** area, a **hundred cubits** each way, in front of the temple. In the center is the **altar.** Opening off the inner court are **two chambers . . . for the priests** which are built on the sides of the northern and southern inner gates.

40:48–41:26. *The Temple Proper.* The sanctuary itself faces the western side of the inner court. It rests on a **raised platform,** or foundation, six cubits high, which extends five cubits beyond the building on each side (41:8). Its entry **pillars** are reached by **ten steps.** Passing between them one enters first the **vestibule,** then the **nave,** and finally the **inner room,** which is the **most holy place.**

41:5-11. Into the exterior walls of the sanctuary are built **three stories of side chambers.** These are entered by northern and southern doors opening on the extended portion of the platform. Access to this is just beyond the entrance pillars. On each side a winding **stairway** leads to the upper stories. These are progressively wider because of the **offset**—the stepped narrowing—in the wall between the chambers and sanctuary.

41:12-15a. The **yard** is the open space **twenty cubits** wide (verse 10) surrounding the sides and back of the temple proper. Beyond this yard **on the west side**—that is, in back of the sanctuary—is a **building** of unspecified use but of enormous size, seventy by ninety cubits. This may be what is called the "precincts" in II Kings 23:11 and the "parbar" in I Chronicles 26:18. Perhaps it did not have a roof but was simply a walled-off place for disposing of the wastes of the sacrifices. This building with its thick walls extends one hundred cubits from north to south. The distance from the outer wall to the rear of the sanctuary is also a hundred cubits, forming a square. The sanctuary stands in a second hundred-cubit square and, still farther to the east, the altar in a third (40:47).

41:15b-26. The interior of the sanctuary is paneled and decorated with **cherubim** (see above on 1:4-28b) **and palm trees,** reminders of the garden of Eden (cf. Genesis 3:22-24). Nothing is said about restoration of the ark of the covenant with its overshadowing cherubs (cf. I Kings 6:23-28; 8:6-7; Jeremiah 3:16). The only furniture mentioned is an **altar of wood.** This is placed **in front of the holy place** and was doubtless the **table** for the bread of the Presence or showbread (cf. Exodus 25:23-30; II Chronicles 13:11). The height of the temple is not given.

However, its **windows** would need to be above the three stories which surround it.

42:1-14. *The Chambers for the Priests.* North and south of the **western building** and of the western end of the **yard** are small chambers. Here the priests eat their sacrificial meals and change from secular to clerical garb and vice versa. The meat is collected at the tables by the gates to the inner court (40:38-43). Some portions are burned on the altar, and some are eaten by the people (see above on 40:17-19). Others—the **most holy offerings**—are eaten by the priests in their chambers.

Three stories probably refers to a split-level arrangement descending from the yard to the outer court in three terraces of unequal width. These do not have extending platforms supported by **pillars.** This explains how the lower wall can be only 50 cubits long while the upper wall is a hundred cubits long. The hundred-cubit-long **passage** may be **inward** in the sense of being at the upper level. The fifty-cubit **wall** may mark a similar passage along the **outer court.** The number of their **chambers** and their connecting corridors are not specified. But the prohibition of going into the outer court without changing clothes (verse 14) shows the need for direct access to the **temple yard** from the priests' chambers.

42:15-20. *Size of the Whole Temple Area.* As a conclusion to the architectural description the angelic guide measures the dimensions around the outside wall. The whole complex is a perfect square, **five hundred cubits** on each side (cf. Revelation 21:16).

43:1-7a. *The Coming of the Divine Glory.* The prophet has last been led out the eastern gate (42:15) and presumably has been standing there while his guide measures the outer wall. His now being **brought** to the **gate facing east** seems to be evidence of editorial rearrangement or revision. No doubt the gate originally intended here is the inner eastern gate. From this place the prophet with his guide **beside** him can view the coming of the **glory** through the outer eastern gate and see it as it passes through the inner court into the sanctuary. The late priestly editors (see Introduction) have inserted verses 3-5 to associate this scene with their elaborated form of the vision in chapter 1 and especially with their interpolations in chapters 8-11. They dispense with the guide. Here the prophet is transported bodily through the air by the **Spirit,** from the outside gate to the inner court.

The coming of Yahweh's glory authenticates the temple. The late editors have tied in with the rest of the book in order to develop a theory of shekinah-glory succession between the pre-exilic temple and that of their own time, traced through the Exile (see Introduction). In doing so they tacitly identify this visionary temple with that built by Zerubbabel after the Exile. However, the description given here is too extensive and elaborate to be embodied fully in that temple.

43:6-12. *The Sanctity of the Temple.* Here is both the conclusion to the preceding description of the temple and a preface to the legal section which follows. The new cult law is spoken from inside the sanctuary of Yahweh (cf. Leviticus 1:1).

The temple thus consecrated by the return of Yahweh's glory is to be Yahweh's only **place** of permanent abode among the people. Since Yahweh's **throne** is there, Yahweh is to rule the people as their king from this place. Therefore Yahweh will now set forth the sacred, priestly law of the land. The temple will be sacred. **Harlotry** must be avoided—that is, idolatry and sacred prostitution. The royal palaces and the royal cemeteries must not adjoin the sacred precincts (cf. I Kings 7:1-12). This regulation agrees with the placement of the royal city at a considerable distance away (48:18-35). But the use of the term **kings** for the future rulers rather than **princes** (as in 44:3 and 45:8-9) suggests that verses 7b-9 may be supplemental.

The prophet will give a full description of the temple and its laws to the people, who will be awed by the splendor and sanctity of the whole scene. They will then **be ashamed of their iniquities.**

43:13-27. *The Altar.* The great altar for burning sacrifices is a stepped pyramid, like a ziggurat. There is a staircase on the eastern side. The lowest stage is the **base,** next the **lower ledge,** then the **smaller ledge,** and at the top the **altar hearth.** The last is twelve cubits square. Since each stage has a **ledge** one cubit broad, each of the lower stages is two cubits longer on a side than the one above. Thus at the ground level the square is eighteen by eighteen cubits. The altar rises eleven cubits above the **base,** which may be a basin **one** cubit deep (not high) to catch **blood.** The horns were upward protuberances at the corners of the altar which were smeared with the blood of the offerings.

This altar has great theological significance. It is at the very center of the temple area and on a platform eight steps higher than the outer court. If the site itself is a **very high mountain** (40:2), the altar hearth is the highest accessible place in the vicinity. The Hebrew word translated "altar hearth" is spelled two ways in this passage. The first spelling (verse 15*a*) is related to "mountain of God." It is probably derived ultimately from an Akkadian word meaning both "mountain of the gods" and "nether world."

Thus at the center of the whole temple is an altar which links heaven and earth, God and humanity, in a bond of reconciliation. This God is also one who reigns over the nether world and will not allow it to triumph.

43:18-27. On the consecration of the altar cf. Exodus 29:36-37; Leviticus 8:11; and I Kings 8:62-64. On the family of Zadok see below on 44:4-31.

44:1-3. *The Shut East Gate.* It may be that this passage is directed against some sort of ritual in which the rising sun on the day of the equinox shone through the eastern gate into the temple. For this purpose it seeks to historicize the entrance of the divine glory into the temple by associating it with the disuse of the eastern approach—which was impractical because of the steep side of the Kidron Valley below it.

The chambers around the outer wall are apparently provided for ordinary lay worshipers, to eat **bread,** meaning the portions of their sacrificial offerings which they are to eat (see above on 40:17-19). But the **vestibule** of the eastern gate is reserved for the **prince,** meaning the ruler of the line of David (37:25). Ezekiel had political reasons for using the term "prince" rather than "king" for Zedekiah (cf. 21:24-27). However, the fact that the later editors prefer "prince" even for the future kings (cf. 45:7-9, 16-17, 22; 46:2, 4, 8-18; 48:21-22) suggests theological reasons, such as the concept of Yahweh alone as king (cf. 43:6-12).

44:4-31. *The True Priesthood.* Those to be **excluded** from the temple are **foreigners**—that is, non-Jews (contrast Isaiah 56:3-7). Now the **Levites,** not foreigners, are to be the temple servants. The Levites were former priests of the now illegitimate high places. As **punishment** for their faithlessness they are to be limited to only the most menial of tasks in the temple. Those who minister in the inner court and in the sanctuary must belong to the **sons of Zadok,** who was chief priest in the time of Solomon. As priests in the preexilic temple they are here said to have remained faithful. But surely Ezekiel would not have forgotten the apostasy which he saw practiced in the temple itself (cf. chapter 8).

Their **linen** garments symbolize purity. The contagion of **holiness** is a power which for ordinary people is as dangerous as uncleanness. On the priests' teaching and judging functions cf. Deuteronomy 1:17; 17:8-13; and 33:8-10. On the other regulations cf. Leviticus 21:1-15. The statement here that the priests are to be supported exclusively by **offerings** and have no **inheritance** is contradicted in the next section (45:4).

45:1-8. *The Holy District.* See below on 48:8-22, where this material is repeated in fuller form.

45:9-17. *Royal Responsibility.* The **princes**—that is, the Davidic rulers, are to have special crown property for their support (verses 7-8; cf. 48:21). Therefore they must refrain from imposing taxes except those which support the temple cult. The King James Version rendering "Take away your **exactions** [taxes] from my people" is better than the Revised Standard Version **Cease your evictions of my people** (verse 9*d*).

The people's religious dues are to be collected by the state for maintaining the daily sacrifices. The "prince" as head of the state will contribute the **offerings** for **sabbaths** and **feasts.** Since contributions by both people and ruler are by specified quantity, it is the obligation of the ruler to enforce honesty in weights and measures lest "man rob God" (Malachi 3:8).

45:18-20. *Atonement for the Sanctuary.* In verse 20 the Septuagint reading "in the seventh month on the first of the month," seems much more probable. Thus semi-annual sacrifices are to purify the sanctuary from any defilement by people who may have unknowingly approached it while in a state of uncleanness. This corresponds to the more elaborate ceremony of the annual day of atonement of the Priestly Code (Leviticus 16:11-22).

45:21-25. *The Feasts of Passover and Booths.* It is strange that only two of the three great annual festivals are mentiond here. The feast of weeks (Pentecost) is omitted (cf. Exodus 23:14-17; Deuteronomy 16:1-17). The ancient rabbis struggled without success to harmonize the rules given here for the sacrifices with those of the Priestly Code (Numbers 28:16-25; 29:12-39). Accordingly at the Council of Jamnia (A.D. 90) some of them wished to exclude Ezekiel from the canon. It is reported that though Hananiah ben Hezekiah used three hundred barrels of midnight oil to explain many of the difficulties of the book, in the end the rabbis decided to await the return of Elijah, who would give the definitive explanations.

46:1-15. *The Ruler's Sacrifices.* Unlike the outer eastern gate, which is permanently closed (44:1-3), the eastern gate leading to the inner court is to be open on the **sabbath** and the day of the **new moon.** It will also be open whenever the prince wishes to present a **freewill offering.** He has special privilege inside this gate. The prince is permitted to watch the sacrifices from the **threshold**—that is, from just outside the inner court. Nevertheless he is a layperson and must return to the outer court by the way he entered. He leads the laity in religious processions at times of festival. To avoid confusion, those entering by the southern gate must exit by way of the northern gate and vice versa. Since the inner court lies in the way, the people must of course go around the eastern side of it. The prince is to provide the **daily** whole **burnt offering** sacrificed each **morning.**

46:16-18. *Property Held in Perpetuity.* Gifts from the king to his sons, if from his own inheritance, may be held by their heirs in perpetuity. Gifts to a servant, however, must be returned to the royal family in the **year of liberty**—that is, the jubilee (cf. Leviticus 25:8-55). Confiscation of property belonging to the people is forbidden (cf. I Kings 21).

46:19-24. *The Kitchen Areas.* This is a return to the tour of the temple area. It may be displaced from an original position in chapters 40–42, perhaps after 42:14. The place for preparing the holy meals of the priests is at the western end of the northern priestly chambers. Likewise, a kitchen would be needed by the southern chambers. Since it is forbidden to carry the holy food into the outer court access to the yard is required. On **communicate holiness to the people** see above on 44:4-31.

Restriction of the lowest row of chambers to fifty cubits (see above on 42:1-14) left room for this kitchen. Kitchens for cooking the people's food (see above on 40:17-19) are located in small **courts** in the **four corners** of the outer court. The ministers who cook for the laity are Levites (cf. 44:10-11).

47:1-12. *The Stream from the Temple.* From the temple flows a stream which for the Judean wilderness and the Dead Sea will be a source of "paradise regained" (cf. Genesis 13:10). The farther this miraculous river flows, the deeper it becomes. The idea of additional springs or tributaries would spoil the picture, for this is life-giving water from the temple. The **trees** growing beside it are the trees of life (cf. Genesis 2:9; 3:22; Revelation 22:1-2). The river sweetens the water of the Dead Sea—which is 26 percent mineral salts—so that it becomes good fishing territory. A few **marshes** are to be kept, however, since **salt** is important for the sacrifices (cf. 43:24).

47:13-20. *Boundaries of the Holy Land.* The northern boundary cuts from the **Great Sea**—that is, the Mediterranean—at a point near Tripolis on the Syrian coast. It runs across the Lebanon mountains to the **entrance of Hamath,** or Riblah, and into Syria. Though at the height of its power Israel extended its sway into Syria, Phoenicia was never a part of Israel.

The eastern boundary angles southwest from **Hazar-enon,** about seventy-five miles north of **Damascus,** to the **Jordan** south of the Sea of Galilee. Thus Transjordan is excluded as unclean (cf. Joshua 22:19). The southern border runs southwest from the southern end of the **eastern sea**—the Dead Sea—at **Tamar** to **Meribath-kadesh**, or Kadesh-barnea. Nor far west from there it follows the **Brook of Egypt** northwest to the Mediterranean, which is the western border.

47:21–48:29. *Tribal Allotments.* Resident **aliens** are to be included with the tribes among whom they dwell. There is to be no brutal conquest in which non-Jews are slain or expelled. The tribes are to be settled in horizontal strips. Seven are to be north of the holy portion (see below on 48:8-22) and five south of it. The tribes descended from Jacob's concubines are placed farthest from the sanctuary, being allowed no closer than fifth position. Reasons for the exchanged places of Judah and Benjamin are probably that Judah after Jerusalem's fall moved farther north, with its capital at Mizpah, and that the name Benjamin means "son of the right hand," meaning "southerner," and is hence put south of the temple.

48:8-22. The **holy portion** (cf. 45:1-8) is **twenty-five thousand cubits**—about eight miles, ninety yards—square. It is divided into three strips. **Priests** and **Levites** each have strips ten thousand cubits wide. South of these lies the capital **city** in a strip five thousand cubits wide. East and west of the holy portion lies the property of the **prince,** the crown property.

The **sanctuary** is **in the midst of** both the priests' portion (verse 10) and the holy portion generally (verse 8). This suggests a central location for the priestly strip. The context, however, proceeds from north and south. The fact that the priests are mentioned before the Levites seems to put them and the sanctuary in the northern strip. In either arrangement the one fixed point is surely the site of the former temple. With the temple in the northern position the capital city would lie fifteen thousand cubits (about) 4.8 miles south at Bethlehem! With the sanctuary in the central location the city would lie five thousand cubits (about) 1.6 miles south. With the width of the city included it would reach beyond Beth-haccherem (Ramet Rahel), where royal buildings have been found by archaeologists.

48:30-35. This city has no temple in it and yet its name is "Yahweh Shamah," **The LORD is there.** Like the temple it is square. But it is nine times as long—about 1.44 miles—on each side. Like the temple also it has a free area around it in which nothing can be built. This is five times as broad as that of the temple. This whole description has a more elaborate parallel—in which city planning is to be undertaken—in the New Jerusalem Scroll, of which several fragmentary copies have been found among the Dead Sea Scrolls. Perhaps both this scroll and Ezekiel lie in the background of Revelation 21:9-22:5.

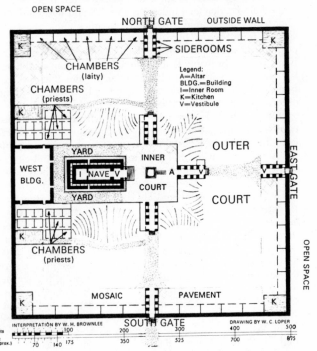

Floor plan of Ezekiel's envisioned ideal temple and surrounding temple area.

THE BOOK OF DANIEL

George A. F. Knight

INTRODUCTION

The book of Daniel is named for its chief character. Most of the stories in chapters 1–6 tell about this person. He himself describes in the first person the visions in chapters 7–11. He is identified as one of the exiled Jews in Babylon who rose to a high position in the government of Nebuchadrezzar (Nebuchadnezzar in the Revised Standard Version) and his successors.

In the English Bible the book appears to head the "minor" prophets or to conclude the "major" prophets. But in the Hebrew the book is not found among the Prophets. It is placed among the Writings, the third and latest division of the Hebrew Scriptures to be canonized.

A large section of the book (2:4b–7:28) has come down to us, not in Hebrew, but in a related Semitic language, Aramaic. The exiles learned to speak Aramaic in Babylon. It then became the people's tongue in the postexilic period, continuing through New Testament times. Hebrew was used only in worship and as a literary and scholarly language. The Aramaic section begins within one of the stories and goes through the first vision. It does not seem to be related to any structural distinction. A number of theories have been put forward to explain the change. Some assume that the author composed the material in two languages. Others assume that one of the languages is a translation.

A combination theory thinks that the author composed the stories and first vision in Aramaic for popular reading but used Hebrew for the remaining visions to appeal to the more learned. Then, later, someone started to translate the Aramaic into Hebrew but got only as far as 2:4*a*. None of these proposed explanations is completely satisfactory.

The Contents

Chapter 1 begins with a reference to the first capture of Jerusalem by the Babylonian army under Nebuchadrezzar. Among the exiles removed to Babylon is a fair young man named Daniel, meaning "God is judge." In the stories of chapters 1–6 Daniel acts as God's wise judge of events. He is able not only to declare the meaning of dreams but also what those dreams are themselves. Three companions of Daniel are introduced, and the story of chapter 3 focuses on them. They display complete courage and loyalty to God when threatened with death—as does Daniel also in the familiar story of the lions' den (chapter 6).

Chapters 7–12 report four visions of Daniel. Chapter 7 portrays the ultimate triumph of God over the cruel nations and the giving of the kingdom to "one like a son of man." This passage has had great theological influence, and the gospels record Jesus as referring to it (Matthew 10:23; Mark 13:26; 14:62). The vision of chapter 8 forecasts the history of the Near East following the Exile. The emphasis here is always on the transcendent rule of Almighty God. Chapter 9 contains a magnificent prayer of confession and trust in God in the face of calamity. This is followed by a divine promise of eventual vindication.

Chapters 10–12 form a unit describing a single vision. After a lengthy statement of the revelation to follow, an outline of about four hundred years of coming events passes before Daniel's eyes. There is greater detail about the events to occur near the end of that time involving a great struggle and an evil king. The final chapter declares that the outcome of this struggle will be the "end" of the present age. It will affect both heaven and earth, time and eternity.

In the Greek versions there are several additions not found in the Hebrew-Aramaic text: the Prayer of Azariah, the Song of the Three Young Men, Susanna, and Bel and the Dragon. In Protestant editions of the Bible these are included in the Apocrypha. In Roman Catholic editions the first two are inserted in the book itself following 3:23 and the last two appear at the end as chapters 13 and 14.

Authorship and Date

Since the visions are told in the first person, Daniel has traditionally been taken to be the author of the whole book. Accordingly it is dated during the Exile in the sixth century B.C. There are many evidences, however, that it was written at a later time and is pseudepigraphic—that is, issued under the name of Daniel by another person. There are a number of Persian and Greek words in the text. For example, the name of one of the musical instruments in 3:5 transcribes a word that is not only Greek, but is found with this meaning nowhere in Greek literature before the second century B.C. The name "Chaldeans" is also used in a special sense it did not acquire till long after the Exile (see below on 1:3-5).

The fact that the book in the Hebrew Bible is placed among the Writings rather than the Prophets indicates a late date. If it had been in existence before about 200 B.C. it probably would have been included among the Prophets, as it now stands in the English Bible. Writing about 180 Jeshua ben Sira lists the heroes of the faith from Enoch, Noah, and Abraham through Nehemiah (Ecclesiasticus 44–49). He makes no mention of Daniel, evidently because he does not know of the book about him. On the other hand Daniel and his three companions are mentioned in I Maccabees 2:59-60, which was probably composed late in the second century. Fragments of the book apparently produced about the same time have been found among the Dead Sea Scrolls.

These data support evidence in the visions pointing to almost the precise year in which the book was composed. We read in I and II Maccabees of a terrible period in Israel's history. Antiochus IV Epiphanes (175-163) was the Seleucid king of Syria. His empire included Palestine and the little "city-state" of Judea—consisting of little more than Jerusalem and the villages in the hills round about. He had the ideal of uniting all his realm culturally and religiously. He planned to do away with local beliefs and customs and force all his subjects to become devotees of the "new" Greek civilization. Many of the Jews resisted, and the king took stern measures to repress the practice of their faith.

It was probably on December 6, 167 that the temple was desecrated by the erection of an altar to Zeus Olympius (I Maccabees 1:54; II Maccabees 6:2-5). In Daniel this event is referred to specifically as the "abomination that makes desolate" (11:31; 12:11), and it is alluded to a number of times. The early reconsecration of the temple and resumption of worship is foretold, but the prediction is too vague to have been written after the actual rededication under Judas Maccabeus, which occurred three years later. Thus the book must have been written within this three-year period, probably near the end of it (see below on 8:9-14).

There has been much discussion about authorship. The differences between narrative and vision, third person and first, Hebrew and Aramaic, have been cited as evidence for two or more authors. But none of these differences can be related to differences in either viewpoint or literary style. These are so much alike that it is simpler to suppose that one man is responsible for the whole book. Thus the theory of some scholars that the stories should be dated a century earlier than the visions has not been widely accepted.

This is not to say that the stories are entirely the author's creation. Basically they no doubt came down to him as oral tradition from the days of Nebuchadrezzar and Cyrus. They may well have been cherished among the Jews scattered in Mesopotamia and elsewhere in the intervening years.

By the author's time their Babylonian setting had become

blurred, and accuracy of historical detail lost. The author was naturally unable to check on four-century-old tales. The important thing he did was to make these old folktales into vehicles that God could use to reveal saving love for Israel in its darkest hour.

Type of Literature

The visions of Daniel belong to the class of writings known as apocalyptic. This literature was concerned with hidden revelations and with the end of the ages. Daniel provided the pattern for most of the apocalypses produced during the following three centuries. Characteristically such works are written in the form of visions, using much symbolism. They predict early catastrophic divine action to end the evils of the present age and inaugurate a new age of justice and vindication for the people of God. Amid the most difficult times—for example, the persecutions which produced both Daniel and the book of Revelation—they sound a clarion call to the faithful to stand fast. They give assurance that even though humanly speaking the situation seems hopeless, God is in control of events.

In such circumstances it was dangerous to be specific with one's references. Instead of naming Antiochus Epiphanes, therefore, the author speaks of a "little horn" (8:9) and a "king of the north" (11:40). It was dangerous also to identify oneself. Hence he takes the name of a hero of the past. Daniel is a name handed down from the second millennium as the type of the wise and good man (see comment on Ezekiel 14:12-23). In the Ugaritic legends of those early days a man named Daniel dispenses justice and protects the widow and orphan. Perhaps a namesake of somewhat the same character lived among the Jewish exiles in Babylon (cf. Ezra 8:2; Nehemiah 10:6). He became the hero of traditions passed down to the author of this book. On the other hand the author may have chosen a respected and appropriate name around which to gather various traditions about unknown exiles.

In any case the author's concern was with the meaning of events rather than with their historicity. This concern was shared by his ancient readers. His purpose was like that of Jesus in teaching by parables. When one asked "Who is my neighbor?" Jesus did not reply with an abstract discussion of brotherhood but with a story of a Samaritan who demonstrated brotherhood in action (Luke 10:29-37). Perhaps he was telling of an actual happening. But if so, factual accuracy in the details would be of no significance—for example, whether the traveler was going from Jerusalem to Jericho or from Nazareth to Capernaum. More likely Jesus made up the parable out of whole cloth. Yet the reality he teaches by it remains just as true and significant.

This kind of story, told to teach a truth, was called a *midrash* in ancient Jewish circles. Midrashic teaching is found throughout all rabbinical literature as well as in the gospels. The story in a midrash may of course be historical fact. Or it may be a tale based on history, as in Daniel. Or it may be wholly made up, as some of Jesus' parables obviously are. It is the truth conveyed by a midrash that is all-important. The story of Daniel in the lions' den (chapter 6) is understood in this light in II Timothy 4:17. Clearly the author's purpose is midrashic in the stories as well as the visions of his book—to preach the power and love and providence of God.

Teachings of Permanent Value

Daniel is highly important for its revelation of God's loving purpose for the people. The persecution by Antiochus Epiphanes presented a profound challenge to the faith of Israel. The question was: Can the distinctive ideas that a handful of peculiar people in the hills of Judea hold about the nature and purpose of the divine Being remain relevant in a new age of reason? The dominant Hellenistic culture seemed about to submerge the Jewish people. "In those days lawless men came forth from Israel, and misled many, saying, 'Let us go and make a covenant with the Gentiles round about us.' " (I Maccabees 1:11).

But there were loyalists in Israel, known as the Hasidim or Hasideans. They remained true to God's *hesed*, his "steadfast love," as the Revised Standard Version usually translates it. This was the loyal love God had bestowed on the chosen people in the covenant made at Sinai. This book seeks to support them in their difficult decision to continue to be loyal to God.

The book shows what loyalty should mean now by referring to past events in Israel's story—events which demonstrate God's completely reliable *hesed* in days that were equally challenging. The God of Israel does not change. If God was faithful to Daniel in the lions' den, God will remain faithful now. God is Lord of all. If arrogant kings seek to dominate the earth without heeding God's purpose, their fall is sure. People matter to God. Even in the rise and fall of great nations the individual remains in God's care. God's covenant with Israel still stood when Jerusalem fell to a heathen monarch. It will continue to stand if the holy city falls again.

God's kingdom is going to embrace not only all people but all creation, and it will endure forever. It will be established when God raises up Israel through its representative head, the "son of man"—that is, the real man. Thus even the dead in Israel will share God's kingdom. For though the "end" will be preceded by a time of trouble, God has promised that all who are written in the book of life, even those now sleeping in the dust of the earth, will enter into everlasting life.

I. STORIES OF DANIEL AND HIS COMPANIONS (1:1–6:28)

A. OBEDIENCE TO THE FOOD LAWS (1:1-21)

1:1-2. *Beginning of the Exile.* The record in II Kings 23:34–24:17 is confirmed and supplemented by Babylonian annals. It shows that **Jehoiakim** became **king of Judah** as a vassal of Pharaoh Neco of Egypt in 609. In 605 **Nebuchadnezzar** defeated Neco at Carchemish, then hurried home to succeed his father as **king of Babylon.** Thereafter he proceeded to take over from Egypt the domination of Syria and Palestine, and Jehoiakim became his vassal for three years before rebelling about 600. Nebuchadrezzar was occupied elsewhere and did not bring his own army against Jerusalem till 598. At that time Jehoiakim died. After three months his young son Jehoiachin surrendered on March 16, 597. A Babylonian capture of Jerusalem in Jehoiakim's **third year**—that is, before Carchemish—can scarcely be fitted into this record. No doubt the author misinterpreted the three years of Jehoiakim's vassalage.

On the other hand II Chronicles 36:5-7, if historical—for the Chronicler was also more interested in theology than in precise history—may indicate that the establishment of Babylonian control over Judah after Carchemish involved some military action. This may have resulted in a few hostages being taken to Babylon. More probably, however, the tradition followed by the author refers to the first body of exiles deported with Jehoiachin in 597.

Nebuchadnezzar represents the Babylonian name Nabu-ku-durri-usur, "Nabu [the god of Nebo] has protected the succession rights." The form Nebuchadrezzar found in Jeremiah and Ezekiel is thus slightly closer to the original. **Shinar** is an old name for southern Mesopotamia. It gives a touch of antiquity as an allusion to the tower of Babel, where human pride and egotism met with God's judgment (cf. Genesis 11:2).

1:3-5. *The Wisdom of Babylon.* The first deportation in 597 took most of Jerusalem's "intelligentsia." Here it is related that some of the younger of these were chosen for higher education in Babylonia. The selection is obviously a great honor for foreigners and demands that the young men be physically and mentally superior.

The **Chaldeans** were a Babylonian tribe. In the seventh century they became dominant in overthrowing the Assyrian Empire and establishing the Neo-Babylonian Empire. In writings before and during the Exile the name is practically synonymous with "Babylonians." In this book it has a meaning acquired later, describing the priestly caste, the intellectual elite of Babylon, who studied and taught the astrology, mathematics, and magic for which the city was famous (cf. Isaiah

47:9, 12). To **stand before the king** was to be available to give him advice on demand.

1:6-7. *The Names of the Young Men.* The Hebrew names of all four youths contain syllables meaning God (el) or Yahweh (iah). But the chief of the royal household gives them Babylonian names. In the ancient world a person's name was meaningful. If the person entered into a new relationship a new name might be received. **Belteshazzar** is understood by the author to contain the name of the Babylonian god Bel (4:8). Probably, however, it represents a Babylonian name meaning "protect his life." **Abednego** is no doubt a corruption of "servant of Nebo" (cf. Isaiah 46:1). The tradition has so far altered **Shadrach** and **Meshach** that their meanings cannot be determined.

1:8-16. *A Test of the Food Laws.* Between the days of the Exile and the second century B.C. the Jews had become increasingly impressed with the importance of keeping the Mosaic law. Notable among this were the regulations about "clean" and "unclean" meats (Leviticus 11; Deuteronomy 14:3-21). Their observance became a mark not only of obedience to the law but also of separation from the Gentiles. Antiochus Epiphanes' program of forced hellenization seems to have included attempts to require abandonment of these food laws.

In this story Daniel challenges the royal officer to prove by a **test** that the will of God revealed in the food laws will accomplish more practical good than the **rich food** prepared in violation of them. Rather than eat "unclean" meats, he and his companions will restrict themselves to **vegetables,** none of which are forbidden in the food laws. **Ten days** is too short a time for any natural effects of a difference in diet. The noticeably healthier **appearance** of the four youths must be attributed to divine approval of their loyalty. This story must have strengthened the resolve of readers who faced hardship and even persecution in their adherence to Jewish customs.

1:17-21. *The Young Men's Reward.* Because of their obedience to the food laws under difficult circumstances God blesses Daniel and his companions. Their development is not only physically but mentally superior, so that they become **ten**

times **better** than the pagan wise men. Even so, if Israel remains loyal to God, there can be no end to God's blessings. The **first year of King Cyrus** marked the end of the Exile and the call to return to Jerusalem (Ezra 1:1). Thus Daniel's career is noted as spanning the whole period of the Exile. The reference is apparently to the length of his service in public office rather than of his lifetime (cf. 6:28; 10:1). Some have thought that this verse is displaced. But at this point it serves as a reminder that God's judgment in the Exile was temporary. Thus it was virtually a promise to the suffering patriots in 165 B.C. that the days of their trial are numbered.

B. NEBUCHADNEZZAR'S DREAM (2:1-49)

Israel shared with its ancient Near Eastern neighbors the belief that dreams were the means of divine communication. A dream in a holy place would most likely be god-given. Therefore it was not uncommon for a king facing a difficult decision to sleep in a temple in hope of receiving guidance. The interpretation of dreams was a profession involving considerable lore, as seen by instruction books discovered in both Egypt and Mesopotamia. Persons skilled in this art were maintained as members of royal courts for frequent consultation. To ancient readers it would not seem at all strange that a king should reward superiority in dream interpretation with high public office.

2:1-13. *The King's Insecurity.* The date **in the second year** is inconsistent with the three-year training period of 1:5, 18. It seems to be evidence of the original independence of the stories. The unusual element in this account is Nebuchadnezzar's demand that his wise men tell him not merely the interpretation of his dream but the dream itself. It is often said that he is purposely withholding information to test the occult powers claimed by his courtiers. But the ancient story may reflect practical experience of what psychologists have now proved scientifically—that most dreams cannot be recalled. Only if one partially wakens during a dream will the memory function.

On **Chaldeans** see above on 1:3-5. Their response in verse 4*b* begins the Aramaic section of the book (see Introduction). It is preceded in the text by the expression "in Aramaic," which may be a part of the introduction (verse 4*a*), meaning that the Chaldeans spoke in that language. More likely it is a parenthetical note of the change of language (see the Revised Standard Version footnote).

2:5-13. Nebuchadnezzar's extremes of threat and promise (verses 5-6) are not too exaggerated a caricature of the behavior of dictators in both ancient and modern times. Many of them have ruthlessly punished those who aroused their displeasure over trifles. Conversely they have rewarded their favorites out of all proportion to services rendered. Though seemingly all-powerful, Nebuchadnezzar feels so insecure that he orders the destruction of all his advisers rather than admit that he demanded too much of them. Daniel and his friends were not among the Babylonian **wise men** consulted, but the order includes them.

2:14-23. *The Wisdom of God.* Verse 16 raises questions. Would Daniel, though one of the royal advisers (cf. 1:19-20), at this stage be able to approach the king directly? If Daniel has already made an appointment as stated here, why must he later (verses 24-25) be introduced by Arioch? Possibly the author has combined variant traditions without bothering to resolve their differences. Possibly the text has been corrupted. For example, it has been suggested that verse 16*a* may originally have read: "And Daniel besought him [Arioch] to appoint him a time." In any case Daniel is confident of God's help in meeting the situation.

2:17-23. Daniel is confronted with a **mystery**—that is, a secret which is divinely **revealed** to him. His hymn of thanksgiving was probably composed by the author of the book as a theological comment on the tradition. It deals with a greater mystery, the **wisdom and might** of God. Babylon could not suppose that one of its gods **removes kings and sets up kings** or **changes times and seasons.** Pagan religion taught people how to change times themselves by magic which manipulated their gods. For example, in Canaanite Baal worship, closely allied to Babylonian religion, people thought they could control the natural processes of autumn rains and spring growth, for their gods were ultimately the deification of nature.

But the God of Israel is absolutely other than the creation which God has brought into being. Behind the mystery of life God's loving purpose is unfolding. One who knows the mind of God therefore learns something of that purpose and thus is given **wisdom and strength.**

2:24-30. *Introduction to the King.* Daniel's first thought is not for himself but for the **wise men of Babylon** with whom he has been condemned. Part of the secret that God has revealed to him is pity for his fellows. This quality was unknown to pagan religion—though it might be possessed by individuals such as Arioch, who seems glad of a chance to be relieved of his duty as executioner.

Daniel does not use God's revelation for his own glory. He immediately disclaims that he or any person can unravel the king's **mystery.** Rather **there is a God in heaven who reveals mysteries,** and God's purpose is to show **what is to be.** The phrase **the latter days** (verse 28) appears in the prophetic books as a designation of the time when God would act in a new and decisive manner for the redemption of the world. Here it refers to the establishment of the kingdom of God (verse 44, cf. 10:14). As evidence of the original independence of the stories, contrast the need for Arioch to introduce Daniel here with Nebuchadnezzar's recognition of the superior wisdom of the four Jewish youths in 1:18-20 (see also above on verses 14-23).

2:31-45. *The Image and Stone.* Daniel first describes the king's dream and then gives its interpretation. The four metals of the statue represent four successive kingdoms, or empires. The first is the neo-Babylonian Empire of Nebuchadnezzar himself, to whom Daniel says, God has entrusted rule over not only all humanity but also the **beasts** and the **birds.** The second is evidently that of the Medes, which was actually contemporary with the Neo-Babylonian Empire rather than a successor to it (see below on 5:30-31). The third is the Persian Empire, which claimed **rule over all the earth.**

2:40-43. The **fourth kingdom** is the Macedonian-Greek empire of Alexander the Great. After his death (323) it was split among four of his generals. The Jews first came under the rule of the dynasty of Ptolemies in Egypt. Then Palestine was seized in 198 by the Seleucid dynasty of Syria, to which Antiochus Epiphanes belonged. That the fourth kingdom is **divided** apparently refers to this division. In the context the word "divided" seems to refer to the composition of **iron** and **clay.** Some scholars have taken these two substances to symbolize respectively the Seleucid and Ptolemaic empires. **Marriage**—if this is what the Aramaic phrase means (see Revised Standard Version footnote)—seemingly alludes to the unsuccessful attempts of the two dynasties to gain peace through intermarriage of the royal lines (see below on 11:5-9, 10-19). In the context this refers to an effort to **mix** iron with clay and thus would support the idea that the substances represent the two dynasties.

On the other hand verse 42 clearly equates the two substances with elements of strength and weakness in a single **kingdom.** This symbolism is probably meant to apply throughout the passage, which therefore presumably describes the Seleucid kingdom. In the author's day this empire would not naturally be viewed as a successor to Nebuchadnezzar's empire.

2:44-45. Verses 37-43 remind the first readers of the book that three empires under which their parents suffered had come and gone. These verses declare that soon God would act to **bring . . . to an end** the whole succession of despotisms with the downfall of the fourth. God is to accomplish this by a **stone . . . cut . . . by no human hand**—that is, divine power. In place of these human kingdoms God will establish a **kingdom,** which will **stand for ever.**

2:46-49. *Nebuchadnezzar's Submission.* Awed by the revelation, Nebuchadnezzar humbles himself before Daniel's God. He attributed the title **Lord of kings** to this God rather than to himself (cf. verse 37). The author reports without disapproval the command to accord Daniel an **offering** (1) sacrifice and **incense,** as if he were a god. No doubt this author thinks of Daniel as the type of all Israel, in whom is God's glory. When the kings of the Gentiles bow down and "lick the dust of your feet" (Isaiah 49:23), they will really be worshiping, not Israel, but Israel's God. Thus Nebuchadnezzar is worshiping Daniel's God.

C. THE FIERY FURNACE (3:1-30)

3:1-12. *The Golden Image.* This story involves only the three companions. It does not even mention Daniel. Perhaps it represents an entirely separate tradition which the author has combined with the Daniel stories. It is a didactic story, or midrash (see Introduction). Therefore it need not require Nebuchadnezzar to remember his humble submission to the God of heaven (2:47) or the **Chaldeans** to recall Daniel's concern to save their lives (2:24).

Ancient statues were sometimes huge, as their remains testify. But **sixty cubits**—about ninety feet—is a great exaggeration. It is no doubt intended to suggest the colossal absurdity of Antiochus' claims to divinity. Informers always flourish in dictatorial regimes. Thus the envious are quick to report the refusal of the three Jewish officials to worship the image. **Satraps,** a Persian term (see below on 6:1-9), is an anachronism applied to neo-Babylonian officials.

3:13-18. *The Courage of Faith.* To the Jews suffering under Antiochus Epiphanes the **furious rage** of Nebuchadnezzar would seem an apt description of their own persecutor. The **burning fiery furnace** would be a fit symbol of the trial they were undergoing. Thus the response of the three young Jews to this threat would suggest the faith in God's saving love that should inspire their own loyalty. Should God deem it best for them to die, they are ready. If not, then God is fully **able to deliver** them even when human beings can see no way of escape. It is only the God of the Bible who can evoke such absolute trust.

3:19-23. *The Furnace.* The prototye of the furnace of the story would be, as archaeology has shown us, a kiln of the type used for smelting metals. Some have been found about nine feet in diameter. **Seven times** is the perfect number and meant what we might express as "to the *n*th degree." The victims are bound and thrown into the furnace from above through the flue. From this issue flames and gases so hot that they kill the unfortunate **mighty** men assigned to the detail. Following verse 23 the Greek versions include a lengthy passage which Protestants include in the Apocrypha. In the Revised Standard Version it is found under the title the Prayer of Azariah and the Song of the Three Young Men.

3:24-30. *The Deliverance.* Apparently a sentence of the text has been lost before verse 24—a statement that Nebuchadnezzar stooped down and peered into the draft opening of the furnace to watch the young men being consumed. Verses 24-25 then tell how he **rose up** to report what he saw—not three men but **four . . . walking** amid the flames.

During the Exile Second Isaiah promised in vivid metaphor:

> When you walk through fire you shall not be burned,
>   and the flame shall not consume you.
> For I am the LORD your God,
>   the Holy One of Israel, your Savior. (Isaiah 43:2*b*-3*a*.)

When Daniel was written it was a fact of history that Israel had not been consumed in the Exile. What Israel's Savior had done before, God could do again. Yet God had not saved Israel at arm's length, as it were. God had been with the people in their sufferings and had shared the pain of the Exile. Many centuries earlier God was revealed to Moses as one who suffered such burning pain as the people experienced, such hurt as Israel went through in Egypt, yet was not consumed (Exodus 3:1-9). So those who trust in God will not be consumed either.

In fact, as Isaiah of Jerusalem knew even in the eighth

century, God is the fire, the fire of judgment, of wrath, of redemption and purification all in one (Isaiah 6:6-7; 31:9; cf. Deuteronomy 4:24). Yet Moses was promised that God would be with him if he ventured into the flames. Israel heard the same promise in its fiery trial in the Exile. Therefore Israel could be assured again that God was with it still as the very fire of wrath and redemption. If Antiochus had thrown Israel into the furnace, God had but thrown it into the suffering, redemptive love of God.

3:28-30. In this chapter Nebuchadnezzar does not turn to sing praises to God. Rather he acknowledges the significance of the witness of three men who **trusted** in their God. It was the faithful witness of a small remnant of the covenant people that preserved Judaism to become the seedbed of the Christian church.

D. NEBUCHADNEZZAR'S INSANITY (4:1-37)

This story develops in detail the theme that there is no such thing as a "divine right of kings." But it also suggests that no human society, whether kingdom or republic, should imagine that rule is vested in it except by God alone. It offers an exposition of such prophetic oracles on the Neo-Babylonian Empire as Isaiah 14–15; 47 and Jeremiah 50–51. Probably the underlying tradition originally concerned, not Nebuchadnezzar, but the last of his successors, Nabonidus (556-539). During most of his reign this king lived away from his capital and spent a number of years at Tema in Arabia. A biased political poem about Nabonidus, written by certain priests to justify the action of the gods in handing his realm over to Cyrus the Persian, declares in one line: "The king is mad."

4:1-3. *A King's Confession.* The story of this chapter is put into the form of a letter from **King Nebuchadnezzar** to his subjects, who are boastfully described as the inhabitants of **all the earth.** Most of what follows carries out the letter idea by being related in the first person by Nebuchadnezzar. Third-person narrative is introduced in verses 19 and 28-33. Nebuchadnezzar announces that he is telling about his experience with the **Most High God.** His hymn of praise in verse 3 represents his viewpoint after the experience. It is repeated and expanded in verses 34-35.

4:4-9. *An Interruption to Complacency.* Before the experience, Nebuchadnezzar declares, he thought he was **prospering** as master of the known world. But he was not master of his own thoughts and fears. God's goodness is severe. God's love may need to send the self-satisfied person a bad dream, or a disease germ, or a national enemy (cf. Isaiah 5:24-30). Nebuchadnezzar's procedure in consulting first the Babylonian **wise men** and then, after their failure, Daniel parallels that in chapter 2. However, it shows no recollection of what happened then—unless his recognition of Daniel's inspiration is to be so understood.

The Aramaic plural **gods** may be intended to represent the Hebrew word for God, *elohim,* which is plural in form (see Revised Standard Version footnote). The assumption that the first syllable of **Belteshazzar** represents the name of a **god**—Bel, title of the god Marduk—is probably incorrect according to the Babylonian etymology (see above on 1:6-7). But the error would not be a problem to the original Jewish readers.

4:10-12. *The Great Tree.* The author builds his symbolism in this passage on Ezekiel 31:3-14, which compares the pharaoh to a towering cedar. His readers would recognize this as a prediction of Egypt's downfall. The figure of a tree whose **top reached to heaven** would also remind them of the tower of Babel and the people who learned they could not build a city and a civilization without God (Genesis 11:1-9). From a material standpoint Nebuchadnezzar's empire seemed a success. His building projects provided work and food for all and produced a capital city of unrivaled magnificence. Yet to knowing readers the very description of the tree's greatness would forecast its fall.

4:13-18. *A Decree of Judgment.* The tree's destruction is ordered by a **watcher,** a "wakeful one," who is a **holy one,** an emissary from the holy God. Yet the **stump** is to be left and **bound** with a metal ring, apparently to protect it (cf verse 26). The angel abruptly shifts from the tree symbolism to a direct order that a person suffer a mental breakdown. This suggests that the author combined differing traditions. A **beast's mind**—that is, the delusion of being an animal—is a not uncommon psychopathic manifestation known as zoanthropy. Such a derangement, though often permanent, might end after **seven times,** or years.

When Antiochus IV took the surname Epiphanes—meaning "manifested one," or a revealed god—some of his enemies called him instead Epimanes, "madman." The Jews especially had reason to believe this nickname justified. In view of the obvious meaning of what Nebuchadnezzar has just related the author might well imply that the failure of the **wise men** to interpret it was due to discretion rather than inability. Instead he chooses to reemphasize Daniel's superior inspiration (cf. verses 8-9).

4:19-27. *Courage to Declare God's Word.* The narrative here shifts from first to third person (see above on verses 1-3). It is understandable that Daniel is **dismayed** at the unwelcome interpretation with which he must confront the proud monarch. As one educated in the court of the most cultured nation of the time, Nebuchadnezzar has a veneer of courtesy (verse 19b). But Daniel is well aware of the despot's ruthless temper (cf. 2:12; 3:13, 19). His opening words (verse 19c) are a vestige of what in earlier times was an attempt to avert the ill effect of bad news and transform it into a curse against **enemies.** But Daniel uses the ancient formula as a way of expressing regret for what he must say (cf. II Samuel 18:32).

4:20-25. The great prophets speak of God's "strange . . . work" (Isaiah 28:21) when in saving love God has to act with seeming cruelty. For in God's wisdom God sees that some people cannot be saved until their pride is broken. Only then can they recognize the truth about themselves and experience the love of God. Thus Nebuchadnezzar must learn that, though he is absolute master of a vast empire, in the sight of God he is only a **beast.** In fact he may be reduced through mental illness to living like one.

4:26-27. It is not inevitable fate that rules on high but a loving God. There is opportunity for restoration when Nebuchadnezzar learns that he reigns under God. Moreover Daniel begs his king to repent at once and acknowledge his submission to God by concern for the **oppressed.** If he thus reforms, the threatened blow may prove unnecessary.

4:28-33. *The Fulfillment.* God gives people time to repent. In this case Nebuchadnezzar is given **twelve months,** yet in spite of the clear warning he remains obsessed with his own **mighty power.** Therefore God must act to destroy his pride (cf. Isaiah 47:8-11), and the predicted doom falls.

4:34-37. *The Mercy of God.* The letter form with which the story began is resumed in the conclusion. Nebuchadnezzar tells in the first person how he recovered his **reason** when he **lifted his eyes to heaven** in acknowledgment of God's rule. In a hymn of praise (cf. verse 3) he confesses that the **Most High** is Lord of all who none may question—**none can . . . say to him, "What doest thou?"** (cf. Job 9:12; Isaiah 45:9). Having submitted to God's **kingdom,** Nebuchadnezzar is restored to his own and finds **more greatness** in ruling under the divine rule. Is the author perhaps suggesting that there is hope yet in God's love for even Antiochus Epiphanes?

E. BELSHAZZAR'S FEAST (5:1-31)

Contemporary Babylonian records show that Belshazzar was the son, not of Nebuchadnezzar, but of Nabonidus (see above on 4:1-37). Some have supposed he was Nebuchadnezzar's grandson, since Nabonidus seems to have married a daughter of Nebuchadnezzar. But this marriage occurred—if at all—only after Nabonidus became king (556), when the records indicate Belshazzar was already an adult. Belshazzar was never **king** but was made coregent by his father. He was no doubt virtual ruler during his father's residence in Arabia. Babylon was taken without a battle in 539 by the army of Cyrus the Persian (see below on verses 30-31). Greek historians report a tradition that its capture followed a night of feasting. The name Belshazzar means "Bel protect the king." It actually includes the designation of the god which the author erroneously assumed to be an element in Daniel's Babylonian name Belteshazzar (see above on 1:6-7).

5:1-4. *Belshazzar's Sacrilege.* At a state banquet Belshazzar unashamedly drinks **in front of the thousand** guests, the officials and leading citizens of his empire. In his drunken state he deliberately commits a sacrilegious act. He calls for the holy vessels stolen from the **house of God,** the Jerusalem temple, so that his guests may drink and pour libations to their pagan gods. The account would of course remind the original readers immediately of Antiochus Epiphanes' desecrations of the temple and its altar (see Introduction).

5:5-12. *The Writing on the Wall.* The walls of ancient palaces were often finished with white **plaster.** Any **writing** would show clearly in the light from a **lampstand,** which might hold a number of oil lamps. Belshazzar's terror at the sight of the **hand** is to be understood as due to guilt, a belated realization of the enormity of his sacrilege. A godless person is always horror-stricken at any invasion of the secure little world from the mysterious beyond whose existence has been denied. The consultation of the Babylonian **wise men** and their failure follows the same pattern as in chapters 2 and 4. Here, however, the eventual calling of Daniel is based on his earlier success.

5:8-9. Why are Babylonians unable even to **read the writing,** which consists of common words in Aramaic (verse 25), a language known to educated persons throughout the ancient Near East? This is a question on which there has been much speculation. Some interpreters suppose the reason is a strange script. For example, the old Hebrew script in which most of the Old Testament was written would be well known to Daniel but presumably unfamiliar to Babylonians. In the author's day the use of this old script for writing Hebrew was giving way to use of the Aramaic script, from which the Hebrew letters we know today developed.

On the other hand the wise men's failure may be due to the fact that Aramaic, like Hebrew and other Semitic languages, was written in a consonantal alphabet. Being unable to make sense of the writing as a whole, they would be uncertain which vowel sounds to insert. Thus, even though they recognized the letters, they would be unable to pronounce them as words.

5:10-12. Probably the **queen** is to be understood as Belshazzar's mother rather than one of his **wives** (verses 2-3). Having just entered the hall, she has not participated in the drunken sacrilege. Therefore she can assess the situation dispassionately. She remembers Daniel's service to Belshazzar's **father** when he faced similar problems. She ascribes to Daniel even greater abilities than stated heretofore. According to her estimate he is the supreme type of the wise man who knows the mind of God.

5:13-29. *Interpretation of the Writing.* As a true man of God Daniel rejects flattery and promised **rewards** and fearlessly tells the ruler the truth about himself. He cites as a warning the experience attributed to Nebuchadnezzar in chapter 4 but perhaps originally told of Nabonidus, historically Belshazzar's **father** (see above on 4:1-37). Each generation has to learn from experience for itself (verse 22). Daniel's reference to **the God in whose hand is your breath** (verse 23) is striking; even the most powerful person on earth lives only by the grace of God.

5:24-28. The words written on the wall as read by Daniel mean respectively **numbered . . . weighed . . . divided.** Read with different vowels as other derivatives of the same roots (see above on verses 8-9), the words are a series of weights: mina, shekel, and half shekels. **Parsin,** literally "halves," sometimes was used of half minas. Here it more likely indicates half shekels, to form a series in order of descending value.

Probably the series was a proverbial expression comparing the abilities of successive rulers—possibly Babylonian kings during the Exile. The coregents Nabonidus and Belshazzar would be the half shekels. There is a further word play in **peres.**

It may mean not only "divided" and "half," the singular of **parsin,** but also **Persians.**

5:30-31. *The Fall of Babylon.* The Babylonian records tell nothing of Belshazzar's death. The Greek historian Xenophon mentions that the "king" was killed when the Persians took Babylon. This may refer to Belshazzar, for the records indicate Nabonidus was captured at a later time. The author's idea that Babylon fell to **Darius the Mede,** who in turn was succeeded by Cyrus the Persian (6:28), accords with his idea of four successive kingdoms (see above on 2:31-45). The second of these was the Median Empire, supposedly coming between the Neo-Babylonian and Persian empires. No doubt this idea stemmed from prophetic oracles against Babylon predicting its destruction by the Medes (Isaiah 13:17-18; 21:2; Jeremiah 51:11, 28). Actually the Median and Neo-Babylonian empires, which arose together after the downfall of the Assyrian Empire, coexisted until both were conquered by Cyrus. The Median Empire fell around 550 and the Neo-Babylonian in 539.

The name Darius is not found in the list of Median kings, which is known from historical records. Evidently it comes from confused traditions of the later Persian king Darius the Great (522-486), who aided the rebuilding of the temple in Jerusalem (Ezra 5–6). Here the name is mistakenly applied to Astyages, the last ruler of the Median Empire (see below on 9:1-2).

F. THE LIONS' DEN (6:1-28)

This story is one of the most familiar in the Bible. It closely parallels in many details the story of Daniel's three companions in chapter 3 and proclaims the same message. God will sustain those who remain loyal in the face of persecution. For the Jews threatened with suffering and even death for persisting in their faith in defiance of Antiochus Epiphanes its application was clear. In succeeding centuries it has given courage to many struggling against overwhelming oppression from without or temptation from within.

6:1-9. *Envy of Daniel's Authority.* Darius the Great (see above on 5:30-31) organized the Persian Empire into provinces governed by **satraps.** His inscriptions indicate that when his conquests brought the empire to its greatest extent the number totaled twenty-nine. Possibly later kings extended the title to subordinates (cf. Ezra 8:36) so that there came to be as many as **a hundred and twenty.** More probably traditions about the size of the empire exaggerated the number of provinces.

Historical records do not mention the **three presidents,** but such a cabinet of top military and civilian officials is not improbable. No reason for Daniel's appointment to such responsibility by a new king to whom he was presumably unknown is given in this case (contrast 1:19; 2:48-49; 5:29). But his integrity and efficiency in office are noted as the basis for Darius' intention to elevate him still further to the post of prime minister.

6:4-5. One who advances above one's fellows, however great one's merit, is likely to arouse jealousy. To this may be added the hatred which sheer goodness provokes in those who prefer darkness rather than light. Daniel's being a foreigner would of course aggravate the resentment—though the author refrains from mentioning such prejudice. Thus the presidents and satraps forget their individual rivalries in an alliance to destroy the common object of their envy. They have searched in vain for any **fault** in Daniel's administration that might be magnified and distorted into a **ground for complaint.** Therefore they conclude that his belonging to a religious minority is the one chink in his armor.

6:6-7. The Aramaic word translated **came by agreement** (verses 6, 11, 15) is of uncertain meaning. That even high officials would dare throng tumultuously (see Revised Standard Version footnote) into the royal court seems unlikely. The Revised Standard Version translators' interpretation of collusion or conspiracy is based on comparison of the several contexts. Thus the envious officers scheme to approach the king together. They will play on his vanity —hoping to obtain his thoughtless assent to an absurd **interdict** they are certain Daniel will violate.

Their proposal has the effect of elevating the king to the status of a god to whom all his subjects must pray. To the book's original readers it would suggest at once Antiochus Epiphanes' pretensions to divinity.

6:8-9. Law of the Medes and the Persians suggests that the author may have supposed the Persians were included in the Median Empire (cf. 5:28; 8:20). Historically this empire took in Elam to the south and extended north and west into Armenia and Asia Minor. It never established rule over the Persians to the east. On the other hand the meaning may be that these peoples independently follwed a legal code that was a common heritage. The idea that a decree issued under this law could not be **revoked** is found also in Esther 1:19 and 8:8. There, as here, it is an essential element in the story. Historical records of the two empires reveal no evidence of unusual legal practice on which such a tradition might be based.

6:10-13. *Faithfulness in Prayer.* As Daniel the exile prays in his **upper chamber**, he looks in the direction of **Jerusalem**—that spot on earth where God chose "to make his name dwell" (Deuteronomy 12:11). Yet it was in exile that Israel learned that God can be addressed in prayer anywhere and at any time. Daniel finds God's strength in this emergency because he has learned to pray to God regularly **three times a day**. But it is his very faithfulness in prayer that provides the plotters with an accusation against him.

6:14-18. *The Sentence of Death.* Darius genuinely admires Daniel (cf. verse 3). He spends the rest of the day trying to **deliver** him, presumably by consulting with his legal advisers. But he has been trapped by his vanity and must give the order for Daniel's execution. Apparently the author visualizes the **den of lions** as a pit somewhat like a cistern; with only a single opening at the top. Over this a **stone** is placed and **sealed**. Its position cannot be **changed** without disturbing a lump of moist clay into which the king's carved **signet** ring has been impressed. Probably the procedure is to tie the stone in place with a rope and enclose the knot in the clay. The king is so distressed that he spends a sleepless night.

6:19-27. *Daniel's Vindication*. The king hurries at dawn to the mouth of the den. His hope to find Daniel alive is based, not on any expectation that the lions may have lacked appetite, but on the realization that Daniel serves a **living God**—one able to take direct action to save. His hope proves justified. Just as God through the **angel,**—literally "messenger" could keep the flames of the furnace from harming the three young men, so now God has **shut the lions' mouths** and kept them from harming Daniel.

God has so acted because Daniel is **blameless**—that is, he is not sinless but he is constant in his observance of the Mosaic law. To the loyal Jews who suffered for their observance of that law in the face of Antiochus Epiphanes this story was calculated to bring fresh hope. Here they would find the assurance that God had been and still was powerful to save those who **trusted** God.

6:24. The author quickly goes on to describe the lions' immediate destruction of Daniel's accusers. The sentencing of the plotters to the same fate they sought for Daniel is in accordance with the mosaic law (Deuteronomy 19:16-19). But the inclusion of their **children** and **wives** is contrary to that law (Deuteronomy 24:16).

6:25-27. Darius' decree follows the form of Nebuchadnezzar's letter and uses some of the same phrases (see above on 4:1-3). His hymn of praise is similar in language and thought to that of Nebuchadnezzar (cf. 4:3, 34-35). This series of stories about Daniel ends with the report that this one man's courageous devotion resulted in the commendation of Israel's God to countless pagans. The author may be meaning to say that an individual's faith is no mere private affair but has a missionary outcome. The loyalty of persecuted Jews in his own day may not only achieve their own salvation but be instrumental in establishing God's kingdom **in all the earth**—as in fact it was.

6:28. *The Beginning of the Persian Empire*. In a concluding note to the stories the author mentions the accession of **Cyrus the Persian.** He evidently understands this event as bringing to an end the Median Empire and inaugurating the Persian Empire. No hint is given of the means by which Cyrus gained the power. The author has already attributed to Darius the Mede the capture of Babylon, which historically occurred under Cyrus (see above on 5:30-31). Probably he knows no other tradition of Cyrus' conquest.

II. DANIEL'S VISIONS (7:1–12:13)

Chapters 1–6 are intended to interpret the faithfulness of God to Jews suffering sorely from persecution. They do so by presenting traditional stories of the past experience of the Babylonian exile. In contrast, chapters 7–12 look forward to the future. Though most of what they predict has already happened, their emphasis is on the divine action that is soon to occur. They declare that just as God has been faithful in the past, so is God to be relied on now and in the unknown days to come. No matter how strong the forces of evil may become, they cannot prevent the living God from bringing divine plans to fruition. This message is presented in symbolic language and apocalyptic imagery that are in striking contrast to the narrative style of chapters 1–6. However, similarities of expression as well as thought are frequent enough to convince most scholars that the same author is responsible.

A. A DREAM OF FOUR BEASTS (7:1-28)

This is one of the most far-reaching passages in the Bible in its influence. Most of the apocalyptic works produced during the next three centuries use some of its language and imagery. It provided a background for much of Jesus' thought about his vocation, as well as a source for many of the symbols with which the New Testament authors speak of God's ultimate triumph.

7:1-8. *The Four Empires.* The dating of the visions (cf. 8:1; 9:1; 10:1) imitates the dates in some of the prophetic books (cf. Jeremiah 26:1; Ezekiel 8:1). **In the first year of Belshazzar** places this dream earlier than the story of that ruler's last night in chapter 5. But since the content shows no connection with his reign, the present position as the first of the visions is more appropriate than a chronological placement among the stories. However, this dream is closely related to the story containing Nebuchadnezzar's dream of an image made of four metals, and it seems to refer to the same four kingdoms (see above on 2:31-45).

7:2-3. The **great sea** here is not the Mediterranean, as elsewhere in the Old Testament. It is the chaotic waters over and under the earth (cf. Genesis 1:7). This chaos is sometimes called the "deep," the Hebrew word being akin to the name of the female dragon of chaos in Mesopotamian mythology, Tiamat. But the God of the Bible is always Lord of chaos, whether conceived in terms of a watery deep or an evil personality. From this sea of chaos rise **four great beasts.** They symbolize human empires that tried to dominate the earth without acknowledging the rule of the living God.

7:4-6. The first beast, resembling a **lion** with **eagles' wings,** represents the neo-Babylonian Empire. The author probably based this symbolism on prophetic metaphors likening Nebuchadnezzar to a lion (Jeremiah 4:7; 50:17) and an eagle (Ezekiel 17:3). Perhaps also he wished to imply a descending order as in the metals of 2:31-45. Thus he chose the most powerful mammal and bird as a parallel to gold. The beast's being **made to stand upon two feet like a man** and being given the **mind of a man** is apparently an allusion to Nebuchadnezzar's regaining his reason (4:34) after he was given a "beast's mind" (4:16).

The second beast, **like a bear,** represents the Median Empire, which the author mistakenly believed had savagely torn at Babylon (see above on 5:30-31). The third, **like a leopard,** known for its swiftness, represents the Persian Empire. Its **four wings** and **four heads** may symbolize the four corners of the earth to which its **dominion** extended (cf. 2:39*b*). This may possibly refer to the four Persian kings of whom the author knew (see below on 11:2-39).

7:7-8. The fourth beast, whose **terrible** appearance is left largely to the reader's imagination (cf. verse 19), represents the Seleucid Empire. In the author's day this controlled Palestine (see Introduction and above on 2:31-45). **Horns** like those of a bull are a common symbol of power in the Old Testament. For example "strength" in I Samuel 2:1*c* and "might" in Lamentations 2:3*b*, are both literally "horn." In this book they are used to symbolize rulers (cf. verse 24), the **little one** here being Antiochus Epiphanes.

During most of the reign of his brother, Seleucus IV (189-175), Antiochus was a hostage in Rome. At length Seleucus' son and heir, Demetrius, was sent to Rome to replace him. While Antiochus was on the way home, Seleucus was killed in a conspiracy of Heliodorus (see below on 11:10-19) to set a younger son on the throne. On hearing the news, Antiochus obtained outside help in Asia Minor, and secured the crown for himself.

The author considered Antiochus a usurper who had contrived all the events that led to his accession. He thus counted Seleucus and Demetrius among the **three of the first horns** uprooted by the little horn, the third being probably the younger son or possibly Heliodorus. To these three he may have added Seleucus' six predecessors in the Seleucid dynasty and Alexander the Great to get the total of **ten.** Other lists of ten have been proposed, however, as well as the possibility that ten is simply a conventional or symbolic number. On the **mouth speaking great things** cf. verse 25; 11:36.

7:9-12. *The Divine Judgment.* The poetic imagery of verses 9-10 is drawn from the psalmists and prophets.

On **ancient of days** cf. Psalm 90:2.

On the whiteness of his **raiment** and **hair** cf. Isaiah 1:18.

On his **throne** cf. Ezekiel 1:15-26.

On **fire** as a symbol of his holiness, wrath, and justice cf. Psalms 50:3; 97:3-5; 104:4; Isaiah 10:17; 33:14.

On his council of **ten thousand times ten thousand**—the square of the highest number for which ancient peoples had a word—cf. I Kings 22:19; Psalm 82.

On his record **books** cf. Psalms 56:8; 69:28; Isaiah 65:6; Malachi 3:16.

7:11-12. The arrogance of the blasphemous **horn** brings the whole beast—the Seleucid Empire—to destruction in the **fire** of God's judgment. But the other three beasts—Babylonia, Media, and Persia, which in the author's day were provinces of the Seleucid Empire, are permitted to survive **for a season**. This apparently referred to an interval envisioned between the fall of the Seleucid Empire and the establishment of the divine kingdom. Contrast 2:44, where the divine kingdom is to be established "in the days of those [Seleucid] kings" and cause the simultaneous breaking of all four kingdoms.

Perhaps the taking of **dominion** from the three beasts symbolizes an end to the kingdoms' rule over others. Thus the author may be thinking here especially of the peoples of these lands, who will live on and come under the rule of God's kingdom.

7:13-14. *The Son of Man.* In place of the beasts there now came—that is, will come—**one like a son of man**. This term as generally used in the Old Testament is simply a poetic synonym of "man." Possibly this is all the author means by it here—a symbol for the coming kingdom that is like a man in contrast to the beasts representing past kingdoms.

In Ezekiel, however, this phrase is used repeatedly as God's way of addressing the prophet. And in Hebrew figurative usage "son" suggests likeness in mind and spirit (cf. Mark 3:17). Thus the author may mean "son of mankind"—one who represents God's intention for humanity, who is truly made in the image of God and is worthy to have **dominion** over all creation.

The dominion over **all peoples** which God gives to this son of man, in contrast to that seized by the beastly rulers, is to be **everlasting.** The implication is that he is in some sense divine. This is suggested by his coming **with the clouds of heaven.** In Canaanite mythological texts from the middle of the second millennium the gods are said to ride on the clouds. Such language is also used of Yahweh in a number of poetic passages of the Old Testament.

7:15-28. *The Rule of the Saints.* This **interpretation** is largely repetition of what has been said or clearly implied in the preceding description of the dream. But it is significant that nothing further is said of the son of man. Instead the **kingdom** is promised to the **saints of the Most High.** "Saint" is literally "holy one," translating the same Aramaic word used earlier of angelic beings (4:13, 17, 23). The reference here is evidently to Israel, called to be a "holy nation" (Exodus 19:6). In ancient Hebrew thought the people of Israel as a whole could be summed up in one representative figure, such as their king, and all together they could be called a "son of man" (Psalm 80:17).

Thus the meaning here may be that the saints are to receive the kingdom through one who is their representative head, yet in whom they are all included as a kind of corporate personality. He is to be the first real man, in contrast to the past rulers who have been like beasts in spirit. As the first real man, or human person, he will institute a kingdom of real people. This expectation that **all dominions shall serve and obey** Israel repeats the promise of Second Isaiah (cf. Isaiah 45:14; 49:7, 23; see above on 2:46-49).

7:19-27. Daniel is to live only under the empires symbolized by the first three beasts. The special concern about the **fourth beast** is to be attributed to the intended readers, Jews suffering under the Seleucid Empire and its last **horn,** Antiochus Epiphanes. By his measures to stamp out Judaism and replace it by Greek religion and culture Antiochus has **made war with the saints.** Seemingly he has **prevailed over them.** His banning of Jewish religious practices has attempted to **change the times**—the festival calendar—**and the law** of Moses. But the prediction is that God will permit this oppression to last for only **a time, two times, and half a time**—that is, three and a half years (see below on 9:27). The promised divine action is therefore not something far off but only a matter of months away. Surely the loyal sufferers can hold out a little longer!

7:28. Possibly **here is the end of the matter** marked the conclusion of an early edition of the book. This may have included only some or all of the stories and this one vision. If so, the author no doubt inserted in his enlarged edition the sentence about being **alarmed** in order to suggest his need for the reassurance of the visions being added. The Aramaic section of the book (see Introduction) ends with this verse.

B. A Vision of a Ram and a Goat (8:1-27)

8:1-4. *The Ram.* The date in verse 1 indicates that this vision follows the preceding by about two years (see above on 7:1-8). **Susa the capital** probably should be translated "the citadel of Susa," referring to a large fortified area separated from the rest of the city. In this area Darius the Great built a magnificent winter palace, which was used by his successors. No doubt the author thought of Susa as the capital of the Persian Empire.

Possibly he knew that the **Ulai** was like the Chebar in being a canal (cf. Ezekiel 1:1; 10:20-22). Thus he considered it an appropriate place for Daniel to be transported in his vision. Some scholars, however, believe the unusual word translated **river** means instead "gate," as in the Septuagint. Thus Daniel in his vision would be standing at the entrance to Susa that faces north or northeast toward the Ulai Canal, which was near rather than adjacent to the city. The **ram** he sees represents the Persian Empire. Its **two horns** symbolize double power (see above on 7:7-8) because of its incorporating the Median Empire (verse 20). The later—that is, Persian—power is **higher.** The Septuagint lists all four directions in verse 4, recognizing that the empire extended all the way to India. However, the author probably visualizes the ram as coming from the east.

8:5-8. *The He-goat.* The rival animal advances **from the west** with such speed that it seems to move **without touching the ground.** It represents the Macedonian force that so quickly conquered the entire Persian Empire (334-326). Its single **conspicuous horn** symbolizes Alexander the Great (verse 21), who died soon afterward (323) and was replaced by **four conspicuous horns,** his generals. They divided his newly won domain **toward the four winds**—into four major kingdoms in Greece, Asia Minor, Egypt, and Mesopotamia. The last of which soon established itself in Syria and later (198) seized Palestine from Egypt.

8:9-14. *Interruption of Sacrifices.* From **one of them,** Seleucus, the general who took over Syria, was descended the **little horn** (cf. 7:8), Antiochus Epiphanes. His growing **great**

toward the south refers to his campaigns in Egypt (see below on 11:25-28). Since there is no record of his campaigning **toward the east** until the two-year expedition during which he died, this reference seems to date the book within very narrow limits (see Introduction). The **glorious land** is of course Palestine.

8:10-12. Not content with earthly conquest, Antiochus assaults the **host of heaven,** the angelic army. He claims divinity and his decrees ban the practice of any religion except his own. The Hebrew text of verses 11-12 is obscure and probably corrupt. But the main reference is clear—Antiochus' suppression of the **continual burnt offerings,** the twice-daily sacrifices on the altar of the temple in Jerusalem. **Overthrown** probably refers, not to physical destruction, but to desecration of the altar by diverting it to the worship of Zeus.

8:13. In using the term **holy one** the author draws no line between the heavenly host and the people of Israel (see above on 7:15-28). Here it evidently refers to two angelic beings. **Transgression,** or "abomination" (11:31; 12:11; cf. 9:27), **that makes desolate** is a word play on the Semitic title of Zeus, "Baal of Heaven." In reading the Scriptures it was a common practice to substitute such words as "shame," "abomination," and "transgression" in references to the old Canaanite god Baal. A mere vowel change transformed "heavenly" into "desolating."

8:14. Worship is to cease for **two thousand and three hundred evenings and mornings**—1,150 days—or three years and about two months (cf. three and a half years, 7:25; 9:27; 12:7). According to I Maccabees (1:54, 59; 4:52-54), Judas Maccabeus and his followers rededicated the altar and resumed sacrifices three years to the day after the desecration. Some scholars point out that Antiochus' prohibition of sacrifices may have been enforced some weeks before the altar was desecrated. Thus 1,150 days may be the actual period during which the daily offerings were suspended. On this basis they maintain that the author knew of Judas' rededication. Therefore this book must have been written in the short period between this event and the news of Antiochus' death.

However, the evidence of this passage is doubtful. It seems to be overweighed, not only by the lack of any sign of such knowledge in 9:27 and 11:31 but also by the expectation throughout of deliverance by God's action rather than by any **human hand** (verse 25).

8:15-27. *The Interpretation.* Again (cf. 7:16) Daniel seeks an explanation of his vision. This time **Gabriel,** meaning "man of God," is instructed to supply it. The naming of angels is a late development which in the canonical Old Testament is found only in this book. In the Apocrypha it can be found in II Esdras; and Tobit 3:17. Both Gabriel and Michael (10:13, 21; 12:1) are among the seven archangels named in intertestamental works, and both are mentioned in the New Testament (Luke 1:19, 26; Jude 9; Revelation 12:7). Gabriel has to waken Daniel from an unnatural **sleep,** such as God imposed on the patriarchs before being revealed to them (cf. Genesis 15:12). He explains that the vision has to do with the **end,** the time of God's **indignation** and intervention on behalf of the people. The implication is that the destruction of Antiochus Epiphanes will be the beginning of this, for it will be accomplished **by no human hand,** but by God's own action.

The instruction to **seal up** the scroll on which the vision is reported is a common convention of apocalyptic works. It is an explanation of why a book supposedly written so long ago has just been published. On the method of sealing ancient documents see comment on Jeremiah 32:9-14. Daniel's return to the **king's** (Belshazzar's, verse 1), **business** is inconsistent with 5:10-16. There he appears to be retired from public office and unknown to Belshazzar before the queen's recommendation.

C. An Interpretation of Prophecy (9:1-27)

This chapter is dominated by a sense of urgency. The day of God's intervention (cf. 8:19), a day of both judgment and mercy, is at hand. God's people are now living at the time of the end. Its imminence is here demonstrated by a new understanding of a well-known prophecy.

9:1-2. *The Prophecy of Seventy Years.* Unlike the preceding dates (see above on 7:1-8) the **first year of Darius** is especially appropriate. Darius supposedly conquered the **realm of the Chaldeans,** who destroyed Jerusalem and carried her people into exile (see above on 5:30-31). This might well cause Daniel to ponder the application of the prophecies in Jeremiah 25:11-12 and 29:10 about God's visiting the people after seventy years. **Ahasuerus** represents the Hebrew equivalent of the name of the Persian king known in Greek as Xerxes, who was the son of Darius the Great. No doubt the author knew about this Persian king (see below on 11:2-4). But here he is referring to a different man, a **Mede** of an earlier time, whom he believed to have borne the same name. Thus he probably knew by this Hebrew name the Median king known through Greek transcription as Cyaxares (around 625–585), who conquered Nineveh and largely created the Median Empire. Cyaxares' **son** was Astyages, who was ruler of this empire when it fell to Cyrus the Persian. Perhaps confused traditions linking the later Ahasuerus (Xerxes) to Darius the Great came to be mistakenly associated also with the earlier Ahasuerus (Cyaxares) and resulted in the misnaming of his son.

9:3-19. *Daniel's Prayer.* This prayer has a distinctive style and uses the divine name Yahweh, not found elsewhere in the book. This may indicate that it is an earlier composition which has been incorporated at this place. The fact that with verses 4-20 omitted, verse 21 would connect well with verse 3 has suggested to some that the prayer is a later addition. Its appropriateness to the context, however, and especially to the situation for which the book was written, favors the more general view that the author chose it to quote at this point. Possibly tradition had already attributed it to Daniel. But the content suggests rather that it was composed in or near **Jerusalem** (cf. verses 7, 12, 16, 19) at a time when the Jews had become scattered in **all the lands.** This would have been late in the Persian period or in Hellenistic times.

The language is comparable with that of the prayers in Nehemiah 1:5-11 and 9:6-37. Each of these prayers places contemporary sinful Israel in focus over against the long history of God's redemptive acts—thus claiming God's redeeming love for the present generation. The hoped-for restoration of communion between God and Israel requires confession of sins. The **prophets** declared sin to be the cause of the Exile. It must be the reason God has permitted Antiochus to prevail over the people for a time. The resulting **calamity** may be either the destruction of God's temple during Daniel's youth or its desecration four centuries later. For all who may be yielding to self-pity because of their hardships, or to self-satisfaction because of their guerrilla victories, or to self-righteousness because of the wickedness of their enemies, the plea is that God may **forgive** and may **act** without further **delay.**

9:20-27. *The 70 Weeks of Years.* In response to his prayer Daniel is given another vision of the angel **Gabriel** (see above on 8:15-27). Here he is called a **man** because he appears in human form (cf. 8:15). He is sent as an interpreter. Unfortunately the text of his interpretation is not only complicated but corrupt. The main point is clear, however. The seventy years of the prophecy (verse 2) are long past at the time of writing. They must be multiplied by seven. Thus the end of the period, bringing God's visitation of the people in Jerusalem and the dawning of the promised new era, will be only a matter of months in the future. Thus, according to the author's calculation, the idea of multiplying the years of punishment may have been suggested by the sevenfold penalties threatened in Leviticus 26:14-39. At any rate **weeks of years** were familiar to the author and his readers from the sabbath year of "rest for the land" in which it was left fallow (Leviticus 25:2-7). This custom was observed by all loyal Jews as the last of each cycle of seven years.

9:25. The end of the first group of **seven weeks**—that is, forty-nine years—brings **an anointed one, a prince.** The reference is probably to Cyrus. Prophecy declared that Cyrus was anointed by God to bring about the return of the exiles to Jerusalem (Isaiah 45:1). Some, however, assume a parallelism with the anointed one of verse 26. They believe this reference is to Joshua, the first high priest anointed after the Exile. A second group of **sixty-two weeks**—434 years—is a **troubled time** of rebuilding the city. The author mistakenly thought this would fit the interval between Cyrus or Joshua and the beginning of the final seven-year period, within which he is writing.

9:26. At the start of the seventieth week an **anointed one,** meaning a high priest, is **cut off.** The allusion is probably to the murder of Onias III about three years after he was deposed by Antiochus Epiphanes. There is evidence that Onias may instead have escaped to Egypt, but in either case a report of his murder spread among the Jews of Palestine. Soon afterward Antiochus invaded Jerusalem and seized treasures in the temple.

9:27. During this final **one week** of years Antiochus is successful in making a **strong covenant** with those Jews who are willing to compromise with his hellenization policy (cf. 11:30, 32). The climax of his persecution is the halting of **sacrifice** in the temple and the desecration of its altar (see above on 8:14).

The author dates this event at the midpoint of the final week of years. He thus predicts that the **decreed end** will occur **half of the week** of years later. Though the observance of a fallow year in Palestine would have to begin and end in the fall, it seems more probable that the author has counted his final sabbath year according to the spring calendar followed by the Jews at this time. Thus he looks forward to its end in the spring of 163. The occurrence of a sabbath year at this time is confirmed in I Maccabees 6:49-54, which tells of food shortages suffered in 162 as stores ran out before the new crop came to maturity. The interval from the desecration on December 16, 167, till the anticipated divine intervention in 163 might be calculated as 1,150 days (see above on 8:14) or less precisely as three and a half years (7:25; 12:7) or half a week of years.

D. A Synopsis of History and Its End (10:1–12:13)

Chapters 10–12 are a single unit. The chapter divisions are unfortunate. The section begins with a prologue in which an angel appears to Daniel. (10:1–11:1). It ends with an epilogue which deals once again with the time of the end (12:5-13). In between is an outline of history leading up to the time of writing.

10:1-12. *The Setting of the Vision.* On the date see above on 1:17-21. This vision begins like the one in chapter 8. The **word** is **true**—that is, from God. Yet it produces a **great conflict** in Daniel's mind. He is again beside a **river** (cf. 8:2). His angelic visitor is presumably Gabriel (see above on 8:15-27). Again this visitor is in the form of a **man** (cf. 8:16), yet he has otherworldly qualities. The visitation overwhelms Daniel. His **deep sleep** is typical of the ecstatic experience of vision (see above on 8:15-27), but the angel reassures him.

10:13-14. *The War in Heaven.* By the second century B.C. the Jews had come to believe that each nation had its heavenly **prince**—a guardian angel. Their own was **Michael** (cf. verse 21; 12:1; Exodus 23:20; see above on 8:15-27). The concept was no doubt rooted in Israel's ancient heritage (cf. Deuteronomy 32:8-9), but much of the later development came from Persian influence.

That there should be conflict among these implies that some of the heavenly beings rebelled against God—an idea seen in Genesis 6:1-4 and Isaiah 14:12. Here then is a mythological presentation of the truth that God has given the whole creation the freedom to be for or against God. Thus the author shows some angels as opposed to the interpretation of God's truth to Daniel.

10:15–11:1. *The Pain of Revelation.* Daniel finds that to be gripped by the truth of God is a painful thing (cf. Jeremiah 4:19). But another angel brings him healing. The angel too feels the urgency of God's calling. He has still to **fight** the guardian angels of both Persia and Greece, with only Michael to help him. This heavenly struggle has been going on since the Jewish exiles first came under the dominion of the Median Empire (see above on 5:30-31). But the author gives no hint of how long he supposed this to be.

11:2-39. *A Synopsis of Past Events.* The author exaggerates the length of the Persian Empire's sway (9:25). But he reduces the number of its rulers to only **three more kings** after Cyrus, during whose reign the revelation is purportedly being spoken (10:1). The Persian kings mentioned in the Old Testament (by Ezra, Nehemiah, Haggai, and Zechariah) were Darius I, Ahasuerus (Xerxes I), and Artaxerxes. Evidently the author supposed these were the only ones.

The **fourth**—meaning the last of the three—is to be **richer** and will **stir up all against the kingdom of Greece.** Historically this would fit Xerxes. But the author had very scanty sources of information about Persian history. No doubt he made these assumptions about the supposed last king of the line to explain the counterattack of the **mighty king,** Alexander the Great. On the division of his kingdom (verse 4) see above on 8:5-8.

11:5-9. In this sketch of about 150 years of history **king of the south** denotes successive rulers of the Ptolemaic dynasty of Egypt. **King of the north** refers to those of the Seleucid dynasty of Syria. Judea lay as a prize between their two kingdoms. Verse 5 describes the two founders of these lines, Ptolemy I and Seleucus I. The latter became for a time one of Ptolemy's **princes** (generals) after he was driven from his own domain by another of Alexander's successors.

After some years—about 250—the Seleucid Antiochus II divorced Laodice to marry Berenice, daughter of Ptolemy II, in an effort to **make peace** (cf. 2:43). But Laodice contrived the assassination of Antiochus, Berenice, and their infant son. For vengeance a **branch from her roots,** Berenice's brother, Ptolemy III, made war on Laodice's son, Seleucus II. He captured the **fortress** of Seleucia, the port of the Seleucid capital Antioch, and seized great booty (verse 8). But then he had to **refrain from attacking** further because of trouble at home. Seleucus hit back (verse 9), but was defeated and had to **return into his own land.**

11:10-19. Seleucus II was succeeded by two **sons** in turn, Seleucus III (227-223) and Antiochus III the Great (223-187). The latter was especially prone to **wage war.** After some successes he suffered a major defeat by Ptolemy IV in 217 (verses 11-12). Later he came back (verse 13) against the forces of the infant Ptolemy V, whose regency was plagued with rebellions (verse 14). These involved some of **your own people,** the Jews. Antiochus succeeded in capturing a **well-fortified city,** Sidon, and winning other victories (verses 15-16). In 198 he wrested the **glorious land,** Palestine, from Egyptian control and incorporated it into the Seleucid Empire. Then he made **peace** with Egypt by marrying his **daughter** Cleopatra to Ptolemy V (verse 17).

Turning to the west, he attempted conquests in the **coastlands** of Asia Minor and Greece (verse 18). There he met with a humiliating defeat in 190 by the Roman **commander** Lucius Cornelius Scipio. This cost him all his territory in these regions and also a huge tribute. He returned to **his own land** and lost his life trying to loot a temple in Elam. He was succeeded by his elder son, Seleucus IV (187-175). This king sent an **exactor of tribute,** Heliodorus, to confiscate funds deposited in the Jerusalem temple. Later he fell victim to a conspiracy of this same Heliodorus.

11:21-24. The author regarded Antiochus the Great's younger son, Antiochus IV Epiphanes, as not only a **contemptible person** but a usurper (see above on 7:7-8). In his view Antiochus was not above contriving the assassination of a **prince of the covenant,** the high priest Onias III (see above on 9:26). He had previously deposed Onias in order to make an alliance with Jewish leaders more willing to cooperate with his program of hellenization. Verse 24 is ambiguous (see Revised Standard Version footnote). It may refer to using **plunder** taken from Egypt to bribe his Jewish allies. Or it may refer to taking plunder from wealthy Jews. At any rate his generosity to those he favored was unprecedented.

11:25-28. These verses concern Antiochus' intervention in Egypt. Rival factions there were supporting the claims of two minor sons of his sister Cleopatra (see above on verses 10-19). He took the side of Ptolemy VI Philometor, and the **two kings** conquered much of Egypt. However they were unable to dislodge the forces of Ptolemy VII Physcon in Alexandria. Returning with **great substance,** booty secured in Egypt,

Antiochus stopped off in Jerusalem to put down a revolt by Onias' brother Jason, whom he had also deposed from the high priesthood. In this he acted **against the holy covenant**—especially in entering the temple and seizing some of its treasures.

11:29-31. The name **Kittim** originally meant Cyprus. Later it came to be used of the Mediterranean coastlands generally, especially of Greece and, as here and in some of the Dead Sea Scrolls, Rome. On a return campaign in Egypt, Antiochus was halted by a Roman emissary, Popilius Laenas, and ordered to **withdraw.** No doubt he was indeed **enraged.** Perhaps his **action against the holy covenant** at this time was motivated by the frustration, as the author implies. On this action see above on 8:10-12, 13.

11:32-39. Having outlined the chief events up to the time of writing, the author here summarizes the situation. Antiochus has been able to **seduce with flattery** a considerable number of Jews who are willing to **violate the covenant.** Yet there are still many **who know their God** and remain **firm** in their loyalty in the face of **sword** and **flame.** To these Judas Maccabeus and his guerrillas, who rose against Antiochus, are only **a little help.** Israel's true help is in God alone.

Meanwhile the **king** continues his blasphemy. He claims divinity for himself and represses the worship of the traditional gods of his realm—including the **one beloved by women,** called alternatively Tammuz or Adonis. He promotes worship of a **foreign god,** probably meaning the Olympian Zeus.

11:40-45. *A Prediction of Coming Events.* At this point the author must leave the known past and present and launch into the unknown future. His guesses do not agree with what actually happened next—a fact which reveals the time of writing within narrow limits (see Introduction). He imagines that a **king of the south**—which Ptolemy he means is uncertain—will begin a new war. Palestine will become the battlefield, though the Transjordan territories will be spared. Forgetting the Roman ban (see above on verses 29-31), he supposes that Antiochus will win and despoil all northeast Africa. Then an alarming report will call him back. He will be encamped in Palestine **between**

the sea and the glorious holy mountain—that is, west of Jerusalem—when God acts to bring the end. Historically Antiochus' death occurred at about the time the author predicted (see above on 9:27), but the place was in Persia.

12:1-4. *The Resurrection.* The Old Testament looks forward, not merely to a day of redemption for God's people, but to the consummation of God's mighty plan for the whole creation. This great end, being beyond space and time and human experience, can be expressed only in symbols and pictures. The author's vision of what God's intervention will mean is not entirely clear. But he does perceive that God is able to bring good out of evil and so life out of death.

The rabbis speak of the "birth pangs of the Messiah" to describe the **time of trouble** that will precede the dawn of the kingdom (cf. Isaiah 66:7-9). Other interpreters have regarded verse 1*b* as referring to the rise of the Antichrist and the outbreak of a great war before the final victory. That day will not dawn, however, just when we expect it. The end of one tyrant such as Antiochus Epiphanes does not preclude the rise of another. But **Michael,** whom God has set over Israel (see above on 10:13-14), is mediating God's care for all those whose names are written in the **book** of life.

12:2-4. The outcome of God's ultimate victory will be the resurrection of **many.** The **wise** who stood firm, did what they knew to be God's will (cf. 11:33), and actively created **righteousness** in other peoples will enter into the **brightness**— the glory—of God. But some will awake to **contempt.** This word, translated "abhorrence" in the last line of Isaiah (66:24), means the opposite of life. In both cases the resurrection is probably of Israel only, since it is brought about by Michael, whose special charge is the covenant people. On **seal the book** see above on 8:15-27.

12:5-13. *The Time of the End.* Daniel asks when the things he has just been told about will occur. He is again told the cryptic expression **a time, two times, and half a time** (cf. 7:25; see above on 9:27). His further question about what will happen then is turned away unanswered. But Daniel learns he is to rest quietly in his grave until **the end of the days** which is in the hands of God. Two notes have apparently been later added to the original ending of the book. These may be attempts to harmonize the period of suspension of sacrifices in 8:14 with the three and a half years denoted in verse 7.

FOR FURTHER STUDY

THE BOOK OF ISAIAH

G. A. Smith, *The Book of Isaiah, 2 vols., rev. ed., 1927. C. R. North, The Suffering Servant in Deutero-Isaiah,* rev. ed., 1956; in *Interpreter's Dictionary of the Bible,* 1962; in *Isaiah 40–55,* rev. ed., 1964. R. B. Y. Scott and James Muilenburg, in *Interpreter's Bible,* 1956. E.J. Kissane, *The Book of Isaiah,* 2 vols., rev. ed., 1960. John Mauchline, *Isaiah 1–39,* 1962. D. R. Jones, *Isaiah 56-66 and Joel,* 1964. J. M. Ward in *Interpreter's Dictionary of the Bible Supplement,* 1976.

THE BOOK OF JEREMIAH

J. P. Hyatt in *Interpreter's Bible,* 1956. James Muilenburg in *Interpreter's Dictionary of the Bible,* 1962. A. S. Peake (Century Bible), 1910-12. J. Skinner, *Prophecy and Religion,* 1922. E. A. Leslie, *Jeremiah,* 1954. H. H. Rowley, *Men of God,* 1963. John Bright (Anchor Bible), 1965. W. L. Holladay in *Interpreter's Dictionary of the Bible Supplement,* 1976.

THE BOOK OF LAMENTATIONS

Israel Bettan, *The Five Scrolls,* 1950. N. K. Gottwald, *Studies in the Book of Lamentations,* 1954.

THE BOOK OF EZEKIEL

C. C. Torrey, *Pseudo-Ezekiel and the Original Prophecy,* 1930; a pioneer analysis of the evidence for a Palestinian locale, widely influential despite its unconvincing view of the book as fiction. I. G. Matthews, *Ezekiel,* 1939. W. A. Irwin, *The Problem of Ezekiel,* 1943; pioneer restoration of Ezekiel's original poetry. C. G. Howie, *The Date and Composition of Ezekiel.,* 1950; C. G. Howie in *Interpreter's Dictionary of the Bible,* 1962; able defenses of the Babylonian locale. H. G. May in *Interpreters Bible,* 1956. W. Zimmerli in *Interpreter's Dictionary of the Bible Supplement,* 1976.

THE BOOK OF DANIEL

J. A. Montgomery, *Daniel*, 1927. R. H. Charles, *Daniel*, 1929. Arthur Jeffery in *Interpreter's Bible*, 1956. S. B. Frost in *Interpreter's Dictionary of the Bible*, 1962. H. H. Rowley, *The Relevance of Apocalyptic*, rev. ed., 1964. A. A. Di Lella in *Interpreter's Dictionary of the Bible Supplement*, 1976.

ABBREVIATIONS AND EXPLANATIONS

ABBREVIATIONS

D — Deuteronomic; Deuteronomist source

E — Elohist source
Ecclus. — Ecclesiasticus
ed. — edited by, edition, editor
e.g. — *exempli gratia* (for example)
ERV — English Revised Version
esp. — especially

H — Holiness Code

J — Yahwist source
JPSV — Jewish Publication Society Version

L — Lukan source
LXX — Septuagint, the earliest Greek translation of the Old Testament and Apocrypha (250 B.C. and after)

M — Matthean source
Macc. — Maccabees
MS — manuscript

N — north, northern
NEB — New English Bible

P — Priestly source
p. — page
Pet. — Peter
Phil. — Philippian, Philippians
Philem. — Philemon
Prov. — Proverbs
Pss. Sol. — Psalms of Solomon
pt. — part (of a literary work)

Q — "Sayings" source

rev. — revised
RSV — Revised Standard Version

S — south, southern

trans. — translated by, translation, translator

viz. — *videlicet* (namely)
Vulg. — Vulgate, the accepted Latin version, mostly translated A.D. 383-405 by Jerome

W — west, western
Wisd. Sol. — Wisdom of Solomon

QUOTATIONS AND REFERENCES

In the direct commentary words and phrases quoted from the RSV of the passage under discussion are printed in boldface type, without quotation marks, to facilitate linking the comments to the exact points of the biblical text. If a quotation from the passage under discussion is not in boldface type, it is to be recognized as an alternate translation, either that of another version if so designated (see abbreviations of versions above) or the commentator's own rendering. On the other hand, quotations from other parts of the Bible in direct commentary, as well as all biblical quotations in the introductions, are to be understood as from the RSV unless otherwise identified.

A passage of the biblical text is identified by book, chapter number, and verse number or numbers, the chapter and verse numbers being separated by a colon (cf. Genesis 1:1). Clauses within a verse may be designated by the letters *a, b, c,* etc. following the verse number (e.g. Genesis 1:2*b*). In poetical text each line as printed in the RSV—not counting runovers necessitated by narrow columns—is accorded a letter. If the book is not named, the book under discussion is to be understood; similarly the chapter number appearing in the boldface reference at the beginning of the paragraph, or in a preceding centered head, is to be understood if no chapter is specified.

A suggestion to note another part of the biblical text is usually introduced by the abbreviation "cf." and specifies the exact verses. To be distinguished from this is a suggestion to consult a comment in this volume, which is introduced by "see above on," "see below on," or "see comment on," and which identifies the boldface reference at the head of the paragraph where the comment is to be found or, in the absence of a boldface reference, the reference in a preceding centered head. The suggestion "see Introduction" refers to the introduction of the book under discussion unless another book is named.

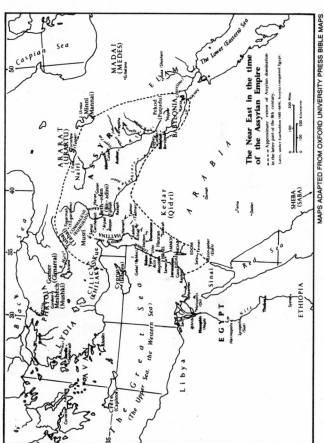

The Near East in the time
of the Assyrian Empire

---- Approximate extent of Assyrian domination
in the latter part of the 8th century.

Later, under Esarhaddon (681-669), Assyria conquered Egypt.

0   100   200 Miles
0   100 200 300 Kilometers

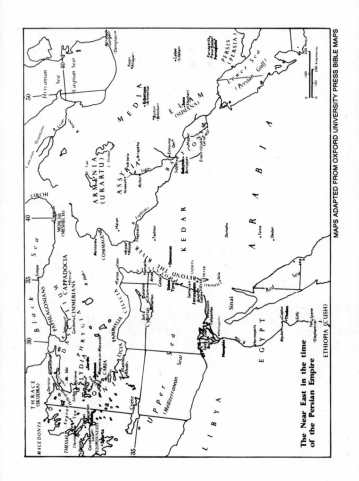

The Near East in the time of the Persian Empire

MAPS ADAPTED FROM OXFORD UNIVERSITY PRESS BIBLE MAPS